'The Governance Space theory is a significant contribution to the complex study of trade, globalisation and human rights.'

Juan Carlos Sainz-Borgo, Dean, United Nations–mandated University for Peace (UPEACE), Costa Rica

'A compelling case for a right to development approach to WTO and human rights linkages.'

Makau Mutua, SUNY Distinguished Professor, University at Buffalo School of Law, New York, USA

THE MULTILATERAL TRADING SYSTEM AND HUMAN RIGHTS

This book contributes an original theory to understanding human rights and international trade. It offers the 'governance space' framework for analysing the linkages and normative relationships between the multilateral trading system (MTS) and human rights regimes. Drawing upon key case studies, the author identifies connecting strands as also gaps in linkage issues. He further examines the 'right to development' approach to resolve tensions between these two regimes and demonstrates how the approach may be the most appropriate road map to finding sustainable solutions in balancing human rights and equitable free trade in a complex globalised world.

Presenting new legal analyses informed by current debates drawn from international organisations – the World Trade Organization, United Nations, International Labour Organization – governments, civil society and academia as well as global commitments such as the Sustainable Development Goals, the book proposes a systematic and holistic policy intervention.

This timely and transdisciplinary text will be of great interest to academics, students and scholars of human rights, international trade, international law, development studies, public policy and governance, economics, politics and international relations. It will also be useful to policymakers, think-tanks, human rights advocates, professionals, lawyers, civil society organisations, non-governmental organisations and trade experts.

Mihir Kanade is Head of the Department of International Law and Human Rights at the United Nations–mandated University for Peace (UPEACE), headquartered in Costa Rica, and Director of the UPEACE Human Rights Centre. He holds an LLB from Nagpur University, India, and master's and doctorate degrees from UPEACE. He is an adjunct faculty at Universidad Alfonso X El Sabio, Spain; Cheikh

Anta Diop University, Senegal; and Long Island University, USA. He serves on the International Advisory Board of the International Bar Association on the topic of Business and Human Rights. He also co-leads an educational project with the UN Office of the High Commissioner for Human Rights on promoting the right to development. Prior to his pursuit in academia, he practised as a lawyer at the Bombay High Court and the Supreme Court of India.

THE MULTILATERAL TRADING SYSTEM AND HUMAN RIGHTS

A Governance Space Theory on Linkages

Mihir Kanade

Routledge
Taylor & Francis Group
LONDON AND NEW YORK

First published 2018 by Routledge

2 Park Square, Milton Park, Abingdon, Oxfordshire OX14 4RN
52 Vanderbilt Avenue, New York, NY 10017

Routledge is an imprint of the Taylor & Francis Group, an informa business

First issued in paperback 2019

British Library Cataloguing-in-Publication Data
A catalogue record for this book is available from the British Library

Library of Congress Cataloging-in-Publication Data
A catalog record has been requested for this book

ISBN: 978-1-138-28001-4 (hbk)
ISBN: 978-0-367-34539-6 (pbk)

Typeset in Sabon
by Apex CoVantage, LLC

CONTENTS

Acknowledgements viii
List of abbreviations x

1 Introduction to the study of linkages 1

2 A 'governance space' theory on linkages 20

3 The normative hierarchy debate and its distractions 51

4 The disputed role of the dispute settlement body 75

5 WTO and the shrinking of governance space 105

6 WTO and the permissive environment to abuse governance space 136

7 WTO and the limiting environment to use governance space 169

8 The way forward: the right to development approach 195

9 Conclusion 231

Appendix: list of cases 237
Bibliography 244
Index 275

ACKNOWLEDGEMENTS

This book is dedicated to my guru, Senior Counsel Subodh Dharmadhikari, in whose chambers I had the privilege of working for more than 10 years as a lawyer in India. He put me through the grind since the first year of law school, dragged me to courts and arbitral tribunals with him all over the country, had me spend nights in the office scavenging through jurisprudence in support of what seemed like impossible propositions (i.e. until I actually found what he wanted) and had me draft pleadings based on laws I hadn't even studied by then. That he was also my uncle never came in the way. He was, and will always be, my teacher in every sense of the term. I am indebted to him and can only aspire to reach the levels of his legal acumen, reasoning and articulation.

Love for institutions – especially if they happen to be international treaty bodies – needs a special kind of conviction, the kind I have with relation to the United Nations–mandated University for Peace (UPEACE). I have always been a firm believer in its mission, its potential and its future. My post-graduate academic life has been shaped significantly by my experiences at UPEACE, and I hope that, through this book, I have managed to contribute to a better understanding of why the world is the way it is in the field of multilateral trade and human rights. I am grateful to the institution and to 'UPEACErs' for all the love and support I have received over the past eight years. In particular, I am grateful to Dr Francisco Rojas Aravena, Rector of UPEACE; my doctoral thesis supervisor and friend Dr Juan Carlos Sainz-Borgo; and my colleagues over the years including Ambassador Gudmundur Eiriksson, Amr Abdalla, the late Mahmood Hamid, Jan Breitling, Natalia Riveros, Juan Amaya Castro, Miriam Estrada, Gal Harmat, Manish Thapa, Mayumi Yamada, Ross Ryan, Olivia Sylvester, Alonso Muñoz, Mirian Vilela, Thomas Klompmaker and others with whom I have had the privilege of working. A special mark of gratitude is due to Karina Loria, our wonderful Academic Support Officer in the Department of International Law. I have also benefitted immensely from debates and discussions on my book with Makau Mutua, Jan Hessbruegge, Joaquín González Ibáñez, Shyami Puvimanasinghe and Jessica Lawrence. I am also thankful to my students at UPEACE and at different universities around the world for giving me the opportunity to develop my thoughts in classrooms.

I must also express gratitude to the WTO for inviting me in March 2016, to address their staff as part of their 'LAD Speaker Series' and for giving me the opportunity to present my research. I have certainly benefitted from their constructive and positive comments. I am equally thankful to the staff of the OHCHR, especially the Right to Development section, for their encouraging thoughts on my research.

Last but certainly not the least, I am indebted to my parents, Yashodhan Kanade and Anjali Kanade, my brother Utkarsh, my sister-in-law Poonam and their little bundle of energy-cum-drama-cum-sweetness Kiara, for always being there for me and supporting me unconditionally. My extended family, the Kanade, the Dharmadhikari and the Akabayov clans, have always been encouraging. Most of all, I am grateful to my wife Samira and our son Orkhan. None of this matters without them. They complete me personally and professionally. This is as much their book as it is mine. They silently tolerated all my tantrums, they egged me on to write another page when I was distracted, they spoiled me when I was happy with a day's work and they celebrated with me when it was all over. Thank you!

ABBREVIATIONS

AB	Appellate Body
ACP	African-Caribbean-Pacific
AFL-CIO	American Federation of Labor and Congress of Industrial Organizations
AfT	Aid for Trade
ATLAS	Agency for Trade and Labor Standards
CIL	Customary International Law
CLS	core labour standards
CTD	Committee on Trade and Development
DC	developed country
DFID	UK Department of International Development
D-LDC	developing and least-developed country
DRTD	Declaration on the Right to Development
DSB	dispute settlement body
DSU	Understanding on Rules and Procedures Governing the Settlement of Disputes
EC	European Communities
ECOSOC	Economic and Social Council
EU	European Union
FTA	free trade agreement
GATS	General Agreement on Trade in Services
GATT	General Agreement on Tariffs and Trade
GDP	gross domestic product
GSP	generalised system of preferences
HRIA	Human Rights Impact Assessment
IC	indigenous community
ICCPR	International Covenant on Civil and Political Rights
ICESCR	International Covenant on Economic, Social and Cultural Rights
ICJ	International Court of Justice

ILC	International Law Commission
ILO	International Labour Organization
IMF	International Monetary Fund
ITO	International Trade Organization
LDC	least-developed country
MDG	millennium development goal
MEA	Multilateral Environmental Agreement
MERCOSUR	Mercado Común del Sur
MFA	multi-fibre agreement
MFN	most favoured nation
MNC	multinational corporation
MTS	multilateral trading system
NAFTA	North American Free Trade Agreement
NGO	non-governmental organization
NT	national treatment
ODA	Official Development Assistance
OECD	Organisation for Economic Co-operation and Development
OHCHR	Office of the High Commissioner for Human Rights
PCG	PVA, cellulose and glass
PPRCs	Peer and Partner Review Committees
PTA	preferential trade agreement
RtD	right to development
S&D	special and differential
SCM Agreement	Agreement on Subsidies and Countervailing Measures
SDG	sustainable development goal
SPS Agreement	Agreement on the Application of Sanitary and Phyto-Sanitary Measures
TBT Agreement	Agreement on Technical Barriers to Trade
TED	turtle extruding device
TMSA	TradeMark Southern Africa
TPRB	Trade Policy Review Body
TPRM	Trade Policy Review Mechanism
TRILS	Agreement on Trade-Related Aspects of Labour
TRIPS Agreement	Agreement on Trade-Related Aspects of Intellectual Property Rights
TWAIL	Third World Approaches to International Law
UDHR	Universal Declaration of Human Rights
UN	United Nations
UNCHR	United Nations Commission on Human Rights

UNCLOS	United Nations Convention on the Law of the Sea
UNCTAD	United Nations Conference on Trade and Development
UNDP	United Nations Development Programme
UNEP	United Nations Environment Programme
UNGA	United Nations General Assembly
UNHRC	United Nations Human Rights Council
UNSC	United Nations Security Council
VCLT	Vienna Convention on the Law of Treaties
WB	World Bank
WTO	World Trade Organization
WWII	World War II

1

INTRODUCTION TO THE STUDY OF LINKAGES

This book seeks to explore a relatively untrodden and difficult path in legal scholarship. It seeks to unravel the complex muddle created by the myriads of interactions between the multilateral trade regime and the international human rights regime and bring some order back to this scattered field of study. That multilateral trade has some adverse impacts on human rights is almost trite today. Contemporary scholarship in this field, however, suffers from a somewhat hollow core. It lacks a theory. It is characterised either by isolated analyses of individual human rights issues arising due to linkages with the multilateral trading system (MTS) or by a collective dealing of all human rights issues affected by trade as if they all deserve a common solution. Unfortunately, neither of these extremes and whatever falls within has been able to offer any rational manner by which one can make sense of the complex ways MTS impacts human rights. This field of study is evidently in search of a 'golden thread' that can tie together all the splinters. It is in search of a comprehensive theoretical framework that can coherently connect the normative elements of the different linkage-issues and yet leave room for different solutions to those issues from a policy perspective. This book, thus, seeks to fill that void by offering a new framework – conceived of as the 'governance space' framework – for analysing the linkages, which can in turn form the foundation for developing a human rights approach, specifically a right to development (RtD) approach, to resolving the tensions between the two regimes.

The context for understanding linkages

The linkages between human rights and multilateral trade have been a subject of considerable debate since the last two decades.[1] The primary cause for the incessant fuelling of these debates relates to the sudden intrusion, led by the emergence of the World Trade Organisation (WTO) in 1995 as the nodal agency for multilateral trade, into many issues which were not hitherto considered to be normally in the domain of trade policy (Sampson 2005: 4). These included rules regulating such new areas as intellectual property rights, sanitary and phyto-sanitary measures and trade in services. Unsurprisingly, this intrusion has over the last few years brought to limelight various tensions caused by overlapping international obligations of States under different legal regimes and international fora. Human rights, in particular, merit special concern, inasmuch as States have undertaken through numerous international treaties under the auspices of the United Nations (UN) and other regional bodies to respect, protect and fulfil human rights. The International Covenant on Economic, Social and Cultural Rights (ICESCR), in particular, requires States to pursue policies and strategies aimed at the realisation for every individual of the right to food, health, shelter, education, work and social security. It is imperative that in the face of these human rights obligations, MTS, its policies and rules need to be developed in a manner which would, at the very least, not be in violation of the former and, in fact, would further them. All members of the WTO are bound by at least one core international human rights treaty (Dine and Fagan 2006: 228) and are generally bound by universal human rights obligations as part of Customary International Law (CIL) (Sohn 1982: 2–9; Meron 1989: 93; Henkin 1990: 19) or as part of General Principles of Law (Simma and Alston 1989: 102–8; de Schutter 2014: 66–71).[2] States, thus, face the clear responsibility of adhering to their human rights commitments while operating at the WTO.[3]

However, no sooner did the WTO come into existence that it quickly became clear that MTS did not necessarily share a harmonious relationship with human rights. The WTO policies and rules began coming under some serious hammering from scholars (Garcia 1999; Tandon 1999; Klein 2000; Gathii 2001; Gray 2002; Stiglitz 2002) as well as civil society organisations (International Federation for Human Rights 1999; Oxfam 2002; Human Rights Caucus 2005) with respect to their human rights impacts. An early report emerging from the UN Economic and Social Council (ECOSOC) unceremoniously branded the WTO as a 'veritable nightmare' for human rights of citizens in the third world (ECOSOC 2000: Para. 15), reportedly leading to an official protest letter being shot off by the WTO to the then UN High Commissioner for Human Rights, Mary Robinson (Institute for Agriculture and Trade Policy 2000). However, the most explicit manifestation of the backlash against economic globalisation spurred by the free trade agenda of the WTO came on 30 November 1999, through the so-called Battle of Seattle, where more than 40,000 people protested against the WTO's Ministerial Conference (Yuen, Burton-Rose and Katsiaficas 2001; Smith 2002; Fominaya 2014: 54–59). As if to reinforce an unfortunate stereotype, police retaliated violently against the protesters, and this response came to be epitomised in popular imagination as representative of a supposed antagonism which WTO nurtures towards human rights.[4]

The historical context for the tensions between the two regimes of human rights and multilateral trade stems from the vision of the victors of World War II (WWII) on how the post-war global framework ought to look like. The 'scourge of war' evidenced by the world, both during and in the immediate aftermath of WWII, witnessed the prelude to a 'New World Order', which was to rest on four pillars – peace and human rights, on the one hand, and trade and finance, on the other (Possel 2008: 192). While the pillars of peace and human rights were necessitated in response to the Holocaust and the catastrophic devastation of the war itself, the pillars of trade and finance were deemed essential as part of the new schema in order to avoid a repetition of the economic instability prevalent during the Great Depression of the 1930s, accompanied by the beggar-thy-neighbour policies which had led to both the emergence and the amplification of WWII (Hoekman and Kostecki 1995: 12; Harrison 2007: 7). The first two pillars of peace and human rights were conceived to be developed and implemented by a global inter-governmental organisation – the UN. In order to develop and implement the other pillar of finance, the Bretton Woods Institutions, including the International Monetary Fund (IMF) and the World Bank (WB), were established in 1944 (Possel 2008: 192). With respect to the fourth pillar of trade, world leaders negotiated the 'Havana Charter for an International Trade Organisation' in 1948 (hereafter, Havana Charter 1948). However, the planned International Trade Organisation (ITO) never saw the light of the day due to refusal by the US to ratify it, despite having taken the lead in its negotiations (Narlikar 2005: 11; Kinley 2009: 39). What did come into effect was the General Agreement on Tariffs and Trade, 1947 (hereafter, GATT 1947), which operated as a de facto trade institution (mostly ad hoc, and without a well-defined institutional structure) until it metamorphosed into the WTO in 1994 by virtue of the Marrakesh Agreement Establishing the World Trade Organisation (hereafter, Marrakesh Agreement 1994). It is for this reason that the UN and the WTO, despite sharing some common objectives (although, obviously, not all), have from the outset adopted different approaches in their functioning – the human rights–centric approach of the UN and the economic approach of the WTO. This difference in approaches of these two institutions since their inception gives us a very good indication of why the two legal regimes of multilateral trade and human rights have developed more or less independently from one another, as against an interdependent and integrated system (Konstantinov 2009: 317–21).

A brief overview of the approach of the UN

Bare perusal of the Charter of the United Nations (hereafter, UN Charter 1945) reveals the importance placed by its drafters on the recognition, protection and advancement of human rights as one of the primary institutional objectives of the UN. The Preamble proclaims that the peoples of the UN are determined 'to reaffirm faith in fundamental human rights, in the dignity and worth of the human person, in the equal rights of men and women and of nations large and small' (UN Charter 1945: Preamble, Para. 2) and 'to promote social progress and better standards of life in larger freedom' (UN Charter 1945: Preamble, Para. 4). Similarly, one of the fundamental purposes of the UN is 'to achieve international co-operation in solving international problems of an economic, social, cultural, or humanitarian character, and in promoting and encouraging respect for human rights and for fundamental freedoms for all without distinction as to race, sex, language, or religion' (UN Charter 1945: Article 1, Para. 3). The Charter also specifically mandates the UN as an organisation to promote 'universal respect for, and observance of, human rights and fundamental freedoms' (UN Charter 1945: Article 55(c)).

In order to operationalise these mandates, the UN Charter, among other things, required the ECOSOC to establish a Commission on Human Rights (UN Charter 1945: Article 68), whose work led to the adoption of the Universal Declaration of Human Rights (UDHR) by the United Nations General Assembly (UNGA) in 1948 (UNGA 1948). The Preamble of the Declaration begins with the solemn recognition by member States that the 'inherent dignity and the equal and inalienable rights of all members of the human family is the foundation of freedom, justice and peace in the world' (UNGA 1948: Preamble, Para. 1). It merely declares what is inherently existing in human beings, just by virtue of their human embodiment.

The UDHR was followed by the adoption of two separate legally binding human rights Covenants on 16 December 1966, namely the International Covenant on Civil and Political Rights (ICCPR) and the

ICESCR. These two Covenants along with the UDHR are today collectively termed as the 'International Bill of Human Rights' as observed by the United Nations Office of the High Commissioner for Human Rights (hereafter, OHCHR) (OHCHR 1996) and, over time, have together come to constitute the bedrock of the international human rights system under the UN.

This working of the UN human rights mechanism is implemented through a comprehensive three-pronged system comprising the Charter-based monitoring bodies, the Treaty-based monitoring bodies and the OHCHR.[5] The Charter-based bodies include the principal organs of the UN and the subsidiary bodies created by those organs, including the Human Rights Council (UNHRC) with its elaborate Special Procedures consisting of Special Rapporteurs and Independent Experts, among other processes. The Treaty-based bodies, on the other hand, consist of all the Committees established under the nine 'core' human rights treaties, which, apart from the ICCPR and ICESCR, include the Convention Against Torture (1984), International Convention for Elimination of All Forms of Racial Discrimination (1966), Convention for Elimination of Discrimination against Women (1979), Convention on the Rights of the Child (1989), International Convention on the Protection of the Rights of All Migrant Workers (1990), Convention on the Rights of Persons with Disabilities (2006) and the International Convention for the Protection of All Persons from Enforced Disappearance (2006). The OHCHR, which forms part of the UN Secretariat, coordinates the human rights work of the UN and provides support to the various Charter and Treaty bodies. Additionally, the various UN organs and specialised agencies have also incorporated human rights objectives as the foundational purpose of their working.[6]

Thus, it is clear from what has been synoptically culled out earlier that the UN as an institution is mandated to adopt a predominantly human rights–centric approach to its functioning and, in compliance thereof, has established a relatively spread-out web of human rights mechanisms.

A brief overview of the approach of the WTO

In contrast, the historical events leading to the emergence of the WTO as an institution explain why it has adopted a predominantly economic approach to its functioning. As noted earlier, the ITO which was supposed to be created as the nodal organisation for regulating international trade at the end of WWII, itself remained stillborn. The 23 countries – 12 developed and 11 developing – involved in the negotiations for exchange of tariff reductions were anxious that implementation of liberalisation not be conditional upon the conclusion of the ITO talks. As a result, they adopted the GATT 1947 as an interim agreement (Hoekman and Kostecki 2001: 38). With the ITO never coming into force, GATT 1947 continued to operate without having an institutional structure, and, over the four decades of its regime, it expanded considerably with many more countries becoming a part of it. However, it also became increasingly fragmented as 'side agreements' or codes were negotiated between subsets of countries (Hoekman and Kostecki 2001: 38). Many new supplementary provisions and special arrangements were added to GATT 1947, yet some important trading sectors like agriculture, textiles and clothing and services were not made subject to MTS.

During the Uruguay Round of negotiations in the 1980s, States deliberated upon a more comprehensive global trading regime bearing an institutional structure. Thus, the WTO was created in order to substitute the hitherto operational GATT 1947. Unlike the latter, the WTO encompassed not only liberalisation of trade in goods (GATT 1947 became part and parcel of General Agreement on Tariffs and Trade 1994; hereafter, GATT 1994) but also trade in services (General Agreement on Trade in Services 1994; hereafter, GATS 1994) and established rules for regulating trade-related aspects of intellectual property rights (Agreement on Trade-Related Aspects of Intellectual Property Rights 1994; hereafter, TRIPS 1994), technical barriers to trade (Agreement on Technical Barriers to Trade 1994; hereafter, TBT 1994), sanitary and phyto-sanitary measures (Agreement on the Application of Sanitary and Phyto-Sanitary Measures; hereafter, SPS 1994), among others. It also created a new and fairly sophisticated system for settlement of multilateral trade disputes (Understanding on Rules and Procedures Governing the Settlement of Disputes 1994; hereafter, DSU 1994) and for periodic review of members' trade policies (Agreement on Trade Policy Review Mechanism 1994). Pertinently, the WTO was not made a part of the UN system and was conceived to operate as an independent international institution.[7]

The WTO proclaims that the economic case for an open trading system based on multilaterally agreed rules rests largely on 'commercial common sense' but is also supported by evidence emerging from the experience of world trade and economic growth since WWII (WTO 2015a: 13). Thus, it points out that tariffs on industrial products have fallen steeply and now average less than 5% in industrial countries. It also points out that during the first 25 years after WWII, world economic growth averaged about 5% per year, a high rate that was partly a consequence of lower trade barriers. It further observes that world trade grew even faster, averaging about 8% during the period.

The 'commercial common sense' case for liberalisation of trade internalised by the WTO finds its genesis in the economic theory of 'comparative advantage' propounded by the classical economist David Ricardo (1817). In its basic form, it simply means that there are gains from trade associated with minimising opportunity costs through the division of labour, that is specialisation (Hoekman and Kostecki 2001: 33). An illustration at the international level may best explain the theoretical underpinnings of comparative advantage. Suppose that the US is better than Costa Rica at making automobiles, while Costa Rica is better than the US at producing coffee. It is clear that both would benefit if the US specialised in automobiles and sold them to Costa Rica, while Costa Rica specialised in producing coffee and traded it with the US. Now, this is a case where both the US and Costa Rica have absolute advantage over each other in the respective products.[8] But what if we assume now that Costa Rica is worse than the US at producing both automobiles and coffee? The theory of comparative advantage states that even in such situation Costa Rica must specialise and produce in what it comparatively does best, which is producing coffee even if it is not as efficient as the US in doing so, and the US must still specialise in what it comparatively does best, which is manufacturing automobiles. This way both can trade in these products and benefit from such international trade.[9] The comparison here is between Costa Rica's relative efficiency in producing coffee versus producing automobiles, compared to the US's relative efficiency in producing the same products. The theory of comparative advantage builds on the proposition that a country does not have to be best at anything to gain from trade (WTO 2015a: 14). It must simply concentrate and invest in what it does better.

This theory can, however, work only if the conditions necessary for ensuring the effective use of comparative advantage of States are guaranteed. Among other things, these conditions require that States enter into reciprocal commitments to reduce trade barriers. For instance, if the US is to enjoy from its comparative advantage in automobiles in the Costa Rican market, it is important that Costa Rica does not create trade barriers which inhibit the access by the US producers to its markets. Similarly, Costa Rica can benefit from its comparative advantage in coffee only if the US allows easy access to its markets to Costa Rican coffee producers. The theory, therefore, suggests that countries desiring to maximise their wealth must not impose trade barriers and that policies which allow the unrestricted flow of goods and services 'sharpen competition, motivate innovation and breed success' (WTO 2015a: 13). Liberalisation is assumed to 'multiply the rewards that result from producing the best products, with the best design, at the best price' (WTO 2015a: 13). This rationale of reciprocal anti-protectionism commitments lies at the heart of the MTS.[10] Indeed, one of the frequently stated objectives of the WTO is for MTS to bring stability and predictability to world commerce, as well as to improve access to markets through the progressive liberalisation of world trade (Robinson 2001: 211).

The WTO's legal architecture is built upon four basic rules which seek to ensure the permissive environment necessary for the theory of comparative advantage to work. The first such rule applicable to trade in goods is that WTO members must 'bind' themselves, pursuant to periodic negotiations, to the maximum tariffs they may charge other WTO members on a particular product (GATT 1994: Article XXVIII bis (1)). These agreed-upon tariff concessions then become 'tariff bindings', which are set out in an Annex to GATT 1994 in the relevant members' tariff schedules. Article II of GATT 1994 requires all members to adhere to their tariff bindings and not impose customs duties exceeding what they have committed to in their schedules. This rule is considered indispensable for the theory of comparative advantage to work because without the predictability it brings with it, no country will know which other country's market it can access.

The second and third rules which form the preconditions for the theory to work are the two limbs of the non-discrimination principle. These are the most favoured nation (MFN) principle and the national treatment (NT) principle, which collectively are viewed as the cornerstone of MTS (Trebilcock 2011: 18). The MFN principle requires that customs duties and charges of any kind imposed by any country on any other member country or any advantage, favour, privilege or immunity granted by such country to any product originating in any other country should be accorded immediately and unconditionally to a 'like' product originating in the territories of all other members (GATT 1994: Article 1).[11] Thus, MFN captures the idea that as part of MTS, countries cannot normally discriminate between their trading partners, and, therefore, no WTO member should be charged a higher customs duty and charges of any kind by a particular country than another WTO member with respect to 'like' products. This principle is considered fundamental to the successful implementation of the comparative advantage theory. For instance, without the MFN principle, the US may be allowed to charge Nicaragua a lower customs duty on its coffee in comparison with what Costa Rica is charged, resulting in a situation where

Costa Rica will not be able to benefit from its comparative advantage, thereby defeating the underlying economic logic behind liberalisation. The second limb of non-discrimination, NT principle, requires that once the customs duties have been paid off by foreign exporters at the border, then no additional burdens may be imposed on them in the domestic market through internal taxes, charges, laws, regulations and so on, if the domestic producers of like products do not bear the same burden (GATT 1994: Article III).[12] Again, this principle seeks to ensure that comparative advantage theory works. For instance, in its absence, the Costa Rican coffee producer who has exported his or her coffee to the US may be unable to benefit from comparative advantage if his or her coffee is charged an internal value added tax in the US, while the domestically produced coffee in the US is not.

The fourth important essential rule, especially in the context of trade in goods, is elimination of quantitative restrictions. Article XI of GATT 1994 prohibits the use of quotas or import or export restrictions on the importation or exportation of goods into or out of any member State. Again, the idea here is that unless such quotas are prohibited, Costa Rica may not be able to benefit from its comparative advantage, if Nicaragua is guaranteed a particular quota in terms of the total imports of coffee into the US or if Costa Rica is prohibited from exporting to the US coffee beyond a particular quantity.

It is in the aforesaid background that Petersmann (2008a: 169) has rightly pointed out that the approach of the WTO as well as its objectives are predominantly economic.

Different approaches, shared objectives and unfortunate tensions

This dichotomised structure has resulted in a rather ambivalent situation for States since they are legally bound to both regimes. At the UN, States adopt (or at least are required to adopt) a human rights–based approach in compliance with their obligations under the UN Charter and various human rights treaties. In the same breath, under the auspices of the WTO, these very States adopt a predominantly economic approach in line with the WTO agreements. The ambivalence in approaches obviously can result in tensions if the WTO obligations lead to undermining the obligations on States cast under international human rights law. In other words, if certain policies or rules adopted by States under the WTO result in undermining human rights, then those States can end up undermining or even breaching their human rights commitments in favour of their trade commitments.

The fact that existing tensions between the two regimes of human rights and multilateral trade can be explained by the initial adoption of different approaches by States at the UN and the WTO, does not either mean that this was inevitable or that it was appropriate. Despite the distinct approaches adopted by States at the two organisations, both, in fact, do share some common objectives. Article 55(a) of the UN Charter provides that the UN 'shall promote higher standards of living, full employment, and conditions of economic and social progress and development'. These are very similar to the expressions present in the Marrakesh Agreement which states that the Parties to the Agreement recognise:

> that their relations in the field of trade and economic endeavour should be conducted with a view to raising standards of living, ensuring full employment and a large and steadily growing volume of real income and effective demand, and expanding the production of and trade in goods and services, while allowing for the optimal use of the world's resources in accordance with the objective of sustainable development, seeking both to protect and preserve the environment and to enhance the means for doing so in a manner consistent with their respective needs and concerns at different levels of economic development.
>
> (Marrakesh Agreement 1994: Preamble, Para. 1)

This similarity in language of the two provisions is no sheer coincidence. The Havana Charter of the stillborn ITO made express reference to Article 55 of the UN Charter, wherein it was recognised that the first purpose and objective for the creation of the ITO was 'the aims set forth in the Charter of the United Nations, particularly the attainment of the higher standards of living, full employment and conditions of economic and social progress and development, envisaged in Article 55 of that Charter' (Havana Charter 1948: Article 1). Almost identical words found expression in GATT 1947 which recognised that the relations of members in the field of trade and economic endeavour should be conducted with a view 'to raising standards of living, ensuring full employment and a large and steadily growing volume of real income and effective demand, developing the full use of the resources of the world and expanding the production and exchange of goods' (GATT 1947: Preamble, Para. 2). Although specific reference to Article 55 of the UN Charter was not made in GATT 1947, the context in which those expressions were mentioned is obvious. As we have seen earlier, these expressions eventually found their way into the Marrakesh Agreement of the WTO as well.[13]

The shared objectives of both MTS and human rights can also be traced to Article 28 of the UDHR, which states that 'everyone is entitled to a social and international order in which the rights set forth in this Declaration can be fully realised' (Possel 2008: 192). This acknowledgement, therefore, captures the intention of the drafters at the time that the international order related to trade as well ought to have been such that the human rights enshrined under the UDHR could be fully realised. This is all the more evident if we consider that the UDHR was proclaimed almost around the same time that GATT 1947 came into effect.

These facts emphasise that although the two organisations were established separately with specialised mandates, it was never the original intention that they develop in 'splendid isolation' from each other. To the contrary, what was sought to be obtained was a unified international social order based on respect for human rights, sovereign equality of states and international cooperation in trade and finance, such that States do not revert back to the circumstances that led to, and escalated, WWII. Indeed, as Howse (2002a: 97) points out, initially, trade liberalisation was embedded within a political commitment to the progressive, interventionist welfare state. Gradually, however, he notes that the 'new trade policy elite' with the bent of 'managers and technical specialists' tended to understand the trade system in terms of the policy science of economics, rather than the original grand normative political vision, leading to systematic isolation of MTS as a regime (Howse 2002a: 98).[14]

There are also good reasons why these two regimes *ought to have* developed in a mutually reinforcing manner. The fields of human rights and trade are interdependent and in many cases overlapping. The fulfilment of human rights depends on generation of wealth and availability of resources, which can result from trade. For instance, exercise of the right to vote, effective functioning of judiciaries, the right to food, clothing and shelter and the right to health all need necessary resources and are thus dependent on successful implementation of trade policies that are aimed at the generation of wealth. Similarly, a healthy population with necessary basic amenities, medicines, access to justice and effective governance are all pre-requisites of a successful MTS.

Yet, as things have developed, WTO policies vis-à-vis human rights have often been severely criticised, including by some who conclude that the WTO itself is antagonistic to human rights (ECOSOC 2000:

Para. 15). Proposed solutions have, therefore, varied from a complete abolition of the WTO (Bello and Legrain 2000), to entirely overhauling the WTO processes by making human rights a central purpose of the same (Dommen 2004). A mapping of the vast landscape of literature on this issue shows that today there definitely exists a widespread concern and recognition among different actors about the adverse effects of MTS and some of its policies on human rights. However, there is no general consensus on how the human rights issues related with MTS must be addressed. There are differences on the role of the WTO itself. There are those who argue that the WTO, being primarily a trade organisation, should not be overburdened with the additional task of handling human rights (Eres 2004; Sampson 2005: 4), while others argue that the WTO has not only moral but legal responsibility to make policies that protect human rights and also promote the same (Howse and Mutua 2000).

On the normative side also, legal scholars differ significantly on how any possible 'conflicts' between trade obligations and human rights obligations of States ought to be resolved.[15] There are scholars who insist that human rights obligations of States 'trump' their WTO obligations in case of a conflict (Howse and Mutua 2000; de Schutter 2011: 176–77; 2014: 72), while others argue that there is no such general normative superiority of human rights in the hierarchy of international legal obligations (Alvarez 2001: 6–7; Marceau 2002: 798). Also, while some scholars argue that the WTO's dispute settlement system is the appropriate forum for States to invoke their human rights obligations to justify breaches of WTO obligations (Pauwelyn 2003a; b), others argue that the DSU prohibits any such invocation of non-WTO law in multilateral trade disputes (Marceau 2001; 2002).

These differences in the moral, legal and political opinions among scholars and policy makers on the role of the WTO in the global society have also manifested themselves in the various solutions proposed to tackle the issue. One of the solutions proposed is strengthening the UN human rights monitoring bodies (Zagel 2005), which do not enjoy the same judicial authority that WTO Dispute Settlement Bodies enjoy. Other solutions include developing a human rights–based approach to the WTO (Petersmann 2001; Robinson 2001; Kong 2005: 232–35; Possel 2008), which involves the whole gamut of proposed reforms, ranging from incorporation of a 'social clause' in the WTO Agreements (Stirling 1996; Sutherland 1998), to changing the objectives of the WTO itself by making human beings the central subject of international trade rather than mere objects (Petersmann 2008a), to conducting human rights impact assessments of trade policies (ECOSOC 2004: Para. 53; UNHRC 2011a), to changing the judicial approach of the Dispute Settlement Mechanism (Howse 1999; Trebilcock and Howse 2005; Harrison 2007; Howse 2008; Petersmann 2008b; Irish 2011), to adopting a Multilateral Agreement on Trade and Human Rights to be annexed to the Marrakesh Agreement (Choudhury *et al.* 2011).

As spelt out at the outset, these proposed solutions suffer from either a complete issue-by-issue segregation so that there is no coherent theoretical framework for analysing the linkages or from a collective dealing of all human rights issues affected by MTS as if they were a single issue which deserve a common solution. What is lacking, therefore, is a comprehensive framework which will coherently link the normative elements of all the different issues and yet leave room for different solutions from a policy perspective.

Most recent books on the topic tend to be compilations of different essays on different topics without a theoretical framework which makes the field coherent enough to suggest sensible policy responses (e.g. Francioni 2001; Compa and Diamond 2003; Cottier, Pauwelyn and Burgi 2005; Abbott, Kaufmann and Cottier 2006; Joseph 2009; Drache and Jacobs 2014). In the alternative, they tend to be studies only on specific trade-related issues impacting human rights, such as on patents and access to medicines (Hestermeyer 2007); human rights–related trade measures (Cassimatis 2007); health, trade and human rights (MacDonald 2006); hunger and trade (Gonzalez-Pelaez 2005); and indigenous cultural heritage and international trade (Graber, Kuprecht and Lai 2012), among several others. Very few general and holistic studies on the relations between multilateral trade and human rights have been undertaken at a systemic level (Harrison 2007; Aaronson and Zimmerman 2008; Hernandez-Truyol and Powell 2009; Joseph 2011). But most of these studies also, despite being quite comprehensive in their coverage of the different linkage-issues, stop short of providing an underlying theoretical framework with policy application in terms of approaching solutions to those linkage-issues. In other words, while they analyse several linkage-issues, each of them remains a mutually exclusive analysis. There is no central theory systematically explaining how and why those diverse linkage-issues arise in the first place and how they might be connected to each other. In metaphorical terms, studying individual planets without understanding the solar 'system' within which they exist can only lead to a scattered and fragmented analysis.

The study which comes closest to what is being attempted in this book is a human rights–based methodology for analysing the linkages between international trade law and human rights law developed by James Harrison (2007). However, the analysis by Harrison is restricted to the ways in which human rights grounds can be raised in legal argumentation within the existing WTO structures, particularly before the dispute settlement body (DSB) of the WTO. His methodology operates very much on the analysis of the 'types of human rights measures which States can take to protect and promote human rights in the trade law context' (Harrison 2007: 61). Thus, his methodology includes dividing the human rights measures which States can legitimately take within existing WTO structures into three typologies, namely conditionality-based, compliance-based and cooperation-based, trade-related measures aimed at the protection and promotion of human rights (Harrison 2007: 62). Unfortunately, this methodology is quite restrictive in terms of analysing the *systemic* linkages between multilateral trade and human rights for three reasons. First, it is by self-proclamation based on a legal positivist approach and, therefore, readily accepts WTO laws and rules as they are without critically questioning their formation or scope (Harrison 2007: 18, 51). The methodology only searches for how human rights arguments can be made compatible with WTO rules as they are. By focusing on WTO laws as they are and not also on how they ought to be, Harrison's methodology does not permit consideration of the linkages at a more holistic level. *Per contra*, the main focus of our study is at the broader level, that is how does the MTS (with the stress on the 'system' and not just its rules) impact human rights adversely, and, therefore, the theoretical framework we need must be capable of analysing WTO laws without binding ourselves to accepting the legitimacy of WTO laws as they are. Additionally, it must permit an analysis of linkages which stem from non-legal aspects of MTS. Second, Harrison's methodology only permits an analysis of which measures can be undertaken by States to protect and promote human rights. The analysis we seek to make is at a more fundamental and, hence, deeper level. We seek not to find only the measures which can be taken by States but also to find the reasons linkage-issues arise in the first place and whether there is any systematic way of categorising them. Third, Harrison's methodology focuses on measures, but only those which are 'trade-related'. Thus, it limits our research to finding measures which can be taken by States within what is permitted by WTO rules. To begin with a framework which restricts us from the outset is not compatible with our objective of a systemic study. Indeed, by focusing on a restricted typology-based methodology, Harrison does not address the underlying need for a very theory on linkages.

Other smaller and more restricted studies have separated human rights issues into those where individuals within a State are affected (inwardly measures) and those where individuals outside a State are affected (outwardly measures) (Charnovitz 1997; Leader 2005). However, for similar reasons mentioned earlier, these methodologies are incapable of permitting systemic analyses of how MTS impacts human rights.

A comprehensive theoretical framework calls for a pragmatic deconstruction of the different linkages between MTS and human rights, and this deconstruction, in turn, needs a rational basis for doing so. These deconstructed linkages then need to be bound together in a systematic theoretical thread which explains the normative, legal and philosophical elements involved in the reconciliation of the two regimes. This book is an attempt to do exactly that. It introduces a new theory – coined here as 'governance space' – for understanding how MTS impacts on abilities of States to fulfil their human rights obligations. The 'governance space' theoretical framework is then used for systematically understanding the broad nature and scope of linkage-issues and how they might be connected. Building on this framework, the book also proposes the way forward to achieve such reconciliation using an approach based on human rights, specifically the RtD approach, and, therefore, is also policy oriented. Indeed, it is aimed at influencing the debates on this topic at the WTO, at the UN and in the civil society and academia with respect to the way forward in this increasingly complex globalised world.

Structure of the book

The full import and structure of the arguments raised in this book can only be clear to the reader once the theoretical framework has been presented in the next chapter. However, to enable a useful head-start, it may not be out of place to briefly outline the structure of this book. The book is divided into nine chapters, including this introduction as the first. Chapter 2 will present the theoretical framework used in this book for deconstructing the web of diverse linkages between MTS and human rights and will also essentially form the foundation for the analytical edifice that will be constructed in the subsequent chapters of this book. The framework introduces a theory on 'governance space' and builds on it. 'Governance space' is defined as the space necessary for governance. This includes the space required by all the different State and non-State actors who play a role in governance. With respect to States specifically, 'governance space' refers to the space which States need to carry out their responsibilities effectively, including the obligation to respect, protect and fulfil human rights. The manner in which WTO rules, policies and structures shape governance space of States determines the impacts on human rights in those States. Using 'governance space' as a central theme, the framework develops three 'linkage-categories' under which different 'linkage-issues' can be arranged and analysed. The first linkage-category includes issues where WTO laws and policies limit the governance space of States in fulfilling their human rights obligations. In these cases, states need governance space but do not have it because WTO laws limit the same. The second linkage-category addresses issues where WTO laws and policies do not limit governance space but create the permissive environment for States to abuse that space. Here, States have the necessary governance space, but MTS creates the environment which enables or permits them to abuse it. The third linkage-category includes issues where MTS inherently creates a limiting environment for States to use the governance space they already have by tapping into their unequal capabilities to benefit from the system. Chapters 5, 6 and 7 explain each of these linkage-categories with the help of one major linkage-issue as a case study. The choice of the three linkage-issues as case studies is based on the impacts these issues have on governance space and human rights in the contemporary world. The two chapters tucked between the theoretical framework and the analyses of each of the linkage-categories deal with the normative aspects of the linkages debate. Chapter 3, thus, analyses the oft-cited argument that human rights obligations of States 'trump' trade law obligations in case of a conflict between the two and argues that this proposition is correct only in very limited circumstances. More importantly, it argues that invocation of the normative hierarchy argument is, in fact, hugely distracting to the human rights project because it diverts attention away from finding solutions and gets caught in polarising and incessant debates which, in any case, serve very little policy purpose. The fourth chapter explores the extent to which international human rights laws can be read into WTO laws, particularly by WTO Panels, as part of their judicial functions. This analysis of the abilities or limitations of WTO Panels is important for us in order to explore whether or not they can play a significant role in efforts to find which human rights friendly policy-oriented solutions are appropriate and pragmatic for the tensions within the three linkage-categories. Chapter 8 of the book proposes the way forward to addressing the three linkage-categories. Building on Chapters 5, 6 and 7, it argues that the two regimes share the common objective of sustainable development and that this commonality necessitates adoption of a RtD approach to reconciling the tensions. Similarly, building on Chapters 3 and 4, Chapter 8 also examines the normative scope of adopting an RtD approach for MTS. Chapter 9 presents the concluding remarks.

Notes

1 The term 'multilateral trade' is consciously preferred in this book since its core analysis pertains to trade within the architecture of the World Trade Organisation. The other commonly used term 'international trade' is avoided since it is capable of including within its fold 'plurilateral trade', 'regional trade' or 'bilateral trade', which are not the foci of this book.

2 A unique feature about WTO as an international organisation is that its members need not be States, but only customs territories. Article XII of the Marrakesh Agreement states that 'any State or separate customs territory possessing full autonomy in the conduct of its external commercial relations and of the other matters provided for in this Agreement and the Multilateral Trade Agreements may accede to this Agreement'. Similarly, the Explanatory Note to the Agreement clarifies that the terms 'country' or 'countries' as used in this Agreement and the Multilateral Trade Agreements are to be understood to include any separate customs territory member of the WTO. In this book, the terms 'members', 'countries' and 'States' will be used interchangeably.

3 The UN human rights system has been quite emphatic in its insistence that States must ensure adherence to human rights even when they operate outside the UN's organisational structure. See, for instance, OHCHR (2002: Para. 5); the UN Committee on Economic, Social and Cultural Rights has also emphasised the obligation on States to ensure that 'agreements concerning trade liberalisation should not curtail or inhibit a country's capacity to ensure the full realisation of the right to water' (UN Committee on Economic, Social and Cultural Rights 2002: Para. 35).

4 For a detailed overview of the civil society protests at Seattle, see Thomas (2000).

5 For an overview of the UN Human Rights system, see OHCHR (2016a).

6 See, for instance, the founding documents of the Food and Agriculture Organisation, World Health Organisation, United Nations Children's Fund, United Nations High Commission for Refugees etc.

7 Article V of the Marrakesh Agreement states that 'the General Council shall make appropriate arrangements for effective cooperation with other inter-governmental organisations that have responsibilities related to those of the WTO'.

8 The Theory of Absolute Advantage was first popularised by Adam Smith in 1776 in his book *The Wealth of Nations*. He gave the following illustration:

> The tailor does not attempt to make his own shoes, but buys them off the shoemaker. The shoemaker does not attempt to make his

> own clothes, but employs a tailor . . . . What is prudence in the conduct of every private family, can scarcely be folly in that of a great kingdom. If a foreign country can supply us with a commodity cheaper than we ourselves can make it, better buy it off them with some part of produce of our own industry, employed in a way in which we have some advantage.
>
> See Smith (1776: 424).

9 Ricardo's famous postulation of the theory of comparative advantage comprised the following scenario, as has been aptly summarised by Trebilcock (2011: 2):

> Portugal can produce a given quantity of wine with 80 units of labour, and a given quantity of cloth with 90 units of labour. England can produce the same quantity of wine with 120 units of labour, and the same quantity of cloth with 100 units of labour. Thus, Portugal enjoys an absolute advantage over England in both wine and cloth. Ricardo argued that trade between the two countries was still mutually advantageous. England is able to export cloth which took 100 units of labour to produce in exchange for wine which it would have required 120 units of labour to produce. Similarly, Portugal, by exporting wine which it took 80 units of labour to produce, gains cloth which would have taken 90 units of labour to produce. Both countries are rendered better off through trade.

Ricardo's theory has been further elaborated by Swedish economists Eli Heckscher and Bertil Ohlin who posit that 'an economy is predicted to have a comparative advantage in producing goods that are intensive in its 'abundant factors of production'. As such, an economy will export goods that are intensive in its abundant factors of production and import goods that are intensive in its scarce factors of production. This proposition is called the Heckscher-Ohlin theorem. For a discussion, see Krugman and Obstfeld (2008: 54–87).

10 For an excellent overview of free trade and comparative advantage theory, see Irwin (1996).

11 MFN is also a fundamental principle of GATS (Article II) and TRIPS (Article IV), although in each agreement the principle is handled slightly differently.

12 See Article III of GATT, Article XVII of GATS, and Article III of TRIPS.

13 In this regard, see *US – Shrimp* (AB Report 1998: Para. 152) observing:

> At the end of the Uruguay Round, negotiators fashioned an appropriate preamble for the new WTO Agreement, which strengthened the multilateral trading system by establishing an international organisation, inter alia, to facilitate the implementation, administration and operation, and to further the objectives, of that Agreement and the other agreements resulting from that Round. In recognition of the importance of continuity with the previous GATT system, negotiators used the preamble of the GATT 1947 as the template for the preamble of the new WTO Agreement.

14 Howse further notes that

> a sense of pride developed that an international regime was being evolved that stood above the 'madhouse' of politics, a regime grounded in the insights of economic 'science', and not vulnerable to the open-ended normative controversies and conflicts that plagued most international institutions and regimes, most notably, for instance, the United Nations.

For a general discussion on the isolated development of trade law from other fields of public international law, see Pauwelyn (2003c).

15 Some scholars even argue that tensions between WTO and human rights obligations are mostly due to misinformation and they do not really exist. For instance, see Mavroidis (2004: 244, 257, 259), arguing that because 'the WTO contract per se does not prejudge regulatory intervention in the field of human rights at all', 'the trade and human rights debate, in the absence of any WTO-dictated policy and consequently any jurisprudence', is due to 'pure misinformation'.

2

A 'GOVERNANCE SPACE' THEORY ON LINKAGES

The WTO is today one of the most important and potent drivers of globalisation. As is the case with other institutional drivers of globalisation such as international financial institutions or multinational corporations, the impacts of MTS can be felt strongly at the local levels. They also tend to permeate into the traditional spaces needed and used by States for policy making. These impacts can be both positive and negative, but what is clear is that there is an obvious tension between the inherently permeating (or, some may argue, invasive) nature of MTS, on the one hand, and the nation-state system, on the other, which tries to guard itself against the adverse impacts of MTS within its own borders.[1] This tension is palpable in the sphere of human rights as well. While MTS has a diverse range of impacts on human rights, under international human rights law, it is primarily the duty of each State to deal with those impacts within their own jurisdictions.[2]

Typically, States are required to exercise their human rights obligations through a variety of administrative, legislative, judicial, budgetary and policy measures which are available to them (UN Committee on Economic, Social and Cultural Rights 1990: Para. 6, 7; UN Human Rights Committee 2004: Para. 7). It is for each State to design and implement the most appropriate combination of these diverse measures in order to deal with potentially adverse impacts of WTO laws. Obviously, therefore, whether a State is able to deal with such adverse impacts as a result of the permeating nature of MTS rests heavily on the 'space' that a State has at its disposal to design and implement such appropriate combination of measures.

This 'space' is applicable not only to human rights obligations of States as such but also broadly to the ability of States to adopt an appropriate mix of strategies in order to ensure economic growth in accordance with their own domestic priorities. The terminology popularly used to denote this ability of States is 'policy space'. Numerous scholars have analysed the question whether MTS limits the policy space of States to adopt the proper mix of domestic policies that they feel is appropriate for their own growth. While this term has now become mainstream as a reference point for analysing WTO laws and whether or not it limits the ability of States to adopt appropriate policy choices for economic development, it has also been used recently in the context of States' abilities to fulfil their human rights obligations (Drache and Jacobs 2014). However, it is suggested in this study that for the specific purpose of analysing human rights linkages, 'policy space' may not be an adequate concept, for it does not capture the entire gamut of linkages between MTS and human rights. It is suggested that, in fact, the term 'policy space' may be misleading in terms of placing a holistic perspective on the nature of human rights obligations of states. It is contended that a new way of conceptualising this space – expressed as 'governance space' in this study – is necessary to denote the appropriate lens for analysing linkages between MTS and human rights.

The concept of policy space in the context of economic development

The term 'policy space' in its current meaning appeared in documents of the United Nations Conference on Trade and Development (UNCTAD) in about 2002 and acquired its first official status in the Sao Paulo Consensus of 2004 (Page 2007a: 14). In the preparatory notes drafted by the UNCTAD Secretariat for that conference, economic policy space was described as referring to 'the extent to which national governments have the authority to make decisions concerning economic policy and, correspondingly, the extent to which such authority is constrained by international disciplines and processes' (UNCTAD 2004a: Para. 1). The Sao Paulo Consensus document, in turn, defined the concept as 'the scope for domestic policies, especially in the areas of trade, investment and industrial development' which might be 'framed by international disciplines, commitments and global market considerations' (UNCTAD 2004b: Para. 8). The expression has continued to gain momentum, particularly in policy circles and scholarly literature, and most recently in the context of the sustainable development goals (SDGs) incorporated in UNGA Resolution entitled 'Transforming Our World: the 2030 Agenda for Sustainable Development' (UNGA 2015: Para. 21, 44, 63, 74, 81 and Goal 17.15).

In its first 'T.R.A.D.E Policy Brief' titled 'Policy Space for the Development of the South', South Centre, the official research think-tank of the G77, described policy space as freedom: 'Policy space is about freedom of choice. For developing countries, it is about their freedom to choose the best mix of policies possible for achieving sustainable and equitable economic development given their unique and individual social, political, economic, and environmental conditions' (South Centre 2005: 1). Referring to the Sao Paulo Consensus, it argued that the concept 'reflects the idea that governments should have the leeway to evaluate the trade-off between the benefits of accepting international rules and the constraints posed by the loss of policy space' (South Centre 2005: 1).

It also provided the principles on which the concept of policy space is founded, namely 'the principles of equal sovereignty of States, the right to development, and the provision of special and differential treatment to developing countries' (South Centre 2005: 1). While critiquing the 'one-size-fits-all' approach of the WTO as not being workable, it stated that 'when applied operationally, recognising policy space means that developing countries should not be required to adhere to international disciplines that they may not be ready to apply or which may yet be inappropriate for them at their respective levels of economic development' (South Centre 2005: 2). In advising the developed countries to support the approach, it stated that 'the focus should be on the preservation of a wide range of policy choices and flexibility that can be used to adjust the pace and direction of economic development initiatives to the country's own economic development needs and priorities' (South Centre 2005: 6–7).

While the term 'policy space' is relatively new, the idea that there is a tension between international economic policies focusing on integration, and the freedom or autonomy that States need to adopt appropriate policies for their economic development, is not necessarily new (Chang 2005). It was well acknowledged, even in the early days of GATT 1947 and other regional integration initiatives, that this tension reflected the dilemma of 'how to keep the manifold benefits of extensive international economic intercourse free of crippling restrictions while at the same time preserving a maximum degree of freedom for each nation to pursue its legitimate economic objectives' (Cooper 1968: 15).

Indeed, the concept has also been analysed from a historical perspective by scholars, most notably by Ha-Joon Chang. In his seminal work, 'Kicking Away the Ladder', Chang (2002) demonstrated through careful empirical analysis that when today's developed countries (DCs) were at the level of development of many of the existing developing and least-developed countries (D-LDCs), they were, in fact, a lot more protectionist than the standards of liberalisation that existing D-LDCs are being pressurised to adopt. In his later work, Chang carried forward his self-described project of 'rewriting the history of capitalism' (Chang 2007: 16). In his work, Chang demonstrates that the US, Britain and other European countries used significant trade protectionism, State-regulated industrial policy and lax intellectual property regimes to develop. The US, for instance, had banned foreign banks from establishing themselves in the US until well into the twentieth century (Chang 2007: 105). Britain was one of the most protectionist countries until the mid-nineteenth century (Chang 2007: 38–40, 54–61). Cheng also highlighted that countries like the Netherlands and Switzerland did not have any patent protection laws until the early twentieth century (Chang 2007: 71), while Germany had a clear policy of non-enforcement of its patent laws for a long time during that period (Chang 2007: 142). As one reviewer of his work puts it, the point of Chang's work is to 'show that economic development, even in its first wave in Europe and North America, was driven not by liberalisation but by varied forms of state intervention that created, nurtured, and sometimes squelched market activity' (Milberg 2008: 119). It was only upon reaching the required threshold of industrialisation that the now - developed countries unleashed themselves for competition in the liberalisation era. In other words, these countries used their policy space to the fullest in the process of their own development, which included their autonomy and freedom to determine their own appropriate policy mix according to their own priorities. The metaphor of 'kicking away the ladder' neatly drives home the point that after having used that policy space, today's D-LDCs are being forced to limit their policy space through WTO policies.[3]

Several other scholars have evaluated the limiting effect of policy space through the mechanism of MTS (Gallagher 2005; Reinert 2007; Wilson Center 2007; Kozul-Wright and Rayment 2008; Gallagher 2013). UNCTAD itself has asserted that the rules and commitments of MTS restrict the de jure ability of D-LDCs to adopt national development policy (UNCTAD 2006: Para. 167). Typically, two main reasons are ascribed for why this limiting effect occurs (Akyuz 2009: 2). First, liberalisation, by its very nature, particularly due to the removal of restrictive regulation over the trans-boundary movement of goods, services and finance, renders economic performance extremely vulnerable to market/financial conditions abroad and thereby seriously circumscribes whatever impacts national policy instruments can have over macroeconomic and development policy objectives. Second, international rules and obligations related to trade, finance and investment 'diminish sovereign control over national policy instruments' (Akyuz 2009: 2).

Of course, not everyone agrees that WTO rules limit policy space of States. Some scholars have argued that under existing rules, States already have enough policy space (Page 2007a: 14; Mayer 2008). However, what no participant in the debate disputes is that the central issue is one of balance. Everyone agrees that 'international agreements on rules necessarily restrict States' freedom to manoeuvre – that is their intention' (Page 2007a: 14). In fact, in the post-WWII period, there was a clear acknowledgement that, in the 1930s, the beggar-thy-neighbour policies adopted by States as a result of protectionism had been an abuse of too much policy space and that this needed to be circumscribed through the adoption of GATT 1947. Today, the debate on policy space is essentially whether the WTO rules have 'gone too far' (Page 2007a: 14). To sum up, whichever side scholars take, the key point is that the debate has revolved around whether there is a balance between the WTO policies and the freedom of States to devise and implement appropriate policies for their own economic development.

Limitations of the concept of 'policy space' in the context of human rights

Given the widespread popularity of the concept of policy space in the context of economic development, it presents itself as a naturally attractive option with respect to the human rights context as well. Indeed, the concept of policy space as central to an analytical framework on the linkages between MTS and human rights has many advantages. First, it uses an existing and fairly sophisticated concept to carry forward the analysis of how WTO rules interact with the ability of States to deal with human rights impacts of such rules. Second, by focusing on the limiting nature of WTO rules of such policy space, it allows for an analysis that exposes the imbalance caused by the tension and, thus, is capable of giving guidance on how States should attempt to preserve or restore the balance. It also vividly brings out the inherent imbalance between DCs and D-LDCs in terms of their abilities to benefit from WTO rules. In that sense, it is a concept that can allow for a development-friendly approach. Third, it can act as the central theme around which a framework to analyse the linkages can be developed.

Despite these advantages, for the purpose of the framework being developed in this book, it is suggested that the concept of policy space does not capture the entire gamut of linkages between MTS and human rights and can sometimes be misleading.

First, in the manner in which the concept is used, policy space is grounded in the 'right' of a State to have the freedom of choice to make appropriate policies that it deems necessary for its economic development. This freedom of choice is, thus, claimed as a 'right' vis-à-vis other trading partners in the multilateral arena. While policy space can also be framed as a 'duty' of States towards their citizens, no one is claiming that it is a reflection of a State's supposed 'duty' to the international community and the other trading partners. It is doubtful whether such a 'duty' is actually cast upon States under international law. In fact, what is claimed through the concept of policy space is the preservation of some sovereign autonomy – quite the opposite of any presumed binding obligation to the international community. It is for this reason that, although the concept of policy space surely fits in nicely with policies for economic development that a country may wish to formulate, it does not fit well with the role of States in the human rights context. This is because the space that we seek to identify for States in order to respect, protect and fulfil human rights is not only a matter of a 'right' of a State vis-à-vis other trading partners, it is also grounded in the 'duty' towards them by virtue of the international obligations that States have undertaken towards each other under human rights treaties and CIL (UN Human Rights Committee 2004: Para. 2).[4] In other words, in the human rights context, a State needs that space not only because it is the autonomous sovereign right of the State to frame development policies but also because it is the duty of that State towards other States to respect, protect and fulfil human rights, in addition to a similar duty towards its own citizens. This duality of the State possessing both rights and duties with respect to the same human rights issue is neither novel nor strange. An analogy can be drawn from the United Nations Declaration on the Right to Development (hereafter, DRTD) (UNGA 1986). Article 2(3) thereof states that 'States have the right and the duty to formulate appropriate national development policies', while Article 3(1) stipulates that 'States have the primary responsibility for the creation of national and international conditions favourable to the realisation of the right to development'. As will also be exhaustively elaborated in Chapter 8, in addition to the right that States have against each other with respect to development, they owe duties to each other as well as to their own citizens. The concept of policy space as it has developed focuses only on the right aspect and because it does not capture the element of duty towards other States as also the reason for having it, it is suggested that it is inadequate in the human rights context.

Second, the concept of policy space is linked more to domestic policies for economic development, and, therefore, the role of States in making policy choices can be constrained by internal factors as much as it can be constrained by external factors. These internal factors may include the political climate, the financial situation, environmental resources and human capital. This does not accommodate the specific nature of human rights obligations of States, because these obligations are not a matter of choice for States, and, irrespective of internal constraints, States are under a duty to respect, protect and fulfil them. This applies not only to civil and political rights but equally to economic, social and cultural rights. The Committee on Economic, Social and Cultural Rights has made it amply clear that, even in the case of the latter set of rights, despite the requirement of progressive realisation thereof, and despite the same being subject to the maximum available resources within a country, the State still needs to fulfil its immediate and core obligations (UN Committee on Economic, Social and Cultural Rights 1990: Para. 1, 10). If a State is constrained due to internal factors, then it is required as a matter of binding international law to seek appropriate international assistance and cooperation with the objective of meeting its human rights obligations (UN Committee on Economic, Social and Cultural Rights 1990: Para. 11, 13).

Third, the concept of policy space, being principally about freedom of States to make policy choices, admits of a possibility for States to make choices that may not adhere to the required standards of human rights under international law. As pointed out earlier, it reflects the idea that governments should have the leeway to evaluate the trade-off between the benefits of accepting international rules and the constraints posed by the loss of policy space. In the case of human rights, States cannot make such a trade-off potentially limiting their duty to respect, protect and fulfil human rights. This point is most evident in case of many D-LDCs adopting policies (de facto, if not officially) ignoring their labour rights standards and obligations in order to benefit from cheap labour which becomes their primary comparative advantage (see Chapter 5 for detailed examination).[5] Under the policy space framework, maintaining lax labour standards can be framed as being within the State's 'right' to ensure its own economic development and, therefore, can also be framed as an acceptable use of its policy space. This wrongly gives the policy itself a positive colour. From a human rights perspective, this trade-off of labour standards by the State can be looked at only as an abuse, not as an appropriate use of space. In other words, the strong focus of the concept of policy space on the limiting characteristic of MTS means that it does not capture the idea that such a 'trade-off' undermining human rights through the use of the concept is not permissible under human rights law.

To sum up, the concept of policy space, as it is understood and used, suffers from a major lacuna. It focuses only on the shrinking of the space that States need to deal with adverse impacts of MTS and calls for more autonomy to States in terms of their ability to frame an appropriate mix of policies. However, the adverse impacts of MTS on human rights are not only a result of this shrinking of autonomy. They also arise when the space so needed is very much present, but States do not use the same, as is the case with non-implementation of labour standards. In addition, there are situations when the space needed is not really shrinking, but MTS creates an inherently limiting environment for States to use the space they already have. This happens mainly because several States are simply not capable enough to use their space as a result of the fact that their technological and infrastructural abilities do not match up with what is required to benefit from MTS.

For these reasons, this book suggests that a more holistic concept of the necessary space for States is crucial, a concept which encompasses the diverse range of linkages between MTS and human rights and, at the same time, fits comfortably within the parlance and discourse on human rights. This is particularly because of the centrality that such a holistic concept will play to the framework being developed here. A new concept needs to be able to evaluate and define this space, not only grounded in the idea that States have a right to freedom of choice but also grounded in the idea that States have a duty towards each other in fulfilling human rights obligations. In other words, the concept that defines the necessary space with respect to human rights needs a paradigm shift from one being founded solely on sovereign autonomy to one that encapsulates both sovereign autonomy and sovereign responsibility.

Conceptualising 'governance space' of states

The concept developed here and suggested as capturing the entire landscape of the space which States need to be able to fulfil their human rights obligations can be framed as 'governance space'. To hit the right chord at the outset, this concept is founded on the argument that the fulfilment of human rights obligations by States is a core function of governance and, therefore, what States need is 'governance space'.

At the broader level, by 'governance space', we simply mean the space necessary for governance. This includes the space required by all the different State and non-State actors who play a role in governance. With respect to States specifically, 'governance space' refers to the space which States need to carry out their responsibilities effectively. In other words, what States need to have is the necessary space to ensure governance, upon which the ability to fulfil their human rights obligations is founded. Without the former, it is impossible to achieve the latter. As will be elaborated presently, the idea of 'governance space', as developed here, addresses the inadequacies of the concept of 'policy space' and, therefore, presents a holistic central theme for designing the appropriate framework for the MTS and human rights linkages. Indeed, 'governance space' encompasses not only 'policy space' but also the duty aspect so central to the human rights context.

The concept of governance space benefits immensely from its close association with the concepts of 'governance' and 'good governance'. Both these terms have become commonplace in institutional policies today as synergetic with human rights. As will be explained in detail later, while the concepts of 'governance' and 'good governance' encompass the performance and quality of performance by States, respectively, including with regard to their human rights obligations, 'governance space' is conceived of here as the precondition for both; that is in reference to States, it is about their very ability to perform. In this analysis, we are essentially concerned with 'governance space' of States because our inquiry is into the question of how MTS interacts with the necessary space which States need to be able to fulfil their human rights obligations. Because of established policy synergies between human rights and governance and good governance, this theory on governance space sits rather comfortably with the prevalent language and discourse on human rights.

For the purpose of our framework, it will be instructive to briefly analyse the concepts of governance and good governance. Neither is well defined, and, therefore, neither enjoys consensus in definitional terms. This might appear surprising because both terms have been shifting rapidly to the very centre of human rights discourse in the last decade and a half. An explanation for this is perhaps that scholars from different fields of study have developed these concepts not entirely in synergy with each other. The idea of governance in the literature in international relations and political science with a strong focus on 'global governance' (Rosenau and Czempiel 1992; Wilkinson and Hughes 2002; Sinclair 2004; Weiss 2013) has developed distinctly from the literature in 'new governance theory' (Karkkainen 2004; NeJaime 2009; Alexander 2010; Ford and Condon 2011), which in turn has been explored by scholars from various fields, including lawyers. On the other hand, as will be discussed later, the literature on the topic of good governance has predominantly evolved in the development field and now has been co-opted increasingly in the human rights field.

Yet, at their core, these two concepts are inter related and indeed feed on each other. It may not be incorrect to argue that these ideas owe their intellectual and policy seeds at the international level to an earlier period in the 1970s and 1980s.[6] In a reference to the growing literature on these terms which had sprouted up before and around the beginning of the new millennium, Thomas Weiss poignantly remarked that 'something of an intellectual cottage industry has arisen around the term over the past two decades' (Weiss 2000: 796). We can only remark that today the cottage industry of the early 2000s is well on course to gaining transnational proportions. Indeed, if contemporary development aid conditionalities are anything to go by, the language of governance, and particularly good governance, has clearly become part and parcel of a multi-billion-dollar transnational industry.

Governance and the role of the state

The frequent usage of the term 'governance', by itself, does not tell us anything about its content. Nor does it mean that there is any one way of defining governance (ECOSOC 2006). One definition on the WB website states as follows:

> Conceptually, governance (as opposed to 'good' governance) can be defined as the rule of the rulers, typically within a given set of rules. One might conclude that governance is the process – by which authority is conferred on rulers, by which they make the rules, and by which those rules are enforced and modified.
>
> (WB 2016a)

This conceptualisation, however, with its focus on rulers may uncomfortably appear to be too State-centric, to the exclusion of the obvious role played by non-State actors in governance, as we shall discuss later. More officially, the WB has defined governance in more neutral terms as 'the manner in which power is exercised in the management of a country's economic and social resources for development' (WB 1994).

Definitions by other organisations and scholars are also less State-centric. For the United Nations Development Programme (UNDP), therefore, governance is defined as:

> the exercise of political, economic and administrative authority in the management of a country's affairs at all levels. Governance is a neutral concept comprising the complex mechanisms, processes, relationships and institutions through which citizens and groups articulate their interests, exercise their rights and obligations and mediate their differences.
>
> (UNDP 1997a)

A simpler definition as adopted from the work of Kaufmann, Kraay and Zoido-Lobaton (1999) is provided by the Worldwide Governance Indicators Project, which defines 'governance' as 'the traditions and institutions by which authority in a country is exercised' (WB 2016b).

The Brandt Commission or the Commission on Global Governance (1995: 2) viewed governance as the 'sum of the ways that public and private institutions and individuals manage their common affairs'.

Apart from institutional definitions, several scholars have employed different ways of expressing the concept. Just a few references might be in order. Mark Bevir (2013: 1) defines 'governance' as a concept referring to 'all processes of governing, whether undertaken by a government, market, or network, whether over a family, tribe, formal or informal organisation, or territory, and whether through laws, norms, power, or language'. Jon Pierre (2000) observes that 'governance refers to sustaining coordination and coherence among a wide variety of actors with different purposes and objectives'. Similarly, Paul Hirst (2000) states that 'governance can be generally defined as the means by which an activity or ensemble of activities is controlled or directed, such that it delivers an acceptable range of outcomes according to some established standard', while Stephen Bell (2002: 2) defines 'governance' as 'the use of institutions, structures of authority and even collaboration to allocate resources and coordinate or control activity in society or the economy'. Finally, Thomas Weiss (2013: 31) defines 'governance' as referring to 'the composite system of authoritative values, rules, norms, procedures, practices, policies and organisations through which an entity manages (or pilots or steers) its common affairs'.

As can be seen, there is a significant amount of diversity in how scholars and institutions have chosen to define the term. But, at its heart, the idea of governance implies a rejection of the term 'government' as the appropriate frame. Thus, today there is a widespread understanding among scholars from all fields that non-State actors, including civil society and corporate entities, are, and ought to be, important actors in governance within a State. The push for increased relevance and role of non-State actors in governance is simultaneously a statement of fact of what exists already in some respects and a critique of its exclusion in some other respects. Thus, the fact that many human rights NGOs providing health care to the disabled may be aiding the fulfilment of the human rights obligations which States have is testimony to their existing role in governance. Simultaneously, a systematic exclusion of civil society from participation in making policies which affect their livelihoods, such as a new investment agreement, represents their exclusion from governance which needs to be corrected. Both situations call for treating civil society as vital to governance. Similarly, non-State actors such as business corporations de facto play an important role in governance. This role can be both positive and negative. It may be positive because businesses do provide jobs and livelihoods to people and contribute to the general economic welfare within the State. On the other hand, their role in governance may be negative where corporate activities harm the environment and human rights without adequate accountability. The latter problem can be more acute in case of weak States which lack the regulatory capacity to enforce their laws or are simply not as powerful as big MNCs in terms of managing the adverse consequences of corporate activities (Kanade 2014: 41–42).

It is in the aforesaid context that the role of the State in contemporary governance needs to be situated. While there has been a clear shift in scholarly thinking of moving away from the sole focus on government to include non-State actors, the decentralised idea of governance still places a vital role on the State. Theories on 'new governance' posit that modern governance models need to be placed at the centre of a spectrum where State regulation through the command-and-control structure is at one end and free market mechanisms are at the other (Lobel 2004). The more governance moves toward either end of the spectrum, the likelihood of failure increases. Thus, the core tenets of governance, according to this theory, are such characteristics as collaboration with non-State actors, deliberation, experimentalism, localism, flexibility and adaptability and non-coerciveness (Lobel 2004; Gunningham 2009). Although it has been noted that a robust body of theory concerning the role of the State under the new governance model is as yet lacking (van der Heijden 2013: 16), there is a significant literature suggesting that while the State must decentralise its own role in governance to make it more effective, it needs to still play the core role of being a facilitator, orchestrator or enabler (van der Heijden 2013). In other words, while recognising and enabling an appropriate place for non-State actors to play their role in effective governance, the paradigm requires the State to ensure that non-State actors are not abusing their respective roles. The structure of the UN Guiding Principles on Business and Human Rights (UNHRC 2011b) is a case in point. The push to promote due diligence, human rights impact assessments and operational level grievance mechanisms by corporations to ensure that they do not harm human rights within a State has been described by Ruggie (2014), the architect of the aforesaid principles, as an example of 'new governance'. More importantly, while this role in governance for corporations is vital, the State is obviously still recognised as bearing the primary duty to ensure that corporations do not actually violate human rights (UNHRC 2011b: Principles 1–10). This duty of States to protect human beings from corporate-related abuses symbolises the role which States must play in new governance theory – as the captain of the ship.

At the other end of this more experimental approach, Natural Law scholars are more direct about the role of the State in governance. For John Finnis (1998: 283), 'public authority is not merely a moral liberty but essentially a responsibility (a liberty coupled with, and ancillary to, a duty)'. Leslie Green (2007: 166–67), therefore, argues that the State has the duty to govern, not just the right to govern. Among other reasons, a core argument for the primary 'non-voluntary' duty to govern placed on the State is that 'authority (and thus the *responsibility* of governing) in a community is to be exercised by those who can in fact effectively settle co-ordination problems for that community' (Finnis 1980: 246). This line of argumentation, of course, does not exclude the role for non-State actors in governance; the stress, however, is on the fact that the State has not only the right to govern but also the duty to do so, and as such must be accountable for non-performance of that duty.

It is not difficult to see why any adequate conception of governance ought to include both the right of the State to govern and the duty to do so, but in a way where it is itself accountable to its citizens, and with respect to human rights, also to the international community. At the same time, this conception of governance must include the ability to ensure that non-State actors are not violating their respective roles in governance, for instance, by harming human rights. The need to incorporate these essential dimensions of how we ought to understand governance is most aptly described by Rajagopal (2013), although in the slightly different context of 'global governance'. In his words, a proper conception of governance is:

> doomed to fail if it is grounded on the idea of disciplining states and celebrating private actors while failing to recognise the centrality of states for positive economic and social outcomes, or if it celebrates a narrow understanding of development while sacrificing accountability of state and private actors. Rather, the challenge we face is the need for a . . . governance agenda that reinstates accountable and embedded statehood as part of the solution, while committing itself to deep democratic structural transformation of such states, private networks, and supranational systems of order, and the creation and strengthening of norms and structures to hold states and other actors accountable to their commitments.
>
> (Rajagopal 2013: 898)

Governance and governance space of states

It is clear from the aforesaid discussion that different actors within a State have a role to play in governance and thus need the space to be able to do so. The precise scope and dimensions of each actor's governance space will necessarily depend on the context. However, in the context of States, given their primary duty to ensure governance, their governance space can be more accurately defined. Thus, in the specific context of States, governance space refers to the space which they need for carrying out their governance responsibilities effectively, including the duty to respect, protect and fulfil human rights. This responsibility includes not only securing, promoting, orchestrating or facilitating adequate governance space for non-State actors as appropriate but also ensuring that they do not abuse their respective governance space.

In the context of States, therefore, if governance is about the processes and structures through which they must ensure governance, governance space is about the space which States need for being able to employ whatever processes and structures are needed to govern. In the human rights context, this space includes the ability to fulfil the human rights obligations which States have undertaken, since that duty is a core element of ensuring governance. The big departure, of course, from policy space is that the concept of governance space developed earlier is embedded in both the right and the duty of States as the reason for having it. In the human rights context, unlike policy space, the reason why States need governance space is not only that they have a right against other States (because it is their duty to govern and they will not be able to do that if they do not have such a right) but also that they have a duty to their citizens as well as to other States to secure human rights through their role in governance.

Good governance

The term which has come to be more closely associated with human rights, and more broadly with the rule of law, is 'good governance'. But like the term 'governance', 'good governance' is also a subject of diverse definitions. What is clear though is that by emphasising on the 'good' aspect of 'governance', the concept directly characterises the quality of governance by an entity – in our case, the State – by linking it with positive and effective governance processes and outcomes.[7] Good governance, therefore, represents the precondition for the fulfilment of human rights in a given State.

Indeed, the UN has in the last one decade placed significant importance on linking human rights with good governance. This concept, however, did not necessarily begin with the field of human rights as its focus. As Weiss and Sornarajah (2012: Para. 1) note, the concept, in fact, 'developed from the discourse between the Bretton Woods Institutions and developing countries, in which good governance represented the standard of public administration expected of developing countries, both as a condition for, and an objective of, assistance'. They further point out that 'the World Bank's adoption of a good governance agenda took place against the background of research in academic circles which argued that poor countries remained poor because their governance structure was poor' (Weiss and Sornarajah 2012: Para. 1). Poor governance structures typically referred to lack of effectiveness and accountability and persistent endemic corruption in recipient countries. As a result, good governance quickly became the keyword that represented the conditions necessary for loans and other assistance to be effective in recipient countries. These were manifested and sought to be employed through conditionalities that were attached to loans from donor institutions.

Quickly, the idea of good governance was also embraced by the European Union (EU), which made use of it for the first time as a policy expression in a 1991 Resolution (Council and Member States of the European Communities 1991). It explicitly linked good governance to human rights and democracy, as being 'part of a larger set of requirements in order to achieve balanced and sustainable development' and that, 'in this context, account should be taken of the issue of good governance' (Weiss and Sornarajah 2012: Para. 46). Conditionalities related to good governance, including human rights, gradually crept into the trade policies of the EU as well, as exemplified by the EU-ACP partnership of 2000.[8] Individual donor States such as Germany, Canada, the UK, the US and Japan, among others, have also focused on good governance as a key component of their development assistance policies.

Today, however, a significant focus on good governance comes from the UN, which has made it a part of its human rights and development agendas. A lot of this, possibly, has to do with efforts to achieve the millennium development goals (MDGs) in the pre-2015 period and, now, the SDGs. Indeed, the 2030 Agenda envisages a world in which 'democracy, good governance and the rule of law as well as an enabling environment at national and international levels, are essential for sustainable development' (UNGA 2015: Para. 9) and further recognises that:

> the need to build peaceful, just and inclusive societies that provide equal access to justice and that are based on respect for human rights (including the right to development), on effective rule of law and good governance at all levels and on transparent, effective and accountable institutions.
>
> (UNGA 2015: Para. 35)

This linking of the good governance agenda to human rights from the earlier focus on economic performance was aptly described by former UN high commissioner for human rights, Louise Arbour. As she put it:

> [W]hereas governance, as a neutral notion, referred to mechanisms, institutions and processes through which authority was exercised in the conduct of public affairs, the normative concept of good governance has expanded over its recent history from concerns over economic performance to include other dimensions, such as political concerns, human development and the realisation of human rights.
>
> (UNCHR 2004a: Para. 8)

It is not surprising that the first official reference to good governance in the human rights context came from the erstwhile Commission on Human Rights (UNCHR) in 2000, around the same time that the UN

Millennium Declaration was adopted (UNGA 2000). In Resolution 2000/64 titled 'The Role of Good Governance in the Promotion of Human Rights', the commission recognised 'the importance of a conducive environment, at both the national and the international levels, for the full enjoyment of all human rights' (UNCHR 2000a: Preamble, Para. 2) and emphasised that:

> the strengthening of good governance at the national level, including through the building of effective and accountable institutions for promoting growth and sustainable human development, is a continuous process for all Governments regardless of the level of development of the countries concerned'.
>
> (UNCHR 2000a: Preamble, Para. 3)

The resolution went on to specifically recognise in its operative portion that 'transparent, responsible, accountable and participatory government, responsive to the needs and aspirations of the people, is the foundation on which good governance rests, and that such a foundation is a *sine qua non* for the promotion of human rights' (UNCHR 2000a: Para. 1). In order to further explore this link between good governance and human rights, the commission requested the UN high commissioner for human rights to invite all States to provide practical examples of activities that have been effective in strengthening good governance practices for the promotion of human rights at the national level (UNCHR 2000a: Para. 3).

Thereafter, several steps have been undertaken within the UN system, not only to explore the linkages between the two concepts but also to outline the best practices. A seminar on good governance practices for the promotion of human rights, jointly organised in 2004 by the OHCHR and UNDP, developed the linkages further and concluded that there is a mutually reinforcing relationship between good governance and human rights (UNCHR 2004a). In 2007, the OHCHR published a study entitled 'Good Governance Practices for the Protection of Human Rights', which outlined experiences from several countries on four broad thematic areas falling within the rubric of good governance, namely strengthening democratic institutions, improving service delivery, the rule of law and combating corruption (OHCHR 2007). The aim was to underline that good governance was a precondition for the realisation of human rights and to 'help fill the gap between human rights standards and principles, on the one hand, and their implementation through governance interventions, on the other' (OHCHR 2007: 1).

This study, in its introductory part, explains how good governance and human rights are linked:

> Good governance and human rights are mutually reinforcing. Human rights principles provide a set of values to guide the work of Governments and other political and social actors. They also provide a set of performance standards against which these actors can be held accountable. Moreover, human rights principles inform the content of good governance efforts: they may inform the development of legislative frameworks, policies, programmes, budgetary allocations and other measures. However, without good governance, human rights cannot be respected and protected in a sustainable manner. The implementation of human rights relies on a conducive and enabling environment. This includes appropriate legal frameworks and institutions as well as political, managerial and administrative processes responsible for responding to the rights and needs of the population.
>
> (OHCHR 2007: 1, 2)

The importance of good governance in creating and maintaining an enabling and conducive environment for the fulfilment of human rights has been recognised by the erstwhile Commission on Human Rights (UNCHR 2004b) and now by the Human Rights Council (UNHRC 2008a; 2012a). Interestingly, while the first resolution 2000/64 by the commission, referred to earlier, focused on the creation of this enabling environment only at the national level, subsequent resolutions have also included the international level (UNHRC 2008a: Preamble, Para. 3, 8; 2012a: Preamble, Para. 4, 5, 7).

Some of the human rights treaty bodies have also emphasised the importance of good governance as the precondition for the realisation of human rights (UN Committee on Economic, Social and Cultural Rights 1999: Para. 23; 2000: Para. 55; United Nations Committee on the Rights of the Child 2013: Para. 99). Therefore, as it stands today, the link between good governance and human rights is firmly established, although the former still is not defined with precision. The website of the OHCHR acknowledges that 'there is no single and exhaustive definition of good governance, nor is there a delimitation of its scope, that commands universal acceptance' and that 'the term is used with great flexibility; this is an advantage, but also a source of some difficulty at the operational level' (OHCHR 2016b). It goes on to say that 'the true test of "good" governance is the degree to which it delivers on the promise of human rights: civil, cultural, economic, political and social rights' (OHCHR 2016b).

The relation between governance space, governance and good governance

Despite these links between good governance and human rights, it is important to emphasise that the concept of governance space that we seek to develop stands at a much different level. We have already noted that there is a difference between governance and governance space. In the context of States, while governance is about the processes and structures through which governments govern, governance space is a step earlier; it is about the space which States need in the first place for their governments to be able to employ whatever processes and structures are needed to govern. Similarly, if good governance is about creating and maintaining the enabling environment for the fulfilment of human rights, governance space is a step earlier; it is about having an enabling environment in the first place, to be able to then create the necessary enabling environment for the fulfilment of human rights.

The relation between governance space and good governance also needs to be situated in another context. The deployment of 'good governance' upon D-LDCs, especially by DCs as part of conditions for development aid, has often been critiqued as an anti–Third World ideology (Rajagopal 2013: 898). Thus, Anghie contends that 'good governance . . . provides the moral and intellectual foundation for the development of a set of doctrines, policies and principles, formulated and implemented by various international actors to manage, specifically, the Third World state and Third World peoples' and that

> the basic task is that of reproducing in the non-Western world a set of principles and institutions which are seen as having been perfected in the Western world and which the non-Western world must adopt if it is to make progress and achieve stability.
>
> (Anghie 2000: 893–94)

There is indeed a widespread sentiment among people in D-LDCs that good governance, with its deeply embedded political overtones, contributes heavily to neo-colonialism (Anghie 1999: 25; Gathii 1999). As Chimni puts it:

> North seeks to occupy the moral high ground through representing the third world peoples, in particular African peoples, as incapable of governing themselves and thereby hoping to rehabilitate the idea of imperialism. The inability to govern is projected as the root cause of frequent internal conflicts and the accompanying violation of human rights necessitating humanitarian assistance and intervention by the North. It is therefore worth reminding ourselves that colonialism was justified on the basis of humanitarian arguments (the civilising mission). It is no different today.
>
> (Chimni 2006: 16)

There are excellent reasons to find such arguments meritorious. And it is in this context that the idea of governance space allows us to shed a deceptively romantic image of good governance and adopt a more grounded and balanced approach to it. It does so by accepting that good governance is a precondition for the fulfilment of human rights obligations by D-LDCs but, at the same time, insists that governance space is a necessary precondition for being able to do so. In other words, it allows for the moral high ground from which the barrage of good governance is deployed to be razed and attention to be instead demanded to governance space. By doing so, the appropriate evaluation can begin with analysing whether or not D-LDCs have the very governance space necessary to ensure good governance, instead of leaping to the assumption that the reason for human rights violations in D-LDCs is due to the lack of good governance despite all the necessary preconditions. Such evaluation will then enable a more revealing and grounded assessment of what the real causes for many D-LDCs not being able to ensure good governance are. In case there is enough governance space and the same is being abused by the State concerned, then obviously the insistence can be on ensuring good governance. In case, however, the State does not have adequate governance space, let's say as a result of the international economic regime or MTS, it may be more appropriate to address that before requiring it to ensure good governance as a condition for loan.

To put the previous discussion in a diagrammatic manner, this is what the picture looks like (Figure 2.1).

Thus, if governance is the precondition for good governance, and good governance is the precondition for the fulfilment of human

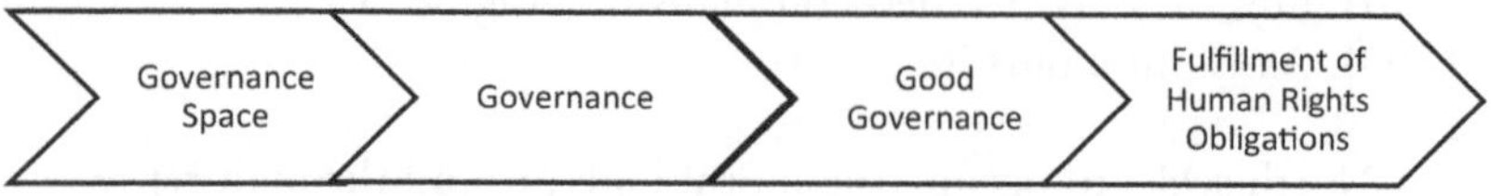

Figure 2.1 The Governance Space-Human Rights Vector
Source: Author.

rights, governance space is the precondition for all of the three. Our inquiry in this book is essentially about the interaction of WTO laws and policies with this governance space, that is, to what extent, and in which manner, does MTS shape and relate to that governance space and how does that influence the ability of States to be able to fulfil their human rights obligations.

As we have seen earlier, the concept of policy space is inadequate and, sometimes, misleading in terms of developing a framework which captures the linkages between MTS and human rights. On the other hand, the concept of governance space, as outlined earlier, helps us to articulate the necessary central theme that we need for developing such a framework. Unlike the former, the concept of governance space is grounded not only in the right of a State vis-à-vis other trading partners; it is also grounded in the duty towards them by virtue of the international obligations that States have undertaken towards each other under human rights treaties. This is because governance space is the precondition for both governance and good governance, which, in turn, are preconditions for the duty of States to fulfil their human rights obligations. The concept allows us to capture the element of duty towards other States as also a reason for having it and, therefore, drives home the point that a State needs that space not only because it is its autonomous sovereign right to promote human rights within by dealing with the impacts of MTS but also because it is its duty towards other States to respect, protect and fulfil human rights. Therefore, while policy space as a concept allows States to present external and, more importantly, internal constraints as a possible valid reason for failing to grow the economy, the concept of governance space does not allow States to resort to internal constraints for failing to respect, protect and fulfil human rights. Moreover, while the concept of policy space being principally about freedom of States to make policy choices admits of a possibility for States to make choices that may not adhere to the required standards of human rights under international law, the concept of governance space does not allow such a possibility. The idea that governments can have some sort of a leeway to evaluate a trade-off potentially limiting their duty to respect, protect and fulfil human rights is not permitted by the concept of governance space. And, finally, the concept of governance space goes much beyond the narrow focus of the concept of policy space on the shrinking of State autonomy. It allows us to also evaluate how MTS, without actually limiting the space needed by States, can, on the one hand, create permissive environments for States to abuse that space, and, on the other hand, also create limiting environment for States to use the space they actually do have. These concepts are further developed in the next section. To conclude, however, it may be helpful to remind ourselves that this holistic analysis of linkages between MTS and human rights is possible because the concept of governance space as we have developed here is founded not solely on sovereign autonomy, but encapsulates both sovereign autonomy and sovereign responsibility.

The governance space framework

Now that we have identified governance space as the central theme for this study, it is possible to begin developing a holistic framework to analyse the diverse linkages between MTS and human rights. A caveat is important at this stage. The framework we seek to develop focuses on the adverse impacts on human rights that MTS has, not on the many benefits it can have. Appropriate approaches to the latter are, of course, the ultimate objective of this book, but the same can happen only if we first focus on areas where MTS is in tension with human rights. The purpose of this book is to find ways not only to reconcile the two regimes but also to ensure that MTS is oriented in a manner that does not undermine human rights and, in fact, promotes the same. As such, while the governance space framework principally addresses how the tensions between the two regimes arise, the book concludes by proposing the way forward in ensuring that MTS promotes human rights.

Most of the critical literature on multilateral trade and human rights we have seen earlier focuses only on how WTO laws shrink the space needed by States to fulfil their human rights obligations. While being one of the major areas of concern, this is not the only way in which the two fields interact in terms of the adverse impacts on human rights. If a comprehensive framework is to be developed, it is important that it is capable of capturing the diverse range of linkages between MTS and human rights that may undermine the latter. The framework put forth in this book attempts to do that and is diagrammatically represented in Figure 2.2.

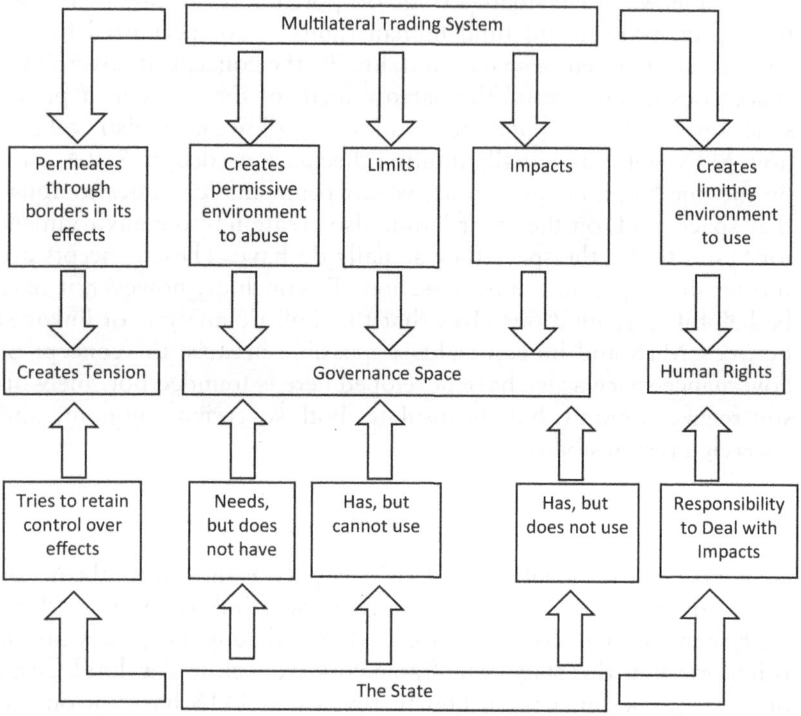

Figure 2.2 The Governance Space Framework
Source: Author.

As can be seen in Figure 2.2, there are three principal ways in which MTS can lead to States not fulfilling their human rights obligations. In the governance space framework, each of these three ways also constitutes a 'linkage-category', signifying that 'linkage-issues' can be placed under one or more of these categories. The first linkage-category relates to the notion that multilateral trade rules limit the governance space that States need in order to fulfil their human rights obligations. This is mostly a function of the laws that States adopt at the WTO as part of the rules underpinning the multilateral trade regime. A classic example of WTO laws limiting the governance space of States is the much-debated argument that patenting of pharmaceutical drugs required under the TRIPS Agreement shrinks the ability of States to ensure access to medicines as part of its human right to adequate standards of health obligations (MacDonald 2006; Hestermeyer 2007). There are clearly many other ways in which MTS and human rights interact within this rubric. Because the patenting issue has been examined in comprehensive depth by other researchers and there is not much to add to existing literature on the linkage-issue, this study will refrain from doing so. Instead, it will explore another and arguably an even more important linkage-issue which relates to the human rights exceptions provided in Article XX(b) of GATT 1994. This provision is designed to give some governance space to States to violate their usual WTO obligations such as the MFN and NT principles, in case such breach is exceptionally necessary to protect certain human rights, such as human health. The study will, however, demonstrate that the manner in which the provision is framed seriously limits the governance space of States to be able to do so. This case scenario will provide an excellent illustration of the types of linkage-issues which fall within this linkage-category.

It is important, however, to point out that if we had adopted the policy space concept as the central theme for our framework, our analysis would have stopped only at exploring how WTO laws actually limit the space needed by States. By adopting the governance space concept as the central theme, we can not only focus on the limiting character of WTO laws but also on two other linkage-categories thereof. This, therefore, brings us to the second manner in which MTS can lead to adverse impacts on human rights. In this case, WTO laws do not limit the governance space that States need. In fact, States have the necessary governance space but end up abusing the same, partly because many States lack the willingness to use it in order to benefit from MTS, and partly because that is the only way they can actually compete on the global market. Thus, here, MTS, while not limiting the governance space of States, ends up creating the permissive environment for States to abuse the governance space they already have. As has been hinted at in the introductory section, this linkage-category typically includes States being lax on their own labour obligations in an attempt to benefit from cheap labour and, therefore, in turn benefit from comparative advantage in the global market. To put this point into context, in the case of labour standards, States do have the governance space to ensure them but are either unwilling to implement those standards or abuse it because that is the only way they can actually compete on the global market. This relationship will be developed more fully later in this book, but another important note is in order at this juncture. The fact that MTS can create permissive environment for States to abuse their governance space and, therefore, violate labour standards does not automatically lead to a conclusion that the appropriate policy solution is at the WTO and not elsewhere. Thus, it remains to be analysed whether amending WTO agreements and incorporating some sort of a 'labour' or 'social' clause allowing States to impose import bans or higher tariffs on products that are manufactured through labour rights violations elsewhere is the appropriate solution. Indeed, as we shall observe later in this book, such an attempt to bring enforcement of labour standards under the WTO framework might be counterproductive and other solutions might be more workable.

The third linkage-category developed in this study focuses on unpacking the phenomenon, whereby MTS creates a limiting environment for D-LDCs to be able to use the governance space they already have for fulfilling their human rights obligations. It is almost axiomatic that because of lower technological and infrastructural capabilities, D-LDCs suffer from a massive disadvantage in benefitting from the MTS. Similarly, it is well known that DCs benefit much more from the system because they possess significantly higher technological and infrastructural capabilities and, therefore, trade in high value-added goods and services. Thus, this linkage-category is characterised by the feature that D-LDCs, despite having the governance space required to fulfil their human rights obligations, especially those which are dependent on the adequacy of resources, are simply not able to make use of that space due to capability deficiencies in equitably enjoying the benefits of MTS. This is precisely also what differentiates this linkage-category from the first where the governance space itself gets limited by WTO laws and from the second where States may not have the willingness to use their governance space. Here, despite having the willingness and the necessary governance space, the limiting environment to use it is created by MTS by requiring States to open their markets irrespective of their capabilities. It is also created by the perpetuation of the existing capability deficiencies in D-LDCs, ironically through the very mechanisms which aim to enhance the competitive capabilities of D-LDCs. By way of case study, the linkage-issue analysed in this study relates to the WTO's Aid for Trade Initiative, which, while being ostensibly aimed at undoing the supply-side capability deficiencies of D-LDCs, ends up reinforcing and perpetuating it due to the distorted manner in which it is actually implemented.[9]

The attempt of this book is not to give an exhaustive list of all possible linkage-issues within each linkage-category where MTS can have an adverse impact on human rights. That is not only overambitious but also probably impossible. What this book attempts to provide is a holistic framework whereby the diverse range of linkages between MTS and human rights can be analysed by deconstructing the ways in which WTO laws and policies interact with governance space of States into three categories. This book suggests that the three-way deconstruction outlined in the previous framework – whether MTS limits governance space, creates permissive environments to abuse governance space or creates limiting environment to use governance space – is capable of providing scholars and policy makers with the appropriate tools to analyse the linkages in a holistic manner.

An analysis of the linkages using the governance space framework also allows us to identify the diverse range of solutions that may or may not be appropriate in resolving the tensions between MTS and human rights. In other words, this framework underpins the point that because the problems related to linkages are different in at least three ways, the solutions to all of those cannot be the same. It is also pertinent to point out that the three linkage-categories are not compartmentalised in a watertight and inflexible manner. It is entirely possible for one linkage-issue to contain strands which may fall under different linkage-categories. For instance, if the linkage-issue is that WTO laws requiring D-LDCs to open up their markets have an adverse impact on human right to livelihood, it could be argued that it falls under the first category because WTO law may limit the governance space of such States by not permitting the adoption of protectionist measures when needed. At the same time, it clearly also falls under the third category, if the focus is on the capability deficiencies of D-LDCs and the resultant limiting environment to use governance space to address the right to livelihood. This overlap is, however, neither superfluous nor inconsequential. It is, in fact, vital if holistic solutions to addressing linkage-issues are to be found. This is because each linkage-category needs a different approach to identifying solutions, and the overlap may simply mean that the linkage-issue needs more than one policy response to be resolved. To put the cart before the horse, Figure 2.2 may mean that the linkage-issue of D-LDCs facing an adverse impact on the human right to livelihood due to opening their markets may require not only more flexibility in the WTO laws but also simultaneously addressing their capability deficiencies.

Glimpse of the end of the tunnel

The governance space framework serves an explanatory function for understanding which linkage-issue can fit into which linkage-category and why. But it also serves an instrumental function, in that it acts as the starting point for devising appropriate policy responses to an issue depending on which category or categories it falls under. This book does not propose solutions for each linkage-issue falling within the interface between MTS and human rights. That prospect is as overambitious, nay impossible, as the prospect of analysing all possible linkage-issues. The study, however, suggests an appropriate *approach* in terms of finding solutions in order to supplement the new framework and to ensure that governance space of States is not used or abused in a way which adversely impacts on their obligations to respect, protect and fulfil human rights. The approach to solutions developed in this book is, thus, not merely an accessory to the framework but is its very soul, guiding the framework to its intended goalpost.

As the arguments unfold in this book, it will become increasingly clear that both States and the WTO Secretariat tend to compartmentalise the nature of rights and obligations falling within the domain of MTS, as distinct from human rights. It will also become clear that the rhetorical and policy disconnect between these areas has led most States to disregard their binding human rights obligations while pursuing trade negotiations. In other words, the adverse impacts of WTO obligations on the use or abuse of governance space of States will emerge as a direct result of States not taking into consideration human rights concerns at any stage of the WTO processes.

The question which arises then is whether there are legal grounds necessitating internalisation of human rights considerations in all WTO processes by States, so that such adverse impacts do not arise in the first place, and, if they do, then they are identified and addressed appropriately. The book argues that there indeed is a legal obligation on States to do so, and the same can be found in the Marrakesh Agreement. The obligation stems from the explicit recognition of 'sustainable development' as one of the principal institutional objectives of the WTO (Marrakesh Agreement 1994: Preamble, Para. 2). If that is the context within which the WTO is to function as an international organisation, it is clear that trade policies and agreements cannot be counterproductive to the very institutional objective of achieving sustainable development, which necessarily and by definition includes respect, protection and fulfilment of human rights. The important point of departure here from current compartmentalised arguments at the WTO is, therefore, acknowledging that free trade is not to be considered as an end in itself, but ought to be considered as a means to achieve sustainable development. MTS is constructed on the hypothesis that WTO laws and policies will lead to sustainable development. It is, therefore, legally obligatory for States to ensure that such is the case, by internalising human rights considerations in all WTO laws and processes.

This study, further, suggests that the appropriate approach for such internalisation must be built on the notion of RtD – the human rights avatar of sustainable development. A case is made explaining why an RtD approach is not only the most appropriate, but indeed the only possible approach to internalisation of human rights considerations within WTO processes. Applying this approach to all three linkage-categories within the governance space framework by no means results in common solutions for the different problems. In fact, the approach insists on understanding and adopting different solutions to linkage-issues depending on their nature and character as is exposed by the category or categories they fall under. Building on the case scenarios developed for each of the three linkage-categories, the study also explains how the RtD approach could be applied to each of those cases in order to find appropriate solutions.

A note on the methodology and the methods

As described earlier, this book will adopt the governance space framework developed and introduced in a previous section for analysing the linkages between MTS and human rights. The actual analysis within the three linkage-categories, and the legal analysis that precedes those chapters, will, however, adopt existing methodologies and methods prevalent in international law. Insofar as methodology is concerned, the analysis will be based on the sources of international law recognised in Article 38(1) of the Statue of the International Court of Justice (1945), which include treaties, CIL and general principles of law, as well as jurisprudence and teachings of various legal scholars from around the world as subsidiary means for the determination of rules of law. Despite the fact that the aforesaid provision governs the applicable law before the ICJ, there is generally a consensus in international law doctrine that, at the very least, Article 38(1) enumerates the most important, if not all, sources of international law (Thirlway 2014). The study will also rely on information from reports and studies published or commissioned by governments, inter-governmental organisations, NGOs and scholars.

Insofar as methods of international law (as distinct from the research methodology) are concerned, the book adopts a mix of various legal techniques. As a distinct terminology, 'methods of international law' may not refer to the information-gathering exercise but to the various techniques used in the legal analysis (Ratner and Slaughter 2004: 2–4). These, therefore, refer to the application of legal theory (abstract) to concrete problems (Ratner and Slaughter 2004: 3). There are several methods used in international legal argumentation, and some of these include Positivism, Critical Legal Theory, Policy-Oriented Jurisprudence, International Legal Process, Third World Approaches to International Law (TWAIL) and Feminist Legal Theory. Despite some stark differences among each of the aforementioned methods, the idea that a legal scholar can compartmentalise his or her research in one of these methods has come under severe challenge from lawyers such as Martti Koskenniemi, who has criticised the 'shopping-mall approach to "method", the assumption that styles of legal writing are like brands of detergent that can be put on display alongside one another to be picked up by the customer in accordance with his/her idiosyncratic preferences' (Koskenniemi 2004: 110). His basic argument is that legal scholars tend to use many or all of these methods in legal argumentation depending on the proposition under analysis. More than one of these methods may, therefore, be employed by lawyers for different argumentations in the same study.

In line with Koskenniemi's position, this book will adopt an approach for analysis that employs many or all of the aforesaid methods for legal argumentation at different points. The analysis is principally legal but will also draw on trans-disciplinary scholarship from the fields of international relations/politics, human rights, economics and development for the purpose of applying the governance space framework to concrete policy solutions.

Limitations and delimitations of the study

Before concluding this chapter, it may be appropriate to also highlight one specific limitation and delimitation of this study. First, this book develops with a clear analytical objective at the systemic level of the multilateral trade and human rights regimes, and as with any study of this nature, it clearly has its own limits. As stated in the previous sections, the book does not pretend, or even aspire, to be a comprehensive catalogue of all possible linkage-issues arising between MTS and human rights, nor does it aim at suggesting solutions to all such linkage-issues. The ambition lies at the broader systemic level of understanding why, how and in which ways does MTS impact human rights, by providing a theoretical framework centred on governance space of States and then using the framework for identifying three broad linkage-categories. The case study of one linkage-issue in each of the three linkage-categories serves an illustrative purpose in explaining the theory and demonstrating how an RtD approach could help resolve those issues.

A delimitation of this study needs to be set out as well. The analysis is restricted to MTS and does not extend to the impacts on human rights of regional/preferential/bilateral/free trade agreements. It is for this reason that the term 'multilateral trade' is preferred in this book over 'international trade'. Having said that, it is indeed difficult to resist the temptation to observe that the governance space framework developed here may be equally applicable to non-multilateral trading systems, as well as to other institutional drivers of globalisation such as the international and regional financial institutions, multinational corporations and even the UN.

Notes

1 John Ruggie has articulated this tension in the Business and Human Rights context through the concept of 'governance gaps'. As he puts it, 'The root cause of the business and human rights predicament today lies in the governance gaps created by globalisation – between the scope and impact of economic forces and actors, and the capacity of societies to manage their adverse consequences' (UNHRC 2008b: Para. 3).

2 Article 2(1) of ICCPR, for instance, states that:

> each State Party to the present Covenant undertakes to respect and to ensure to all individuals within its territory and subject to its jurisdiction the rights recognised in the present Covenant, without distinction of any kind, such as race, colour, sex, language, religion, political or other opinion, national or social origin, property, birth or other status.

This is not to say that States do not have extra-territorial human rights duties. The point made is that they definitely have duties within their own jurisdictions at the very least.

3 In using the metaphor 'kicking away the ladder', Chang (2002: 31) confesses to being inspired by the German economist, Friedrich List, who, in 1841, criticised Britain for preaching free trade to other countries, while having achieved its economic supremacy through high tariffs and extensive subsidies. He argued that 'it is a very common clever device that when anyone has attained the summit of greatness, he kicks away the ladder by which he has climbed up, in order to deprive others of the means of climbing up after him' (Friedrich 1841, as translated by Sampson 1885: 295–96).

4 The UN Human Rights Committee noted that 'the contractual dimension of the treaty involves any State Party to a treaty being obligated to every other State Party to comply with its undertakings under the treaty'.

5 For a general historical overview of the topic, see Charnovitz (1987).

6 At a non-international level, 'the concept of governance has deep historical roots, as, for example, in the Arthashastra, an ancient Indian treatise on

governance attributed to the Mauryan empire in 400 BCE, which emphasised justice, ethics and anti-autocratic tendencies, in the ancient Greek city states, or in other ancient treatises and empires' (Weiss and Sornarajah 2012: Para. 2).

7 For an overview of good governance indicators, see Kaufmann and Kraay (2008).

8 'The Partnership Agreement between the members of the African, Caribbean and Pacific Group of States of the One Part, and The European Community and its Member States, of the Other Part, Signed in Cotonou on 23 June 2000' (the Cotonou Agreement) made several references to good governance, democracy, human rights and respect for the rule of law from the ACP countries.

9 For an overview by the WTO of the Aid for Trade Initiative, see WTO (2016a).

3

THE NORMATIVE HIERARCHY DEBATE AND ITS DISTRACTIONS

The previous chapter developed a theoretical framework for analysing the linkages between MTS and human rights using 'governance space' as the central theme. Any further analysis of those linkage-categories can, however, be situated in the proper perspective only after unpacking the legal normative milieu within which the tensions arise. For instance, it is difficult to fully appreciate the import of cases where WTO laws may limit governance space of States to fulfil their human rights obligations, unless we resolve the controversy whether there is a hierarchy between human rights and multilateral trade norms in international law. Similarly, it is pertinent to analyse the role of the WTO's dispute settlement mechanism and understand its limits before we analyse why some of the linkage-issues turn out to be bigger challenges to resolve. This chapter and the next, therefore, deal, respectively, with the aforesaid normative aspects of the linkages debate and set up the necessary pedestal for a fuller and proper understanding of the linkage-categories.

A rather perpetual discussion in the MTS and human rights interface has been on the question whether a normative hierarchy exists between obligations undertaken by States under these two legal regimes. This question has emerged often in the context of providing the legal justification for why is it that States cannot be allowed to violate their human rights obligations while participating in MTS and fulfilling its rules. The normative hierarchy argument states that human rights obligations 'trump' trade obligations, and, therefore, there is a normative superiority of the former over the latter in international law. Two reasons are generally ascribed for this, namely that human rights norms are *jus cogens* and, therefore, hierarchically superior to WTO norms and that human rights obligations of States are UN Charter obligations and, therefore, prevail over WTO obligations by virtue of Article 103 of the Charter (Howse and Mutua 2000: 60; de Schutter 2011: 176–77; 2014: 72). The natural corollary to this argument is that in case there is a conflict between obligations of States under the two regimes, then their human rights obligations must prevail over their WTO obligations. For some scholars, however, the proposition that there is such a clear hierarchy in international law is specious (Alvarez 2001: 6–7; Bartels 2002: 363; Marceau 2002: 798). Although both these opposing positions have continued to be invoked intermittently in scholarly literature, there is hardly any in-depth analysis of the rationale justifying either of these propositions. This chapter, thus, provides an extensive analysis of the normative hierarchy argument. It finds that the proposition that human rights obligations of States trump their WTO obligations is indeed correct, but only under a very limited set of circumstances. As such, it urges caution to be exercised in applying the hierarchy argument to existing linkages between MTS and human rights and suggests that such invocation is more distracting than helpful to the human rights project because it diverts attention away from finding solutions and gets caught in polarising and incessant debates which ultimately serve very little policy purpose.

From a moral perspective, the primacy of human rights values over commercial values is indeed an attractive proposition, and most would agree with the ethical underpinnings behind such a claim. While in Hartian terms, it may be sound to argue that these ethical and moral values underlying human rights inspire the creation of international human rights law (Hart 1955), the fact is that when it comes to legal normativity, the accepted concrete sources of international law, not abstract morality, remain the primary determinant. Human rights obligations of States from an international law perspective are shaped by the sources of international law, including treaty obligations, obligations under CIL (Sohn 1982: 2–9; Meron 1989: 93; Henkin 1990: 19) and those flowing from the general principles of law (Simma and Alston 1989: 102–8; de Schutter 2014: 66–71). Similar is the case with obligations of States with respect to WTO law. The question of normative hierarchy of international legal norms is, therefore, a subject which must be analysed with reference to the principles and techniques of international law.

As stated earlier, the literature on this issue reveals that there are different opinions among scholars on whether or not human rights obligations prevail over or supersede trade obligations in terms of their 'relative normativity'.[1] Unsurprisingly, the legal arguments behind such conclusions are also quite varied. But more importantly – and this is where the debate becomes so mushy – many of the arguments put forth on either side are not always compelling. Additionally, scholars who have researched extensively on the nexus between human rights and MTS tend to avoid answering the question definitively on the ground that it is unnecessary to do so while analysing existing linkages (Joseph 2011: 50). The question is nevertheless important to address because from the perspective of some scholars, the foremost logical method for resolving linkage-issues is by insisting on normative hierarchy of human rights obligations over trade obligations.

Fragmentation of international law and the question of normative hierarchy

The most comprehensive analysis on the question of normative hierarchy comes from a study group of the International Law Commission (ILC) in its 2006 report on fragmentation of international law (ILC 2006a), which is accompanied by an exhaustive 'analytical study' finalised by Martii Koskenniemi, on behalf of the study group (ILC 2006b). The ILC, however, did not specifically answer the question with reference to human rights regime and WTO regime in either of the documents. By its own acknowledgement, the study did not aim 'to set up definite relationships of priority between international law's different rules or rule-systems', and 'to that extent, its results may seem unsatisfactory or at least inconclusive' (ILC 2006b: Para. 484).

Fragmentation of international law is the inevitable outcome of increased number of specialised treaties related to specialised regulation of different social and economic issues emerging in the globalised world. Thus, fragmentation of international law is nothing but a reflection of the fragmentation of the 'international social world' (ILC 2006b: Para. 8). As the ILC study noted:

> One of the features of late international modernity has been what sociologists have called 'functional differentiation', the increasing specialisation of parts of society and the related autonomisation of those parts. It is a well-known paradox of globalisation that while it has led to increasing uniformisation of social life around the world, it has also led to its increasing fragmentation – that is, to the emergence of specialised and relatively autonomous spheres of social action and structure.
> (ILC 2006b: Para. 7)

The ILC study further noted that the fragmentation of this international social order described earlier, has had legal ramifications as well, since 'it has been accompanied by the emergence of specialised and (relatively) autonomous rules or rule-complexes, legal institutions and spheres of legal practice' (ILC 2006b: Para. 8). An example of this is the emergence of 'human rights law' and 'trade law' as relatively isolated rule-systems, with their own foci and institutions, which do not always operate in harmony with each other or with knowledge about the activities in each other's fields. This is also manifested in the creation of laws specific to these regimes which are not drafted with cross-fertilisation of principles underpinning the other regime. This obviously leads to fragmentation of what once could be called as 'general international law' (Marceau 2006). As the ILC study puts it, 'The result is conflicts between rules or rule-systems, deviating institutional practices and, possibly, the loss of an overall perspective on the law' (ILC 2006b: Para. 8). The phenomenon, however, does not only lead to fragmentation of substantive norms of international law, but also to fragmentation of authority in international law, including institutional authority (Broude 2008).

Increased specialisation of the WTO's legal regime in 'splendid isolation' from the human rights regime has meant that States are left with specific sets of obligations under the two rule-systems. This can, in turn, lead to fragmentation of their own international legal obligations such that those under WTO may come into conflict with those under human rights law. The question then arises of what rules of interpretation of international law must be applicable for resolution of such conflicts between obligations of States under the two regimes.

The question of resolving the hierarchy issue may be important for two key actors – States themselves and the WTO Panels which decide trade disputes between States. Whether and to which extent is this a pertinent question for the Panels to deal with has been a subject of much debate and is discussed more extensively in the next chapter. However, what is clearly not debatable is that States themselves must be in a position to resolve these tensions, because it is States that have the primary responsibility to fulfil the obligations under both regimes. As Harrison (2007: 56) has pointed out aptly, human rights issues do not arise only in dispute settlement, but at the levels where States must make legally compatible policy decisions as well. The resolution of this legal problem is, therefore, vital for a State to make an informed use of its governance space in a way that its policy decisions do not violate its international legal obligations.

It cannot be stressed enough that the function of a State to make these decisions is more important than a possible similar function of the WTO Panels. This is because the question of resolution of conflicts between obligations of States should logically come up before the Panels *only after* a State has made an informed trade policy decision based on an assessment of how it should manage its WTO obligations in the face of its human rights obligations. As we shall argue in Chapter 8 of this book, there is a duty on States not only to resolve conflicts after they arise but even to ensure that such conflicts with human rights obligations do not arise in the first place. This is because States are legally bound to negotiate and design multilateral trade obligations in a manner compatible with their human rights obligations. The question of fragmentation is, therefore, first and foremost, important for States themselves, even before the question can potentially come up before the Panels. Second, the question of this issue coming up before the Panels is triggered only when other States, in fact, question a trade policy of a given State. If another State/s does not question the validity of a trade policy of the given State, then the Panels' interpretative function is not set into motion. For the State, however, the resolution of the question of how it should manage its different sets of obligations is not so triggered by objections from other States. Because it is a core issue which needs to be resolved by a State in determining the options it has within its governance space, every State needs to undertake this exercise irrespective of such triggers. The question is, therefore, all the more important from the perspective of States themselves, rather than the Panels. Third, except in the limited number of cases described later in this chapter, the gamut of questions relating to resolution of conflicts between norms arising out of fragmentation may not be within the functional mandate of the Panels. As will be more extensively analysed in the next chapter, its mandate may be limited to interpretation and application of WTO Agreements. Of course, the Panels may need to interpret human rights treaties as well under certain circumstances. However, the interpretative function of the Panels may not extend to adding or diminishing the rights and obligations of States as are mentioned under the WTO agreements (DSU 1994: Article 3.2). In other words, it may not be within the interpretative functions of the Panels to hold a breach by a State of its WTO obligations as valid, by finding that the State did so to fulfil its human rights obligations, except in the limited circumstances described later where a clear hierarchy exists, and unless such human rights exception is expressly allowed by the WTO agreements such as Article XX(b) of GATT 1994. States on the other hand, do not have this interpretative limitation that the Panels suffer. To the contrary, States are required to go beyond mere interpretation as a technique of conflict resolution and translate such resolution into actual governance decisions, by making the best use of its governance space, such that it may manage its obligations under both regimes in the best manner possible. The question of dealing with fragmentation of its own obligations under different regimes is, thus, a governance issue for a State and much broader than the scope of Panels' functions.

Rules for resolving conflicts of norms

What then, are the rules of international law that a State must apply in order to navigate its way through managing its different legal obligations, particularly when there is a conflict between the two? Before we get into that question, it is important to make a note of what is meant by the term 'conflict'. Would a conflict arise only when a WTO law makes it impossible for a State to fulfil an obligation under it without violating its human rights obligations? Or, would such a conflict arise even when the effect of a WTO agreement might mean frustrating the goals of a human rights treaty obligation without there being any strict incompatibility between their provisions? The former is a 'strict notion' of the term 'conflict', while the latter is a 'looser understanding of conflict' (ILC 2006b: Para. 24). After taking note of these two ends of the spectrum, the ILC study adopted the definition of conflict, as a 'situation where two rules or principles suggest different ways of dealing with a problem' (ILC 2006b: Para. 25). To put this into context, what this means is that in case WTO laws and human rights laws impose obligations on a State in such a way that the two regimes imply different ways of dealing with a social problem, then a conflict of norms may arise. For instance, if a State is in the process of formulating appropriate governance mechanisms for ensuring public health for its citizens, then it may have to look at its human rights obligations as well as any WTO obligations and then evaluate whether there are different ways required by these regimes to deal with the problem. If there do exist such different ways, then a conflict may arise. Conversely, if the ways suggested by the two regimes are not necessarily different, then there is no conflict of norms. In other words, there is no conflict if the obligations under the two regimes can be simultaneously achieved through an informed use of governance space.

While this proposition appears straightforward, there is an additional problem which we must grapple with. What if only one regime suggests a way to deal with a problem, while the other regime does not prescribe any particular way, but allows States to choose among a host of options available to it to fulfil its obligations? Is there still a conflict if the WTO regime requires particular means of conduct which, if adopted, may exclude not all, but only one (or few) among a range of options available to States to take measures to fulfil their human rights obligations? To illustrate this conundrum, the debates on patenting of pharmaceutical drugs and their impacts on access to medicines is very helpful (Hestermeyer 2007; Joseph 2011: 214–44). Under the TRIPS Agreement, all members are under a general obligation to adopt and enforce laws protecting patents (TRIPS 1994: Article 27). It is well known that patenting of pharmaceutical drugs can generally create a monopoly in favour of the patent-holder in terms of both the pricing of the medicine and the exclusion of others from producing generic versions thereof (Drahos and Braithwaite 2003; Oxfam 2006). As a result, access to medicines protected by patents, many of which can relate to life-threatening diseases, can be seriously circumscribed for patients around the world thereby adversely impacting on their right to health (Marks 2009). The argument has, therefore, often been raised that by requiring patents to be generally protected, the TRIPS Agreement, despite some flexibilities related to public health having been introduced (WTO 2006a), still effectively excludes the option of permitting cheap generic copies of the patented drugs to be produced in order for a State to ensure the right to highest attainable standard of health (UNHRC 2009a; South Centre 2011). However, under human rights law, States have a wide range of options spread across a variety of administrative, legislative, judicial, budgetary and policy measures available to them to ensure that right (UN Committee on Economic, Social and Cultural Rights 1990: Para. 6, 7; UN Human Rights Committee 2004: Para. 7), and excluding patent protection is just one of such possible options. The question which emerges here then is whether the WTO regime which excludes lax patent protection as a possible option for States within their governance space, 'conflicts' with their human rights obligation relating to the right to health.

The answer to this question is not a straightjacket 'yes' or 'no' like the previous proposition. Whether or not there is a conflict of norms will depend on an objective evaluation of each case. For instance, if the WTO way of dealing with a problem makes it extremely difficult for a State to reasonably use non-onerous means of fulfilling its human rights obligations among a host of options that it has, then a conflict of norms may still arise. The conflict may arise in this case because the governance space of a State in fulfilling its human rights obligations using reasonable and non-onerous means is severely limited. The degree of conflict will depend on the severity of such limitations on the governance space. Conversely, if the WTO way of dealing with a problem leaves enough options open for a State to fulfil its human rights obligations in a reasonable manner, then there may not be a conflict. Thus, with respect to the patenting debate, if the TRIPS obligations on States leave open other options to ensure access to medicines, but if the use of such options is unreasonably onerous for a State, it may be fair to say that a conflict may still arise. If States can fulfil both their patenting obligations and their human right to health obligations reasonably well through means other than excluding patent protection, then there is no conflict. The question of conflicts is important because if it does exist, a State will probably be in a position where it has to give priority to one set of obligations over another, using interpretative techniques which give guidance to it, on which laws will prevail over the other and which considerations it should take into account in designing its governance choices. As stated earlier, in case there is no conflict, the State will have to fulfil both its sets of obligations without having the privilege of arguing that one set of laws prevails over another.[2]

With this backdrop, let us examine what are the rules of interpretation applicable in case there is indeed a conflict that arises between WTO obligations and human rights obligations of States. As is otherwise also well established, the ILC study lists three known techniques of interpretation for answering conflicts between legal norms, whether they be within the same rule-system or between two different rule-systems (ILC 2006b: Para. 36). The first is the rule of *lex specialis* (ILC 2006b: Para. 46–122). By this, we mean that a special law will prevail over a general law when both sets of laws deal with the same subject matter. The second rule is the rule of *lex posterior* (ILC 2006b: Para. 223–323). This means that the latter law will prevail over the former law when both sets of laws deal with the same subject matter (VCLT 1969: Article 30). The third rule is the rule of *lex superior* (ILC 2006b: Para. 324–60). This means that in some cases, international law creates a clear hierarchy between different sets of norms in a vertical manner, with the normatively superior norm being applicable at the cost of the normatively inferior norm. It is this last rule of interpretation which has been pressed into service by some scholars when dealing with conflict resolution between WTO obligations and human rights obligations of States. We shall deal with this argument in the present chapter and revert back to the other two techniques of *lex specialis* and *lex posterior* in the following chapter.

In terms of *lex superior*, the ILC study notes two important sets of legal norms accompanied by obligations flowing therefrom which are hierarchically superior to all other legal norms and their accompanying obligations (ILC 2006b: Para. 327). The first, and indeed the more analytically complex by a fair margin of such *lex superior* norms, flows from Article 103 of the UN Charter, while the second flows from the concept of *jus cogens*.[3] The following sections will deal with both of these sequentially, because scholars have used both concepts to claim that human rights obligations of States are *lex superior* as compared to their WTO obligations.

Lex superior and Article 103 of the UN Charter

The first argument is that human rights obligations of States fall within the ambit of Article 103 of the UN Charter and are, therefore, hierarchically superior to WTO obligations (de Schutter 2011; 2014). As such, the argument is that in case of a conflict between the two, the former would prevail.

Article 103 of the UN Charter states that 'in the event of a conflict between the obligations of the members of the UN under the Charter and their obligations under any other international agreement, their obligations under the UN Charter shall prevail'. The word 'prevail' has been interpreted by the ILC not to imply that the lower-ranking provision would become automatically null and void or even suspended. The ILC study points out that the State is merely 'prohibited' from fulfilling an obligation arising under that other norm and that, in case of a conflict, 'the State in question should fulfil its obligation under the Charter and perform its duties under other agreements in as far as compatible with obligations under the Charter' (ILC 2006b: Para. 334).

Therefore, in our context, the principle of *lex superior* enshrined in Article 103 means that when obligations under WTO Agreements conflict with obligations of States under the UN Charter, States must fulfil their obligations under the WTO agreements only as far as they are compatible with obligations under the Charter. If they are not compatible (i.e. there is a conflict), then States are 'prohibited' from fulfilling their WTO obligations. The word 'prohibited' also suggests that in case of such a conflict arising, the objection of other States is not required to trigger Article 103. A State is obliged, irrespective of whether another State has an issue with the exercise of the given State's governance choices or not, to not perform its duties under the non-Charter agreement. Article 103 is, therefore, self-executing and not dependent on another State raising an objection. This also lends credence to our observation earlier that the question of resolving the conflict of norms question is first and foremost important for States themselves.

Article 103 and the human rights argument

This primacy of Article 103 has been invoked, most vocally by Olivier de Schutter (2011; 2014), to argue that human rights obligations of States must prevail over conflicting trade obligations, because the former are UN Charter obligations. Despite such invocation, a detailed analysis of this proposition, its nature, scope and applicability is generally absent from scholarly literature. We, therefore, need to first examine whether the Charter indeed imposes human rights obligations on States and, if so, what is the nature and extent of such obligations. We then further need to examine whether, in light of the nature of such human rights obligations under the Charter, a conflict with WTO laws is possible and if yes, what are its characteristics.

The provisions which are typically invoked for the argument that human rights obligations of States are Charter obligations – Article 55(c) and Article 56. Article 55 of the Charter, discussed in depth in the following section, imposes certain human rights obligations on the UN as an institution and reads as follows:

> With a view to the creation of conditions of stability and well-being which are necessary for peaceful and friendly relations among nations based on respect for the principle of equal rights and self-determination of peoples, the United Nations shall promote:
>
> a higher standards of living, full employment and conditions of economic and social progress and development;
> b solutions of international economic, social, health and related problems; and international cultural and educational cooperation; and
> c universal respect for, and observance of, human rights and fundamental freedoms for all without distinction as to race, sex, language or religion.

This is followed by Article 56 which states that 'all Members pledge themselves to take joint and separate action in co-operation with the Organisation for the achievement of the purposes set forth in Article 55'. On a combined reading of these two provisions in conjunction with Article 103, it has been argued that the human rights obligations of States as enshrined in Articles 55(c) and 56 of the UN Charter, enjoy a hierarchical superiority over the obligations of the same States under any other treaty law (Loukaides 1995: 220), including WTO law. What follows from this argument is that in the contingency of a WTO obligation not being capable of being interpreted in a manner consistent with a human rights obligation, the latter must prevail over the former because of the latter's hierarchical superiority in the normativity of international law (International Federation for Human Rights 2005: 1).

In order to test the validity of this proposition, it is important to deconstruct what sort of human rights obligations are entailed by Articles 55 and 56 upon States, and based on that, what specific human rights obligations fall within the ambit of 'obligations under the Charter' as enshrined in Article 103.

First look at Articles 55 and 56

Article 55 is distinct from Article 56 in at least one important respect. While Article 55 is an obligation on the UN as an organisation, Article 56 is aimed at States. Although there was some doubt in the early organisational history of the UN whether the 'pledge' by States in Article 56 translates into a legal obligation (Crowell 1950: 1059; Kelsen 1950: 29), more contemporarily, there rightly appears to be no serious opposition to an interpretation of the provision as containing a binding legal obligation on States (Sohn 1975: 131; Arend and Riedel 2012: 1573). This conclusion, however, does not tell us anything about the scope of such an obligation on States with respect to human rights. In order to determine the scope of such States' obligations, we need to examine the language of both the provisions more closely, which task is not easy, since the Charter provisions were intentionally kept vague and the strict obligation to protect human rights was specifically prevaricated (Schwelb 1965: 362; Lauren 1983: 1).

Article 56 has three important parts to it which give context to what States have pledged to. The first part is that States must take joint action, the second is that they must take separate action and the third is that such action/s must be in cooperation with the Organisation. The clear operative part relating to the pledge comes from the words 'take action'. Thus, the pledge by States is with respect to 'taking action' – jointly, separately and in cooperation with the UN. The purpose of 'taking action' is also culled out in Article 56; the pledge of States to 'take action' is with respect to 'achievement of the purposes set forth in Article 55'. Thus, the text and context of the pledge by States to 'take action' in Article 56 is directly related to the text and context of Article 55. It is, therefore, now important to examine what 'the purposes set forth in Article 55' are, before we make a conclusion on the nature and extent of the pledge by States flowing from a conjoint reading of both provisions.

'Purposes set forth in Article 55'

At this stage, only clause (c) of Article 55 is pertinent for our purposes, and it may be helpful to reproduce, as follows, only the relevant portions of the said provision at the risk of repetition:

> With a view to the creation of conditions of stability and well-being which are necessary for peaceful and friendly relations among nations based on respect for the principle of equal rights and self-determination of peoples, the United Nations shall promote: universal respect for, and observance of, human rights and fundamental freedoms for all without distinction as to race, sex, language, or religion.

The problem of determining the 'purposes set forth in Article 55' stems from the language of the provision itself. There are at least four different tiers of 'purposes' which are set forth in the previous statement, even without taking into account clauses (a) and (b) of Article 55. The first tier is the broadest purpose, namely peaceful and friendly relations among nations based on respect for the principle of equal rights and self-determination of peoples. The second tier is the purpose which is 'necessary' for achieving the first tier, that is the 'creation of conditions of stability and well-being'. The third tier of the purposes set forth in the Article is required to be fulfilled 'with a view' to achieving the second tier, which in turn is 'necessary' for achieving the first tier. This third tier of purposes is also the operative obligation on the UN enshrined in the provision, namely *the UN shall promote* 'universal respect for, and observance of, human rights and fundamental freedoms for all without distinction as to race, sex, language or religion'. The focus of this third tier in terms of the purposes of the provision is on the UN being the subject of the positive obligation to promote certain goals. The fourth tier of purposes that could possibly be deciphered from Article 55 is the 'promotion' of goals mentioned in the three clauses (a), (b) and (c). If the promotion of these goals by itself is considered as 'the purposes set forth in

Article 55', then it is immaterial whether the agent is the UN or the States.

A conjoint reading of Article 56 with Article 55(c), therefore, leaves us with the following options on how to read the nature and extent of the pledge by States:

a The pledge by States is to take action for the achievement of peaceful and friendly relations among nations based on respect for the principle of equal rights and self-determination of peoples;
b The pledge by States is to take action for the achievement of creation of conditions of stability and well-being;
c The pledge by States is to take action for the achievement by UN of promotion of universal respect for, and observance of, human rights and fundamental freedoms for all without distinction as to race, sex, language or religion;
d The pledge by States is to take action for the achievement of promotion of universal respect for, and observance of, human rights and fundamental freedoms for all without distinction as to race, sex, language or religion.

Now, each of the afore-mentioned options is probably a valid interpretation of the two provisions with respect to the pledge by States, and, indeed, there is no interpretative reason whatsoever to restrict the same to one of these four purposes only. The words 'purposes set forth in Article 55' are in the plural and, therefore, they may clearly cover all the purposes mentioned earlier. Obviously, the most relevant of these interpretations for invoking Article 103, specifically in the context of human rights, is the fourth interpretation despite its promotional nature.

It may, nevertheless, be argued that there is one more tier of purpose which can be deciphered from Article 55. The fifth tier of purposes which could thus be interpreted are the three goals in clauses (a), (b) and (c) themselves, without the focus on the 'promotion' of these goals. Thus, these goals by themselves are then the purposes which States have pledged themselves to achieve, not just the promotion of these goals.[4] If that is correct, the fifth interpretation which should be added to the list would read as follows:

e The pledge by States is to take action for the achievement of universal respect for, and observance of, human rights and fundamental freedoms for all without distinction as to race, sex, language or religion.

It is, therefore, possible to argue that Articles 55(c) and 56, together impose binding obligations on States not only of a promotional nature but also directly with respect to achieving universal respect for and observance of human rights. The distinction between an obligation which is promotional in nature and one which is in the nature of achieving results may be important because the former admits of the possibility to not obtain a result and yet not violate the obligation to promote. For instance, it is entirely possible for a State to promote universal observance of the right to non-discrimination against the girl child through laws and awareness campaigns and yet not be able to achieve it entirely. In this case, while the State may be in violation of its obligation to achieve observance of the right to non-discrimination, it may not be in violation of its obligation to promote such observance.

There is, however, a clear indication that States have gradually moved away from an understanding of the purposes of Article 55 in promotional terms only, to understanding it more as actual protection of human rights. For instance, the Preambles of the UDHR, the ICCPR as well as the ICESCR, indicate that States had initially understood the obligations related to human rights under the Charter only in promotional terms. The Preamble of UDHR states: 'Whereas Member States have pledged themselves to achieve, in co-operation with the United Nations, the promotion of universal respect for and observance of human rights and fundamental freedoms' (UNGA 1948: Preamble, Para. 6). Similarly, the Preambles of both the ICCPR and ICESCR contain the following words: 'Considering the obligation of States under the Charter of the United Nations to promote universal respect for, and observance of, human rights and freedoms; . . . agree upon the following articles' (ICCPR: Preamble, Para. 4; ICESCR: Preamble, Para. 4).

These early documents may, however, only be a hangover of the opposition from some quarters during the drafting of Article 55(c) to mention an obligation to 'protect' human rights along with the obligation to 'promote' (Schwelb 1965: 362; Lauren 1983: 1). However, it has been pointed out that the early fixation on only promotion of human rights as the purpose of Article 55 has evolved over time as part of a dynamic interpretation undertaken by States, such that now the purposes of the provision may be considered to include 'protection' as well (Ramcharan 1989: 350). Indeed, the 1993 Vienna Declaration and Programme of Action may support this line of argument. Thus, in its Preamble, States reaffirm:

> the commitment contained in Article 56 of the Charter of the United Nations to take joint and separate action, placing

> proper emphasis on developing effective international cooperation for the realisation of the purposes set out in Article 55, including universal respect for, and observance of, human rights and fundamental freedoms for all.
>
> (World Conference on Human Rights 1993: Preamble, Para. 4)

As can be seen here, the word 'promotion' is not even mentioned as part of the purposes of Article 55. On the other hand, the purposes set out in Article 55 are clearly articulated as 'universal respect for, and observance of, human rights and fundamental freedoms'. Further, in the operative portion, the Declaration includes 'protection' as well, along with 'promotion' of human rights 'as a priority objective of the United Nations in accordance with its purposes and principles, in particular the purpose of international cooperation' (World Conference on Human Rights 1993: Para. 4). Thus, there are strong reasons to argue that today the purposes set forth in Article 55 go beyond just promotion and include the actual respect and observance of human rights as well.

Nature of obligations on States under Article 56 with respect to 'purposes set forth in Article 55'

The broad interpretation of the 'purposes' of Article 55, however, does not give us a clear or complete picture of the actual obligations on States under Article 56. If we revert back to the five possible interpretations of a conjoint reading of Articles 55(c) and 56 mentioned earlier, we will notice that there is one important common denominator in each of them, which essentially defines the scope of the obligations of States related to human rights. 'The pledge by States is *to take action* for the achievement of . . .' are the words which are present in each of the interpretations. This is by far the most ignored aspect of the debate on the nature and extent of the human rights obligations imposed by the Charter on States. Thus, the obligation that the Charter imposes on States is the obligation to 'take action' for achievement of all of the purposes mentioned in Article 55, including those related to human rights. In other words, the operative part in Articles 55(c) and 56 regarding the Charter obligation on States for the purposes of Article 103 is the obligation to 'take action'. Taking action means that States are required to take steps to achieve something; quite different from ultimately achieving the results. It signifies that States are obliged to work on the means (taking of action) by which they will achieve the ends (purposes set forth in Article 55). Thus, irrespective of whether the purposes set forth in Article 55(c) are promotional in nature or more than that, the obligation is still that of taking action.

Importantly, the Charter leaves it to the discretion of States by which means they would achieve the purposes set forth under Article 55; what they are required to do is to take action using the options at hand to achieve the ends in the manner deemed effective and appropriate by the State. In determining their own means, States generally have a variety of options available, including legislative, administrative, judicial, institutional or budgetary means (Stoll 2012: 1604).

The obligation to 'take action' is clearly not the same type of obligation which States have under the ICCPR, ICESCR or any of the other seven core human rights treaties or even regional human rights treaties, because under these instruments, the obligation goes far beyond 'taking action' to actually achieving results. In fact, the very emergence of human rights treaties is an expression of States 'taking action' to achieve the purposes set forth in Article 55.

Now, given this rather clear distinction, the question arises whether it is productive to characterise any further the 'obligation to take action' under the Charter or the obligations under human rights treaties. International law scholars, especially those influenced by the French civil law system, often tend to divide States' obligations into two types, namely 'obligations of conduct/means' and 'obligations of results/ends'. On plain linguistic common-sense, one might even be tempted to characterise the 'obligation to take action' as an 'obligation of conduct/means'. However, this chapter consciously avoids using these concepts because they lack sufficient clarity from an international law perspective and have often been source of confusion. Because the two terms have specifically been used in the human rights context by none other than the UN Committee on Economic, Social, and Cultural Rights (1990: Para. 1), it will only be proper to explain why this chapter chooses not to employ them.[5]

The concepts of 'obligations of conduct/means' and 'obligations of results/ends' seem to have been introduced into mainstream international legal language by Roberto Ago, the former Special Rapporteur of the ILC on 'The Internationally Wrongful Act of the State, Source of International Responsibility'. In his report to the ILC in 1977 concerning 'State Responsibility', Ago summarised the distinction as follows:

> 'International obligations of conduct' [are] those obligations which require a State to adopt a specific course of conduct, whether an action or an omission, as opposed to those

> obligations which impose on the State the generic requirement that it should bring about a certain result but leave to it the choice of the ways and means by which the results are to be achieved, and which could be characterised as 'obligations of result'.
>
> (ILC 1977: Para. 12)

However, in the footnote section, he hastened to observe that:

> while in most cases an 'obligation of conduct' in the meaning which we favour is at the same time an 'obligation of conduct' in the meaning which would be borrowed from civil law, this is not always the case; the same is true of 'obligations of result'. According to the civil law criterion which, for example, holds that the obligation of a doctor to treat a patient without necessarily being able to ensure his cure is an obligation of conduct, one would have to characterise as an international obligation of conduct the obligation of the State to protect foreigners, and particularly certain foreign persons, against attempts by third parties, an obligation which, on the contrary, would appear to be an obligation of result according to the criteria favoured in this section.
>
> (ILC 1977: Footnote 27)

With the lack of clarity infused since the outset, it was no surprise then that the distinction proposed by Ago turned out to be a subject of heated discussion later in the ILC, with the subsequent Special Rapporteur on the topic, James Crawford, suggesting deletion of the terms from the Draft Articles on Responsibility of States for Internationally Wrongful Acts (ILC 1999: Para. 132–35).[6] Indeed, because of the ensuing serious opposition among several ILC members to characterising State obligations into these two typologies for the purpose of identifying accountability, the final adopted text of the Articles refrained from using them (ILC 2001).

It is not difficult to see why the distinction as proposed by Ago is similarly problematic for our purposes. According to his criteria, it would be difficult to characterise the 'obligation to take action' as an 'obligation of conduct/means' because Article 56 does not provide any specific course of conduct for States to follow. From a broader perspective, there does not seem to be any good reason to restrict the types of States' obligations under international law to the two outlined by Ago and in the fashion that he did. An indication of this, in fact, came from the ICJ in its advisory opinion on the *Legality of the Threat or Use of Nuclear Weapons* (1996: Para. 98–103) where, after stating that the obligation on States to negotiate in good faith a nuclear disarmament, as enshrined under Article VI of the Treaty on the Non-Proliferation of Nuclear Weapons, goes beyond that of a mere obligation of conduct, the court went on to observe that the obligation is to achieve a precise result – nuclear disarmament in all its aspects – by adopting a particular course of conduct, namely the pursuit of negotiations on the matter in good faith. Going by Ago's conceptualisation of an obligation of result, the ICJ would be wrong to characterise the obligation to achieve nuclear disarmament as one of result, because negotiations were also provided as the specific means to achieve the result. It is in the backdrop of the random and intermittent nature of the use of these concepts in international law, that Wolfrum (2011: 366–69) has argued that States' obligations must be systematically distinguished into five types, namely obligations of result, obligations of conduct, goal-oriented obligations, obligations which, in fact, address natural and juridical persons and international obligations of conduct as well as result.

Given the lack of consensus on the scope of these two concepts, it might simply be counterproductive to use them with any certainty in our context. As such, we will proceed on the basis of the simple but sufficient understanding of the distinction outlined earlier between the 'obligation to take action' stipulated under the Charter, as compared to the specific obligations enshrined under human rights treaties.

Bringing back Article 103 into the analysis

Given that the obligation under the UN Charter is one of taking action, it is now important to put that in the context of Article 103. In order for the Charter obligations to prevail, it is important that there be a conflict with a non-Charter obligation. Therefore, given the specific nature of obligations under the Charter with respect to human rights, for a conflict to arise, it will be necessary for the non-Charter obligation to either negate the ability of States to 'take action' or to put serious restrictions on the same. However, as we have seen earlier, given the wide array of choices which States have in terms of 'taking action', such a conflict will occur in extremely narrow set of circumstances. Even if a non-Charter law eliminates one manner of taking action to promote or achieve a particular human right, it still may not be in conflict if there are other ways of taking action available to the State to achieve the same result. Surely, the range of policy choices of States will be shrunk because one of the options to 'take action' is eliminated, but does not equate with a conflict.

If, on the other hand, several options for taking action are eliminated because of a non-Charter obligation, or if a non-Charter obligation makes it unreasonably onerous for a State to take several of the actionable options available to it, then there may still be a conflict because the Charter obligation of taking action may be rendered non-implementable or otiose. The possibility of a conflict with the Charter's human rights obligations will, therefore, depend on the severity and scope of the impact of the non-Charter obligation on the ability of States to 'take action'.

Putting this in the context of the trade-human rights interface, a conflict will arise within the meaning of Article 103 only when a WTO obligation makes it impossible or unreasonably onerous for a State to 'take action' under Article 55 of the Charter. Even if a WTO obligation eliminates one among a range of options for States to take action to promote or achieve a human right, it still may not amount to a conflict, although the policy choices of the State will essentially be limited or shrunk.

Would this then mean that if a WTO obligation clearly violates a human rights obligation of a State under a human rights treaty, there will not be a conflict within the meaning of Article 103? Note that here we are comparing a conflict between two non-Charter obligations, namely WTO obligation and a human rights treaty obligation which goes beyond the obligation to take action. In this case, it is indeed still possible that a conflict arises with the Charter obligation of taking action. This may happen because the violation by WTO obligation of a human right may be to such an extent that it makes the Charter obligation of taking action non-implementable or otiose. This is simply because if a human rights result is made impossible or unreasonably onerous to achieve because of a WTO obligation, any possible means to achieve that result may be non-existent.[7]

The aforesaid discussion then leads us to the following two conclusions. First, the Charter obligations with respect to human rights are those of taking action, which are quite distinct from obligations to achieve specific results. Second, given that States have a variety of actionable options to take, it is extremely difficult for a WTO obligation to be in conflict with the Charter's human rights obligation of taking action. In the extreme circumstance where the human rights obligation to achieve a result itself is made impossible or unreasonably onerous by virtue of a WTO obligation, it may directly conflict with the Charter obligation of taking action as well. The applicability of Article 103 for the WTO obligation to be prevailed over will thus be in very limited set of circumstances. In other words, human rights obligations of States do 'trump' WTO obligations of States, but not as a general all-encompassing rule because the conflict of norms applies only in very limited number of cases, if any. The normative hierarchy can, therefore, operate only depending on the context and impact of the WTO obligation on human rights.

Article 103, human rights and the WTO

Now, what does all of this mean when we contextualise the nature of human rights obligations under the Charter in light of Article 103 and then relate that to WTO obligations? Quite clearly, under Article 103, States' human rights obligations of taking action do prevail over those WTO obligations which may come into conflict with the former. In that sense, there indeed is a normative hierarchy between the two. But reaching to such a point will be a huge rarity, if it ever is possible, because this would require an obligation under the WTO to either negate the possibility of States to 'take action' to promote or achieve human rights or to make such taking of any action unreasonably onerous so as to render the very obligation to 'take action' otiose. In reality, States have a variety of options available to them in terms of 'taking action'. This is what we have called governance space.

Indeed, as part of the research for this book, not a single instance where a WTO obligation has been found to be in this type of a conflict with the Charter's human rights obligation of taking action could be identified. Because it is impossible for us to prove the negative, the only conclusion which can be drawn is that the tensions between WTO laws and human rights are not a result of an irreconcilable conflict between norms, but rather due to the limitation of governance space of States as a result of WTO obligations. As will be demonstrated in Chapter 5, there indeed are instances where WTO laws, by requiring a particular trade obligation to be fulfilled in a particular manner, obviously remove the option to use governance space in the contrary manner. In other words, if the trade obligation were not present, States would have wider governance space to fulfil human rights obligations. In that sense, a WTO obligation can limit the range of choices which States have in order to fulfil their human rights obligations. This, does not, however, mean that the WTO obligation comes into conflict with the human rights obligation of taking action under the Charter.

An unlikely admission of the above comes from de Schutter, who as noted earlier, has been quite proactive in raising the Article 103 argument. Yet he concedes that 'even if [the doctrine] were successful at seeking to achieve the recognition of the primacy of human rights obligations of States over any of their other obligations . . . this would still only concern a relatively limited range of human rights' (de Schutter 2010: 44–45). He further reminds readers that 'the difference between a decision adopted by an international organisation which is in direct conflict with any human rights obligations of its member States, and such a decision which merely impedes the realisation of human rights by the member States concerned' (de Schutter 2010: 44–45) should be borne in mind. Developing this observation further, he notes that 'direct, "open" conflicts will not occur frequently' and that:

> much more frequent will be the situations where the law-making or dispute-settlement activities of the international organisation will restrict the policy space available to its member States, which they need in order to realise a number of human rights under their jurisdiction – for instance, to improve the affordability of education, to provide a decent work to all members of its active population, or to make medicine more accessible.
>
> (de Schutter 2010: 44–45)

Lex superior and *jus cogens*

Apart from Article 103, the other *lex superior* argument which has been made by some scholars is based on the concept of *jus cogens*. Like the former, the peremptory norms of international law from which no derogation is permitted under any circumstances whatsoever are placed at the highest level of the hierarchy of international law. However, unlike Article 103, the analytical task with respect to the *jus cogens* argument is relatively straightforward. It is axiomatic now that treaties or their provisions which are in conflict with *jus cogens* norms are void. Article 53 of Vienna Convention on the Law of Treaties (VCLT) captures this principle: 'A treaty is void if, at the time of its conclusion, it conflicts with a peremptory norm of general international law.' Similarly, VCLT stipulates that an existing treaty will also become void if it conflicts with new *jus cogens* norms (VCLT 1969: Article 64).

In other words, *jus cogens* norms have the very highest normative value in international law. As such, any obligations of States which run contrary to *jus cogens* norms will cease to exist. The absolute primacy of these norms is also borne out from the fact that any conflict therewith renders a treaty void; whereas, in case of Article 103, the

Charter obligations only 'prevail'. The ILC study observed further that despite what is mentioned in Article 103, even the UN Charter is not above *jus cogens* (ILC 2006b: Para. 360).

It is in this backdrop that some scholars have argued that all human rights obligations of States are *jus cogens* and, therefore, a WTO obligation which comes into conflict with any human rights obligation is void. In an influential article written by Howse and Mutua, the authors controversially stated that 'although there is no list, as such, of rules that constitute *jus cogens*, prohibitions against the slave trade or slavery, genocide, piracy and violations of human rights are regarded as peremptory norms of international law or *jus cogens*' (Howse and Mutua 2000: 60). Similarly, de Schutter has often argued that all human rights are *jus cogens* norms (de Schutter 2014), including in his capacity as the UN Special Rapporteur on the Right to Food (UNHRC 2011a: 6).

However, this argument is fraught with dispute.[8] Marceau (2002: 798), for instance, rightly points out that only a few human rights are recognised as acquiring the status of *jus cogens*, providing them with hierarchical superiority over WTO provisions in cases of conflict. The ILC study, while acknowledging that the list of *jus cogens* norms is malleable, listed the 'most frequently cited candidates for the status of *jus cogens*' (ILC 2006b: Para. 374). These were the prohibition of aggressive use of force, the right to self-defence, the prohibition of genocide, the prohibition of torture, crimes against humanity, prohibition of slavery and slave trade, the prohibition of piracy, the prohibition of racial discrimination and apartheid and the prohibition of hostilities directed at civilian population.

It is clear that any WTO obligation which comes into conflict with a *jus cogens* norm such as any one of those mentioned earlier will be essentially rendered void. However, the fact is that most human rights which become an issue in the context of the WTO-human rights linkages can hardly fit within the *jus cogens* category. Indeed, there is no research which could be found which identifies a conflict between a WTO obligation and one of the aforesaid norms. Thus, to say that all human rights have automatic and unbounded legal primacy over WTO agreements because they all are *jus cogens* norms cannot be the correct interpretation of international law. It can be concluded, therefore, that the *lex superior* argument in this case may simply be a hopeful human rights advocacy strategy at placing the goal post beyond the goal line, rather than a substantively accurate legal position.

The distractions of the normative hierarchy debate

We have concluded earlier that human rights obligations of States under the Charter do stand at a normatively higher level than WTO obligations of States by virtue of Article 103. However, this proposition cannot be applied as a general rule without reference to context. It is only through the facts of a particular case that a determination can be made whether a conflict arises between WTO obligations and the Charter's human rights obligations. Because the Charter's human rights obligations are those of taking action, it is extremely difficult for a situation to arise whereby WTO obligations will 'conflict' with those, for Article 103 to be applicable. We have likewise concluded that the invocation of *jus cogens* as a ground for claiming *lex superior* is also possible in very limited number of cases. However, the types of linkages which WTO obligations have with human rights obligations of States are not such that they involve *jus cogens* norms.

As such, it is contended that attempts to push for a general proposition of normative hierarchy of human rights norms over WTO norms, without detailed analysis of whether a conflict arises or not in the facts of a specific case, is only a distraction to the larger human rights project. It leads to polarisation of views among different actors, including scholars, civil society organisations and functionaries of the UN and WTO. By doing so, the debate diverts the focus away from the crux of the issue – how to find solutions. We may, therefore, conclude from this chapter that the current linkages between WTO obligations of States and human rights obligations of States are better analysed within the framework of governance space, rather than in terms of 'conflicts' of norms.

Notes

1 The term 'relative normativity' to signify hierarchies in international legal norms appears to have been introduced by Prosper Weil (1983). Interestingly, Weil critiqued the development of hierarchies in international legal norms as 'pathological' because of the uncertainties it may bring about in establishing rights and obligations of States (Weil 1983: 416, 418, 440). For a critique of Weil's arguments and a position that 'relative normativity' in international law is unavoidable and merely a reflection of fact, see Fastenrath (1993: 141).

2 A State must fulfil all its existing international law obligations, and in case of breach of any of them, the same will amount to 'an internationally wrongful act', making the State liable. See, generally, Articles on Responsibility of States for Internationally Wrongful Acts (ILC 2001). Specifically, see Article 2: 'There is an internationally wrongful act of a State when conduct

consisting of an action or omission: (b) constitutes a breach of an international obligation of the State.'

3 In addition to Article 103 and *jus cogens*, the ILC study (2006b) also deliberated upon the concept of 'obligations *erga omnes*' in the context of *lex superior*. It, however, was quick to point out that the concept does not form part of the *lex superior* principle.

> The *erga omnes* nature of an obligation, however, indicates no clear superiority of that obligation over other obligations. Although in practice norms recognised as having an *erga omnes* validity set up undoubtedly important obligations, this importance does not translate into a hierarchical superiority similar to that of Article 103 and *jus cogens*.
>
> (ILC 2006b: Para. 380)

4 This is an interpretation preferred by some of the early commentators in the debate over the legally binding force of the provisions. See Lauterpacht (1950: 149) and Schachter (1951: 652).

5 The Committee stated that the obligations of States under the ICESCR 'include both what may be termed (following the work of the ILC) obligations of conduct and obligations of result' (UN Committee on Economic, Social, and Cultural Rights 1990: Para. 1). The reference to ILC's work was obviously to the period prior to 1990. In view of subsequent developments, it can only be conjectured whether the Committee would have incorporated the distinction had it drafted General Comment No. 3 after 2001.

6 For the debates among members of ILC, see ILC (1999: Para. 145–72).

7 Take, for instance, the following metaphor. Consider that A and B create an organisation, under the Constitution of which they undertake an obligation to 'take action' to reach a particular mountain. Suppose that A enters into an agreement with B, with the purpose of implementing the previous contract, whereby both agree to build a road to reach the mountain. Now, suppose further that there is another agreement between A and B, the implementation of which results in the destruction of the mountain. The consequence of this is necessarily that A will not be able to fulfil his obligation to build a road to reach the mountain. This also necessarily means that A will not be able to fulfil his obligation to 'take action' to reach the mountain under the Constitution of the organisation. If the mountain is destroyed, neither is there any road which can lead there nor can any action be taken to achieve that result.

8 Olivier de Schutter has acknowledged that there is 'doctrinal uncertainty' over this point. See de Schutter (2010: 43; 2014: 88).

4

THE DISPUTED ROLE OF THE DISPUTE SETTLEMENT BODY

Background to the debate

In the previous chapter, one of the conclusions we reached was that Article 103 of the UN Charter does not apply to cases where a WTO obligation conflicts with only one way of fulfilling a human rights obligation, if it leaves open a number of other possible and reasonable ways in which States can 'take action' to fulfil their human rights obligations. This conclusion can, however, be made only for a 'conflict' which arises within the meaning of Article 103. What, then, about a conflict of norms outside the hierarchical context of that provision? In other words, what about that smaller individual conflict between a WTO obligation and one of the possible ways in which States can fulfil a human rights obligation? It is clear that the inapplicability of *lex superior* does not mean that the individual conflict does not exist anymore. It simply means that *lex superior* may not be the appropriate technique for resolving that conflict.

To illustrate this, we may again take recourse to the debates on patenting of medicines we discussed in the previous chapter. We noted that it is possible for a State to argue that the obligation to patent medicines conflicts with its obligation to ensure the right to an adequate standard of health to its citizens under Article 12 of the ICESCR. In this case, if one reaches the conclusion that there are no reasonable non-onerous ways available for the State to 'take action' to fulfil its right to health obligation other than not respecting patents, then a conflict within the meaning of Article 103 may arise and the normative hierarchy argument may apply. However, if one reaches the conclusion that other ways are available to 'take action', it does not mean that the conflict does not arise at all. It only means that the conflict may arise in a context outside of Article 103. In these cases, therefore, in the absence of a normative hierarchy, the conflict must be understood to arise between norms having the same value.

In the absence of *lex superior* as the applicable tool, what are the rules of international law that enable a resolution of conflicts between international legal norms which have the same value? To which extent can such rules be employed by the WTO Panels when faced with issues of normative conflicts between two normatively equal obligations under WTO law and human rights law? These are some of the questions which will be discussed in this chapter. Three specific conclusions will be arrived at. First, the techniques for resolution of conflicts between norms having the same value (*lex specialis* and *lex posterior*) are not helpful in convincingly resolving norm conflicts which may arise between WTO obligations and human rights obligations. Second, even if they were capable of resolving possible conflicts, it is doubtful whether the Panels could be the appropriate forum for so adjudicating. Third, and despite the first two conclusions, States continue to be under an obligation to ensure that they do not violate their human rights obligations while fulfilling their WTO obligations. It is here that the governance space framework developed in Chapter 2 and elaborated in Chapters 5, 6 and 7 enables policy makers within and beyond States to understand the nature of diverse linkages and devise appropriate approaches to solutions.

Lex specialis and *lex posterior* in the context of human rights and WTO rules

As noted in the previous chapter, the two known techniques for resolving conflicts between legal norms having the same value, whether they be within the same rule-system or between two different rule-systems, are *lex specialis* and *lex posterior* (Sadat-Akhavi 2003; Borgen 2005; ILC 2006b: Para. 36). The principle of *lex specialis* means that special law derogates from general law and is a widely accepted maxim of legal interpretation and technique for the resolution of normative conflicts (ILC 2006b: Para. 56). The rule is considered fundamental to treaty interpretation and conflict resolution, although it does not find a specific mention in the VCLT. The rule suggests that 'if a matter is being regulated by a general standard as well as a more specific rule, then the latter should take precedence over the former' (ILC 2006b: Para. 56).

However, when discussing how conflicts between WTO norms and human rights norms might be resolved using the *lex specialis* principle, two specific problems arise. First, the principle applies only when the subject matter of the general law and the specific law are the same (ILC 2001: 140). The determination of whether specific provisions within human rights law and those within WTO law constitute the same subject matter needs a case-by-case analysis and the principle cannot be applied in general terms. The ILC study has thus rightly stressed 'the relational character of these attributes and the way in which their specific operation is always dependent on the context in which they are applied' (ILC 2006b: Para. 222). But what constitutes the 'same subject matter' and whether or not human rights obligations and WTO obligations fall within that rubric is far from resolved. Some scholars have argued that the terms 'same subject matter' should be construed strictly (Vierdag 1988: 100; Aust 2013: 204). In line with these arguments, Joseph (2011: 49) contends that human rights and WTO law are not the same subject matter and, therefore, the principle of *lex specialis* does not apply. The ILC study, on the other hand, adopts an expansive meaning to the terms 'same subject matter' leaving open the question of whether WTO law and human rights law, in a given context, may fall within that category. In giving guidance on how a legal interpreter may understand the term 'same subject matter', the study states that:

> the test of whether two treaties deal with the 'same subject matter' is resolved through the assessment of whether the fulfilment of the obligation under one treaty affects the fulfilment of the obligation of another. This 'affecting' might then take place either as strictly preventing the fulfilment of the other obligation or undermining its object and purpose in one or another way.
>
> (ILC 2006b: Para. 254)

However, even with this expansive, and arguably, the correct interpretation of what constitutes 'same subject matter', we do not reach far enough in resolving the types of norm conflicts that may emerge in the interface between WTO and human rights laws. This is because of the second problem which arises in the application of the *lex specialis* principle, namely it does not apply when the conflict of norms is between two *lex specialis*. It applies only when one is *lex specialis* and the other is *lex generalis* (ILC 2006b: Para. 57). In the case of WTO and human rights obligations, what could the latter be considered as? According to Joseph, both WTO law and human rights law are *lex specialis* and as such, she argues that 'in addressing the issue of patents on medicine, it is unconvincing to claim that TRIPS is the *lex specialis* in preference to the right to health in Article 12 of ICESCR, or vice versa' (Joseph 2011: 49). Indeed, there is some value in the argument that when conflicts between a WTO norm and a human rights norm may arise, there is no a priori reason to assume that one of these is *lex specialis* and the other is *lex generalis*.

The other rule of treaty interpretation and conflict resolution between international norms – *lex posterior* – is specifically enshrined under Article 30 of the VCLT. This principle states that later law supersedes earlier law when the two deal with the same subject matter. Article 30 of VCLT codifies the principle that when States enter into a subsequent treaty that is contrary to the provisions of the former treaty, then the subsequent treaty must be deemed to prevail over the former treaty. However, even in this case, a broader interpretation of the terms 'same subject matter' as proposed by the ILC study does not allow us to take the principle much further in resolving conflicts between WTO norms and human rights norms. For, it is impossible to determine whether human rights treaties and obligations thereunder should be treated as *lex posterior*, or whether WTO agreements and obligations thereunder ought to be treated as such. Indeed, if WTO laws are considered to have come into existence after the establishment of the organisation in 1994, it will be problematic to argue that human rights treaties which came into existence much earlier are *lex posterior*. The UDHR, which arguably for the most part reflects CIL on human rights today, was adopted in 1948. Also, the ICCPR and ICESCR came into force only in 1976, that is much earlier than the coming into force of the WTO Agreements. On the other hand, some of the core human rights treaties have come into force after the WTO Agreements.[1] As such, the *lex posterior* principle is very limited in terms of its ability to resolve conflicts between WTO obligations and human rights obligations.

The conclusion we can reach from the aforesaid analysis is that, much like *lex superior* is not a very helpful technique for resolving a conflict between WTO obligation and human rights obligation of States within the meaning of Article 103 of the Charter, the twin techniques of *lex specialis* and *lex posterior* are not very helpful either outside of the Article 103 context.[2] Even when WTO obligations and human rights obligations are of equal normative value, the two techniques are not of much help in convincingly resolving the norm conflicts.[3] This does not, however, mean that in a potential scenario which may come up in the future, a possible conflict may be incapable of being resolved using the two techniques. That, then, brings up the question of whether the Panels can determine WTO law to be prevailed over in case of a conflict with human rights law. In other words, our inquiry is into the functional mandate of the Panels and whether they suffer from any sort of limitations prohibiting them from applying human rights obligations of States as justification for breaching WTO obligations.

Making human rights arguments before WTO panels – five potential scenarios

One of the hallmark achievements of the Uruguay Rounds was the adoption of the DSU as part of the single undertaking under the Marrakesh Agreement. Indeed, by virtue of Article 23 thereof, the DSU established the first compulsory third-party adjudication system in the history of international law. This system comprises the Panels which make recommendations in the first stage (DSU 1994: Articles 6–16), the Appellate Body (AB) to which findings of the Panel can be appealed on questions of law in the second stage (DSU 1994: Article 17) and the DSB which then formally adopts the recommendations of the Panels/AB (DSU 1994: Article 16(4)). The system is considered the most robust in international law till date, leading Charnovitz (2002: 29) to quip that WTO has become a 'magnet for expansionist ideas' whereby there are constant calls for broadening the scope of the WTO.

In order to determine the scope of the functional mandate of the Panels, it is important to outline five potential scenarios when a Panel might be asked to apply human rights law in cases before it. The first scenario is when a human rights exception to WTO law is specifically permitted under a WTO agreement, such as under the General Exceptions Clause in Article XX of GATT 1994. In other words, this scenario deals with cases where State A complains before a Panel that State B is violating a WTO law, and State B invokes an exception to the law which is specifically permitted under the WTO agreements. In such cases, however, there is no conflict because the WTO laws themselves incorporate the non-WTO exception, including some touching on human rights. We shall deal with those cases extensively in Chapter 5.

The second scenario is when State A complains before the Panel that State B is violating non-WTO law. There is general consensus among scholars that Panels do not have the mandate to consider such a claim, because, the rules and procedures of the DSU apply only to claims that are based on violations of the WTO 'covered agreements' (DSU 1994: Article 1(1); Marceau 2002: 763; Pauwelyn 2003a: 910; Harrison 2007: 188). The list of WTO Agreements which fall within the category of 'covered agreements' are outlined in Appendix 1 of the DSU and do not include non-WTO agreements, much less any human rights treaty. In *EC – Poultry*, Brazil claimed that the EU had violated terms of the so-called Oilseeds Agreement. The AB held the said Agreement was not a 'covered agreement' within the meaning of the DSU since it was a bilateral agreement negotiated by the EC and Brazil, was not part of the multilateral obligations accepted by Brazil and the EC pursuant to the Marrakesh Agreement and was not cited in any Annex thereof (*EC – Poultry*, AB Report 1998: Para. 79).[4] This may be logically justified on the ground that the DSB was created to enforce WTO agreements and not agreements under other regimes.

The third scenario is when State A complains against a WTO violation by State B, and State B justifies it on the ground that State A has violated a non-WTO agreement. This argument has also been rejected. In *Mexico – Soft Drinks*, the US challenged certain tax measures and bookkeeping requirements imposed by Mexico on soft drinks and other beverages that use sweeteners other than cane sugar. The US and Mexico are both parties to the North American Free Trade Agreement (NAFTA), 1992. As part of its defence, Mexico argued that the applicability of its WTO obligations towards the US would be called into question as a result of the US having prevented Mexico, by an illegal act, namely the alleged refusal by the US to nominate panellists to the NAFTA panel, from having recourse to the NAFTA dispute settlement mechanism to resolve a bilateral dispute between Mexico and the US regarding trade in sweeteners (*Mexico – Soft Drinks*, AB Report 2006: Para. 55). In other words, the argument by Mexico was that it was justified in violating its obligations towards the US under the WTO because the US had violated its obligations under NAFTA. The AB held that if Mexico's arguments were accepted, then it would entail a determination whether the US has acted consistently or inconsistently with its NAFTA obligations and would imply that the WTO dispute settlement system could be used to determine rights and obligations outside the covered agreements (*Mexico – Soft Drinks*, AB Report 2006: Para. 56). This scenario will also be dealt with in depth in Chapter 6, albeit in the different context of the raging debate whether States should be allowed to impose trade sanctions on countries which violate labour standards.

The fourth scenario arises when State A complains against a WTO violation by State B, and State B seeks to justify it on the ground that it is obliged to State C to do so. This argument has also been rejected. In *Turkey – Textiles*, for instance, India had challenged certain import restrictions by Turkey on textiles and clothing products. Among other grounds raised in defence, Turkey argued that it was 'required' by the terms of its customs union agreement with the EC to adopt the WTO compatible import restrictions of the EC in the sector of textiles and clothing. The Panel rejected this argument and held that a bilateral agreement between two members, such as that between the EC and Turkey, 'does not alter the legal nature of the measures at issue or the applicability of the relevant GATT/WTO provisions' (*Turkey – Textiles*, Panel Report 1999: Para. 9.178). In coming to this conclusion, the Panel recalled Article 41 of the VCLT which states that:

> two or more parties to a multilateral treaty may conclude an agreement to modify the treaty as between themselves alone if . . . (b) the modification in question is not prohibited by the treaty and (i) does not affect the enjoyment by the other parties of their rights under the treaty or the performance of their obligations.

The Panel concluded that 'even if the Turkey – EC customs union agreement did require Turkey to adopt all EC trade policies . . . we consider that such requirement would not be sufficient to exempt Turkey from its obligations under the WTO Agreement' (*Turkey – Textiles*, Panel Report 1999: Para. 9.182).

The fifth scenario arises when State A complains against a WTO violation by State B, and State B seeks to justify it on the basis of a human rights obligation either under treaty law or customary international law. In such cases, a clear conflict may arise between the obligations of State B under the WTO agreement and those under non-WTO law such as human rights law. It is this last scenario which has formed the major bone of contention among scholars, in terms of whether or not Panels are authorised to permit a WTO-inconsistent measure in light of a State's human rights obligations. Indeed, scholars have been polarised into two separate camps. One camp, led by Joost Pauwelyn, has argued vehemently that States may be able to successfully use human rights arguments as defence in WTO disputes to wriggle out of their WTO obligations (Howse and Mutua 2000; Pauwelyn 2001; Howse 2002b; Pauwelyn 2003a, b, c; 2005). Based on an evaluation of the functional mandate of Panels as enshrined under the DSU, Pauwelyn has argued that a Panel is required to *apply* human rights law, if raised in defence by Party B against a claim related to violation of WTO law made by Party A, in such a way that it may even reject an otherwise rightful claim by party A.

The other camp led by Gabrielle Marceau has argued that the scope of Panels' functions is limited to rulings and recommendations related to violations of WTO agreements only and that they has no mandate to allow WTO-inconsistent measures by a State on the ground that they are justified or required under human rights law (except, of course, under the first scenario outlined earlier) (Trachtman 1999; Alvarez 2001; Marceau 2001; 2002: 798; Trachtman 2004; Mavroidis 2008; Bartels 2011; 2014).[5] Indeed, Marceau differentiates between what may be the actual relationship of a WTO norm vis-à-vis a human rights norm and the legal capacity of a Panel to hold so in a ruling or recommendation. Her suggestion is that even if according to legal reasoning, a WTO law may be deemed to be prevailed over by a human rights law after applying the principles of conflict resolution, a Panel may be constrained in so holding in light of the DSU which prohibit Panels and the AB from adding to or diminishing rights and obligations pursuant to the WTO treaty (Marceau 2001: 1100).

The dispute over the dispute settlement understanding

As stated earlier, Article 1(1) of the DSU outlines the coverage and applicability of the provisions of the DSU and states that its rules and procedures apply to disputes brought pursuant to the consultation and dispute settlement provisions of the 'covered agreements'. As we have also seen earlier, the term 'covered agreements' refers only to specific WTO agreements and does not include non-WTO agreements such as human rights treaties. Article 3(2) then identifies the main purpose of the dispute settlement system of the WTO by stating that it 'is a central element in providing security and predictability to the multilateral trading system'. It further states that 'the Members recognise that it serves to preserve the rights and obligations of Members under the covered agreements, and to clarify the existing provisions of those agreements in accordance with customary rules of interpretation of public international law' and that 'recommendations and rulings of the DSB cannot add to or diminish the rights and obligations provided in the covered agreements'.

The 'customary rules of interpretation of public international law' have generally been understood to be codified by Articles 31 (*Libyan Arab Jamahiriya v. Chad* 1994: 6; ILC study 2006: Para. 167) and 32 (*Constitution of the Maritime Safety Committee of the IMCO* 1960: 161; *Libyan Arab Jamahiriya v. Chad* 1994: 20) of the VCLT. In *US – Gasoline*, the very first case decided by it, the AB agreed that the 'general rule of interpretation' in Article 31 of VCLT 'has attained the status of a rule of customary or general international law' (AB Report 1996: 17). In *Japan – Alcoholic Beverages II*, the AB further acknowledged that 'Article 32 of the Vienna Convention, dealing with the role of supplementary means of interpretation, has also attained the same status' (AB Report 1996: 10).[6]

Article 31 of VCLT lays down the general standards for interpretation of a treaty, namely that a treaty should be interpreted in good faith in accordance with the ordinary meaning to be given to the terms of the treaty in their context and in the light of its object and purpose. In addition to the text of a treaty, including its preamble and annexes, other factors which should be considered by a treaty interpreter to determine the context for the purpose of the interpretation of a treaty are any agreements relating to the treaty made between all the parties in connection with the conclusion of the treaty and any instruments which were made by one or more parties in connection with the conclusion of the treaty and accepted by the other parties as an instrument related to the treaty. Human rights treaties generally will not fall within the aforesaid two categories when interpreting WTO agreements. However, Article 31(3)(c) further states that together with the context, the treaty interpreter 'should take into account . . . any relevant rules of international law applicable in the relations between the parties'.

It is here that disagreement between scholars arises when discussing whether Panels are required, by virtue of Article 31(3)(c) of VCLT, to not only *interpret* WTO law in light of non-WTO law, but also to *apply* non-WTO law in a manner that a State may be allowed to derogate from its WTO obligation. This principal disagreement over the scope of functional mandate of Panels stems from how scholars have understood differently the concepts of 'interpretation', 'applicable law' and 'jurisdiction' in the context of the DSU.

Pauwelyn has convincingly argued that there is a distinction between 'jurisdiction' of a DSB and the 'applicable law' which must be used to resolve conflicts. Using the example of the decision by the ICJ in *Questions of Interpretation and Application of the 1971 Montreal Convention Arising from the Aerial Incident at Lockerbie* (*Libya v. US*) (1998), he points out that despite the 'jurisdiction' of the ICJ to consider the case being limited to the Montreal Convention, the ICJ, in fact, examined other international law also as part of the 'applicable law', particularly UN Security Council Resolution 748 which was invoked in defence by the UK and the US (Pauwelyn 2003b: 1000). Thus, in 'interpreting' the Montreal Convention, the ICJ 'applied' other international law binding on the parties to the dispute, although its 'jurisdiction' was found under the Montreal Convention only.

Interpretation and applicable law

Puwelyn's arguments mentioned earlier raise the question whether use by Panels of non-WTO law in 'interpreting', that is 'clarify[ing] the existing provisions of [covered] agreements in accordance with customary rules of interpretation of public international law' (DSU 1994: Article 3(2)), necessarily means that such non-WTO law is also part of the 'applicable law' between the disputing parties.

In answering this question, it appears important to note that some judicial bodies are explicitly required to 'apply' other international law in determining disputes. For instance, Article 38 of the Statute of the ICJ clearly stipulates which international law it must 'apply' in deciding disputes before it, and this includes general principles of law as well (Statute of the ICJ 1945: Article 38(1)). Similarly, the United Nations Convention on the Law of the Sea (UNCLOS), 1982 stipulates explicitly that the Tribunal 'shall apply this Convention and other rules of international law not incompatible with this Convention' (UNCLOS 1982: Article 293(1)). The DSU, on the other hand, does not explicitly make non-WTO law applicable. Whether or not such non-WTO laws are applicable, nevertheless, is the main bone of contention.

When a judicial body is required to 'apply' other international law while deciding on the rights and obligations of parties to the dispute, it necessarily involves the process of 'interpretation'. This is because such 'application' of other law, may require the judicial body to resolve norm conflicts between the treaty under which the violation is claimed and the other international law which may be invoked by a defendant. It is in this context that the ILC study rightly observes that the process of conflict resolution and interpretation are inseparable and whether there is a conflict and what can be done with it depends on the way the relevant rules are interpreted. It further states that 'interpretation does not intervene only once it has already been ascertained that there is a conflict' and that 'rules appear to be compatible or in conflict *as a result of interpretation*' (ILC 2006b: Para. 412).

The aforesaid observations can be applied directly to the decision of the ICJ in *Lockerbie*. The ICJ was required by Article 38 of its Statute to apply law which was binding on the parties other than the Montreal Convention also. As such, when it applied other international law, it also necessarily undertook the process of interpretation. Here, the application of other international law was a result of interpretation.

However, this does not necessarily lead to a conclusion that any use of other international law for the purpose of interpretation of a treaty, necessarily also requires that the other law must be applied in determining the very rights and obligations of the parties under that treaty. In other words, where other international law may not be part of the applicable law, its use may be restricted only to interpreting the provisions of the treaty which is invoked.

In the context of the DSU, this distinction assumes life, specifically because of the language of Article 3(2). It is now well settled that by virtue of Article 31 of VCLT, a relevant non-WTO law may be used by the DSB to interpret the provisions of covered agreements.[7] Thus, in *US – Shrimp*, the interpretation of the terms 'exhaustible natural resources' mentioned in Article XX(g) of GATT was in contention, and India, Pakistan, Thailand and Malaysia had argued that only 'finite resources such as minerals, rather than biological or renewable resources' would qualify (AB Report 1998: Para. 127). As such, their contention was that the species of sea turtles which were sought to be protected by the US through the measure under challenge were not 'exhaustible natural resources'. The AB, however, adopted an 'evolutionary' approach to defining the term and concluded that it included not only non-living natural resources but living ones such as sea turtles as well (*US – Shrimp*, AB Report 1998: Para. 128–34). Importantly, in order to interpret the term 'exhaustible natural resources' in Article XX(g), the AB referred to various non-WTO treaties such as the UNCLOS, the Biodiversity Convention as well as the Convention on International Trade in Endangered Species of Wild Fauna and Flora (*US – Shrimp*, AB Report 1998: Para. 132). Additionally, it also referred to 'soft law' instruments such as the 1992 Rio Declaration and Agenda 21 (*US – Shrimp*, AB Report 1998: Para. 132).

US – FSC (21.5) is another example where the AB used non-WTO law to interpret terms in WTO provisions. In this case, the issue related to the meaning of the terms 'foreign-source income' in footnote 59 of the Agreement on Subsidies and Countervailing Measures (hereafter, SCM Agreement), which was a 'covered agreement'. In order to give meaning to the term as referring to 'income which is susceptible of being taxed in two States' (*US – FSC (21.5)*, AB Report 2002: Para. 138), the AB relied on how the term has been used in a series of bilateral and multilateral treaties relating to avoidance of double taxation (*US – FSC (21.5)*, AB Report 2002: Para. 142).

Marceau (1999: 131; 2006: 31) has pointed out that panels may also look at other treaties and reports of other international bodies as 'factual matters' to assess compliance with WTO provisions. In *EC – Asbestos*, the import ban by France on asbestos and asbestos containing products was challenged by Canada. France sought to justify the ban on the ground that it was necessary to protect 'public health' within the country, since asbestos was carcinogenic. In determining that asbestos is indeed toxic and can have serious adverse impacts on public health, the AB relied on conventions under the World Health Organisation (*EC – Asbestos*, AB Report 2001: Para. 114, 135).

However, the question remains whether Panels can go beyond using non-WTO law as an interpretative tool for clarifying existing WTO provisions and allow such non-WTO law to be successfully raised in defence in a WTO dispute. Typically, Panels and the AB have been extremely cautious by restricting themselves to the former. For instance, in *EC – Bananas III*, the facts were that since 1992, at the request of the EC and of the 49 ACP States that were also GATT contracting parties, the WTO Contracting Parties had granted the EC a waiver, known as the Lomé waiver, from certain obligations it had under GATT 1947. Since the waiver incorporated a reference to the Fourth ACP-EC Convention of Lomé (Lomé Convention), the Panel observed that the meaning of the said Convention had become a GATT/WTO issue and that it had no alternative but to examine the provisions of the said Convention 'in so far as it is necessary to interpret the Lomé waiver' (*EC – Bananas III*, Panel Report 1997: Para. 7.98). The AB agreed with this statement (*EC – Bananas III*, AB Report 1997: Para. 167).

An explicit expression of the distinction between 'interpretation' and 'application' was presented by the AB in *US – Anti-Dumping and Countervailing Duties (China)*. In this case, one of the questions was whether the term 'public body' in Article 1.1(a)(1) of the SCM Agreement could be interpreted in light of the ILC Articles on State Responsibility. The AB observed as follows:

> The question in the present case, however, is not whether certain of the ILC Articles are to be applied, that is, whether attribution of conduct of the SOEs and SOCBs at issue to the Government of China is to be assessed pursuant to the ILC Articles instead of Article 1.1(a)(1) of the SCM Agreement. There is no doubt that the provision being applied in the present case is Article 1.1(a)(1). Rather, the question is, whether, when interpreting the terms of Article 1.1(a)(1), the relevant provisions of the ILC Articles may be taken into account as one among several interpretative elements. Thus, the treaty being applied is the SCM Agreement and the attribution rules

> of the ILC Articles are to be taken into account in interpreting the meaning of the terms of that treaty.
>
> (*US – Anti-Dumping and Countervailing Duties (China)*, AB Report 2011: Para. 316)

Pauwelyn, despite being on the other side of the Marceau camp, has also distinguished between use of non-WTO law in interpretation of WTO provisions and its use as applicable law. According to him:

> WTO panels may be called upon to refer to non-WTO rules of international law pursuant to Articles 31 and 32 of the Vienna Convention, in particular, Article 31.3(c) referring to 'any relevant rules of international law applicable in the relations between the parties'.
>
> (Pauwelyn 2003a: 910)

However, in his view, the non-WTO rules that may thereby be referred to in the process of interpreting WTO terms are limited to those non-WTO rules reflecting 'the common intentions of all WTO members' (Pauwelyn 2003a: 910). On the other hand, he also argues that 'although the jurisdiction of WTO panels is limited to WTO claims, all international law binding on both parties to a dispute may, in principle, be part of the applicable law before a WTO panel' (Pauwelyn 2003a: 910). According to him, non-WTO law is part of this applicable law and may, in particular, provide a defence against violation of WTO law. However, while non-WTO law:

> referred to when interpreting WTO terms ought to be limited to law that reflects the common intentions of all WTO members, . . . the applicable law in a particular dispute may also include law binding only between the two disputing parties (it need not be binding on all WTO members).
>
> (Pauwelyn 2003a: 910)

Therefore, the distinction between the role of non-WTO law in interpretation of WTO provisions, and as applicable law in deciding rights and obligations of parties under the WTO, is now well accepted. The difference in arguments is that while the Marceau camp argues that the role on non-WTO law is limited to the former, the Pauwelyn camp argues that it extends also to the latter (albeit with a different scope).

Jurisdiction, interpretation and applicable law

The distinction which Pauwelyn makes between 'jurisdiction' and 'applicable law', using the *Lockerbie* case as an example, has also found favour with the ILC (2006b: Para. 44–45). Even Marceau agrees that there is a distinction between the two concepts (Marceau 2002: 766). However, that is where the agreement ends. Pauwelyn argues that while there is a limitation on the jurisdiction of Panels in terms of claims only under the covered agreements, there is nothing in the DSU which restricts the applicable law only to WTO covered agreements (Pauwelyn 2003b: 1000–1005). Marceau, on the other hand, argues that not only is the jurisdiction of Panels limited to covered agreements, the applicable law is also so limited, and, therefore, no non-WTO law can be brought in as defence by a party to avoid WTO obligations (Marceau 2002: 767).

In order to understand why there is a difference of opinion between the scholars, it is also important to highlight some other provisions of the DSU. Pauwelyn argues that Article 3(2) of the DSU only lays down the 'rather obvious limits a WTO panel must observe in interpreting WTO covered agreements' and that the provision 'does not limit the applicable law before WTO Panels, nor does it deal with the relationship between WTO covered agreements and all past and future law' (Pauwelyn 2003b: 1003). According to him, the provision which lays down the applicable law is Article 7 of the DSU, which requires panels 'to examine, in the light of the relevant provisions in . . . the covered agreement(s) cited by the parties to the dispute' (Pauwelyn 2003b: 1000). He contends that just by confirming the relevance of some rules – *in casu* those that Panels will most commonly be asked to apply, that is WTO rules – does not preclude that Panels may apply also other, non-WTO rules in particular circumstances (Pauwelyn 2003b: 1001). This conclusion, however, in my view, is not convincing for reasons spelt out later.

Pauwelyn sets out four main reasons for arriving at this conclusion. First, he argues that Panels and the AB have already referred to general principles of law, CIL and even other, non-WTO treaties. However, as we have seen earlier, references to general international law and even to non-WTO treaties have been limited to either interpreting existing WTO provisions or as a factual matter to decide whether a WTO obligation has been complied with or not, or on occasions, to guide issues on procedural issues.[8] Therefore, the fact that such references have already been made can hardly lead to a conclusion that non-WTO law can also be applicable law.

Second, in concluding that non-WTO law can be applicable law in a WTO dispute, he refers back to Article 3(2) of the DSU and the incorporation of customary rules of interpretation of public international law to clarify WTO provisions. He rightly points out that because Article 31(3) of the VCLT is thus incorporated, in interpreting a treaty, account must be taken not only of the WTO treaty itself but also of any subsequent agreement between the parties regarding the interpretation of that treaty or the application of its provisions, in addition to any relevant rules of international law applicable in the relations between the parties (Pauwelyn 2003b: 1001). However, it is unclear how this fact can lead to an automatic conclusion that non-WTO law is not only a rule of interpretation of a treaty but also the applicable law. This is particularly so because, as pointed out earlier, he himself argues that Article 3(2) of the DSU is not a provision highlighting the applicable law but only a provision outlining the scope of the Panel's mandate for interpreting WTO provisions. But additionally, it is important to highlight that Article 7(1) of the DSU goes further to state that the mandate of the Panels is not only limited to examining the provisions of the covered agreements, but to also making 'such findings as will assist the DSB in making the *recommendations or in giving the rulings provided for in that/those agreement(s)*' (emphasis supplied). Further, Article 7(2) stipulates that 'Panels shall address the *relevant provisions in any covered agreement or agreements cited by the parties to the dispute*' (emphasis supplied). In the teeth of these provisions, therefore, the argument by Pauwelyn that non-WTO law can also be applicable law in a WTO dispute is rather tenuous and, to my mind, untenable.

Third, Pauwelyn argues that because WTO agreement is a treaty part of public international law, it cannot be applied in isolation from other rules of international law, including human rights treaties (Pauwelyn 2003b: 1001). He argues that despite the fact that the DSU does not explicitly include other rules of international law as applicable law unlike Article 38 of the ICJ or Article 293 of UNCLOS, there is no need to do so (Pauwelyn 2003b: 1002). In other words, he contends that:

> there was no need for Article 7 of the DSU to explicitly include also other rules of international law as part of the applicable law before WTO Panels; to the extent that those other rules were not deviated from in the WTO treaty, this is automatically the case.
>
> (Pauwelyn 2003b: 1002)

The underlying premise behind this argument, therefore, is that human rights treaties as part of general international law applicable between WTO members is not excluded – members have not contracted out of them – and, therefore, they continue to be applicable law even at the WTO.

The proposition that unless a treaty contracts out of general international law, the latter continues to apply has also found favour with the ILC (2006b: Para. 172–85).[9] Whether or not, and to what extent, has the WTO contracted out from non-WTO law explicitly or implicitly was not specifically answered by the ILC study. Similarly, it did not specifically answer the question whether human rights treaties would be applicable law for the purpose of being invoked as a defence against a claim alleging the violation of WTO law. It did observe, however, that:

> even as it is clear that the competence of WTO bodies is limited to consideration of claims under the covered agreements (and not, for example, under environmental or human rights treaties), when elucidating the content of the relevant rights and obligations, WTO bodies must situate those rights and obligations within the overall context of general international law (including the relevant environmental and human rights treaties).
>
> (ILC 2006b: Para. 170)

This observation that WTO bodies must 'situate' WTO rights and obligations for the purpose of 'elucidating their content' in the overall context of human rights treaties, unfortunately, does not answer whether such treaties are also applicable law. To the contrary, it only reiterates the rule of interpretation enshrined in Articles 31 and 32 of VCLT that human rights treaties do add to the overall 'context' for 'elucidation' of WTO provisions.

It may also be relevant to refer at this stage to an observation by a WTO Panel in *Korea – Procurement*, reliance on which was placed by Pauwelyn to buttress his arguments that WTO rules do not 'contract out' of other international law. In this case, the Panel observed as follows:

> We take note that Article 3.2 of the DSU requires that we seek within the context of a particular dispute to clarify the existing provisions of the WTO agreements in accordance with customary rules of interpretation of public international law. However, the relationship of the WTO Agreements to

> customary international law is broader than this. Customary international law applies generally to the economic relations between the WTO Members. Such international law applies to the extent that the WTO treaty agreements do not 'contract out' from it. To put it another way, to the extent there is no conflict or inconsistency, or an expression in a covered WTO agreement that implies differently, we are of the view that the customary rules of international law apply to the WTO treaties and to the process of treaty formation under the WTO.
> (*Korea – Procurement*, Panel Report 2000: Para. 7.96)

However, if these observations are contextualised with the facts of the case, it is clear that no inference could be drawn that non-WTO treaties such as human rights treaties can be brought in as valid justifications for violating a WTO obligation. First, the customary rules of international law to which the Panel was referring to as being applicable to WTO members also, were the principles of good faith and error in treaty negotiations (*Korea – Procurement*, Panel Report 2000: Para. 7.101), which the Panel observed are an extension of the doctrine of *pacta sunt servanda* (Para. 7.93, 7.99). This doctrine is specifically enshrined in Article 26 of the VCLT and states that 'every treaty in force is binding upon the parties to it and must be performed by them in good faith'. It is well known that States through treaties cannot 'contract out' of the principle of *pacta sunt servanda* (ILC 2006b: Para. 176). The aforesaid observations by the Panel, therefore, were made with reference to such fundamental principles of CIL which cannot be contracted out by States in any treaty. No general conclusion can be drawn from these observations that non-WTO law, including human rights law, was not 'contracted out' by WTO members as being part of 'applicable law'. The latter part of the previous passage also lends credence to these conclusions when the Panel states that the customary rules of international law apply to the WTO treaties and to the process of treaty formation under the WTO, but only 'to the extent there is no conflict or inconsistency, or an expression in a covered WTO agreement that implies differently'. As such, the Panel only reiterates the point that in case of conflict between WTO obligations and non-WTO obligations, the latter cannot be brought in as justification to prevail over the former.

Pauwelyn's argument that non-WTO law is also applicable law in WTO disputes when raised in defence has been countered most effectively by Marceau. She agrees with Pauwelyn that the jurisdiction of panels is limited to covered agreements but disagrees that similar is not the case with respect to applicable law. According to her, 'The provisions on the limited jurisdiction of panels mirror those on the applicable law between WTO members' (Marceau 2002: 767). These include not only Articles 1, 3 and 7 of the DSU mentioned earlier, but also Articles 11 and 19 thereof.

Article 11 of the DSU defines the functions of the Panels. It states that:

> The function of panels is to assist the DSB in discharging its responsibilities under this Understanding and the covered agreements. Accordingly, a panel should make an objective assessment of the matter before it, including an objective assessment of the facts of the case and the applicability of and conformity with the relevant covered agreements, and make such other findings as will assist the DSB in making the recommendations or in giving the rulings provided for in the covered agreements.

The terms 'applicability of and conformity with the relevant covered agreements', therefore, leave no measure of doubt that the covered agreements are the applicable law. Similarly, like Articles 3 and 7, the recommendations and rulings that the Panels can make are only those provided for in the covered agreements.

Article 19 of the DSU completes the circle and, to my mind, indeed clinches the issue. It reads as follows:

1 Where a panel or the Appellate Body concludes that a measure is inconsistent with a covered agreement, it shall recommend that the member concerned bring the measure into conformity with that agreement.;
2 In accordance with paragraph 2 of Article 3, in their findings and recommendations, the Panel and Appellate Body cannot add to or diminish the rights and obligations provided in the covered agreements.

It is again clear, therefore, that the non-WTO law, including human rights treaties, cannot be the applicable law before the Panels when they are raised in defence as justifications for violations of WTO obligations. As Bartels bluntly puts it, 'Disapplying a valid WTO norm because of a contrary non-WTO right does diminish those rights and obligations', and, therefore, he concludes that 'Article 19.2 precludes a straightforward application in WTO dispute settlement proceedings of any rule that results in the disapplication of WTO law' (Bartels 2014: 10).

The overall purpose of the WTO's dispute settlement system was summarised by the AB in China – Publications and Audiovisual Products, when it observed that 'the purpose of WTO dispute settlement is to resolve disputes in a manner that preserves the rights and obligations of WTO Members and clarifies existing provisions of the covered agreements in accordance with the customary rules of interpretation of public international law' (China – Publications and Audiovisual Products, AB Report 2009: Para. 213). As Marceau puts it, 'WTO members can be seen as having set up a system that contains a specific applicable law, a lex specialis system' (Marceau 2002: 767). Because WTO law is a specific subsystem of international law with its own specific rights and obligations, remedies and dispute settlement mechanism, 'WTO provisions cannot be overruled by situations and considerations belonging to another subsystem, such as those of human rights law' (Marceau 2002: 767).[10]

Her approach can also be discerned from the limited case law of the WTO on this point, albeit only implicitly. In *EC – Commercial Vessels*, Korea had questioned the EC Temporary Defensive Mechanism for Shipbuilding (the TDM Regulation) as being in violation of their WTO obligations. Among other points raised by the EC in defence was that Korea had decided to ignore its bilateral commitments on injurious pricing agreed with the EC, referred to as the 'Agreed Minutes' of 2000. In this connection, the Panel emphasised that 'its review of the text of the Agreed Minutes only serves the purpose of enabling it to decide a factual issue on which the parties disagree and that it is not interpreting the Agreed Minutes in order to determine the rights and obligations of the parties under that bilateral agreement' (*EC – Commercial Vessels*, Panel Report 2005: Para. 7.131). The stated reason for this was that the 'Agreed Minutes' were not 'covered agreements' within the meaning of Articles 1 and 2 of DSU (*EC – Commercial Vessels*, Panel Report 2005: Footnote 275).

In *Argentina – Poultry Anti-Dumping Duties*, Argentina raised a preliminary issue that Brazil's claim of violation by Argentina of its WTO obligations should be rejected at the outset, since Brazil had already challenged a similar issue before the Mercado Común del Sur (MERCOSUR) tribunal. Argentina argued that the Panel ought to rule in line with the MERCOSUR decision. In response, the Panel observed that:

> Argentina would have us apply the relevant WTO provisions in a particular way, rather than interpret them in a particular way. However, there is no basis in Article 3.2 of the DSU, or

> any other provision, to suggest that we are bound to rule in a particular way, or apply the relevant WTO provisions in a particular way.
>
> (*Argentina – Poultry Anti-Dumping Duties*, Panel Report 2003: Para. 7.41).

In *EC and Certain Member States – Large Civil Aircraft*, the US had challenged certain types of subsidies granted by some European countries to Airbus as being in violation of WTO agreements. One of the defences raised by the EC was that such subsidies were permitted under a '1992 Agreement' entered into between the US and the EC. Interestingly, the invocation of the 1992 Agreement was not only for interpreting provisions of the SCM Agreement (*EC and Certain Member States – Large Civil Aircraft*, Panel Report 2011: Para. 7.72), but also as applicable law (Para. 7.71). In response to the argument that the non-WTO law was applicable law, the Panel stated:

> Article 7.2 of the DSU requires panels to 'address the relevant provisions in any covered Agreement or Agreements cited by the parties to the dispute'. The 'covered Agreements' cited by the United States in document WT/DS316/2 include the DSU, the GATT 1994 and the SCM Agreement. As the 1992 Agreement is not a covered Agreement cited by the United States in document WT/DS316/2, or contained in the list of covered Agreements in Appendix 1 to the DSU, or one of the instruments included in the GATT 1994, we do not have jurisdiction to determine of the rights and obligations of the parties under the 1992 Agreement.
>
> (*EC and Certain Member States – Large Civil Aircraft*, Panel Report 2011: Para. 7.89)

But, having observed that it did not have *jurisdiction* to determine the rights and obligations of parties under the 1992 Agreement, the Panel proceeded to examine the argument by the EC that said Agreement may constitute law that the Panel may apply in order to resolve the claims under the covered Agreements. In essence, here, the EC's argument was that by virtue of the 1992 Agreement, the US had waived its rights under WTO Agreements to challenge certain measures in WTO dispute settlement proceedings. The question, therefore, as the Panel put it was:

> whether it is possible for a Member to have waived its rights under the WTO Agreements in an agreement which it entered

> into *prior to* entering into the WTO Agreements, and if so, whether and on what basis a WTO panel could enforce such a waiver.
>
> (*EC and Certain Member States – Large Civil Aircraft*, Panel Report 2011: Para. 7.91)

However, the Panel observed that they 'did not need to and do not decide' the issue of whether the WTO panel can enforce such a presumed waiver under the 1992 Agreement in a WTO proceeding (*EC and Certain Member States – Large Civil Aircraft*, Panel Report 2011: Para. 7.94), because it rejected the first claim of the EC itself that a WTO right could be waived by the US in a *prior* agreement (Para. 7.98).

The question later again came up before the Panel with respect to another issue, when the EC invoked an agreement called Tokyo Round Subsidies Code as a defence to justify its measures. On this occasion, although the EC acknowledged that the Tokyo Round Subsidies Code was not a 'covered agreement', they argued that it was relevant to the dispute because it fell within the scope of the 'agreements' that parties are entitled to cite under the terms of Article 7.2 of the DSU (*EC and Certain Member States – Large Civil Aircraft*, Panel Report 2011: Para. 7.317). Indeed, their argument was that the EC measures challenged by the US cannot be assessed for compliance with Article 5 of the SCM Agreement, but must instead be examined in the light of the 1979 Tokyo Round Subsidies Code (*EC and Certain Member States – Large Civil Aircraft*, Panel Report 2011: Para. 7.325). The Panel rejected this argument and it is important to reproduce the response of the Panel *ad verbatim*:

> It is clear to us that the word 'agreements' in Article 7.2, which is joined to the words 'covered agreement' that immediately precede it by the conjunction 'or', refers to the plural of a 'covered agreement'. Therefore, it should not, as the European Communities suggests, be understood as referring to international agreements that are not WTO covered agreements. As we have already noted in our preliminary ruling, Article 7.2 does not give us jurisdiction to determine the rights and obligations of the parties under non-covered agreements for the purpose of the recommendations or rulings envisaged under Article 11 of the DSU. Such recommendations or rulings must relate to the parties' rights and obligations under the WTO covered agreements, not the rights and obligations

> of parties under international agreements that are not WTO covered agreements. Additional support for this view is found in Articles 3.2, 3.4 and 19.1 of the DSU, which, as noted by the United States, also envisage panel findings and recommendations in respect of WTO covered agreements, not non-covered agreements. There is therefore no legal basis to support the European Communities' contention that, in the context of the present dispute, the challenged measures must be evaluated under the terms of the Tokyo Round Subsidies Code.
>
> (*EC and Certain Member States – Large Civil Aircraft*, Panel Report 2011: Para. 7.324)

The aforesaid paragraph is, therefore, probably the closest enunciation by a WTO Panel of the proposition that neither does it have jurisdiction with respect to non-WTO law, nor can such non-WTO law be the applicable law in WTO disputes. These are entirely in line with the arguments by Marceau pointed out earlier.

None of the aforesaid observations by the Panel were, however, specifically examined by the AB for their veracity. With respect to the Tokyo Round Subsidies Code, the AB did not address and decide whether or not the said document applied to the dispute because it was not a 'covered agreement'; it merely stated that the SCM Agreement applied to the measure under question (*EC and Certain Member States – Large Civil Aircraft*, AB Report 2011: Para. 689). With respect to the 1992 Agreement, the EC did not argue before the AB that the said document was applicable law. Instead, it restricted its arguments to the use of the 1992 Agreement either for interpreting certain words in the SCM Agreement or 'as part of the facts' to establish the relevant market benchmark at the time the measures under challenge were granted by the EU (*EC and Certain Member States – Large Civil Aircraft*, AB Report 2011: Para. 839). However, even with respect to the use of the 1992 Agreement for interpretation or as facts, the AB did not consider it as a 'relevant' document within the meaning of Article 31(3)(c) of VCLT. It observed that 'for the 1992 Agreement to qualify under Article 31(3)(c) of the Vienna Convention, it must be shown to be "relevant"' and further, that 'a rule is "relevant" if it concerns the subject matter of the provision at issue' (*EC and Certain Member States – Large Civil Aircraft*, AB Report 2011: Para. 846). It then proceeded to conclude that because the subject matter of the 1992 Agreement was different, it was not relevant for the purpose of interpretation either (*EC and Certain Member States – Large Civil Aircraft*, AB Report 2011: Para. 851).[11]

Recently, in *Peru – Agricultural Products*, the AB appears to have taken a clear position that the relevance of Article 31(3)(c) of VCLT and Article 3(2) of DSU with respect to non-WTO law is restricted to interpretation of WTO agreements. In this case, Peru argued that the terms 'shall not maintain' under Article 4(2) of the WTO Agreement on Agriculture should be understood as 'may maintain' by virtue of a particular provision in a subsequent FTA between Peru and Guatemala. The AB observed that:

> while Peru has brought arguments on appeal under Article 31(3)(a) and (c) of the Vienna Convention concerning the Panel's interpretation of Article 4.2 of the Agreement on Agriculture and Article II:1(b) of the GATT 1994, in fact, Peru's arguments go beyond the interpretation of these provisions in accordance with Article 3.2 of the DSU and Article 31 of the Vienna Convention, and amount to arguing that, by means of the FTA, Peru and Guatemala actually modified these WTO provisions between themselves.
>
> (*Peru – Agricultural Products*, AB Report 2015: Para. 5.107)

Therefore, based on the aforesaid analysis, it can be concluded that as the WTO jurisprudence stands today, it is very reluctant to consider non-WTO law as applicable law for WTO disputes, especially when raised in defence by a party whose measures are being challenged as being WTO inconsistent.

Meaning of 'parties' in Article 31(3)(c) of VCLT

At this juncture, it will be important to highlight yet another aspect to this discussion. Assuming that non-WTO law can be applicable law in WTO disputes, it will still have to fulfil some of the other requirements of Article 31(3)(c) of the VCLT, especially whether such non-WTO law is applicable in the relations between 'the parties'. Article 31(3)(c) of VCLT provides that when interpreting a treaty 'there shall be taken into account, together with the context: . . . (c) any relevant rules of international law applicable in the relations between the parties'. Whether the term 'the parties' means parties to the VCLT, or parties to the WTO Agreement under consideration, or only parties to the WTO dispute concerned, has been a subject of much debate. This question assumes significance in the context of our discussion because if the non-WTO law can be taken into account under the aforesaid provision only when *all* WTO members are also parties to it, then very few, if at all any, non-WTO agreements can be applied in WTO disputes. This aspect, therefore, adds yet another layer of complexity to the discussion.

In *EC – Approval and Marketing of Biotech Products*, the US challenged a moratorium which had been applied by the EC since October 1998 on the approval of biotech products on the ground that it violated the SPS Agreement. As justification, the EC invoked the provisions of the Biosafety Protocol to the Convention on Biodiversity, and the question arose whether and to which extent did the said protocol play a role in deciding whether the EC's measures were justified. In this case, however, the EC did not argue that the Protocol was inconsistent with the SPS Agreement and that a conflict arose. In fact, it stated that 'the Biosafety Protocol and the SPS Agreement . . . are so closely connected that they should be interpreted and applied consistently with each other, to the extent that is possible' and that 'there is no *a priori* inconsistency between the WTO agreements (SPS Agreement, TBT Agreement, GATT 1994) and the Biosafety Protocol; that the two instruments are complementary' (*EC – Approval and Marketing of Biotech Products*, Panel Report 2006: Para. 7.55). Therefore, this case is not one that dealt with a defence where a non-WTO treaty was sought to be applied in the face of a conflict with a WTO treaty. Nevertheless, the Panel proceeded to consider whether the Protocol could be 'taken into account' at all as rules of international law 'applicable in the relations between the parties' as required by Article 31(3)(c) of the VCLT. Because the US was not a party to the Biosafety Protocol, the question before the Panel was whether the Protocol could be considered 'applicable between the parties'. This is what the Panel held:

> In considering this issue, we note that Article 31(3)(c) does not refer to 'one or more parties'. Nor does it refer to 'the parties to a dispute'. We further note that Article 2.1(g) of the Vienna Convention defines the meaning of the term 'party' for the purposes of the Vienna Convention. Thus, 'party' means 'a State which has consented to be bound by the treaty and for which the treaty is in force'. It may be inferred from these elements that the rules of international law applicable in the relations between 'the parties' are the rules of international law applicable in the relations between the States which have consented to be bound by the treaty which is being interpreted, and for which that treaty is in force. This understanding of the term 'the parties' leads logically to the view that the rules of

> international law to be taken into account in interpreting the WTO agreements at issue in this dispute are those which are applicable in the relations between the WTO Members.
>
> (*EC – Approval and Marketing of Biotech Products*, Panel Report 2006: Para. 7.68)

Thus, based on these observations, the Panel did not consider that 'in interpreting the relevant WTO agreements [they] are required to take into account other rules of international law which are not applicable to one of the Parties to this dispute' (*EC – Approval and Marketing of Biotech Products*, Panel Report 2006: Para. 7.71). It, however, declined to make any observations on whether such other rules of international law could be taken into account when the parties to the dispute are bound by it, but not all WTO members are so bound. Neither the scholarly literature nor WTO jurisprudence is conclusive on this issue.

As mentioned earlier, Pauwelyn has suggested that non-WTO law can be used to interpret WTO provisions, but only when such rules reflect 'the common intentions of all WTO members' (Pauwelyn 2003a: 910). However, when it comes to non-WTO law being applied as defence, he contends that not all WTO members need to be parties to it. If both parties to the dispute are bound by such non-WTO law, it will suffice (Pauwelyn 2003a: 910). Pauwelyn's dichotomy between the requirements of 'parties' in order for non-WTO law to be used for interpretation and as applicable law has been questioned by Marceau. In her words,

> It is difficult to understand why such a non-WTO norm, enforced by WTO adjudicating bodies and thus newly part of the legal context of other WTO provisions, could not be "taken into account" in the interpretation of a WTO provision while it is forced into the WTO applicable law.
>
> (Marceau 2002: 782)

She points out that such a requirement with respect to interpretation would lead to 'inconsistencies and incoherence between systems of law' because almost no international agreement with have identical membership with WTO and that it will lead to a paradoxical result that with growth in membership of the WTO, it would become more isolated from other international systems of law (Marceau 2002: 781). Her critique of Pauwelyn's argument relating to interpretation also finds support from the ILC (2006b: Para. 471). Instead of Pauwelyn's approach to interpretation, Marceau suggests another way of reading the terms 'applicable in relations between parties' in Article 31(3)(c) of VCLT. She argues that the words 'parties' should be understood in a way which 'allows consideration of treaties signed by a subset of the WTO membership that is less than all the parties, but more than one of the parties, that is accepted by the other parties' (Marceau 2002: 782). Her approach seems to also be the one which the AB has used, although without specifically outlining it in that fashion. For instance, in *US – Shrimp*, reliance was placed by the AB on the generally accepted understanding by WTO members of the terms 'exhaustible natural resources' in the Convention on Biological Diversity and the Convention on the Conservation of Migratory Species of Wild Animals for interpreting provisions of GATT, even though not all WTO members were party thereto. Similarly, in *EC – Computer Equipment*, the AB referred to the Harmonised System of Classification treaty when interpreting the WTO Schedule of the US, although not all WTO members were parties to the said treaty.

WTO jurisprudence so far, however, does not give a conclusive opinion on either of the aforesaid interpretations. In *EC and Certain Member States – Large Civil Aircraft*, the AB was asked to consider whether the 1992 Agreement entered into between the US and the EC, could be considered an agreement applicable in relation between 'the parties'. The AB first noted that under existing jurisprudence, it has made no statement as to whether the term 'the parties' in Article 31(3)(c) refers to all WTO members, or rather to a subset of members, such as the parties to the dispute (*EC and Certain Member States – Large Civil Aircraft*, AB Report 2011: Para. 844). Having said that, it did not, however, resolve this question itself. It held that 'in this dispute, the resolution of the European Union's arguments regarding the 1992 Agreement need not turn on the proper meaning to be ascribed to the term "the parties"' (*EC and Certain Member States – Large Civil Aircraft*, AB Report 2011: Para. 844). Nevertheless, the following observations made by the AB point to the inconclusive nature of the debate on this point:

> An interpretation of 'the parties' in Article 31(3)(c) should be guided by the Appellate Body's statement that 'the purpose of treaty interpretation is to establish the common intention of the parties to the treaty'. This suggests that one must exercise caution in drawing from an international agreement to which not all WTO Members are party. At the same time, we recognise that a proper interpretation of the term 'the parties'

> must also take account of the fact that Article 31(3)(c) of the Vienna Convention is considered an expression of the 'principle of systemic integration' which, in the words of the ILC, seeks to ensure that 'international obligations are interpreted by reference to their normative environment' in a manner that gives 'coherence and meaningfulness' to the process of legal interpretation. In a multilateral context such as the WTO, when recourse is had to a non-WTO rule for the purposes of interpreting provisions of the WTO agreements, a delicate balance must be struck between, on the one hand, taking due account of an individual WTO Member's international obligations and, on the other hand, ensuring a consistent and harmonious approach to the interpretation of WTO law among all WTO Members.
>
> (*EC and Certain Member States – Large Civil Aircraft*, AB Report 2011: Para. 845)

In *Peru – Agricultural Products*, the AB declined to resolve the question, however, it made the following passing observation:

> we express reservations as to whether the provisions of the FTA . . ., which could arguably be construed as to allow Peru to maintain the PRS in its bilateral relations with Guatemala, can be used under Article 31(3) of the Vienna Convention in establishing the common intention of WTO Members underlying the provisions of Article 4.2 of the Agreement on Agriculture and Article II:1(b) of the GATT 1994. In our view, such an approach would suggest that WTO provisions can be interpreted differently, depending on the Members to which they apply and on their rights and obligations under an FTA to which they are parties.
>
> (*Peru – Agricultural Products*, AB Report 2015: Para. 5.106)

Based on the previous overall analysis, one can conclude safely that Panels and the AB have been very reluctant to *apply* non-WTO law by way of a justified defence for violations of WTO obligations. The provisions of the DSU as analysed earlier also appear to provide no reason why the approach might be diametrically changed. Furthermore, assuming that they do decide in the future that such non-WTO law can be applicable law, it remains to be seen whether it will require the said non-WTO law to be binding on not merely the two WTO members who are parties to the WTO dispute, but to a much larger membership.

Conclusion

In this chapter, we have concluded, first, that techniques for resolution of conflicts between norms having the same value (*lex specialis* and *lex posterior*) are not very helpful in convincingly resolving norm conflicts which may arise between WTO obligations and human rights obligations. Second, we have concluded that even if they were capable of resolving possible conflicts, it is extremely doubtful whether the DSB could be the appropriate forum for so adjudicating. This then brings up the question of whether States can violate their human rights obligations while implementing their WTO obligations. The answer to this is a resounding no. As we have noted in the previous chapter, States continue to be under an obligation to ensure that they do not violate their human rights obligations while fulfilling their WTO obligations. This is because States have undertaken both sets of obligations, and since they have equal normative value, both must be fulfilled. As the Articles on Responsibility of States for International Wrongful Acts stipulate, 'There is an internationally wrongful act of a State when conduct consisting of an action or omission . . . constitutes a breach of an international obligation of the State' (ILC 2001: Article 2).[12] Thus, the obligation on a State to manage its international obligations in the best possible manner is irrespective of, and indeed much more important than, any role of the DSB to resolve a potential conflict. But, in order to manage their international obligations, it is a *sine qua non* that States must first be able to understand the nature and scope of the linkage-issues, how they arise and what impacts are had on their abilities to fulfil their human rights obligations. How can they go about doing that? It is here that the governance space framework developed in Chapter 2 enables policy makers within and beyond States to understand the nature of the diverse linkages and devise appropriate approaches to solutions. And, it is to a detailed examination of each of the three linkage-categories in the governance space framework using a case study that we shall now turn our attention to.

Notes

1 For instance, the International Convention on the Protection of the Rights of All Migrant Workers and Members of their Families, 1990, came into force on 1 July 2003; the Convention on the Rights of Persons with

Disabilities, 2006, came into force on 3 May 2008; and the International Convention for the Protection of All Persons from Enforced Disappearances, 2006, came into force on 23 December 2010.

2 For a strong argument that current rules are grossly inadequate for clear and systematic solutions to treaty conflicts and that 'VCLT's treaty conflict provisions are neither an accurate description of current state practice, nor are they adequate prescriptions for how states should act', see Borgen (2005: 578).

3 Pauwelyn (2003a: 909) has argued that when none of the previous rules may offer a way out, 'in that case, I would not rule out a *non liquet*, i.e., a ruling not so much that there is no law, but that there is too much law and that it cannot be resolved which of the conflicting norms applies'.

4 Also see *EC – Hormones (22.6)* (Arbitration Report 1999: Para. 50).

5 For similar arguments under GATT, see Kuijper (1994: 227–57).

6 See also *EC – Computer Equipment* (AB Report 1998: Para. 92); *Canada – Dairy* (AB Report 1999: Para. 138); *EC – Chicken Cuts* (AB Report 2005: Para. 282); *China – Intellectual Property Rights* (Panel Report 2009: Para. 7.260).

7 For a discussion, see Lennard (2002: 41).

8 For a discussion on the use of general international law for filling gaps related to procedural questions, including on the allocation of burden of proof, legal standing, temporal/retroactive application of treaties, as well as on the use of principles of international law such as good faith, *abus de droit in dubio mitius*, effectiveness and contemporaneity, see Delimatsis (2011: 99–100).

9 The term 'general international law' appears to have been used with some fluidity by the ILC in its study. At one place, the study states that '[g]eneral international law (that is, general custom and general principles of law) fulfil gaps in the special regime' (ILC 2006b: Para. 194). On another occasion, it observes, 'WTO bodies must situate those rights and obligations within the overall context of general international law (including the relevant environmental and human rights treaties)' (ILC 2006b: Para. 170). Yet the ILC report, which culls out the conclusions of the ILC study, states that:

> there is no accepted definition of 'general international law'. For the purposes of these conclusions, however, it is sufficient to define what is 'general' by reference to its logical counterpart, namely what is 'special'. In practice, lawyers are usually able to operate this distinction by reference to the context in which it appears.
>
> (ILC 2006a: Footnote 6)

10 The ILC study contends that it is problematic to have denominations such as 'trade law' or 'environmental law' since they have no clear boundaries. In order to explain this, the study hypothesises and observes that:

> maritime transport of oil links to both trade and environment, as well as to the rules on the law of the sea. Should the obligations of a ship owner in regard to the technical particularities of a ship, for instance, be determined by reference to what is reasonable from the perspective of oil transport considered as a commercial activity

or as an environmentally dangerous activity? The responses are bound to vary depending on which one chooses as the relevant frame of legal interpretation.

(ILC 2006b: Para. 55)

While it is true that generic expansive names for legal regimes are problematic, the passage cannot be interpreted to mean that for the purposes of WTO disputes governed by the DSU, WTO law is not *lex specialis*.

11 See also *Peru – Agricultural Products* (AB Report 2015: Para. 5.100–5.105).

12 Article 1 also states that '[e]very internationally wrongful act of a State entails the international responsibility of that State' (ILC 2001: Article 1).

5

WTO AND THE SHRINKING OF GOVERNANCE SPACE

This chapter begins with an exploration of the first of the three linkage-categories in the governance space framework developed in Chapter 2 of this book, namely the shrinking of governance space. As we have noted earlier, this linkage-category relates to the notion that multilateral trade rules can limit the governance space which States need in order to fulfil their human rights obligations. This shrinking of governance space is often a function of the laws which States adopt at the WTO as part of the rules underpinning MTS. In other words, when States undertake legally binding obligations at the WTO to conduct themselves in a particular fashion in their multilateral trading relations, they may end up limiting their governance space and the choices they may have in order to fulfil their human rights obligations. Thus, as argued in Chapter 3, even if there is no 'conflict' between the WTO and human rights obligations of a State *per se*, the shrinking of governance space may be a common occurrence. The point is best illustrated through the much-debated argument that patenting of pharmaceutical drugs required under the TRIPS Agreement (1994) shrinks the ability of States to ensure access to medicines as part of its human right to health obligation (MacDonald 2006; Hestermeyer 2007). Here, even though there may be no scholarly consensus on whether patenting obligations create a normative 'conflict' with the right to health obligations of States, there can be no disagreement that their governance space is reduced. This necessarily happens because States lose the unfettered ability to ignore patent claims, a policy option which they may otherwise well have been able to use in order to produce or import generic drugs in an unshackled manner and ensure access to medicines to its citizenry.

The patenting issue is, however, just one of several possible examples of ways in which MTS interacts with human rights within the first linkage-category. In this study, it is obviously not possible to explore the range of different linkage-issues where governance space of States is limited by WTO laws. The same holds true for the other two linkage-categories in which cases also it isn't possible to explore the range of linkage-issues where MTS creates the permissive environment for States to abuse/not use their governance space and where MTS creates the limiting environment for States to use their governance space. However, since the purpose of the book is to understand the nature and characteristics of each of these three linkage-categories in order to develop appropriate approaches to solutions, it is ideal to use a case study approach. This, and the next two chapters, therefore, presents a case study on each linkage-category and then bring them all together in Chapter 8 for a final analysis on the way forward.

The choice of case studies for each of the three linkage-categories has been made on the combined basis of its importance, contemporaneity and the possibility of contributing a new perspective on the issue selected. Therefore, some of the important issues which have been explored already by scholars in depth have not been considered as ideal candidates for the case studies. For instance, as explained in Chapter 2, the issue of patenting of drugs has already been analysed in comprehensive depth by other researchers and there is not really much that can be possibly added to the already existing literature. As such, in this chapter, the case study will be based on another and arguably an even more important linkage-issue. The case study relates to an analysis of the General Exception Clauses in Article XX of GATT 1994, which allow States to take measures for protection of some human rights which would otherwise be WTO inconsistent. The interaction between these General Exception Clauses and the ability of States to use them will be analysed to demonstrate that despite the presence of these provisions, the governance space that States need to be able to make use of them successfully is seriously circumscribed.

Introduction to the case study and the rationale for choosing it: the general exceptions clause in Article XX of GATT 1994

WTO Agreements, in general, are aimed at ensuring a rule-based trading system whereby States have agreed to enter into 'reciprocal and mutually advantageous arrangements directed to the substantial reduction of tariffs and other barriers to trade and to the elimination of discriminatory treatment in international trade relations' (Marrakesh Agreement 1994: Preamble, Para. 3). As explained in Chapter 1, the

WTO's legal architecture to ensure the aforesaid is built upon four basic rules which seek to create the permissive environment necessary for the theory of comparative advantage to work. These include tariff bindings, MFN, NT and prohibition on quantitative restrictions. Based on these provisions, the entire scheme of the WTO, and GATT, in particular, is to ensure that States do not engage in protectionist measures which would violate the basic idea of moving towards free trade globally.

This general structure of WTO laws has deep implications for our discussion on governance space of States. If States bind themselves to one particular template of multilateral trade without leaving any space whatsoever to adopt protectionist measures when really needed, then their governance space will obviously be non-existent. Such a situation will militate against the very ability of governments to function effectively, and, therefore, in order to prevent such an extreme limitation of governance space, GATT permits States to adopt measures, under certain circumstances, which would otherwise be inconsistent with their obligations under the agreement. The 'General Exceptions' clause in the GATT, enshrined in Article XX thereof, specifically lists several policy objectives, for the promotion of which, States may be allowed to adopt protectionist measures. In *US – Gasoline*, the AB highlighted that the exceptions listed in Article XX . . . relate to all of the obligations under GATT, not only the NT and MFN obligations, but others as well (*US – Gasoline*, AB Report 1996: 24). Therefore, in general, Article XX does not prohibit an importing State conditioning access to its domestic market on 'whether exporting Members comply with, or adopt, a policy or policies unilaterally prescribed by the importing Member' (*US – Shrimp*, AB Report 1998: Para. 121). On first blush, therefore, it might appear that GATT, through Article XX, does allow for States to use their governance space effectively. However, as will be discussed presently, adoption of such exceptional measures is an extremely difficult task and is subject to several caveats that are imposed by the text of Article XX. It is important, therefore, to analyse the text of Article XX and analyse to which extent it permits effective governance space to States to adopt WTO-inconsistent measures when needed.

There are two clauses in Article XX which directly relate to human rights. Clause (b), which is the most directly applicable provision in our context, permits States to deviate from WTO obligations when such measures are 'necessary to protect human, animal or plant life or health'. It is this provision and the WTO jurisprudence on it which we shall focus on in the current analysis to drive home the point that despite being on paper as a potential avenue for States to utilise their governance space to respect, protect and fulfil an extremely important human right – the right to health – such governance space is, in fact, vastly limited. The other important provision relating to human rights is clause (a), which permits States to deviate from WTO obligations when such measures are 'necessary to protect public morals'. The human rights linkage here is that potentially all human rights values may fall within the category of public morals of citizens in a State, and, therefore, the clause may potentially permit a State to adopt WTO-inconsistent measures to protect human rights.[1] For the purpose of this chapter, however, it is sufficient that we restrict our analysis to clause (b) not only because it is enough for the case study, but also because we will analyse clause (a) in the subsequent chapter. In our analysis of clause (b), we will not only rely on WTO jurisprudence to understand its scope, but also juxtapose it with clause (g) of Article XX, to highlight how the former limits the governance space of States to an extent which makes it very difficult for States to make use of the human health exception effectively.

In order to begin our analysis of clause (b), it is important to reproduce only the relevant portions of Article XX:

> Subject to the requirement that such measures are not applied in a manner which would constitute a means of arbitrary or unjustifiable discrimination between countries where the same conditions prevail, or a disguised restriction on international trade, nothing in this Agreement shall be construed to prevent the adoption or enforcement by any contracting party of measures:
>
> . . .
>
> (b) necessary to protect human, animal or plant life or health; . . .
>
> (g) relating to the conservation of exhaustible natural resources if such measures are made effective in conjunction with restrictions on domestic production or consumption.

As can be seen from the aforesaid text, Article XX not only contains the clauses outlining the policy objectives for which exceptions may be made, but also the Chapeau of the provision, which enumerates general caveats on how the exceptional measure must be applied in order to successfully pass the test. In *US – Gasoline*, the AB clarified that:

> in order that the justifying protection of Article XX may be extended to it, the measure at issue must not only come under

> one or another of the particular exceptions – paragraphs (a) to (j) – listed under Article XX; it must also satisfy the requirements imposed by the opening clauses of Article XX.
>
> (*US – Gasoline*, AB Report 1996: 20)

The assessment of a defence under Article XX, thus, involves a tiered analysis in which a measure must first be provisionally justified under one of the subparagraphs of Article XX and then shown to be consistent with the conditions of the chapeau of Article XX (*US – Gasoline*, AB Report 1996: 20; *Brazil – Retreaded Tyres*, AB Report 2007: Para. 139; *EC – Seal Products*, AB Report 2014: Para. 5.169). The AB has noted that this 'sequence of steps' in the analysis of a claim of justification under Article XX reflects 'not inadvertence or random choice', but rather the fundamental structure and logic of Article XX (*US – Shrimp*, AB Report 1998: Para. 119; *China – Rare Earths*, AB Report 2014: Para. 5.86).

In general, provisional justification under one of the subparagraphs of Article XX requires that a challenged measure 'address the particular interest specified in that paragraph' and that 'there be a sufficient nexus between the measure and the interest protected' (*US – Gambling*, AB Report 2005: Para. 292; *China – Rare Earths*, AB Report 2014: Para. 5.87; *EC – Seal Products*, AB Report 2014: Para. 5.169). It is important to note, however, that Article XX uses different terms 'in respect of the various categories of governmental acts, laws or regulations which WTO Members may carry out or promulgate in pursuit of differing legitimate state policies or interests outside the realm of trade liberalisation' (*US – Gasoline*, AB Report 1996: 16). In this respect, the AB has noted the following – 'necessary' in paragraphs (a), (b) and (d); 'essential' in paragraph (j); 'relating to' in paragraphs (c), (e) and (g); 'for the protection of' in paragraph (f); 'in pursuance of' in paragraph (h); *and* 'involving' in paragraph (i) (*US – Gasoline*, AB Report 1996: 16).

This difference in the language used in different clauses in Article XX has prompted the AB to reject a supposition that WTO members intended to require, in respect of each category, the same kind or degree of relationship between the measure under appraisal and the state interest or policy sought to be promoted or realised (*US – Gasoline*, AB Report 1996: 16; *China – Rare Earths*, AB Report 2014: Para. 5.87).

Based on these general observations, three main points will be made in the foregoing analysis. First, in order for a State to invoke clause (b) to protect human health, the requirement that such WTO-inconsistent measures must be 'necessary' leads to a significant shrinking of governance space for States. WTO jurisprudence on clause (b) will be analysed to demonstrate that such shrinking of governance space is as a result of the language of clause (b), in particular, the requirement of 'necessary'. Second, the aforesaid conclusion will be analysed by comparing clause (b) with the requirements of clause (g) relating to environment to point out that justifications for a State to invoke the latter are easier to prove and that there is no legitimate policy reason that the requirements for proving human health exceptions must be stricter than the requirements from proving environmental exceptions. Third, the requirements of the Chapeau of Article XX make it extremely difficult for a State to invoke clause (b) successfully, even if the challenged measure may pass the requirements of 'necessary'. In sum, the overall conclusion will be that despite being on paper, the flexibility in order to utilise the governance space that States need to protect human health is extremely limited.

Clause (b) of Article XX: a textual and jurisprudential analysis

Because Article XX is an exception to the general rule, the overall burden of proving that requirements of clause (b) are fulfilled lies on the State invoking the exception (*EC – Seal Products*, AB Report 2014: Para. 5.169). In examining whether the challenged measure is designed to achieve the stated health objectives, the Panels need to consider not only the express provisions of the instrument containing the measure, but also the design, architecture and structure of the measure (*Japan – Alcoholic Beverages II*, AB Report 1996: 29; *EC – Tariff Preferences*, Panel Report 2003: Para. 7.200). Enough jurisprudence has now emerged from the WTO to provide clarity on the test for determining 'necessity' within the meaning of Article XX(b), a term used in Articles XX(a) and XX(d) as well. In *US – Section 337*, a GATT Panel had stated that:

> a contracting party cannot justify a measure inconsistent with another GATT provision as 'necessary' in terms of Article XX(d) if an alternative measure which it could reasonably be expected to employ and which is not inconsistent with other GATT provisions is available to it. By the same token, in cases where a measure consistent with other GATT provisions is not reasonably available, a contracting party is bound to use, among the measures reasonably available to it, that which

> entails the least degree of inconsistency with other GATT provisions.
>
> (*US – Section 337*, Panel Report 1989: Para. 5.26)

The GATT Panel in the *Thailand – Cigarettes* followed this reasoning and held that a ban by Thailand on import of foreign cigarettes was not 'necessary' to protect human health, since less trade-restrictive measures were available to Thailand, including a ban on advertisements related to tobacco products, labelling requirements and ingredient disclosure regulations (*Thailand – Cigarettes*, Panel Report 1990: Para. 77–78). The WTO Panel in *US – Gasoline* adopted the same logic in its interpretation of the term 'necessary' in Article XX(b) to conclude that because less trade-restrictive measures were available to the US, its measures putting certain restrictions on the import of Gasoline to protect 'clean air' as a human health issue were illegal. The solitary focus on 'least trade restrictiveness' of a measure has, however, been watered down in subsequent decisions. In order to understand how much exactly this easing up of the strict test has happened, it may be instructive to analyse more recent jurisprudence from the WTO.

In *Korea – Various Measures on Beef*, with reference to the identical term used in Article XX(d), the AB stated that:

> Measures which are indispensable or of absolute necessity or inevitable to secure compliance certainly fulfil the requirements of Article XX(d). But other measures, too, may fall within the ambit of this exception. As used in Article XX(d), the term 'necessary' refers, in our view, to a range of degrees of necessity. At one end of this continuum lies 'necessary' understood as 'indispensable'; at the other end, is 'necessary' taken to mean as 'making a contribution to'. We consider that a 'necessary' measure is, in this continuum, located significantly closer to the pole of 'indispensable' than to the opposite pole of simply 'making a contribution to'.
>
> (*Korea – Various Measures on Beef*, AB Report 2000: Para. 161)

In view of the aforesaid, the AB noted that 'the word "necessary" is not limited to that which is "indispensable"' (*Korea – Various Measures on Beef*, AB Report 2000: Para. 161). On a combined reading of the aforesaid observations, it is clear that although 'necessary' does not limit itself to 'indispensable', for a measure to qualify as such, it still needs to be 'significantly' closer to the pole of 'indispensable'. In

Brazil – Retreated Tyres (AB Report 2007: Para. 141), the AB quoted the aforesaid observations with approval.

In terms of the analytical process itself through which Panels must evaluate whether a challenged measure is 'necessary', the AB has now developed a fairly stable approach. In *Korea – Various Measures on Beef*, it explained that determining whether a measure is 'necessary' within the meaning of Article XX(d) involves in every case a process of 'weighing and balancing' a series of factors which prominently include the contribution made by the compliance measure to the enforcement of the law or regulation at issue, the importance of the common interests or values protected by that law or regulation and the accompanying impact of the law or regulation on imports or exports (*Korea – Various Measures on Beef*, AB Report 2000: Para. 164). In its applicability to Article XX(b), this approach of weighing and balancing was approved by the AB in *Brazil – Retreaded Tyres* (2007: Para. 142). The AB approved the proposition that the weighing and balancing process inherent in the necessity analysis 'begins with an assessment of the "relative importance" of the interests or values furthered by the challenged measure' and also involves an assessment of other factors, which will usually include 'the contribution of the measure to the realisation of the ends pursued by it' and 'the restrictive impact of the measure on international commerce' (*Korea – Various Measures on Beef*, AB Report 2000: Para. 163; *Brazil – Retreaded Tyres*, AB Report 2007: Para. 143).

In line with the aforesaid, a step-by-step process of 'weighing and balancing' has been developed by the AB. As the AB put it:

> In order to determine whether a measure is 'necessary' within the meaning of Article XX(b) of the GATT 1994, a panel must assess all the relevant factors, particularly the extent of the contribution to the achievement of a measure's objective and its trade restrictiveness, in the light of the importance of the interests or values at stake. If this analysis yields a preliminary conclusion that the measure is necessary, this result must be confirmed by comparing the measure with its possible alternatives, which may be less trade restrictive while providing an equivalent contribution to the achievement of the objective pursued.
>
> (*Brazil – Retreaded Tyres*, AB Report 2007: Para. 156)

Thus, the weighing and balancing process must normally include an evaluation of whether possible alternatives which may be less trade restrictive are available. However, unlike the previous strict 'least trade restrictive' test, the weighing and balancing process is more holistic and incorporates an analysis of the importance of the interests or values at stake, the extent of the 'contribution' to the achievement of a measure's objective, as well as the trade restrictiveness of the measure. As the AB has observed, such an analysis involves a 'holistic' weighing and balancing exercise 'that involves putting all the variables of the equation together and evaluating them in relation to each other after having examined them individually, in order to reach an overall judgement' (*Brazil – Retreaded Tyres*, AB Report 2007: Para. 182; *EC – Seal Products*, AB Report 2014: Para. 5.214). In *EC – Seal Products*, the AB discussed the holistic nature of this weighing and balancing process. In response to an argument that a measure's contribution to the policy objective must be given predominant weight, the AB observed as follows:

> A measure's contribution is thus only one component of the necessity calculus under Article XX. This means that whether a measure is 'necessary' cannot be determined by the level of contribution alone, but will depend on the manner in which the other factors of the necessity analysis, including a consideration of potential alternative measures, inform the analysis. . . . Indeed, the very utility of examining the interaction between the various factors of the necessity analysis, and conducting a comparison with potential alternative measures, is that it provides a means of testing these factors as part of a holistic weighing and balancing exercise, whether quantitative or qualitative in nature.
>
> (*EC – Seal Products*, AB Report: Para. 5.215)

The AB further stated that 'the flexibility of such an exercise does not allow for the setting of pre-determined thresholds in respect of any particular factor'.

With respect to an analysis of the importance of the interests or values at stake, the Panels and AB have generally deferred to the determination of the State invoking the exception concerned. In *EC – Asbestos*, the AB noted that 'it is undisputed that WTO Members have the right to determine the level of protection of health that they consider appropriate in a given situation' (AB Report 2001: Para. 168). It accepted the right of France to determine that its chosen level of health protection is a 'halt' to the spread of asbestos-related health risks and not just a reduction. Similarly, in *Brazil – Retreaded Tyres*, the AB noted that 'it is within the authority of a WTO Member to set the public health or environmental objectives it seeks to achieve, as well as the level of protection that it wants to obtain, through the measure or the policy it chooses to adopt' (AB Report 2007: Para. 140). However, this does not mean that the Panels or AB will automatically accept the characterisation of the objectives of a measure under challenge by the State invoking the measure without any independent analysis of its own (*EC – Seal Products*, AB Report 2014: Para. 5.144).

With respect to the analysis of the extent of the 'contribution' to the achievement of a measure's objective, the AB has clarified that 'such a contribution exists when there is a genuine relationship of ends and means between the objective pursued and the measure at issue' (*Brazil – Retreaded Tyres*, AB Report 2007: Para. 145). This genuine relationship of ends and means has been articulated by the AB as a requirement that there should be a 'material' contribution by the measure concerned to the achievement of the policy objective of human health, or where the contribution of a measure forms part of a broader policy scheme and was not yet having, or likely itself to produce, an immediately discernible impact on its objective, the measure must at least be 'apt to produce such a material contribution' to the achievement of the objectives (*Brazil – Retreaded Tyres*, AB Report 2007: Para. 150; *China – Rare Earths*, AB Report 2014: Para. 5.115; *EC – Seal Products*, AB Report 2014: Para. 5.213). Hence, the notion that a measure in order to qualify as 'necessary' must be significantly closer to the pole of 'indispensable' is given shape by the requirement of the actual presence or aptness of the measure's 'material' contribution to the achievement of the policy objectives of human health. Clearly, therefore, Article XX(b) by its very language, imposes on States a significantly high degree of expectation with respect to the measure's contribution to the achievement of the objectives. A small or minor contribution of the measure to the improvement of human health will not suffice for the test of 'necessity' in Article XX(b).

In *Brazil – Retreaded Tyres*, the AB recalled its statement in *Korea – Various Measures on Beef* that the word 'necessary' is not limited to that which is 'indispensable'. However, it proceeded to observe that when a measure produces restrictive effects on international trade as severe as those resulting from an import ban, it would be difficult to find that measure necessary unless the measure is apt to make a material contribution to the achievement of its objective (*Brazil – Retreaded Tyres*, AB Report 2007: Para. 150). It, therefore, rejected the argument by Brazil that because its aim was to reduce risk exposure to the maximum extent possible, an import ban that brings a small or marginal contribution to reducing such risk can nevertheless be considered necessary. What this demonstrates is that with respect to the extent of contribution of a measure to the achievement of the objectives of human health, Article XX(b) imposes a very high threshold and that the higher the trade restrictiveness of the measure, the lesser is the chance that such measure will be found 'necessary'.

Indeed, the third element of the weighing and balancing process requires an analysis of the trade restrictiveness of the measure concerned. This is generally accompanied by a process of evaluating whether there are possible alternative less trade-restrictive measures that the State may undertake. The burden of initially identifying possible alternatives that the responding member could have undertaken rests with the complaining State, whereafter the responding State can demonstrate that such measures are not 'reasonably available' (*EC – Seal Products*, AB Report 2014: Para. 5.169; *US – Gambling*, AB Report 2005: Para. 311). In *US – Gambling*, while interpreting the term 'necessary' in Article XX(a) relating to public morals, the AB clarified that in order to qualify as an alternative, a measure proposed by the complaining member must be not only less trade restrictive than the measure at issue but should also 'preserve for the responding Member its right to achieve its desired level of protection with respect to the objective pursued' (AB Report 2005: Para. 308). Further, the AB clarified that in order for a measure to be 'reasonably available', it must not be 'merely theoretical in nature, for instance, where the responding Member is not capable of taking it or where the measure imposes an undue burden on that Member, such as prohibitive costs or substantial technical difficulties'. In *Brazil – Retreaded Tyres*, the AB adopted these observations as equally applicable with respect to Article XX(b) (AB Report 2007: Para. 156). The AB, in *EC – Seal Products*, interpreted the aforesaid language to highlight that it 'does not foreclose the possibility that there may be other indications that the alternative measure is "merely theoretical in nature"' (AB Report 2014: Para. 5.277). This, it said, could mean that an assessment of the reasonable availability of an alternative measure could potentially include the burden on the industries concerned, including cost factors which might affect their ability or willingness to comply.

On the basis of the jurisprudence developed by the AB, there have been two cases under Article XX(b) thus far where such alternative measures have been considered not reasonably available. In *EC – Asbestos*, France had imposed an import ban on asbestos containing products to achieve its chosen level of health protection, which was a halt in the spread of asbestos-related health risks. In its challenge,

Canada had asserted that 'controlled use' represented a reasonably available measure that would serve the same end. The AB, however, rejected this argument and observed that 'France could not reasonably be expected to employ any alternative measure if that measure would involve a continuation of the very risk that the Decree seeks to "halt"' and that 'such an alternative measure would, in effect, prevent France from achieving its chosen level of health protection' (*EC – Asbestos*, AB Report 2001: Para. 173–74). Similarly, in *Brazil – Retreaded Tyres*, Brazil had imposed an import ban on retreaded tyres, the objective being, reduction of the 'exposure to the risks to human, animal or plant life or health arising from the accumulation of waste tyres' (AB Report 2007: Para. 170). Brazil's chosen level of protection was 'the reduction of these risks to the maximum extent possible'. In its challenge, the EC had proposed several waste management measures as reasonably available alternatives. While rejecting the alternatives proposed by the EC, the AB observed that 'non-generation measures are more apt to achieve this objective because they prevent the accumulation of waste tyres, while waste management measures dispose of waste tyres only once they have accumulated' (*Brazil – Retreaded Tyres*, AB Report 2007: Para. 174). Further, the AB agreed with the Panel that account needed to be taken of specific risks attached to the proposed alternative, such as the risk of leaching of toxic substances that might be associated to landfilling or the risk of toxic emissions that might arise from the incineration of waste tyres.

In *US – Gasoline*, the US had imposed certain regulations relating to import of gasoline, including establishment of statutory baselines for foreign refineries. The US argued that one of the grounds for taking these measures was to preserve clean air, which was an essential element of protecting human health under Article XX(b). In its challenge, Venezuela and Brazil argued that in the impugned measure, the US had required individual baselines for domestic refineries, and, therefore, by way of reasonably available alternative measures, the same could have been established for foreign refineries as well. They further argued that in any case, the US could have designed the measures in a way which was not as trade restrictive as establishing statutory baselines for foreign refiners. The Panel undertook an examination of several alternative measures such as 'established techniques of checking, verification, assessment and enforcement of data' to conclude that there were reasonably available alternatives to the US instead of statutory baselines (*US – Gasoline*, Panel Report 1996: Para. 6.28). It, thus, concluded that the measures were not 'necessary' under Article XX(b). These findings were not appealed by the US before the AB (*US – Gasoline*, AB Report 1996: 9).

In *EC – Tariff Preferences*, the EU had extended certain tariff preferences under its Drug Arrangements to only select developing countries on the ground that this was necessary to fight against drug production and trafficking and that this fell within the objective of protecting human health under Article XX(b). The preferences were, however, not extended to all developing countries, including India. With respect to the justification for the exceptional measures under Article XX(b) put forth by the EC, India argued that the measures were not, in fact, designed for the stated objective of protecting human health. The Panel agreed with India's contention but proceeded to discuss whether reasonably available alternatives were available to the EC. The Panel observed that at least one, less-inconsistent alternative was available to the EC to achieve its health objective, 'that of financial and technical assistance combined with multilaterally negotiated tariff reductions that provide sufficient tariff reductions on products of export interest to drug-affected countries' (*EC – Tariff Preferences*, AB Report 2003: Para. 7.222). As such, it held that the measure was not 'necessary' within the meaning of Article XX(b). Like *US – Gasoline*, the findings of the Panel related to Article XX(b) were not appealed before the AB.

In *China – Raw Materials*, the US, the EU and Mexico had challenged China's use of certain export restraints on the exportation of some forms of bauxite, coke, fluorspar, magnesium, manganese, silicon carbide, silicon metal, yellow phosphorus and zinc. Among the defences which China presented, one was that these restrictions were necessary to protect human health under Article XX(b) because 'they reduce the pollution emitted when the raw materials are extracted or produced' (*China – Raw Materials*, Panel Report 2011: Para. 7.470). In determining whether alternate measures were reasonably available to China, the Panel considered various other measures such as investment in more environmentally friendly technologies, recycling of consumer goods, increasing environmental standards, investing in manufacture necessary to facilitate recycling of scrap, stimulating greater local demand for scrap without discouraging local supply and introduction of production restrictions or pollution controls (*China – Raw Materials*, Panel Report 2011: Para. 7.569–7.580). The Panel concluded, on the basis of these available alternative measures, that China had 'not been able to justify why less trade restrictive and WTO-consistent alternatives available, as identified by the complainants and acknowledged to exist by China, cannot be used in lieu of applying export restrictions' (Panel Report 2011: Para. 7.590) and further held that the measures were not 'necessary' (Panel Report 2011: Para. 7.615–7.616). Like the previous two cases, this question was not appealed by China before the AB (*China – Raw Materials*, AB Report 2012: Footnote 20).[2]

A similar question came up also in *China – Rare Earths*, where China's use of export quotas and export duties on various forms of rare earths, tungsten and molybdenum were challenged. Among the several grounds raised by China in its defence, one was based on Article XX(b). Nevertheless, the Panel considered the argument by China that the measures were necessary to protect human health under clause (b). In response and as part of its analysis, the Panel considered the availability of other alternative measures, including increasing volume restrictions on mining and production, increasing pollution controls on mining and production and increasing resource tax and/or pollution tax and held that China had not met its burden of demonstrating that the alternative measures identified by the complainants were not reasonably available to China (*China – Rare Earths*, Panel Report 2014: Para. 7.186–7.187). Like the previous case, this issue was also not appealed against by China before the AB (*China – Rare Earths*, AB Report 2014: Para. 2.80).

The aforesaid cases demonstrate that there have been mixed results for States in fulfilling the requirement of demonstrating that there are reasonably available alternate measures as part of the 'necessity' test under Article XX. This, combined with the requirements in the weighing and balancing process, including the importance or value of the objective pursued, the contribution of the measure in achieving the objectives pursued and trade restrictiveness of the measure concerned, impose significant burden on any WTO member in justifying the exceptional measures under Article XX(b). This, therefore, also means that the strict requirements of justifying proper invocation of Article XX(b), create extremely strict conditions for States to use their governance space for designing measures to protect human health. The question that needs to be answered, however, is whether such strict conditions for even the possibility of using governance space to protect human health is warranted. The importance of this question assumes life when we compare the significantly less strict requirements imposed by Article XX with respect to environmental concerns under clause (g). The following section will highlight why and how clause (g) incorporates a much lower threshold for States to justify a measure under the said provision in comparison with clause (b). In order to situate this discussion in proper context, it may be helpful to extrapolate a quote by the Panel in *Brazil – Retreaded Tyres* that is directly applicable to our comparison here. In that case, the Panel observed that 'few interests are more "vital" and "important" than protecting human beings from health risks, and that protecting the environment is no less important' (*Brazil – Retreaded Tyres*, Panel Report 2007: Para. 7.108). This observation has found approval in other Panel and AB reports (*Brazil – Retreaded Tyres*, AB Report 2007: Para. 144, 179; *China – Raw Materials*, Panel Report 2011: Para. 7.482; *China – Rare Earths*, Panel Report 2014: Para. 7.194). It is rather odd that, on the one hand, protection of human beings from health risks and protecting the environment are equally important objectives and, on the other hand, the requirement to invoke the human health exception is significantly stricter than the requirement to invoke the environmental exception. With this general observation, let us analyse the threshold vis-à-vis Article XX(g).

Comparison with clause (g) of Article XX

Article XX(g) specifically states that the measure must be 'relating to the conservation of exhaustible natural resources if such measures are made effective in conjunction with restrictions on domestic production or consumption'. Even on first blush, it is clear that the 'relating to' test is not as strict as the 'necessary' test under Article XX(b). A number of commentators have questioned the more stringent 'necessity' test for measures to protect human health under Article XX(b) as compared to a lower threshold of 'relating to' for environmental protection under Article XX(g) (Garcia 1999: 83; Bal 2001: 97; Cleveland 2001: 240; Howse 2003: 1371; Harrison 2007: 217–18; Joseph 2011: 114). WTO jurisprudence confirms this interpretation, as will be pointed out presently. Indeed, there is no requirement under Article XX(g) to even search for the availability of other reasonable alternatives which are less trade restrictive – a requirement under Article XX(b). But it is not only the 'relating to' test that renders the invocation of Article XX(g) comparatively easier. The other part of the provision, namely 'made effective in conjunction with restrictions on domestic production or consumption', requires 'even-handedness' between the requirements of a measure on foreign producers and those on domestic producers. However, this does not mean that the measures applicable to domestic producers need to be the same as those required of foreign producers. Indeed, the former can be less strict than the latter.

The AB in *China – Raw Materials* observed that the term 'relating to' in first part of Article XX(g) is 'defined as having some connection with, "being connected to"' (AB Report 2012: Para. 355). This is a far cry from the strict 'necessity' test under Article XX(b). Indeed, WTO jurisprudence brings out the distinction between the requirements of the two clauses quite starkly. In *Canada – Herring and Salmon*, a GATT Panel had held that the 'relate to' test requires that the impugned measure be 'primarily aimed at' the conservation of an exhaustible natural resource (Panel Report 1988: Para. 4.6). In WTO disputes, this interpretation has been carried forward and has been given further shape. Thus, in *US – Gasoline*, the Panel observed that:

> while a trade measure did not have to be necessary or essential to the conservation of an exhaustible natural resource, it had to be primarily aimed at the conservation of an exhaustible natural resource to be considered as 'relating to' conservation within the meaning of Article XX(g).
>
> (Panel Report 1996: Para. 6.39)

In appeal, the AB observed that in order to satisfy the 'primarily aimed at' test, the measure must not be regarded as 'merely incidentally or inadvertently aimed at' the conservation.[3] Based on these principles, it concluded that the US measure that was under challenge – the baseline establishment rules – cannot be regarded as 'merely incidentally or inadvertently aimed at' the conservation of clean air in the US for the purposes of Article XX(g) (*US – Gasoline*, AB Report 1996: 19). It is pertinent to specifically highlight that while the AB thus held that requirements of Article XX(g) were fulfilled, it came to the opposite conclusion with respect to Article XX(b).

In *US – Shrimp*, the AB observed that in making a determination on the 'relate to' test, 'the treaty interpreter essentially looks into the relationship between the measure at stake and the legitimate policy of conserving exhaustible natural resources' (AB Report 1998: Para. 135). Referring to its observations in *US – Gasoline*, the AB noted that 'the substantial relationship we found there between the EPA baseline establishment rules and the conservation of clean air in the United States was a close and genuine relationship of ends and means' (*US – Shrimp*, AB Report 1998: Para. 137). In order to determine the relationship of ends and means, the AB analysed the design and structure of the measure impugned and its relationship with the goal of conservation of sea turtles. Based on this analysis, the AB concluded that 'focusing on the design of the measure here at stake, it appears to us that *Section 609*, cum implementing guidelines, is not disproportionately wide in its scope and reach in relation to the policy objective of protection and conservation of sea turtle species' and that 'the means are, in principle, reasonably related to the ends' (*US – Shrimp*, AB Report 1998: Para. 141). It, therefore, held that Section 609 was a measure 'relating to' the conservation of an exhaustible natural resource under Article XX(g).

The AB has underscored the importance of analysing the design and structure of the challenged measure in order to make a proper assessment of whether a measure 'relates to' the conservation objective. In *China – Rare Earths*, China argued before the AB that an assessment of the 'relating to' criteria requires also taking into account the effects of such measures, not just its design and structure, and that because the Panel in that case had not done so, the decision needed to be reversed. In response, the AB recalled that it 'has consistently emphasised the primacy of the design and structure of the measure at issue in the assessment of whether that measure is related to the conservation of exhaustible natural resources' (*China – Rare Earths*, AB Report 2014: Para. 5.111). Therefore, the AB rejected China's argument by observing that the text of Article XX(g) does not 'require' an evaluation of the actual effects of a measure, although Panels are not precluded from 'considering evidence relating to the actual operation or the impact of the measure at issue in an assessment under subparagraph (g)' (*China – Rare Earths*, AB Report 2014: Para. 5.114). In observing that the actual or predictable effects of a measure on conservation are not 'required' to be evaluated in determining whether the measure 'relates to' conservation objectives, the AB observed that under Article XX(g), there is no requirement to apply an 'empirical effects test'. It referred to its observations in *US – Gasoline*, where the AB had identified two primary challenges that a panel, as trier of fact, would face if it were required to evaluate 'effects':

> In the first place, the problem of determining causation, well-known in both domestic and international law, is always a difficult one. In the second place, in the field of conservation of exhaustible natural resources, a substantial period of time, perhaps years, may have to elapse before the effects attributable to implementation of a given measure may be observable.
> (*US – Gasoline*, AB Report 1996: 21)

The AB further observed that:

> although 'predictable effects' might be understood also to encompass future effects projected on the basis of empirical data of actual effects, reliance upon such effects in assessing a measure's compliance with Article XX(g) would also be fraught with the causation difficulties identified by the Appellate Body in *US – Gasoline.*
>
> (*China – Rare Earths*, AB Report 2014: Para. 5.100)

It is clear from the aforesaid jurisprudence that the 'relating to' requirement under Article XX(g) requires a much lower threshold of justification than the 'necessary for' test under Article XX(b). Article XX(g) also requires a close and genuine relationship of ends and means, however, it is important to distinguish this from what is required under Article XX(b). Under the latter, we have seen that as part of the 'necessity' test, the measure's contribution to the desired goal of human health is vital. In making a determination on this, Panels may consider not only the actual material contribution of the measure but also its aptness at making a material contribution. Thus, the effect of the measure on achieving the policy objective of health is quite crucial in the analysis under Article XX(b). As the AB has clarified in the previous passage from *China – Rare Earths*, such is not the case in an analysis under Article XX(g). Indeed, in that case, China had sought to bring in the contribution analysis required under Article XX(b), into an analysis of Article XX(g) as well. Specifically, China had expressed the view that 'a measure relates to conservation whenever the measure "contributes" to the realisation of a Member's conservation goals' and that 'a measure's contribution to such goals might be demonstrated through a showing of that measure's aptness to contribute to conservation, since the results of regulatory actions aimed at conservation may not be immediately observable' (*China – Rare Earths*, AB Report 2014: Para. 5.115). China went on to argue that owing to the similarities between the language that the AB has used in discussing the 'contribution' element of the 'necessity' test in Article XX(b), on the one hand, and that used in the context of the 'relating to' test in Article XX(g), on the other hand, the concepts of 'relating to' and 'contribution' are closely linked (*China – Rare Earths*, AB Report 2014: Para. 5.115). In rejecting this argument, the AB held that because Article XX(b) uses the connecting word 'necessary' while Article XX(g) uses the connecting word 'relating to' 'a mixing of the different tests under Article XX(b) and Article XX(g), absent of context, would result in an approach that ignores the important distinctions between the various subparagraphs of Article XX' (*China – Rare Earths*, AB Report 2014: Para. 5.116).

Thus, quite clearly, the governance space that States have in order to design and structure measures to achieve the policy objective of conservation under Article XX(g) is much wider than what they have in order to achieve the policy objective of human health under Article XX(b). This conclusion is also confirmed by the language of the second part of Article XX(g), which further requires that the conservation measures be 'made effective in conjunction with restrictions on domestic production or consumption'. In *China – Raw Materials*, the AB expanded upon the ordinary meaning of the terms in this phrase. It stated that 'the word "effective" as relating to a legal instrument is defined as "in operation at a given time"' (*China – Raw Materials*, AB Report 2012: Para. 356). It further observed that 'the term "made effective", when used in connection with a legal instrument, describes measures brought into operation, adopted, or applied' and that 'the term "in conjunction" is defined as "together, jointly, (with)"' (*China – Raw Materials*, AB Report 2012: Para. 356). In *China – Rare Earths*, the AB stated that 'taking both of these elements together, the second clause of Article XX(g) refers to governmental measures that are promulgated or brought into effect, and that operate together with restrictions on domestic production or consumption of exhaustible natural resources' (AB Report 2014: Para. 5.92).

In *US – Gasoline*, the AB introduced the idea of 'even-handedness' in determining whether the second part of Article XX(g) is satisfied. It stated that 'the clause is a requirement of "even-handedness" in the imposition of restrictions, in the name of conservation, upon the production or consumption of exhaustible natural resources' (*US – Gasoline*, AB Report 1996: 21). It, however, hastened to point out that the requirement of even-handedness does not require identical treatment of foreign and domestic products. It stated the rationale behind this interpretation as follows:

> Indeed, where there is identity of treatment – constituting real, not merely formal, equality of treatment – it is difficult to see how inconsistency with Article III:4 would have arisen in the first place. On the other hand, if *no* restrictions on domestically-produced like products are imposed at all, and all limitations are placed upon imported products *alone*, the measure cannot be accepted as primarily or even substantially designed for implementing conservationist goals. The

> measure would simply be naked discrimination for protecting locally-produced goods.
>
> (*US – Gasoline*, AB Report 1996: 21)

Thus, it is quite clear that the treatment to foreign products by the measure concerned can be more exacting as compared to those required of domestic products under Article XX(g). Indeed, in *US – Gasoline*, the baseline establishment rules affected both domestic gasoline and imported gasoline, such that individual baselines were established for domestic refiners and blenders and statutory baselines were established for importers. Because identical treatment was not required, the AB held that 'thus, restrictions on the consumption or depletion of clean air by regulating the domestic production of "dirty" gasoline are established jointly with corresponding restrictions with respect to imported gasoline' (*US – Gasoline*, AB Report 1996: 21), and, therefore, the impugned measures fell within the requirements of even-handedness under the second part of Article XX(g). The same line of analysis was followed by the AB in *US – Shrimp* as well. In that case, the AB held that because the US required its shrimp trawlers to use approved TEDs in areas and at times when there is a likelihood of intercepting sea turtles, the measure was 'even-handed', although what was imposed on foreign shrimp trawlers was not identical (*US – Shrimp*, AB Report 1998: Para. 143).

In *China – Rare Earths*, the question was raised whether the burden of conservation must be evenly distributed between foreign consumers and domestic producers or consumers, for the measure to fulfil the requirements under the second part of Article XX(g). The AB rejected and reversed the Panel's observations that the burden of conservation must be evenly distributed by observing that although the clause 'made effective in conjunction with restrictions on domestic production or consumption' requires that, when GATT-inconsistent measures are in place, effective restrictions must also be imposed on domestic production or consumption, 'it does not require a Member seeking to justify its measure to establish that its regulatory regime achieves an even distribution of the burden of conservation' (*China – Rare Earths*, AB Report 2014: Para. 5.136).

Finally, with respect to the second part of Article XX(g), in *China – Raw Materials*, the AB was posed with an argument by the US, Mexico and the EU that the terms 'made effective in conjunction with' meant that Article XX(g) requires the measure to be primarily aimed not only at conservation but also at making effective the restrictions on domestic production or consumption (*China – Raw Materials*, AB

Report 2012: Para. 352). However, the AB rejected this argument by stating that:

> we see nothing in the text of Article XX(g) to suggest that, in addition to being 'made effective in conjunction with restrictions on domestic production or consumption', a trade restriction must be aimed at ensuring the effectiveness of domestic restrictions, as the Panel found.
>
> (*China – Raw Materials*, AB Report 2012: Para. 360)

Thus, the AB found that Article XX(g) permits trade measures relating to the conservation of exhaustible natural resources if such trade measures 'work together with' restrictions on domestic production or consumption, which operate so as to conserve an exhaustible natural resource.

The aforesaid evaluation of Article XX(g) demonstrates that a 'holistic assessment' of both parts of the clause requires a much lower threshold of justification than what is required under Article XX(b).[4] The natural corollary to this is that the governance space that States have with respect to designing and structuring measures for conservation goals is much broader as compared to those for protecting human health. Given that both the AB and the Panels have observed that human health and conservation goals are equally important, there is no valid justification for restricting the governance space of States for achieving the former in comparison with the latter. This comparison with Article XX(g) only fortifies our analysis earlier that even on its own, the provisions of Article XX(b) seriously limit the governance space of States to protect human health.

Chapeau of Article XX: a textual and jurisprudential analysis

Our analysis cannot be complete without an appraisal of the Chapeau of Article XX, since in reality, it is this part of the provision which has proved to be the demise of most attempts to invoke the exceptional measures (Joseph 2011: 115). Indeed, with respect to Article XX(b), there is only one case, *EC – Asbestos*, which has thus far successfully managed to pass the scrutiny of both clause (b) and the Chapeau. The obvious implication is that the Chapeau further limits the governance space that States need to protect human health under Article XX(b), a fact confirmed by WTO jurisprudence on the point.

The Chapeau of Article XX states that the exceptions provided in clauses (a) to (j) can be adopted or enforced by States 'subject to the requirement that such measures are not applied in a manner which would constitute a means of arbitrary or unjustifiable discrimination between countries where the same conditions prevail, or a disguised restriction on international trade'. The AB has pointed out that the chapeau addresses, not so much the questioned measure or its specific contents as such, but rather the manner in which the measure is applied, and, as such, its basic objective is generally the prevention of abuse of the exceptions provided in the clauses (*US – Gasoline*, AB Report 1996: 22). In order to prevent such abuse of the exceptions, the Chapeau imposes additional disciplines on measures that have been found to violate an obligation under GATT, but that have been found to be provisionally justified under one of the subparagraphs of Article XX (*Brazil – Retreaded Tyres*, AB Report 2007: Para. 215; *EC – Seal Products*, AB Report 2014: Para. 5.296). In *US – Shrimp*, the AB stated that the Chapeau embodies the recognition on the part of WTO members of the need to maintain a balance of rights and obligations between the right of a member to invoke one or another of the exceptions of Article XX, on the one hand, and the substantive rights of the other members under GATT, on the other hand (AB Report 1998: Para. 156). It also highlighted the rationale behind this recognition. In the words of the AB, 'Because the GATT 1994 itself makes available the exceptions of Article XX, in recognition of the legitimate nature of the policies and interests there embodied, the right to invoke one of those exceptions is not to be rendered illusory' (*US – Shrimp*, AB Report 1998: Para. 156). The Chapeau has been recognised as one expression of the general international law principle of good faith (*US – Shrimp*, AB Report 1998: Para. 158) and a way to ensure that the exceptions are not invoked 'as a means to circumvent one Member's obligations towards other WTO Members' (*Brazil – Retreaded Tyres*, AB Report 2007: Para. 215). As the AB has noted, 'One application of this general principle, the application widely known as the doctrine of *abus de droit*, prohibits the abusive exercise of a state's rights and enjoins that whenever the assertion of a right impinges on the field covered by a treaty obligation, it must be exercised bona fide, that is to say, reasonably' (*Brazil – Retreaded Tyres*, AB Report 2007: Para. 215).

It is well settled that the burden of demonstrating that a measure provisionally justified under the exceptions does not, in its application, constitute abuse of the chapeau, rests on the party invoking the exception (*EC – Seal Products*, AB Report 2014: Para. 5.297). The AB has noted that this is, 'of necessity, a heavier task than that involved in showing that an exception . . . encompasses the measure at issue'

(*US – Gasoline*, AB Report 1996: 22–23). In our context, this means that although the burden of proving that a measure fulfils the requirements of clause (b) is already very heavy, the task of proving that the Chapeau is also satisfied is even heavier.

The scheme of Article XX, therefore, is such that 'each of the exceptions in paragraphs (a) to (j) of Article XX is a limited and conditional exception from the substantive obligations contained in the other provisions of the GATT 1994' (*US – Shrimp*, AB Report 1998: Para. 157). The exceptions invoked by a State will not be available unless the requirements of the Chapeau are also complied with.

In terms of the Chapeau itself, the requirements are three-fold: the measures should not be applied in a manner which would constitute a means of (a) 'arbitrary discrimination' (between countries where the same conditions prevail), (b) 'unjustifiable discrimination' (with the same qualifier) or (c) 'disguised restriction' on international trade (*US – Gasoline*, AB Report 1996: 23; *US – Shrimp*, AB Report 1998: Para. 150).

Importantly, the AB has also acknowledged that 'the text of the chapeau is not without ambiguity, including one relating to the field of application of the standards its contains: the arbitrary or unjustifiable discrimination standards and the disguised restriction on international trade standard' (*US – Gasoline*, AB Report 1996: 23). As such, the interpretation and the scope of these terms has been developed predominantly by the Panels and the AB. In the forthcoming analysis, two features of the Chapeau will emerge, which clearly limit the governance space of States even further in terms of invoking Article XX to protect human health. First, the requirements of Article XX are not free from ambiguity as the AB itself has noted. Second, it has also empirically proved to be extremely difficult for States to successfully demonstrate that they have fulfilled the requirements of Article XX. The obvious implication is that the Chapeau tilts the balance quite heavily in favour of trade interests as compared to the interests of achieving the policy objectives mentioned in the clauses of Article XX, including human health.

Insofar as the first two requirements are concerned, 'countries where the same conditions prevail' is the qualifier for the application of the measure to be considered arbitrary or unjustifiable discrimination. In *EC – Seal Products*, the AB observed that 'only "conditions" that are relevant for the purpose of establishing arbitrary or unjustifiable discrimination in the light of the specific character of the measure at issue and the circumstances of a particular case should be considered under the chapeau' and, therefore, 'the question is . . . whether the conditions prevailing in different countries are relevantly "the same" ' (AB Report 2014: Para. 5.299). Further, it observed that the identification of the relevant 'conditions' under the chapeau 'should be understood by reference to the applicable subparagraph of Article XX under which the measure was provisionally justified and the substantive obligations under the GATT 1994 with which a violation has been found' (*EC – Seal Products*, AB Report 2014: Para. 5.301).

The interpretation of the terms 'arbitrary or unjustifiable discrimination between countries' and 'disguised restriction on international trade' in the WTO era began with the somewhat shaky and rather exploratory analysis conducted by the AB in *US – Gasoline*. There, the AB observed that ' "arbitrary discrimination", "unjustifiable discrimination" and "disguised restriction" on international trade may, . . . be read side-by-side; they impart meaning to one another' (*US – Gasoline*, AB Report 1996: 25). The exploratory nature of the interpretation of these terms and the analysis that would be needed, therefore, is best demonstrated in the following passage of the AB in that case, an *ad verbatim* reproduction of which will be helpful in developing our argument here. The AB observed:

> It is clear to us that 'disguised restriction' includes disguised discrimination in international trade. It is equally clear that concealed or unannounced restriction or discrimination in international trade does not exhaust the meaning of 'disguised restriction'. We consider that 'disguised restriction', whatever else it covers, may properly be read as embracing restrictions amounting to arbitrary or unjustifiable discrimination in international trade taken under the guise of a measure formally within the terms of an exception listed in Article XX. Put in a somewhat different manner, the kinds of considerations pertinent in deciding whether the application of a particular measure amounts to 'arbitrary or unjustifiable discrimination', may also be taken into account in determining the presence of a 'disguised restriction' on international trade. The fundamental theme is to be found in the purpose and object of avoiding abuse or illegitimate use of the exceptions to substantive rules available in Article XX.
>
> (*US – Gasoline*, AB Report 1996: 25)

Based on these observations, the AB identified two omissions on part of the US 'to explore adequately means, including in particular cooperation with the governments of Venezuela and Brazil, of mitigating the administrative problems relied on as justification by the United States for rejecting individual baselines for foreign refiners' and to 'count the costs for foreign refiners that would result from the imposition of statutory baselines' (*US – Gasoline*, AB Report 1996: 28). It held that because of these omissions, the resulting discrimination must have been foreseen and was not merely inadvertent or unavoidable. Interestingly, in line with its observations in the previous passage, the AB did not carry out separate analysis for the three requirements of the Chapeau. It simply observed that 'in the light of the foregoing, our conclusion is that the baseline establishment rules in the Gasoline Rule, in their application, constitute "unjustifiable discrimination" and a "disguised restriction on international trade"' (*US – Gasoline*, AB Report 1996: 29).

In *US – Shrimp*, the AB attempted to develop the interpretation and application of these terms further. With respect to 'arbitrary or unjustifiable discrimination', it observed that:

> the application of a measure may be characterised as amounting to an abuse or misuse of an exception of Article XX not only when the detailed operating provisions of the measure prescribe the arbitrary or unjustifiable activity, but also where a measure, otherwise fair and just on its face, is actually applied in an arbitrary or unjustifiable manner.
>
> (*US – Shrimp*, AB Report 1998: Para. 160)

It, therefore, observed that the standards of the chapeau project both substantive and procedural requirements. Based on these general observations, the AB held that the impugned measure amounted to unjustifiable discrimination for the following reasons. First, 'the actual application of the measure, . . . required other WTO Members to adopt a regulatory program that was not merely comparable, but rather essentially the same, as that applied to the US shrimp trawl vessels' and, therefore, the effect of the application of the measure was to create a 'rigid and unbending standard' (*US – Shrimp*, AB Report 1998: Para. 163). Second, shrimp caught using methods identical to those employed in the US had been excluded from the US market solely because they have been caught in waters of countries that had not been certified by the US (*US – Shrimp*, AB Report 1998: Para. 165).[5] Third, the US had negotiated seriously with some countries regarding the application of the measure affecting export of shrimp to the US, but not with other States including the appellees, resulting therefore in 'unilateral and non-consensual procedures' (*US – Shrimp*, AB Report

1998: Para. 171–72). Fourth, the US had permitted a phase-in period of about three years to fourteen countries in the Caribbean/western Atlantic region, while the appellees were allowed only four months to conform to the new requirements of the impugned measures (*US – Shrimp*, AB Report 1998: Para. 173–74). Finally, there were significant differences in the levels of effort made by the US in transferring the required TED technology to the 14 Caribbean/western Atlantic countries and to the appellees (*US – Shrimp*, AB Report 1998: Para. 175). Importantly, the AB placed significant value to the 'cumulative' effect of these discriminations to come to a conclusion that the application of the measure amounted to unjustifiable discrimination (*US – Shrimp*, AB Report 1998: Para. 176).

The AB then proceeded to analyse whether the application of the measure impugned also amounted to arbitrary discrimination. Following reasons were provided to hold that it does so. First, the AB noted that the unjustifiable discrimination amounting from the fact that the measure in its application imposed a single, rigid and unbending regulatory programme on countries seeking certification from the US for export of shrimp, also amounted to arbitrary discrimination (*US – Shrimp*, AB Report 1998: Para. 177). Second, it noted that the measures did not entail a transparent, predictable certification process that is followed by the competent US government officials (*US – Shrimp*, AB Report 1998: Para. 180) and that the certification processes followed by the US appeared to be 'singularly informal and casual' and were 'conducted in a manner such that these processes could result in the negation of rights of Members' (*US – Shrimp*, AB Report 1998: Para. 181).

Based on the aforesaid findings, the AB concluded that the measure was applied in a manner which constituted not just of unjustifiable discrimination, but also of arbitrary discrimination and, therefore, did not deem it necessary to analyse whether the measures were applied also in a manner which constituted a disguised restriction on international trade (*US – Shrimp*, AB Report 1998: Para. 184).

The observations and findings of the AB in the *US – Shrimp* case, however, do not give any clear indication of the actual difference or scope between the three terms in the Chapeau. Indeed, any of the aforesaid findings could be used to conclude that any of the three requirements of the Chapeau are violated. The ambiguity in the language of the Chapeau that was noted in *US – Gasoline* by the AB, was not necessarily resolved in *US – Shrimp*.

In *Brazil – Retreaded Tyres* also, the AB did not make any conclusions on whether the application of the impugned measures amounted to a disguised restriction on international trade.[6] However, it did conclude that the measures were applied in a manner which constituted arbitrary or unjustifiable discrimination between countries where the same conditions prevailed. In this case, the global import ban on retreaded tyres by Brazil was challenged before the MERCOSUR tribunal by Uruguay on the ground that it constituted a new restriction on trade prohibited under MERCOSUR. The MERCOSUR tribunal found Brazil's restrictions to be a violation of its obligations under MERCOSUR. In compliance of this decision, Brazil exempted the MERCOSUR members from the ban, while continuing to apply it for rest of the world. The EC challenged this measure before the WTO on the ground that this amounted to violation of the MFN principle. In response, Brazil argued that the exemption to MERCOSUR members was justified under clause (b) of Article XX and that, in terms of the Chapeau, the application of the measure did not constitute an 'arbitrary discrimination' because it was the result of a judicial decision. The AB observed that 'the analysis of whether the application of a measure results in arbitrary or unjustifiable discrimination should focus on the cause of the discrimination, or the rationale put forward to explain its existence' (*Brazil – Retreaded Tyres*, AB Report 2007: Para. 226). Accordingly, it held that the ruling issued by the MERCOSUR arbitral tribunal was not an acceptable rationale for the discrimination, because it bore no relationship to the legitimate objective pursued by the import ban that fell within the purview of Article XX(b) and even went against this objective, to however small a degree (*Brazil – Retreaded Tyres*, AB Report 2007: Para. 228). The AB rejected the Panel's finding that the discrimination resulting from the MERCOSUR exemption was not arbitrary because it was adopted further to a ruling within the framework of MERCOSUR and, therefore, could not be said to be 'capricious' or 'random' (*Brazil – Retreaded Tyres*, AB Report 2007: Para. 231). It found that 'discrimination can result from a rational decision or behaviour, and still be "arbitrary or unjustifiable", because it is explained by a rationale that bears no relationship to the objective of a measure provisionally justified under one of the paragraphs of Article XX, or goes against that objective' (*Brazil – Retreaded Tyres*, AB Report 2007: Para. 232). Based on this analysis, the AB concluded that 'the MERCOSUR exemption had resulted in the Import Ban being applied in a manner that constitutes arbitrary or unjustifiable discrimination' (*Brazil – Retreaded Tyres*, AB Report 2007: Para. 228).

Again, here, the exact scope of the terms 'arbitrary discrimination', 'unjustifiable discrimination' and 'disguised restriction on international trade' is quite blurry. Indeed, the AB in the *Brazil – Retreaded Tyres* case came to a collective determination that the measures were applied in a manner which constituted both arbitrary and unjustifiable discrimination, without carrying out any separate analysis.

In *EC – Seal Products*, the AB observed that 'the relationship of the discrimination to the objective of a measure is one of the most important factors, but not the sole test, that is relevant to the assessment of arbitrary or unjustifiable discrimination' (AB Report 2014: Para. 5.321). In this case, the EU had imposed a different regulatory treatment of seal-hunts by the Inuit indigenous community (IC) in the EU as compared to the general ban on imports resulting from commercial hunts. The EU explained that based on the rights of indigenous peoples, it had decided not to impose the ban on the importation and placing on the market of seal products derived from Inuit hunts, however, the AB did not accept that this did not amount to arbitrary or unjustifiable discrimination. The AB observed that the EU had failed to demonstrate 'how the discrimination resulting from the manner in which the EU Seal Regime treats IC hunts as compared to "commercial" hunts can be reconciled with, or is related to, the policy objective of addressing the EU public moral concerns regarding seal welfare' (*EC – Seal Products*, AB Report 2014: Para. 5.320).

Additionally, the AB found other reasons for concluding that the measures were applied in a manner which would constitute arbitrary or unjustifiable discrimination. First, it found considerable ambiguity in certain criteria of the IC exception and observed that because of this and the broad discretion that the recognised bodies consequently enjoy in applying them, 'seal products derived from what should in fact be properly characterised as "commercial" hunts could potentially enter the EU market under the IC exception' (*EC – Seal Products*, AB Report 2014: Para. 5.338). Second, the AB found that the EU had not sufficiently explained how such instances can be prevented in the application of the IC exception. Third, the AB was not persuaded that the EU had made 'comparable efforts' to facilitate the access of the Canadian Inuit to the IC exception as it did with respect to the Greenlandic Inuit. Finally, the AB noted that setting up a 'recognised body' that fulfilled the requirements of the EU Regulation 'may entail significant burdens in some instances' (*EC – Seal Products*, AB Report 2014: Para. 5.338). Similar to *Brazil – Retreaded Tyres*, having made a finding on 'arbitrary or unjustifiable discrimination', the AB did not analyse whether the measures were applied also in a manner which constituted disguised restriction on international trade. But, like that case, *EC – Seals* also came to a determination on 'arbitrary or unjustifiable discrimination' in a collective manner without examining the two separately.

Irrespective of which exception has been invoked under clauses (a) to (j) of Article XX, *EC – Asbestos* and *US – Shrimp (21.5)* are the only two cases where the requirements of the Chapeau have been held to have been fulfilled. In *EC – Asbestos*, however, the facts were indeed such where any other conclusion would have been impossible; the French ban on asbestos applied to everyone, including France itself, and, as such, the Panel noted that the measure was being applied without discrimination, let alone, arbitrary or unjustified discrimination (Panel Report 2000: Para. 8.237). However, the Panel again used the reasoning for 'arbitrary or unjustifiable discrimination' to conclude that there was no disguised restriction on international trade. These findings of the Panel on the question of whether the requirements of the Chapeau were fulfilled were not, however, appealed before the AB by Canada, and, as such, the AB did not have the occasion to address the issue (*EC – Asbestos*, AB Report 2001: Para. 58.c). In *US – Shrimp (21.5)*, the Panel and the AB held that the US had rectified the flaws identified in the original dispute through its new Revised Guidelines and, therefore, the new measures conformed with the Chapeau. In particular, the AB observed that unlike the original proceedings, the US had now made serious good faith efforts to negotiate an international agreement and, therefore, 'Section 609 is now applied in a manner that no longer constitutes a means of unjustifiable or arbitrary discrimination, as identified by the Appellate Body in its Report' (*US – Shrimp (21.5)*, AB Report 2001: Para. 134). Similarly, it also found that unlike the original measures, the new measures did not require exporting countries to use only TEDs recognised by the US in order to be certified by US authorities, but only required measures of 'comparable efficiency' to be taken to protect sea turtles (*US – Shrimp (21.5)*, AB Report 2001: Para. 144). As such, it agreed with the Panel's conclusion that 'conditioning market access on the adoption of a programme comparable in effectiveness, allows for sufficient flexibility in the application of the measure so as to avoid "arbitrary or unjustifiable discrimination"' (*US – Shrimp (21.5)*, AB Report 2001: Para. 144). Again here, the AB merely clubbed its observations together to arrive at a collective conclusion on both 'arbitrary' and 'unjustifiable' discrimination. Regarding 'disguised restriction on international trade', Malaysia had unsuccessfully raised arguments before the Panel, but did not appeal against them before the AB (*US – Shrimp (21.5)*, AB Report 2001: Para. 82). The Panel, however, made no effort to distinguish between the analysis which might be required to conclude on this requirement as distinct from the other two. Indeed, it used the same arguments which it had used to conclude that the revised measures did not amount to 'arbitrary or unjustifiable discrimination', to also conclude that they do not amount to 'disguised restriction on international trade' (*US – Shrimp (21.5)*, Panel Report 2001: Para. 5.143).

From the aforesaid discussion, it is clear that the requirements of Article XX are not free from ambiguity as the AB itself has noted. Despite significant jurisprudence emerging from the Panels and the AB, it is still unclear on how the three requirements of the Chapeau differ from each other and what their exact scope is. Obviously, this ambiguity means that States do not have clear interpretational standards on the basis of which they can design their exceptional measures. Second, the fact that only one case under Article XX(b) and two cases under any of the clauses (a) to (j) have thus far successfully passed the Chapeau's test, empirically demonstrate how difficult it has been for States to use the general exceptions provision to protect human health.

Conclusions on Article XX and the limiting of governance space

The aforesaid discussion thus leads us to three important conclusions. First, in order for a State to invoke clause (b) to protect human health, the requirement that such WTO-inconsistent measures must be 'necessary' leads to a significant shrinking of governance space for States. In particular, this is a result of the strict requirements of the 'necessity' test. Second, the 'relating to' test under clause (g) for environmental measures is significantly more lenient than the 'necessity' test under clause (b). As such, justifications for a State to invoke the former are easier to prove. However, there is no a priori legitimate policy reason that the requirements for proving human health exceptions must be stricter than the requirements for proving environmental exceptions. Third, the requirements of the Chapeau of Article XX make it extremely difficult for a State to invoke clause (b) successfully, even if the challenged measure may pass the requirements of 'necessary'. The only inevitable conclusion which can be made is that despite Article XX being on paper, the flexibility in order to utilise the governance space that States need to protect human health is extremely limited. Indeed, it is the manner in which Article XX is couched which limits the governance space that States really need to address human health concerns.

One of the purposes of this chapter was to use the case study to demonstrate how MTS in general can limit the governance space which States need to fulfil their human rights obligations. The case study is thus an example of many other ways in which the obligations which States undertake at the WTO may result in the shrinking of the necessary governance space required to fulfil their human rights obligations. To that end, the case study has served the purpose.

The other purpose of this chapter was to also lay the platform for a better exploration of the appropriate approach to finding solutions to issues within this linkage-category in Chapter 8. The detailed discussion and conclusion on the case study has thus enabled us to use it also for illustrating how an appropriate approach to solutions can help resolve the issue of Article XX(b). This will in turn enable us to evaluate possible application of a similar approach for resolving other issues which may fall within this linkage-category.

Notes

1 For a detailed discussion on the public morals exception and the challenges of invoking human rights concerns through clause (a) of Article XX, see Harrison (2007: 200–19).

2 In any case, the question might have been moot in view of the concurrent findings by the Panel and the AB that a defence under Article XX(b) was in fact not even open to China to justify its export restrictions as a result of its commitments under its Accession Protocol to the WTO (*China – Raw Materials*, Panel Report 2011: Para. 7.159; *China – Raw Materials*, AB Report 2012: Para. 307).

3 See also *China – Rare Earths*, AB Report (2014: Para. 5.90).

4 The AB in *China – Rare Earths* stated that 'the text of Article XX(g), particularly its use of the conjunctive "if", suggests a holistic assessment of its component elements' (AB Report 2014: Para. 5.94).

5 The AB further observed that

> discrimination results not only when countries in which the same conditions prevail are differently treated, but also when the application of the measure at issue does not allow for any inquiry into the appropriateness of the regulatory program for the conditions prevailing in those exporting countries.

6 Although the AB reversed the findings of the Panel that the application of the impugned measures amounted to disguised restrictions on grounds that there was legal error in the approach, it did not itself analyse whether the measures were applied in such a manner.

6

WTO AND THE PERMISSIVE ENVIRONMENT TO ABUSE GOVERNANCE SPACE

In the previous chapter, we discussed questions relating to the first linkage-category where WTO laws can limit the governance space of States to be able to fulfil their human rights obligations. As noted in Chapter 2, this is not the only way in which governance space of States is affected in the interface between MTS and human rights such that adverse impacts on the latter can be occasioned. In this chapter, we will develop the second manner in which such governance space is affected. The inquiry here rests on an analysis of those cases where the interaction between MTS and human rights obligations of States results not from a limitation of the governance space that States need, but rather because MTS creates the permissive environment for States to abuse the governance space they already have. This abuse of governance space occurs partly because many States lack the willingness to use it in order to benefit from MTS and partly because that is the only way they can actually compete on the global market. While, as we saw in the previous chapter, the first category comprises cases where WTO laws place limitations on States to *use* the governance space they need but do not have, this linkage-category rests on the foundation that States already have that necessary governance space and that WTO laws do not limit the same. Instead, the WTO regime creates a permissive environment for States to *abuse* that governance space. The difference in the nature and scope of this linkage-category from the former is not relevant only as a typology of ways in which linkages emerge. Indeed, it is central to how we understand and evaluate governance space and suggest appropriate solutions thereto. Distinguishing this linkage-category from the others, by understanding how the central theme of governance space is impacted differently, allows us to also appreciate that solutions to linkage-issues within different linkage-categories may need to be approached differently.

Introduction to the case study and rationale for choosing it: MTS and labour standards

The case study which screams for being considered within this linkage-category is the controversial MTS-labour issue. As is well known, this linkage-issue emerges because many States are typically lax on their own labour obligations in an attempt to benefit from cheap labour and, therefore, in turn benefit from comparative advantage in the global market. This is not a case where States, typically D-LDCs, who adopt lax labour standards do not have the governance space they need in order to improve them. Instead, they have the necessary governance space to improve labour standards but are either unwilling to use it in order to benefit more from MTS or because they have no other choice if they wish to compete on the global market. The former case could be viewed as situations where some D-LDCs (arguably the emerging economies) may make a voluntary and conscious choice to be lax on their international and domestic labour rights obligations to benefit more from global markets, while the latter case could be viewed as one where MTS plays a coercive role in forcing D-LDCs (arguably those other than the emerging economies) to lower their labour rights standards because not doing so leads to loss of any possible export opportunities. In either case, however, the governance space which States already have to improve labour standards ends up being abused, willingly or unwillingly.

It is important to hasten and add, however, that the fact that MTS can create permissive environment for States to abuse their governance space and, therefore, violate labour standards, does not automatically lead to a conclusion that the appropriate policy solution is at the WTO and not elsewhere. Indeed, as Chapter 7 of this book will argue, an attempt to bring enforcement of labour standards under the WTO framework might be counterproductive and other solutions might be more workable.

An institutional history of the MTS and the labour standards debate

The debates on MTS and labour standards have quite a long history dating back to much before WWII (Charnovitz 1987: 574; Leary 1996: 182–83). However, these debates have gradually flared up in both academic and policy circles over time. Diverging viewpoints have been raised over whether trade and labour standards are linked, how they are linked, who should address the linkages and in which manner. That there are inherent linkages between trade and labour standards to some extent is not so much in contention, as the question of what the extent of those linkages is. We begin our analysis with the institutional attempts post-WWII to link trade and labour standards, before moving on to the underlying justifications presented by the range of different actors involved in this debate.

Although the International Labour Organization (ILO) was established in 1919 to codify and promote labour standards, it survived the 'scourge' of WWII. Not only that, labour standards which had been agreed upon under the aegis of the ILO also made it to Article 7 of the Havana Charter of the stillborn ITO. That provision entitled as 'Fair Labour Standards' has been described by some commentators as an explicit recognition by the drafters that labour standards were related to trade (Chartres and Mercurio 2012: 676). However, a closer examination of Article 7 indicates the actual purpose of the provision. It stated that 'unfair labour conditions, particularly in production for exports, create difficulties in international trade [. . . and] each member shall take whatever action may be appropriate and feasible to eliminate such conditions within its territory' (Havana Charter 1948: Article 7). Thus, while a linkage was indeed recognised, the rationale behind it was a concern for eliminating distortion in markets as a result of the comparative advantage that some States may attain because of lower labour standards, rather than a concern for dignity of labourers.

Unlike the ill-fated Havana Charter, GATT 1947, did not contain any such reference to labour standards (Bhala 1998). Immediate attempts thereafter in 1953 by the US for the inclusion of a provision which would provide for the nullification of a State's benefits under the GATT if it maintained unfair labour standards were rejected by GATT parties (Charnovitz 1987: 574). When the Uruguay Round of negotiations for the establishment of the WTO began in the 1980s, the US, with some support from the EC and Nordic countries, again proposed the inclusion of a 'social clause', but no agreement could be reached on the issue (Hepple 2007: 171).

The US persisted, and, with support from DCs, it requested at the Marrakesh Ministerial Conference in 1994 that a 'WTO Committee on Labour Standards' be established to facilitate future negotiations on the issue (Chatterjee 2007: 476). However, while a 'Committee on Trade and Environment' was set up, no similar Committee was created on labour standards and trade due to the opposition from D-LDCs.

The ILO had also become centre stage during the discussions at this juncture. While D-LDCs were keen on keeping labour standards out of WTO, DCs were arguing that the ILO did not have enforcement mechanisms, and as such non-incorporation of a 'social clause' in the WTO would essentially leave protection of these standards in the hands of a weak organisation (Cappuyns 1998). The ILO itself formally entered the linkages debate in 1994 and set up a 'Working Party' on the social dimensions of the liberalisation of international trade (Trebilcock and Howse 2005: 262). In the meantime, labour ministers from 85 D-LDCs gathered together in New Delhi in January 1995 at a conference entitled 'Labour Ministers of Non-Aligned and Other Developing Countries'. The outcome statement of the Conference adopted a firm stance against a potential 'social clause' in the WTO describing it as 'coercive' and declaring that such a clause would negate the benefits of trade liberalisation and aggravate problems of unemployment (Kolben 2010: 469). This unflinching position adopted by D-LDCs eventually reverberated at both the ILO and the WTO. Thus, at the ILO, the governing body concluded in 1995 that the Working Party which it had created would not pursue the question of trade sanctions and that further discussion of a link between international trade and social standards or a sanction-based social clause mechanism would be suspended (Trebilcock and Howse 2005: 262).

At the WTO, the saga began to reach its final chapter in the Singapore Ministerial Conference in 1996. In fact, the controversy over the 'social clause' had reached such serious levels that an invitation to Michel Hansenne, the then Director-General of the ILO, to address the ministers had to be unceremoniously withdrawn due to objections from D-LDCs (Leary 1997: 119). In the end, the final Ministerial Declaration put to rest all demands made by DCs for linking trade and labour standards at the WTO. It stated as follows:

> We renew our commitment to the observance of internationally recognised core labour standards. The International Labour Organisation (ILO) is the competent body to set and deal with these standards, and we affirm our support for its work in promoting them. We believe that economic growth and development fostered by increased trade and further trade liberalisation contribute to the promotion of these standards. We reject the use of labour standards for protectionist purposes, and agree that the comparative advantage of countries, particularly low-wage developing countries, must in no way

> be put into question. In this regard, we note that the WTO and ILO Secretariats will continue their existing collaboration.
>
> (WTO 1996: Para. 4)

As some commentators have rightly noted, the Singapore Ministerial Declaration thus provides the WTO's final word on the matter (Leary 1997: 119; Collier and Bamu 2012: 331).

In the meanwhile, at the ILO, other attempts to link trade and labour standards continued to be thwarted by D-LDCs, primarily based on their fears that such linkages may permit DCs to deny market access benefits to them. Thus, in 1997, even a proposal by its Director-General that ILO promote and administer a country-based certification and labelling programme for products from countries complying with core labour standards was rejected by ILO members (Cullen 1999: 15; McCrudden and Davies 2000: 47). ILO, however, moved ahead to get its own house in order with respect to defining the content of 'core labour standards' (CLS), which had already become a flash point in the discussions on trade and labour. Thus, in June 1998, the 'Declaration on Fundamental Principles and Rights at Work' was adopted (ILO 1998). This Declaration identifies four distinct rights as having a special status within the international labour law hierarchy (ILO 1998: Para. 2), because they are obligatory on all ILO members irrespective of whether they have ratified or not the relevant Conventions. The four principles articulated in the Declaration, and commonly known as CLS, are the right to (a) freedom of association and the effective recognition of the right to collective bargaining, (b) the elimination of all forms of forced or compulsory labour, (c) the effective abolition of child labour and (d) the elimination of discrimination in respect of employment and occupation. These four principles echo some of the universal human rights recognised in the UDHR, ICCPR and ICESCR (Stirling 1996: 16–17; Trebilcock and Howse 2005: 263; Chartres and Mercurio 2012: 691). For instance, Article 4 of the UDHR prohibits slavery; Article 25(2) provides for the special protection of childhood; and Article 26 guarantees the right to education which is the counterpart of the abolition of child labour. Under ICCPR, Article 8 prohibits forced or compulsory labour; and Article 21(1) guarantees the right to freedom of association with others, including the right to form and join trade unions. Similarly, ICESCR provides in Article 7 for fair working conditions; Article 10 provides for the protection of children from social and economic exploitation; Article 20 guarantees the right of association; Article 23(4) guarantees the right to join trade unions and Article 23(2) ensures the right to work in a profession of one's choosing. In addition, the most widely ratified human rights instrument – Convention on the Rights of the Child – contains several provisions aimed at the right to education and protection of children from child labour.

Despite agreement on the contents of CLS and their obvious status as human rights, the hangover of the 1996 Singapore Ministerial Declaration at the WTO permeated its way through the ILO's Declaration as well. Thus, ILO members thwarted any attempted interpretation of the ILO Declaration to revive the trade-labour discussion at the WTO by stressing that:

> labour standards should not be used for protectionist trade purposes, and that nothing in this Declaration and its follow-up shall be invoked or otherwise used for such purposes; in addition, the comparative advantage of any country should in no way be called into question by this Declaration and its follow-up.
>
> (ILO 1998: Para. 5)

The final attempt by DCs, especially Canada, the US and the EC, to rake up the issue at the WTO was made in the 1999 Seattle Ministerial Conference. DCs, however, did not have a united front or even a consensus on how the issue should be addressed at the WTO. Thus, for instance, while Canada proposed a WTO working group to examine the links between trade, development and social and environmental policies, the EC proposed the establishment of a hybrid ILO/WTO Standing Working Forum on 'Globalisation and Labour', and the US, on its part, proposed the establishment of a WTO Working Group on Trade and Labour to investigate 'the effects of the multilateral trading system on the living standards and employment opportunities of working men and women around the world' (WTO 1999: 152–53, 175, 186). D-LDCs, on the other hand, put up a united front and rejected all the proposals. Indeed, like the Singapore Ministerial Conference, they even frustrated an effort to invite the ILO Director-General to address the Seattle WTO meeting (Kolben 2010: 470).

With the aforesaid attempt at Seattle vehemently rejected, and with the Bush administration in the US refusing to revive the issue again in the Doha round of negotiations (Chartres and Mercurio 2012: 667), the issue eventually fizzled out entirely from the WTO agenda. The Doha Ministerial Declaration of 2001 makes a perfunctory reference to labour but that is simply to reaffirm the Singapore Ministerial Declaration (WTO 2001: Para. 8).

This has, however, not mellowed down scholars, policy makers and civil society organisations from engaging in vociferous discussions and debates on the topic. Indeed, as shall be pointed out, admirably novel and unique (but several of them ultimately unpragmatic) proposals have been presented, particularly by academics, on how the issue should be addressed in the future. Additionally, with the exponential proliferation of preferential trade agreements (PTAs) in recent years and the increasing incorporation of labour standards provisions therein, the issue of linkages itself is far from buried. The ILO, unshackled as it is in conducting research on linkages between non-WTO trade agreements and labour standards, has recently come out with a number of working and discussion papers on the topic (Ebert and Posthuma 2011; Boie 2012; Haberli, Jansen and Monteiro 2012). Even remote attempts in those reports to justify conditioning market access to performance on labour standards through PTAs has met with outrage from the developing world (Anuradha and Dutta 2012).

But what exactly are the underlying theoretical and political bases for scholars to take such divergent views on the question of linkages? It is to this question that we shall now turn.

Arguments by proponents of linking MTS with labour at the WTO

In the post-WTO era, the first systematic scholarly study on linkages between MTS and labour standards was pioneered by Bhagwati and Hudec (1996). The Bhagwati-Hudec volumes have since led to a proliferation of scholarship on the topic, with proponents and opponents of linkages often speaking past each other. Nevertheless, the main justifications for linking the two fields mostly put forth by DCs can be clearly deciphered from scholarly and policy publications (Langille 1997).

The first of these justifications is that lower labour standards in D-LDCs create an unfair form of competition because the resultant low cost of production deprives producers in countries where labour standards are respected of legitimate market share (Hiatt and Greenfield 2004). Scholars point out that because labour is by nature an 'intrinsic part of the production process that culminates in the manufacture of goods and services for trade' (Ehrenberg 1995: 364; Hughes and Wilkinson 1998: 381), failure by a government to regulate the means by which labour is utilised constitutes a trade distortion. As such, this sort of 'social dumping' or 'implicit and illicit subsidisation' can lead to distortion of MTS (Trebilcock and Howse 2005: 266), which is the very antithesis of the WTO's objectives (Zaheer

2004: 75). Greater global integration has also meant that States are increasingly able to use poor labour standards as a means of gaining a competitive advantage for their country's goods on the international market (Standing 1999: 68). Indeed, some scholars have argued that lower labour standards are associated with higher trade (Granger and Siroen 2006: 820).

The second justification pressed into service is that lower labour standards in D-LDCs will lead to an overall 'race to the bottom' in DCs as well (Kaufmann 2007: 9). This argument posits that competition from imports made in low-wage D-LDCs will lead to loss of jobs for workers in DCs, and the resultant loss of comparative advantage would drive the DCs to lower their labour standards as well (Alben 2001: 1413; Anuradha and Dutta 2012: 9). This trend will then precipitate a 'race to the bottom' where the DCs will eventually get trapped into some form of prisoner's dilemma. This argument assumes that importing countries, rather than maintaining the status quo with respect to their higher labour standards and accepting a loss of market share, would instead also progressively lower them to avoid losing market share to imports from countries with lower labour standards (Trebilcock and Howse 2005: 270). In order to prevent such a global deterioration, the 'race to the bottom' argument stresses on the need for labour standards to be enforced through MTS. In other words, this justification for the trade-labour link 'effectively requires countries to raise standards to the level desired by importing countries or face trade sanctions by the latter' (Panagariya 2001: 5).

The third justification for linkages is that lower labour standards in D-LDCs will not only lead to a 'race to the bottom' in DCs, but within D-LDCs as well. Because D-LDCs will compete with each other for more market share, the desire to lower costs of production and attract more investment, particularly from MNCs, will lead them to increasingly lower their labour standards (Maskus 1997: 16; Stone 2008: 123). An extensive exposition of this argument is presented by Kevin Banks who incidentally dismisses the 'race to the bottom' argument vis-à-vis DCs, but makes a strong pitch for its applicability to D-LDCs (Banks 2006: 78). He contends that vertical competitive pressures will result where D-LDCs rely heavily on low labour costs to compensate for shortcomings in other factors that attract investment and gain market share, and, because of this, such jurisdictions will face significant pressures to hold labour standards down (Banks 2006: 88). As a result, he argues that far greater share of employers in D-LDCs is likely to rely on low labour costs for competitiveness, and they will face obstacles in pursuing other strategies (Banks 2006: 90).

The fourth justification for linkage is based on the concept of 'embedded liberalism' enunciated by John Ruggie in his seminal work in the 1980s on explaining the modern international economic system (Ruggie 1982: 379–415). The theory suggests that international markets are grounded in some sort of a compact between States who agree to liberalise their markets globally, while simultaneously maintaining a degree of control over their regulatory space through domestic regulatory interventions. This theory is similar to the notion of 'policy space', in that, in Ruggie's analysis, the domestic regulatory interventions by a State are more concerned with this being their right rather than duty. Based on this concept of 'embedded liberalism', it has been argued that States have the ability to regulate around social issues in a non-protectionist manner and, therefore, labour standards are rightly linked by DCs to MTS (Howse, Langille and Burda 2006: 157). In other words, the argument suggests that because DCs have retained their right to regulate on social issues, they are justified in insisting that trade rules regulate labour standards, even if they pertain to standards in other countries (Kolben 2010).

The fifth justification for linkages is based on the argument that consumers ought to be allowed autonomy in the choices they make regarding products, except when such choices are based on illegitimate grounds such as protectionism. This argument is couched in the language of 'consumer autonomy' or 'consumer citizenship' (Kolben 2010: 461–62) and is often presented in the context of debates whether products manufactured by methods which result in violations of CLS can be considered as distinct from those manufactured without such violations so that MFN and NT principles would not apply to them (Howse and Regan 2000: 253). It is further argued that because the market and the consumer are central to public policy in the post-WTO era, it is, in fact, the role of the State to act as a facilitator to ensure effective consumer citizenship by permitting discrimination between products and services based on the methods by which they are made.

The sixth justification for linkages is based on the freedom-based capability approach to development espoused by Amartya Sen in his landmark book *Development as Freedom* (Sen 1999). Development, in this approach, must look beyond economic growth and must focus on enhancing the freedoms that people value and cherish. Thus, economic growth through trade, at the cost of labour standards, militates against development because it reduces rather than enhances the freedoms that people value. As Kolben has put it, 'A development approach to trade and labour asks how the freedoms of workers, defined more richly than a thin account, can be expanded, and how institutions can be created or expanded to achieve those goals' (Kolben 2010: 466). In this context, scholars have presented economic arguments attempting to demonstrate that linkages will most likely benefit everyone, both DCs and D-LDCs, but particularly the latter, rather than hurt them (Bagwell and Staiger 2000; Summers 2001; Elliot and Freeman 2003: 2, 9; Staiger 2003). This is because, at least with respect to CLS, the welfare effects of compliance are likely to be positive in D-LDCs themselves (OECD 1996: 98; Trebilcock and Howse 2005: 268). Some scholars have even suggested that although labour costs indeed tend to go up as standards become more stringent, there is little evidence that lax labour standards create comparative advantages or that they encourage FDI (Rodrik 1997: 52–59). In sum, the argument, therefore, is that labour standards and trade need to be linked if we are to focus on true development in poorer countries, namely going beyond short-term interests of comparative advantage and focusing more on enhancing the freedoms of workers. It is worthwhile to point out though that the 'development approach to trade and labour' argument is 'externally focused' on the development of others, unlike the arguments based on 'embedded liberalism' and 'consumer autonomy', which Kolben categorises as 'reflexive' justifications (Kolben 2010: 462).

Seventh, another 'externally focused' argument put forth by scholars is based on human rights of workers in D-LDCs. The main proponents of this argument are Trebilcock and Howse, who while supporting linkages are incidentally not too enamoured by the justifications founded on the 'unfair competition' and 'race-to-the-bottom' arguments since they are 'largely spurious and inconsistent with the central predicates of a liberal trading system' (Trebilcock and Howse 2005: 272). Instead, they argue that the concern with basic or universal human rights falling within CLS is because the failure to respect them in any country 'either does not reflect the will of the citizens but rather decisions of unrepresentative or repressive governments', or 'majoritarian oppression of children, women, racial or religious minorities', or 'paternalistic concerns that citizens in other countries have made uninformed or ill-advised choices to forego these basic rights' (Trebilcock and Howse 2005: 271–72). They contend that trade sanctions for promoting labour standards, which are human rights, are entirely consistent with the central tenets of a liberal trading regime, because the latter also seeks to ensure other human freedoms such as the right of individuals to engage in market transactions with other individuals on the basis of country or location. In highlighting and further promoting the pre-eminent status that they wish to ascribe to the human rights argument for linkages, they even insist that:

> competitiveness-based claims about 'social dumping' have become less prominent, and the notion that the objective should be to achieve some kind of 'level playing field' between developed and developing countries is now heard less frequently, even from labour rights advocates on the left of the political spectrum.
>
> (Trebilcock and Howse 2005: 300)

Instead, they stress that the discussion in the international policy community on the relationship between liberal trade and labour rights has focused on the issue of compliance with core universal rights. This conclusion appears, however, to be not quite accurately reflective of current discourse which continues to place extensive attention to the 'unfair competition' and 'race to the bottom' arguments as is noted in other parts of this chapter.

And finally, as is evident from the historical context of the debate already highlighted, the argument has consistently been made that linkages between trade and labour standards at the WTO are justified, including through trade sanctions, because the ILO's enforcement mechanisms are quite weak. While the ILO is the global nodal organisation responsible for overseeing and promoting better working conditions and improving labour law enforcement in its member countries, it is often considered a 'toothless tiger – a tripartite, do-nothing organisation that is somewhat effective in generating norms but falls far short in ensuring their respect due to its lack of meaningful sanctions power' (Kolben 2010: 461). One reason ascribed for this is that several of its agreements are not consistently ratified by States, including most importantly by the US, and this has resulted in a 'patchwork of inconsistent legal obligations' (Thomas 2004: 350) which hampers its effective enforcement capabilities. Even if they have been ratified, many States do not implement them (Sengenberger 2006: 332). On its part, the ILO also adopts in practice a rather soft approach to the enforcement of its norms, relying mostly on naming and shaming and, of course, on promoting compliance by providing technical assistance. It has been noted that the ILO does not even do this very well, as the ILO's 'special list' of transgressions of CLS garners little international publicity and even less government attention and has not produced any substantial improvements in compliance (Chartres and Mercurio 2012: 687).

Arguments by opponents of linking MTS with labour at the WTO

The opponents of linking trade and labour standards, on their part, however, also pose a series of vehement arguments debunking the justifications put forth by the proponents. As has been aptly put, the opponents of linking labour standards and trade believe that such linkages are akin to 'spreading peanut butter on your steak: the two have little to do with each other, and when mixed together disastrous consequences can result' (Kolben 2010: 461).

Among the most important reasons for such strong opposition, as previously noted in this chapter, is a belief that efforts by DCs to link trade and labour standards at the WTO is nothing but a disguise for protectionism masquerading as a humanitarian concern (Salazar-Xirinachs 2000: 380; Bhagwati 2002: 127–28; Grimwade 2004). D-LDCs argue that such attempts to link the two are meant to essentially nullify the comparative advantage that they enjoy as a result of low labour costs (Blackett 2007). Bhagwati, who has been an unflinching and scathing critique of the linkages argument, characterises it as nothing but an attempt at 'export protectionism' (Bhagwati 2008: 78). To him, the language of altruism and concern for worker's rights in D-LDCs is simply a facade, and the real motive behind claims for linkages is self-interest of those in the west who are terrified from competition and who hope that raising standards and therefore costs abroad will neutralise the competitive ability of D-LDCs. What resonates most with scholars and NGOs from D-LDCs is Bhagwati's conviction that the language of altruism is hypocritical and offensive (Bhagwati 2002; 2008). He contends that it is very easy for lobbyists of linkages to sell the idea to domestic constituencies in DCs under the comfort of altruism: 'You need not feel guilty if you can deceive yourself into thinking you are flogging the foreigner in his own interest' (Bhagwati 2007). Indeed, in 1999, a group of 99 influential academics and NGOs from D-LDCs, led by Bhagwati, issued a statement which was eloquently titled as 'Third World Intellectuals and NGOs Statement Against Linkage' (Bhagwati *et al.* 1999). What is noteworthy is that the opposition to linkages in D-LDCs pervades through a variety of stakeholders and is not limited to governments. For instance, based on their interviews in India, both Bhagwati (2002: 131) and Kolben (2006) have separately concluded that there is indeed a genuine and well-founded fear among policy makers, scholars, NGOs, as well as trade unionists that DCs will abuse any linkage for protectionist purposes. Display of concerns in the west for worker's rights in the poorer countries has also been characterised as 'inappropriately paternalistic or culturally patronising' (Watson 1994) or more bluntly, as 'neo-colonialism' (Kolben 2006: 251–53).

Opponents of linkages also take issue with the proponents with respect to the 'unfair competition' argument (Block, Roberts and Ormiston 2002: 418). Panagariya (2001), for instance, has pointed out that the argument that DCs will have to face unfair competition from D-LDCs where costs of production are lower is in direct conflict with the basic principle of comparative advantage. As he contends, this 'pauper-labour argument' is a common fallacy because high-wage countries are perfectly capable of competing against low-wage countries due to their higher productivity, higher capital, as well as technological and infrastructure advances (Panagariya 2001: 10). These are, of course, areas where DCs have a comparative advantage over the D-LDCs and, therefore, a linkage between trade and labour standards is not a win-win policy and may very well lead to a decline in world welfare (Panagariya 2001: 10). Interestingly, some of the staunchest proponents of linkages agree with this analysis. For instance, Trebilcock and Howse also point out that it is equally unfair for D-LDCs to have to compete with firms and workers in DCs that depend on highly skilled labour, developed infrastructure, large public investments in health, law and order, education and research and superior institutions, which reflect collective or public investments on a scale that far exceeds the capacity of most D-LDCs (Trebilcock and Howse 2005: 269).

Some scholars further point out that even if the 'unfair competition' argument were theoretically possible, in reality, there is no empirical evidence demonstrating that countries with low CLS enjoy a better export performance (Anuradha and Dutta 2012: 9). In fact, an Organisation for Economic Co-operation and Development (OECD) study also concludes to the same effect (OECD 2000: 33). As such, the 'unfair competition' argument is not only misplaced but its relentless invocation only lends further credence to claims that it is a smokescreen for protectionism or for other foreign policy interests of DCs amounting to neo-colonialism.

According to the opponents of linkages, the same holds true for the 'race to the bottom' argument. Empirical studies by scholars have almost always unanimously debunked the theory that increased trade is linked to declining labour standards, both in DCs and in D-LDCs (Gould IV 2001: 725–26; Smarzynska and Wei 2001). Flanagan (2003: 15; 2006: 81–83) has demonstrated that there is very little empirical evidence that trade liberalisation without labour safeguards leads to downward wage pressures or generally to increased pressures to weaken labour regulatory regimes in DCs. In his research, he has also demonstrated an almost complete lack of empirical evidence that foreign direct investors are investing in D-LDCs with weak CLS and has concluded that although improvements in actual labour conditions may raise productivity and compensation, there is no evidence that adoption of international labour standards has, in fact, produced such improvements.

In the specific case of DCs, scholars have demonstrated that the adverse effect of trade with poor countries on the wages of unskilled workers in the rich countries is minuscule and that most of the increase in the wage gap between skilled and unskilled workers is attributable to technological change and, in the case of the US, also to rapidly declining rates of unionisation (Brown 2000: Para. 69). Bhagwati (2000: 131) has suggested that trade may even have moderated the decline in real wages that would have occurred from unskilled labour-saving technological change, while others like Feenstra and Hanson (1999) have suggested that the effect on earnings of US American unskilled workers from the outsourcing of labour-intensive inputs to D-LDCs is definitely not adverse, but may, in fact, be slightly favourable. Finally, it has been pointed out that there is almost no evidence that the reduction in relative earnings of unskilled workers in DCs which is reasonably attributable to increased trade with D-LDCs relates to non-compliance with CLS rather than simply lower wages (Trebilcock and Howse 2005: 267). Insofar as D-LDCs are concerned, Stern and Terrell (2003: 7) have pointed out that mandatory standards have not and will not improve working conditions of workers in poor countries, including wages, if they raise the cost of labour above its level of productivity. To the contrary, they argue that workers may suffer *negative* consequences when their wages are raised above the market value of their productivity. Thus, from whichever side one may look at the race-to-the-bottom argument, the poignant words of Bhagwati may perhaps be the best expression of the belief underlying the approach of opponents of linkages: 'The rhetoric of globalisation is used by both its enemies and its friends to create the mythology of such a race to the bottom' (Bhagwati 2002: 131).

Perhaps the more ethical argument by the proponents of linkages, as discussed earlier, focuses on the fact that this will enhance development and human rights in poorer countries with lax labour standards. However, from empirical evidence presented by scholars as narrated earlier, the assumption that forcing labour standards to increase in poorer countries will lead to development and improvement of human rights may itself be questionable. Skyes (2003: 4), for instance, has argued that rising real incomes and greater openness tends to promote human rights and, therefore, if the intention is to improve human rights in poorer countries, it is best to rely on the benefits of free trade and not block it. Trebilcock and Howse, proponents of the human rights argument as the justification for linkages, themselves have pointed out that according to economic theories, immediate imposition of international labour standards would lead to a reduction in the total economic welfare worldwide including in D-LDCs, as well as DCs and industrialised nations (Trebilcock and Howse 2005: 268). Moreover, as will be discussed later, there is a compelling case presented by scholars that the process of improving labour standards, much like the process of economic change itself, is very complex because it is conditioned by a variety of ground-level realities existing in D-LDCs which need to be changed through a long process of economic and social development, and as such the expected results cannot be achieved through mere mandates for linkages (Stern and Terrell 2003: 11).

Another reason for scepticism against linkages, although not shared necessarily by all opponents, is that there may be no general consensus on what labour rights ought to be covered if trade is to be linked to the former. Panagariya, for instance, has pointed out that the US is not a party to several of the core ILO Conventions other than the Convention (No. 105) Concerning the Abolition of Forced Labour, 1957 and the Convention (No. 182) Concerning the Prohibition and Immediate Action for the Elimination of the Worst Forms of Child Labour, 1999 and that 'this fact alone should alert us to the falsehood of any claims that there is general agreement among nations on a set of core labour standards' (Panagariya 2001: 3). He concludes that there are perhaps shared values but precisely how these values are to be translated into action is quite contentious. With respect to the four CLS outlined in the ILO Declaration on Fundamental Principles and Rights at Work (ILO 1998) as well, there is no common understanding of their scope. In fact, Alston (2004: 458) has argued that the Declaration does not even reflect labour rights, but only principles.[1] Thus, despite a general agreement on the shared values or principles, there is no consensus on the finer details like whether forced or compulsory labour includes cases amounting to slavery only or to a lower threshold as well, or what the minimum working age for child labour should be, or what is the exact relation between the right to strike and the right to freedom of association or collective bargaining, or for that matter, what is the exact scope of non-discrimination in respect of employment and occupation. The lack of consensus is probably only reflective of the heterogeneity in ground realities in D-LDCs and DCs. Panagariya rightly points out that 'in abstract, most parents are likely to share the value that child labour is "wrong", . . . but when forced to choose between child starvation and child labour, most will choose the latter' (Panagariya 2001: 6). There is especially a strong support for this line of argument in light of evidence that employment of older children can indeed be productive and humanely combined with schooling (Brown 2000: Para. 145). The role of culture in the perceptive differences is also evident in Panagariya's comment that in the US, 'no one questions the morality of children distributing newspapers in the neighbourhood or working as babysitters' (Panagariya 2001: 6). Also, it has been argued that the very expectation that labour standards can be enforced through trade measures is unrealistic given the level of economic development in the poorer countries. That is because, unlike richer countries who can choose to pay the cost of eradicating child labour by forgoing the output produced by potential child workers and by committing resources to educational facilities for them, the poorer countries are not in a position to do so because the adjustment can be exorbitantly expensive (Panagariya 2001: 6). Therefore, unless the richer countries are willing to bear the costs of these adjustments in poorer countries, it is unrealistic to expect that any benefits will accrue out of mere linkages.

Finally, in sync with the official position of the D-LDCs at the WTO, many scholars have also pointed out that ILO is the more appropriate forum to enforce labour standards, because that is indeed the organisation created for that purpose, not the WTO. This point will be discussed more fully later in this chapter. However, with reference to the argument that ILO is a toothless tiger with no bite because it relies on moral suasion, it might be in order to quote the riposte presented by Bhagwati: 'God gave us not just teeth but also a tongue. A good tongue lashing today, with the ubiquity of CNN and civil society groups, can be very effective' (Bhagwati 2002: 132).

Having presented the views of the opponents of linkages, it is vitally important to properly qualify this opposition and the boundaries thereof in order to carry forward the analysis in the appropriate perspective. The opposition to linkages cannot and should not be understood as a claim by D-LDCs that there is no connection whatsoever between MTS and labour standards. Indeed, the stand by D-LDCs in the 1996 Singapore Ministerial Declaration that the comparative advantage of countries, particularly low-wage D-LDCs, must in no way be put into question because of trade measures, is indicative of the fact that labour standards and trade indeed have a nexus. For, how else would lower wages constitute a comparative advantage for

D-LDCs? Therefore, the opposition to linkages is really about the use of trade measures to nullify this comparative advantage, meaning that labour standards should not be sought to be enforced through trade measures at the WTO. This is an opposition to the choice of WTO as the forum for enforcing labour standards and not the ILO. As stated earlier, a lot of this opposition is based on a well-grounded suspicion that labour-related trade measures will be used by DCs only for protectionist purposes. This fear is particularly real because, as has rightly pointed out, there is no natural or self-evident baseline or rule that can solve the basic dilemma of what the true intentions of a DC are, when it decides to impose a trade sanction on a D-LDC on the ground of labour violations (Tarullo 1985: 171; Howse 2007: 12; Lang 2011: 171).

WTO rules and exclusion of labour standards

The discussion on linkages between MTS and labour presented earlier, as well as calls for inclusion of a 'social clause' in the WTO Agreements, are obviously a result of the fact that WTO rules, as they stand, do not allow WTO members to enforce labour standards in other countries. A closer look at WTO rules and relevant jurisprudence reveals that, in fact, not only is such express permission to invoke labour standards as a ground for validating trade sanctions absent, States are actually prohibited from doing so.

'Like' products, most favoured nation and national treatment

One way in which trade measures could be justified under WTO rules is if they do not violate the non-discrimination provisions. Both the MFN and the NT principles permit discrimination between products from an exporting country, on the one hand, and products from another exporting country or domestic products from the importing country, on the other hand, if the products are not 'like'. Thus, because plantains and bananas are not 'like products', different treatment, say higher customs duty on plantains as compared to bananas, is not *per se* a violation of the MFN principle. In our context, the question arises whether products, let's say shoes, manufactured with violations of CLS and those manufactured without such violations are 'like products'. If they are not 'like products', then some amount of discrimination may not be a violation of MFN or NT principles and, thus, may be permitted. On the other hand, if they are considered to be 'like products', such discrimination will be deemed a breach of WTO provisions. The Panels and AB have not had the occasion to directly deal with the question as related to labour standards till date, however, current jurisprudence clearly suggests that a distinction between products based on labour standards may be a violation of MFN and NT principles. In other words, products manufactured with violations of labour standards and those manufactured without must be considered 'like products' and resultantly, no discriminatory treatment can be meted out to the former without violating MFN and NT principles.

With respect to MFN, the term 'like product' appears in Article I:1 of GATT 1994, and, with respect to NT, it appears in Articles III:2 and III:4. It also appears in Articles II:2, VI:1, IX:1, XI:2(c), XIII:1, XVI:4 and XIX:1 of GATT 1994. The term is also a key component in the scheme of some other WTO Agreements such as the SCM Agreement. The interpretation of the term is not, however, identical for all the provisions or agreements where it is used. In *Japan – Alcoholic Beverages II*, the AB observed:

> There can be no one precise and absolute definition of what is 'like'. The concept of 'likeness' is a relative one that evokes the image of an accordion. The accordion of 'likeness' stretches and squeezes in different places as different provisions of the WTO Agreement are applied. The width of the accordion in any one of those places must be determined by the particular provision in which the term 'like' is encountered as well as by the context and the circumstances that prevail in any given case to which that provision may apply.
>
> (*Japan – Alcoholic Beverages II*, AB Report 1996: Para. 114)

Nevertheless, in *EC – Asbestos*, the AB has also crystallised the 'general criteria, or groupings of potentially shared characteristics', which 'provide a framework for analysing the "likeness" of particular products on a case-by-case basis' (*EC – Asbestos*, AB Report 2001: Para. 102). These four criteria for determining 'likeness' of products are (a) the properties, nature and quality of the products; (b) the end-uses of the products; (c) consumers' tastes and habits and (d) the tariff classification of the product. The AB noted that these four criteria:

> comprise four categories of 'characteristics' that the products involved might share: (i) the physical properties of the products; (ii) the extent to which the products are capable of

> serving the same or similar end-uses; (iii) the extent to which consumers perceive and treat the products as alternative means of performing particular functions in order to satisfy a particular want or demand; and (iv) the international classification of the products for tariff purposes.
>
> (*EC – Asbestos*, AB Report 2001: Para. 101)

It further observed that Panels must examine *each* of the four criteria and, then, weigh all of that evidence, along with any other relevant evidence, in making an overall determination of whether the products at issue could be characterised as 'like' (*EC – Asbestos*, AB Report 2001: Para. 109).

When these criteria are applied to an analysis of whether products manufactured with violations of labour standards and those without are 'like products', it is clear that they are. Thus, when comparing shoes manufactured in sweatshops to those manufactured in countries where labour standards are complied with, the physical properties of the shoes as reflected in the property, nature and quality of the two sets of shoes may be the same. Similarly, the extent to which the shoes are capable of serving the same or similar end-uses is the same. The international classification of the products for tariff purposes is also the same. Thus, three of the four criteria mentioned earlier are not fulfilled in the analysis of likeness. This suggests that the overall determination which Panels must make after weighing in all the evidence will typically tilt to a finding of the shoes being like. The only criteria where there might be some room for debate is the criteria related to consumers' tastes and habits. As the AB has explained, this includes an analysis of the extent to which consumers perceive and treat the shoes as alternative means of performing particular functions in order to satisfy a particular want or demand. It might be argued that consumers in a particular importing country might disdain shoes manufactured with labour violations and might overwhelmingly prefer those manufactured without. Based on these specific tastes and habits, it might be argued that the two sets of shoes are not 'like products'. However, there are several problems with reaching such a conclusion. First, the argument based on consumers' tastes and habits assumes the presence of widespread consumer awareness in the importing country, which can only come from concerted efforts to gain or provide such awareness. Proving that such consumer awareness exists in a widespread manner with relation to specific labour violations in the manufacture of a specific product from a specific country may be extremely difficult. Second, even if consumer awareness exists, the supposition that consumers may have an aversion to specific products manufactured in a specific country with violations of specific labour standards can only stand scrutiny if the tastes and habits are based on full and accurate information about these circumstances in the exporting country. A conclusion on what the tastes and habits of consumers are in a particular case need to be grounded on specific facts and cannot be based on vacuum. Therefore, if the consumers' aversion to specific products manufactured with violations of labour standards is to be considered as a key determinant of likeness, it obviously cannot be based on ill-informed or even contentious facts. Proving the availability, accuracy and adequacy of such facts will be very difficult to accomplish. Third, as Trebilcock and Howse have acknowledged, consumers, even if fully informed about conditions under which imports are being produced and violations of CLS that particular modes of production may entail, in fact, do not care enough about the intrinsic values reflected in these CLS 'to put their money where their mouth is' (Trebilcock and Howse 2005: 276). Indeed, for most consumers, price and quality (what some may call as 'value for money') is typically what determines whether they purchase a product or not. *EC – Seal Products* provides some sort of a validation to these arguments presented earlier. In that case, the question arose before the Panel whether the type or purpose of the seal hunt affects in any way the 'likeness' of the final products. It held that it did not so affect the products' physical characteristics, end-use or tariff classification. As regards the criterion of consumers' tastes and habits, the following is what the Panel observed:

> The complainants presented evidence to demonstrate that, prior to the EU Seal Regime, consumers did not make any distinction between seal products based on the type or purpose of the hunt. This evidence consists of statements by manufacturers and producers of seal products who maintain that the quality of the product, rather than the type or purpose of the hunt, was the main factor for consumers' choice. We note that the European Union has not contested this evidence.
>
> (*EC – Seal Products*, Panel Report 2013: Para. 7.139)

Thus, even when the AB held that EU citizens in general considered seal-welfare as part of public morals, the consumers of those products did not actually make a distinction between seal products based on the type or purpose of the hunt. Instead they chose seal products based on their quality.

A final point related to an analysis of consumers' tastes and habits is determining who the consumers under consideration are. This will, of course, depend on the specific case at hand. With specific reference to Article III:4 of GATT, the AB has held that 'a determination of "likeness" under Article III:4 is, fundamentally, a determination about the nature and extent of a competitive relationship between and among products' (*EC – Asbestos*, AB Report 2001: Para. 99; *Philippines – Distilled Spirits*, AB Report 2011: 119–20). Thus, the issue is which group of consumers ought to be taken into account in order to determine the tastes and habits with reference to competition and substitutability between products. In *EC – Asbestos*, the question was whether chrysotile asbestos fibres, import of which was banned by EC, and PCG (PVA, cellulose and glass) fibres were 'like products'. In determining the criterion of consumers' tastes and habits, the AB observed that the 'consumer of the fibres is a *manufacturer* who incorporates the fibres into another product, such as cement-based products or brake linings' and that the tastes and habits of the manufacturer; that is the 'manufacturers' decisions in the marketplace' may be influenced by the preferences of the ultimate consumer of the products (*EC – Asbestos*, AB Report 2001: Para. 122). The manufacturers, effectively the importers of the fibres, were deemed to be the key consumer group whose tastes and habits were considered by the AB to be important to the analysis. What this demonstrates is that, when it comes to imported products which are then used for manufacturing something else in the importing country, the manufacturers in the latter are considered as the relevant group of consumers. For instance, in *EC – Seal Products*, as stated earlier, in determining consumer tastes and habits, the evidence which the Panel took into account consisted of statements by manufacturers and producers of seal products. In other cases, however, where the imported products are end-use products, the end-users of the products have been considered as the consumers whose tastes and habits must be taken into consideration. For instance, in *Korea – Alcoholic Beverages* (Panel Report 1999), consumers of Soju and Whiskey were compared to determine whether they were like; in *Thailand – Cigarettes (Philippines)* (Panel Report 2010), consumers of imported and domestic cigarettes were compared; in *Philippines – Distilled Spirits* (Panel Report 2011), consumers of liquor made from sugar cane and those without were compared; and in *US – Clove Cigarettes* (Panel Report 2011), smokers of clove cigarettes and menthol cigarettes were compared. There is some dispute on whether the Panels and AB have in cases decided by them correctly taken into account both marginal consumers and captive consumers within the relevant consumer groups

(Iacovides 2014). In principle, however, the AB has taken a position that tastes and habits of '*all relevant* consumers of the product at issue' must be considered in the analysis (*US – Clove Cigarettes*, AB Report 2012: Para. 144). The important point from this discussion is that the relevance of all those consumers whose tastes and habits need to be taken into account will vary depending on the end-use of the product and that, even within those 'relevant' consumer groups, a widespread aversion to a particular product manufactured with labour violations must be prevalent. This is indeed an extremely difficult proposition to prove. If the imported product constitutes raw material for some other product manufactured domestically in the importing country, then those domestic manufacturers may only consider the quality and price of the imported raw material as guiding factors for their choice. Even if the ultimate end-users' tastes and habits may not be ignored by the said manufacturer in determining the marketability of the end-product, as we have seen earlier, it may be extremely difficult to show that there is widespread aversion among end-users to purchase products manufactured with lower labour standards than in the importing country. Taken from any perspective, therefore, WTO rules and jurisprudence prohibit any distinction to be made between products manufactured with violations of labour standards and those without.

Extra-territorial measures under Article XX(b) of GATT

The other option which needs to be inquired into is whether the General Exception provisions allow such measures to be taken. Again, here, the answer is in the negative. It may be argued that violations of labour standards such as occupational health and safety may fall within the 'human health' exception under Article XX(b). However, WTO jurisprudence does not suggest that measures with extra-territorial effect can be justified under the provision. In other words, while 'inwardly measures' to protect human health in the importing country are justified under the provision, 'outwardly measures' to protect human health in the exporting country are not necessarily permitted. The unadopted *US – Tuna Dolphin* cases decided by GATT Panels remain till date the most explicit rejection of the extra-territorial application of Article XX exceptions. In *US – Tuna Dolphin I* (Panel Report 1991: Para. 5.27), the Panel held that the US was prohibited from adopting measures designed to enforce its environmental standards extra-territorially.[2] In *US – Tuna Dolphin II* (Panel Report 1994: Para. 5.27), the Panel held that such extra-territorial measures could not be applied if they intend to coerce policy changes in other States.[3]

This GATT-era jurisprudence relating to extra-territoriality has not changed under the WTO. The closest that the issue has come to being settled was in *US – Shrimp*, where the US had imposed trade restrictions on imports of shrimp from countries which did not require turtle extruding devices (TEDs). The AB held that the US measures fulfilled the requirements of Article XX(g) because the species of turtles in question were highly migratory and were known to occur in waters over which the US exercised jurisdiction (*US – Shrimp*, AB Report 1998: Para. 133).[4] Thus, because there was a territorial nexus between the turtles sought to be protected and the US, the trade measures were held to fulfil the requirements of Article XX(g). On the question of 'whether there is an implied jurisdictional limitation in Article XX(g), and, if so, the nature or extent of that limitation', the AB decided not to examine the question (*US – Shrimp*, AB Report 1998: Para. 133). Similarly, in *EC – Seal Products* (AB Report 2014: Para. 5.173), with reference to Article XX(a), the AB decided not to examine the issue of any implied jurisdictional limitation. As such, there is no jurisprudence which recognises the extra-territorial application of measures under Article XX. Specifically, in light of the vociferous opposition by D-LDCs, there is also no reason to believe that Article XX(b) may someday be interpreted by the Panels and AB to permit such extra-territorial measures. Indeed, the 1998 Singapore Ministerial Declaration can only be understood as a rejection of such an interpretation of Article XX, because the contrary would mean that DCs can adopt trade measures conditioned on labour standards in D-LDCs. It may only be helpful to note the spirit of Article IX:2 of the Marrakesh Agreement (1994), which gives the Ministerial Council the exclusive authority to adopt interpretations of covered agreements.

Labour standards as 'public morals' under Article XX(a) of GATT

Some scholars have also argued that if 'outwardly' trade measures for protecting labour rights elsewhere are not permitted under Article XX(b), 'inwardly' trade measures might be justified under Article XX(a) on the ground that such measures are necessary to protect public morals of citizens in the importing country (Howse 1999: 142–44; Trebilcock and Howse 2005: 289–90; Harrison 2007: 200–19). Trebilcock and Howse (2005: 290) have canvassed use of 'dynamic interpretation' to suggest that 'public morals' should be interpreted broadly by Panels by recognising that violations of labour standards by exporting countries can affect morals of public in the importing country. Harrison (2007: 200–19) has also taken a similar view. The use of dynamic or evolutionary or teleological interpretation has now become mainstream in the WTO dispute settlement proceedings, ever since the AB used post-GATT non-WTO law to give a modern interpretation to the terms 'exhaustible natural resources' in Article XX(g) in *US – Shrimp*. Thus, a good case can be made that the term 'public morals' in Article XX(a) cannot a priori exclude cases of violations of labour standards in the exporting country. Having said that, the actual successful use of Article XX(a) for justifying trade measures conditioned on labour violations is negligible. That is because, first, it will be impossible to demonstrate that trade measures on countries violating labour standards are 'necessary' to protect public morals and that other alternative measures are not available, as required by the provision. There are always other ways through which countries can advance such goals other than protectionist trade measures (Vasquez 2003). Second, in the unlikely event that such measures are deemed to be necessary to protect public morals, it will be impossible to apply the measure in a way which satisfies the requirements of the Chapeau unless such measures are applied on products from all countries where labour standards are violated, including domestic products from the importing country itself. Given that majority of the countries in the world do not have a clean chit with respect to observance of CLS, it is almost impossible not to violate the 'arbitrary or unjustifiable discrimination' or 'disguised restriction on international trade' criteria in the Chapeau without isolating oneself from participating in MTS (Ewing-Chow 2007: 166; Joseph 2011: 117).

The previous discussion demonstrates that WTO rules not only do not permit, but they prohibit any trade measures being imposed on products from countries which may have lax labour standards. It is precisely for this reason that calls for a 'social clause' to be introduced in WTO agreements have been put forth time and again by scholars (Lim 2001). This approach has been described as 'incorporation through legislation' (Thomas 2004: 374–90). The implication of such a clause would be that trade sanctions for countries violating labour standards would then be permissible under the WTO framework. However, there are very strong reasons that such a 'social clause' would not only be politically impossible but also counterproductive.

A potential 'social clause' and its problems

As noted earlier, attempts to allow trade sanctions at the WTO conditioned upon labour standards has been vehemently opposed by

D-LDCs. Given the 'single undertaking' nature of WTO negotiations, there is no possibility of a consensus being achieved among all members to amend the WTO Agreements and incorporate a 'social clause'. D-LDCs continue to harbour fears that such a potential 'social clause' will be used by DCs to impose trade sanctions for protectionist purposes. What is more, continuous lobbying by trade unions in richer countries for a 'social clause' permitting trade sanctions on D-LDCs have only exacerbated these fears over the years since the 1998 Singapore Ministerial Declaration. Importantly, the prime motivation for demands for such sanctions has not been a concern for labour rights of fellow workers in D-LDCs, but loss of jobs at home.

The most visible expression of this was a petition filed by the American Federation of Labor and Congress of Industrial Organizations (AFL-CIO) in March 2004 under Section 301 of the US Trade Act alleging that the 'brutal repression' by China of internationally recognised workers' rights constituted an 'unfair trade practice' (AFL-CIO 2004). The primary motivation for the petition was that such repression 'burdened or restricted US commerce' and not concern for the rights of Chinese workers (Alston 2004: 474). The petition alleged that the benefit accrued by China due to such lax labour standards, including lack of right to form independent unions, artificially low wages, unpaid overtime and unsafe working conditions, was directly responsible for reduction of 268,345 to 727,130 jobs in the US (AFL-CIO 2004). For this reason, among other reliefs prayed for, AFL-CIO asked that the USTR and the president 'impose commensurate trade sanctions' on China (AFL-CIO 2004).

This petition only validates the fear that a 'social clause' will be utilised by DCs for protecting their own constituencies by undoing the comparative advantage which D-LDCs enjoy and not for the welfare of workers elsewhere. The 'race to the bottom' argument indeed found a prominent mention in the petition when the AFL-CIO demanded a direction to the USTR 'to enter into no new WTO-related trade agreements, until the WTO requires each of its members to comply with the core labour rights of the ILO' and that 'labour rights must be enforced against all countries, not just China, to end the international race to the bottom' (AFL-CIO 2004: 6).

More recently, in the context of regional trade and investment agreements negotiated by the US, the AFL-CIO has insisted that the labour provisions must be 'fully and effectively enforceable – using trade sanctions if necessary – in a timely manner' (AFL-CIO 2013). It has also demanded that the rules of international trade and globalisation must also allow for mechanisms that level the playing field so that 'the choices by which nations organise their economies' cannot be used as weapons in an effort to achieve growth through a 'beggar thy neighbour' approach (AFL-CIO 2013; 2014).

Considering these protectionist intentions, it is simply a political impossibility for D-LDCs to agree to a 'social clause' (Kolben 2010: 469, 471). Apart from the aforesaid political conundrums, there is ample evidence that such a 'social clause' allowing imposition of trade sanctions would, in fact, be counterproductive. One end-of-the-spectrum argument is that any labour-related trade sanctions would themselves be a violation of the rights to property and contract and must therefore be avoided (McGee and Yoon 2009). But even empirically, several scholars have demonstrated that trade sanctions, while purporting to be aimed at human rights or labour rights protection, hardly ever have the desired effect (Hufbauer, Schott and Elliott 1990). To the contrary, they almost always hurt the very populations they seek to protect (Kryvoi 2008).

To put it in simple terms, if trade sanctions are imposed for products manufactured by violations of labour rights, the producers will lose their markets and the workers who are sought to be protected by the sanctions will, in fact, lose whatever livelihood they had. Panagariya (2001: 14) has illustrated this phenomenon by observing that if countries are imposed with trade sanctions for failing to meet child labour standards, the gains from trade will necessarily be reduced in that country, no improvement in labour standards will be achieved, and world welfare will also be necessarily reduced. Similarly, if child workers are simply shifted from producing exports into alternative activities, again world welfare will be reduced because there will be no net reduction in the aggregate volume of child labour while the wages received by the children in alternative employments will be lower or working conditions worse (Panagariya 2001: 14). Also, with respect to child labour, as Bhagwati (2002: 132) has pointed out, trade sanctions are not even a properly targeted policy because only 5% of the output of child labour in the world is exported.

Finally, the very assumption that trade sanctions will compel D-LDCs with weak labour standards to improve and enforce them is probably based on a simplistic understanding of ground realities in such countries. As has been rightly pointed out, 'The domestic labour governance deficit in most developing countries is not primarily one of *de jure* law' but is often related to 'a larger set of complex issues related to rule of law, lack of resources, the close economic and social ties between governments and employers, cultures of noncompliance, the technical capacity of labour inspectorates' as well as 'highly dysfunctional labour courts' (Kolben 2010: 482–84). Other relevant factors affecting enforcement of labour standards, such as unaffordability of social insurance schemes in the absence of international transfer of payments or the inflexibility of international immigration policies which inhibit labour flexibility, are related to international conditions rather than domestic ones (Charny 2001: 328). As such, in the face of these multidimensional complexities, merely assuming that a straitjacket sanctions model will undo all these impediments at once is misleading.

Other options

Given that both the 'social clause' and 'dynamic interpretation' of existing WTO provisions are not feasible options to address the trade and labour standards linkages, some scholars have proposed other mechanisms. Chartres and Mercurio (2012), for instance, have proposed the adoption of an Agreement on Trade-Related Aspects of Labour (TRILS), on similar lines as the TRIPS Agreement. However, despite the sophistication of their proposal, they themselves acknowledge that in view of the political opposition by D-LDCs to any linkages within the WTO, such an Agreement is a non-starter (Chartres and Mercurio 2012: 723).

Trebilcock and Howse (2005: 285) have rooted for some form of horizontal coordination with specialised international agencies with expertise and legitimacy in the labour standards or human rights fields. Their suggestion would entail that the ILO will make determinations of systematic and persistent violations of labour norms, and in the context of Article XX, also whether the 'necessity' test is fulfilled (Trebilcock and Howse 2005: 285). The WTO panel should then 'accept these agencies' determination as presumptively dispositive of the referenced issues' (Trebilcock and Howse 2005: 285). Of course, while this suggestion is interesting, such a radical procedural and substantive shift will have to be authorised within the DSU. That, as we have seen earlier, is a political impossibility.

Also, as Guzman (2003: 888) has pointed out, the issue of international labour standards fundamentally requires a political solution and not a judicial one. But while acknowledging that the judicial path suggested by scholars like Trebilcock and Howse is not a viable option, he proposes an equally unviable political solution. In his vision, an independent trade and labour department should be created within the WTO (Guzman 2003: 888–89). This department would be staffed by specialists in labour issues and would hold periodic negotiations leading to binding obligations. Periodic 'mega-rounds' would be held in which labour and other trade negotiations occur simultaneously to allow for a political solution to the issue (Guzman 2003: 900–1). Obviously, this proposal is also a non-starter because of the opposition by D-LDCs. It was precisely such attempts that were rejected in the Seattle Ministerial Conference.

Barry and Reddy (2008) have written an entire book in an attempt to establish a unique institutional mechanism for linking international trade and labour standards. In this, they have proposed the creation of an 'Agency for Trade and Labor Standards' (ATLAS) which would be jointly governed by the ILO and WTO (Barry and Reddy 2008: 81). Such an agency would not only have developmental functions, in that, it will assist countries in developing and implementing policies for promoting labour standards, but would also have adjudicative functions. In the former case, a Peer and Partner Review Committees (PPRCs) would be created to make an assessment of the progress made by a country with respect to labour standards (Barry and Reddy 2008: 83). This process may include both country reports and on-site monitoring by the PPRC. The PPRCs would then make recommendations for actions that the reviewed country should take to improve its compliance with ATLAS requirements. Based on these recommendations, countries may propose a time-bound plan of action. The PPRC may provide its observations and comments on the proposal. A burden-sharing fund will be created which the PPRC can utilise for financing the implementation of the proposal by the country (Barry and Reddy 2008: 83). In the case of the adjudicative role, an Advocate's office is proposed who can investigate cases of potentially egregious instances of indifference to agreed labour standards' and can set in motion complaints through an Adjudicative Tribunal, which would then make findings of violations and determine what steps a country must take to remedy them (Barry and Reddy 2008: 84). The Tribunal could recommend initially technical and/or financial assistance for the country in question, which would be released from the burden-sharing fund. The Tribunal would ultimately also have the power to authorise trade sanctions on recalcitrant States (Barry and Reddy 2008: 84). Participation of countries is initially voluntary in this scheme of things (Barry and Reddy 2008: 84–85).

The obvious problem is that this proposal is also a non-starter, since it will need amendments to the WTO Agreements to permit trade sanctions, which as we have seen D-LDCs are opposed to. Second, the idea of a burden-sharing fund would also probably be a political non-starter, given that DCs would have to primarily fund it, and there is no reason to believe that they would accept this. Third, apart from the impossibility to adopt a sanctions model even as a last resort, 'it is not entirely clear how the functions of ATLAS are materially different than those of the ILO's supervisory mechanisms, especially since most of the ILO's activities are related to reporting and commenting' (Kolben 2010: 487). Finally, the proposal would also mean that several of the core functions of the ILO would now partly be relegated outside the organisation and would require massive political will to remodel the ILO structures also, conjointly with the WTO structures. As we know the political will to do this is scarce.

Another option which has been suggested as an alternative is through PTAs. Indeed, an increasing trend has been to incorporate 'social clauses' or 'labour clauses' in PTAs (Ebert and Posthuma 2011), and it has been suggested that if the multilateral forum – the WTO – is not an option, then such non-WTO Agreements are the appropriate place to get what the DCs want. Since this book is restricted to an analysis of MTS, it is not possible to do justice to a discussion on the various models adopted by different PTAs and their successes and failures; however, it would suffice to point out that D-LDCs and their think-tanks are not necessarily delighted by this development (Anuradha and Dutta 2012). The same arguments for opposing 'social clauses' in WTO Agreements apply also to PTAs. Additionally, other non-institutional means such as social labelling, corporate social responsibility as well as increased role for civil society organisations have been proposed as viable alternatives. The main limitation of these mechanisms, however, is that they do not have any institutional foundation and are pretty much dependent on consumer, corporate and civil society awareness and willingness (Basu 2001).

Addressing the permissive environment to abuse governance space: the WTO or the ILO?

This brings us back to the avenue most preferred by D-LDCs – the ILO. Indeed, it would only be logical that being the international nodal body created for codifying and enforcing labour standards worldwide, it should be the ILO which is primarily responsible for monitoring and enforcing the progressive improvement of labour standards in all countries.

It may be recalled that the violations of labour standards are not a direct result of member states complying with their WTO obligations. The WTO rules nowhere require States to be lax on labour standards for their own workers. In other words, WTO laws do not create a limitation on the governance space that States have in enhancing labour standards domestically. What they do, however, is create the permissive environment for States to abuse the governance space needed for improving labour standards, which they already have. This is precisely what makes this category so distinct from the first linkage-category. Violations of labour and associated rights, unlike other linkages, are *not* caused due to provisions of WTO Agreements. They are caused because States do not enforce their ILO obligations.

There is no need to amend GATT or GATS to make it illegal for States to violate labour rights. These obligations already exist under labour rights instruments and must be followed in any case. But, more importantly, when scholars talk about countering these violations of labour rights by inclusion of 'social clause' in WTO Agreements, they are really seeking creation of enforcement mechanisms for labour rights through the WTO, an organisation created for a completely different purpose, and not through the body that was created to deal with the issue of labour rights – the ILO. As such, WTO Agreements do not really need to be amended to hold States accountable for violation of labour rights. The focus should instead be on the ILO.

It is apparent that not much can be achieved by thrusting additional responsibility on the WTO to address this category of human rights abuses. WTO neither has the mandate, nor the resources or expertise to follow up on these issues. This job can be best done by the ILO itself and must not be transferred to the WTO. As Zagel puts it, 'If the human rights community wanted the enforcement of standards through trade restrictions, this would have been established through the existing human rights instruments, not in an entirely different organisation – whose task is to promote free trade' (Zagel 2005: 20).

The UN and its specialised agencies are charged with advancing human rights, and a case can be made that these institutions should be strengthened and given the resources they need to carry out their tasks successfully, so that the WTO does not have to deal with the wider agenda that it now seems to be acquiring (Sampson 2005: 11). It is indeed true that presently the ILO does not have the enforcement mechanisms necessary to effectively hold State actors to their obligations (International Federation for Human Rights 2005: 8–9). But that is precisely where the efforts must be directed. Enforcement of labour standards should be a result of strengthening the ILO and its mandate and not linking it to trade sanctions within the WTO.

The approach urged earlier is also necessary, because amending GATT Article XX to incorporate a new 'social clause' is an extremely complex process. Article X of the Marrakesh Agreement (1994) requires a consensus to be built within the Ministerial Conference, or in its absence, a two-thirds majority, for even tabling the amendment proposal for consideration of the members. It is highly unlikely that a proposal for amending Article XX or analogous WTO provisions to include a 'labour clause' would find a two-thirds majority at the WTO under the prevailing circumstances. Additionally, the 'single undertaking' nature of WTO negotiations mean that in reality not even a two-thirds majority would suffice because a consensus would be needed. It would be far more pragmatic to advocate for amending the Constitution of the ILO (1919) in accordance with Article 36 thereof, in order to put in place strong enforcement and supervisory mechanisms. Advocacy strategists must realise that it is a significantly easier process to amend the ILO Constitution than amending a WTO Agreement.

This does not mean that other international institutions should have no role whatsoever. As Stern and Terrell (2003) have pointed out, improving labour rights in poor countries will also require continuing with the many economic and social development efforts deployed by other international organisations such as the OECD, WB and other UN agencies. However, to try and enforce ILO standards through the WTO is to misunderstand how governance space in this linkage-category is impacted by the WTO regime. Fortunately, some impartial think-tanks in DCs as well have called for a delinking of trade and labour standards, abandoning trade sanctions and social clauses in trade agreements and focusing future efforts at the ILO (Carnegie Endowment for International Peace, and Trade Policy Group of the Inter-American Dialogue 2001).

Conclusions on labour standards and the permissive environment to abuse governance space

From the aforesaid discussion, it can be concluded that the linkage-issue of MTS-labour standards is vastly distinct from the types of linkage-issues which may fall under the first linkage-category. There is nothing in MTS, including in WTO laws, which limits the governance space needed by States to fulfil their own international and domestic labour rights obligations. This does not mean that labour standards and MTS are not related at all. Their relationship, however, is characterised by the permissive environment which MTS creates for States to abuse their governance space with respect to labour standards. Being lax on labour obligations in an attempt to benefit from cheap labour can be an expression of either unwillingness by some D-LDCs to use their existing governance space in order to benefit more from MTS or it can simply be an expression of lack of any other available choice. In either case, MTS creates the permissive environment for the governance space to be willingly or unwillingly abused by States.

Before concluding, it may be pertinent to note that this case study has exhaustively explored the MTS-labour linkage, primarily because this is the issue which covers most of the scope of the second linkage-category. This does not, however, mean that there may be no other issues which may fall within this category. While without an exhaustive case study it will be irresponsible to speculate which other linkage-issues might find a place here, we can safely assume that human rights issues which are contextually associated with labour standards, such as gender and child rights at the workplace, will be covered by this linkage-category.

With respect to the case study explored, it should be evident that if the adverse impact on human rights in this category is not a result of WTO laws limiting the governance space of States, then the solutions cannot be the same. It has already been indicated in this chapter that the ILO might be the better alternative to enforcing labour standards through the WTO. In Chapter 8 of this book, we shall revert back to this case study and evaluate whether this approach is appropriate through a human rights lens as well.

Notes

1 For a rebuttal of Alston's arguments, see Langille (2005).

2 The Panel rejected extra-territorial application of Article XX(b) because otherwise,

> each contracting party could unilaterally determine the life or health protection policies from which other contracting parties could not deviate without jeopardising their rights under the General Agreement. . . . The General Agreement would then no longer constitute a multilateral framework for trade among all contracting parties.

3 The Panel also did not rule on whether extra-territorial application of Article XX(b) was permitted, only holding that 'the policy to protect the life and health of dolphins in the eastern tropical Pacific Ocean, *which the United States pursued within its jurisdiction over its nationals and vessels*, fell within the range of policies covered by Article XX (b)' [emphasis added] (*US – Tuna Dolphin II*, Panel Report 1994: Para. 5.33).

4 The *US–Shrimp* case is sometimes misconstrued as a rejection of the *US–Tuna Dolphin I* principle which excludes extra-territorial application of Article XX. The *US–Shrimp* decision only rejected the finding in the

previous case that unilateral measures under Article XX were prohibited. In Para. 121, the AB held that

> it appears to us, however, that conditioning access to a Member's domestic market on whether exporting Members comply with, or adopt, a policy or policies unilaterally prescribed by the importing Member may, to some degree, be a common aspect of measures falling within the scope of one or another of the exceptions (a) to (j) of Article XX.

This does not, however, mean that it accepted an extra-territorial application of Article XX. A unilateral measure under Article XX can have both territorial and extra-territorial application. *US–Shrimp* only accepted the former, while expressing no opinion on the latter, as is clear from Para. 133.

7

WTO AND THE LIMITING ENVIRONMENT TO USE GOVERNANCE SPACE

Introduction to the linkage-category

The first two categories of linkages between WTO and human rights discussed in the preceding chapters focused first on how WTO rules limit the governance space which States need and second on how they create a permissive environment for States to abuse the governance space they have. In contrast to both, the third linkage-category discussed in this chapter focuses on unpacking the phenomenon whereby MTS inherently creates a limiting environment for D-LDCs to use the governance space they have to fulfil their human rights obligations. The tensions between MTS and human rights in this linkage-category arise are a result of the imbalance between the economic and social costs of undertaking commitments under WTO rules, on the one hand, and the capability of those States in benefitting from the resultant MTS, on the other hand. The main thrust of this linkage-category is that while not directly limiting the governance space of States, MTS, through its laws and policies, can, nevertheless, in some cases, create a limiting environment for States to use the governance space that they already have by tapping into their incapabilities to benefit from the system.

That MTS creates an inherent limiting environment for D-LDCs to compete with DCs is a direct result of equal rules being applied to unequal political and economic entities. We have already highlighted the theoretical aspects of this phenomenon in the first two chapters. However, an elaboration of the factual aspects is necessary here as well in order to fully comprehend the linkage-category.

This chapter is organised in the following manner. We will first discuss how MTS inherently creates the limiting environment for D-LDCs to use their governance space to fulfil their human rights obligations, in contrast to DCs. It will then look at how the WTO has responded to the need to address this inherent imbalance, focusing specifically on its Aid for Trade Initiative (hereinafter AfT), which is aimed at mitigating the incapacities of D-LDCs to equally benefit from MTS by providing them trade-related aid. The discussion on the case study of AfT which follows, seeks to situate it in the context of the political economy of WTO members, particularly the DCs, and engages with reasons that D-LDCs have increasingly become disillusioned with it. It also lays the platform for exploring in Chapter 8, the appropriate approach to resolving this linkage-issue, which may also be the most appropriate approach for addressing the entirety of issues within this linkage-category.

WTO and the limiting environment to use governance space

The Ricardian theory of free trade, modernised by Paul Samuelson (1938) early in the twentieth century, posits that free trade will lead to economic growth for countries that embrace it, which, in turn, will lead to increased welfare, aggregate wealth and reduction of poverty in such countries (Dollar 1992; Sachs and Warner 1995; Edwards 1998). The free trade agenda codified into binding agreements under the WTO is thus founded on the presupposition that free trade is the engine which leads to development and alleviation of poverty (Joseph 2011: 142). Indeed, a recent joint publication by the WTO Secretariat and WB assuredly entitled 'The Role of Trade in Ending Poverty' insists on the need to sustain efforts to keep global trade open and to do more to lower trade costs by further integrating markets in order to alleviate poverty (WTO and WB 2015). At the same time, it is clear that elimination of poverty and fulfilment by States of their human rights obligations are inextricably linked (UNHRC 2012b). This is especially true of obligations related to economic, social and cultural rights (UNHRC 2016). Today, the multidimensional links between poverty and human rights violations are too well established to necessitate an exhaustive analysis here (Pogge 2008). What is clear though is that poverty itself can be seen as a denial of human rights (UNDP 2003). More importantly from our perspective, poverty should not be seen as deprivation of income or wealth only, but as deprivation of capabilities as well (Sen 1999). And it is in this interface that the links between MTS, poverty and human rights assume significance. As will be argued later, MTS creates an inherently limiting environment for D-LDCs to use their governance space to benefit equally from it by tapping into their existing incapabilities and exacerbating them, which ultimately can result in their incapability to alleviate poverty and fulfil their human rights obligations.

As already discussed in Chapters 1 and 2, WTO's underlying economic logic of comparative advantage which prescribes that liberalisation of multilateral trade is beneficial to all participating States, is only partially true, in that, it benefits DCs much more than it benefits D-LDCs. This imbalance in the results of liberalisation is only a logical extension of the imbalance in the starting positions of these countries at the time they undertook their WTO commitments. As such, there are very good reasons to question the prescription that the template set out by the WTO Agreements is indeed the appropriate course of action for all States, irrespective of whether they are DCs or D-LDCs. This prescription is predicated upon an assumption that all States have equal capabilities to appropriately benefit from MTS and, obviously, that is not necessarily true. As Stiglitz and Charlton (2013: 367) have noted, symmetric agreements can have asymmetric effects because of the asymmetries of different countries.

However, apart from the fact that asymmetric starting points in terms of infrastructural and technological development have meant that DCs have benefitted through trade in high value-added goods far more than D-LDCs, several scholars have questioned whether free trade actually has led to economic growth at all and, thus, to alleviation of poverty. For instance, an influential research by Rodriguez and Rodrik (2000), cast serious doubts on empirical studies which had shown that free trade led to economic growth. In particular, they critiqued the methodological aspects of such studies, arguing that in many cases, the indicators of 'openness' used by those studies were poor measures of trade barriers or were highly correlated with other sources of bad economic performances, and, in other cases, the methods used to ascertain the link between trade policy and growth had serious shortcomings (Rodriguez and Rodrik 2000: 261–338). Their damning critique has indeed contributed to continuing lack of consensus among economists on the link between free trade and economic growth. Thus, while scholars such as Stiglitz and Charlton (2013) continue to question this link, some others such as Wacziarg and Welch (2008) provide updated evidence that liberalisation has on average led to some economic growth. The latter, however, while finding that there is an average increased effect of liberalisation on growth, investment and openness, have also acknowledged that these average findings mask differences in the individual responses of countries to trade liberalisation. For instance, they found that roughly half of the countries in their survey experienced zero or even negative changes in growth post-liberalisation.[1] Thus, at the very least, researchers agree that liberalisation has not led to economic growth for all and that there is vast heterogeneity among countries and their internal situations, pointing again to the fact that not everyone has the capabilities to benefit from MTS.

Additionally, there is ample evidence that even if free trade may have led to economic growth for some, it has not necessarily reduced poverty in the poorer countries and has led to increased income inequality (Winters, McCulloch and McKay 2004; Topalova 2010). For instance, the Global Wealth Report 2014, by Credit Suisse (2015) and endorsed by Oxfam (2015), points out that despite the financial crisis of 2008, income inequality is so stark today that only 1% of the global population holds as much wealth as the remaining 99%.

One of the reasons that several D-LDCs have not been able to benefit from trade liberalisation is that 'trade liberalisation increased risk, so much so that everyone could be worse off' and that 'these concerns were especially relevant in developing countries, where risk markets were imperfect' (Stiglitz and Charlton 2013: 364). But, more importantly, scholars have pointed out that making structural adjustments to liberalisation is an extremely costly affair, which D-LDCs are hard pressed to find revenue for. The theoretical loopholes in the neoclassical model of liberalisation have been exposed by Stiglitz and Charlton, pointing out that 'neoclassical theory (upon which most of the pro-liberalisation analyses were based) simply presumed that workers would move from inefficient protected sectors to efficient unprotected sectors, without cost' (Stiglitz and Charlton 2013: 364). This, they argue, was a fundamental flaw because in reality, at least for the poorer countries, they moved from inefficient protected sectors into unemployment. Unpacking the flawed assumptions in the neoclassical models, they point out that such models 'did not describe economies in which there were, even before liberalisation, high levels of unemployment' (Stiglitz and Charlton 2013: 364). As such, they argue that pre-existing unemployment increased and thereby put downward pressure on wages, output decreased, government revenue from tariffs decreased and, resultantly, governments were forced to cut back investments in education and infrastructure, further impairing development.

The evidence post-WTO also exposes the fact that adjusting to new commitments under MTS was very costly for D-LDCs. Apart from cuts in tariffs and thus loss of government revenue, the WTO agreements created several new undertakings in several new areas for D-LDCs, such as in sanitary and phyto-sanitary measures, intellectual property and customs valuation, which cost huge sums of money. Hungary, for instance, spent USD 40 million to upgrade the level of sanitation of its slaughterhouses in compliance with the SPS Agreement, and Mexico spent USD 30 million on upgrading its intellectual property laws in compliance with the TRIPS Agreement (Finger and Schuler 2000). Finger and Schuler (2000) estimated that the collective implementation costs of just three areas (customs valuation, TRIPS and SPS) would cost each developing country around USD 150 million. For LDCs, in particular, such sums of money were unimaginable. The authors noted that implementing these inappropriate commitments would cost up to a year's budget for eight of the 12 LDCs they examined. According to some estimates, it has been suggested that the 48 LDCs had actually lost a total of USD 600 million a year as a result of the Uruguay Round, which was around 5% of their gross domestic product (GDP) (Stiglitz and Charlton 2013: 362). In 1997, the UNDP estimated that Sub-Saharan Africa stood to lose about USD 1.2 billion till then as a result of the Uruguay Rounds (UNDP 1997b: 82).

In contrast, there was quickly a realisation that it was the DCs who benefitted from most market access gains in areas of their interest such as services, intellectual property and advanced manufacturing. The areas of interest for poorer countries, such as elimination of agricultural subsidies by DCs and streamlining of the textiles regime, particularly the phasing out of the trade-distorting multi-fibre agreement (MFA) which allowed bilateral MFA quotas, were not covered (Hallaert 2013: 655). This was despite an understanding that in return for giving the DCs a financial services agreement and an intellectual property rights agreement, D-LDCs would get what they wanted, that is a marked reduction in agricultural subsidies and an end to the MFA (Stiglitz and Charlton 2004). However, while D-LDCs did not end up getting what they wanted, DCs did. Even today, there is no end to agricultural subsidies in DCs, while the phasing out of MFA happened only in 2005, by which time several poorer countries had already lost out. What led D-LDCs to ever reach such a situation has been a subject of analysis among scholars as well. Cadot and de Melo (2014: 1) point out that WTO Agreements were rules derived from international conventions developed by industrial countries that were well beyond the needs of D-LDCs in their current stage of institutional development. As Cai (2008: 287) points out, until very recently, D-LDCs played little, or no, role in the shaping of MTS. Indeed, the role of LDCs particularly, in the negotiations increased only closer to the launch of the Doha Development Round in 2000.

Ironically, while the neoclassical theories of liberalisation seem to ignore the heterogeneity and specificities of poorer countries, the WTO's

Marrakesh Agreement gives adequate hints that developing countries, and particularly LDCs, were always going to find it difficult to adjust to the free trade regime and would need assistance from DCs to compete on reasonable terms. Thus, the Marrakesh Agreement explicitly recognises that 'there is need for positive efforts designed to ensure that developing countries, and especially the least developed among them, secure a share in the growth in international trade commensurate with the needs of their economic development' (Marrakesh Agreement 1994: Preamble, Para. 2). The initial response to this imbalance in starting points between DCs and D-LDCs was to grant special and differential treatment (hereafter, S&D treatment) to the latter. S&D Treatment included a range of options, the most prominent ones being longer time periods to D-LDCs for implementing Agreements and commitments and preferential treatment to increase their trading opportunities. A large part of S&D treatment focused on increasing market access for export of products from D-LDCs to DCs. These included preferential market access schemes such as the EU's 'Everything but Arms' initiative, the US 'African Growth Opportunity Act' and similar schemes in other OECD countries. These also included preferential market access provided to certain D-LDCs under the generalised system of preferences (GSPs). However, despite the easing of tariff barriers under these schemes in DCs for imports from D-LDCs, it soon became clear that this was not a sufficient condition for increasing exports from the latter. Indeed, LDCs which have for long been enjoying preferential market access for goods into most high-income markets, have constantly decreased their share in world exports over the last three and a half decades (Cali and te Velde 2011: 726). For instance, Sub-Saharan Africa's share of world exports decreased dramatically between 1980 and 2006, falling from 3.9% to 1.9%, while African LDCs did even worse, seeing their average share fall from 0.06% to 0.02% over the same period (Stiglitz and Charlton 2013: 365).

It was in this context that D-LDCs approached the Doha Round of negotiations with a lot of scepticism about MTS. With unsolicited but helpful support from civil society protestors, they had managed to block the first attempt to begin new round of negotiations in Seattle. They were growing extremely wary of undertaking additional market access commitments through a new round, especially when there was so much evidence that opening up trade, including benefitting from preferential market access, was not showing results in terms of development. They, therefore, insisted that the new round which began in Doha in 2001 must focus firmly on development interests of D-LDCs. The Ministerial Declaration adopted in November 2001 acknowledged that 'the majority of WTO Members are developing countries' and that the Ministers 'seek to place their needs and interests at the heart of the Work Programme adopted in the Declaration' (WTO 2001: Para. 2). The round even came to be labelled as the Doha Development Round.

However, it soon became clear that DCs wanted to turn the main agenda of the Doha round into focusing more on liberalisation in newer areas and implementation of previous ones. Burdened with the fears mentioned earlier, D-LDCs walked out of the meeting in Cancun in 2003. To them, additional liberalisation was not how their 'needs and interests' could be 'placed at the heart' of the Doha agenda. Their sentiments were echoed by the now much-cited observations of the UN secretary general at the time, Kofi Annan, who stated that:

> trade liberalisation is no panacea for developing countries. For many of them, it involves considerable adjustment and social costs. There is a need for synergy and proper sequencing – between the capacities of the developing countries, the level of obligations they are to take on, the cost of implementation, and the adequacy of financial and technical resources available to them.
>
> (Annan 2003: 3)

Come 2005, the Doha Development Round had reached an almost irreversible deadlock, as 'the early fascination with trade liberalisation for its own sake began to fade, particularly amongst many developing countries' (UNEP 2009: 88).

It was at this juncture that the discourse that S&D measures, including market access improvements or disciplines ensuring a more level playing field, were not sufficient to lift everyone onto the path of sustained trade growth, became prominent. It had become clear that unless the most important supply-side constraints of D-LDCs were addressed, preferential treatment or greater market access to their products was inconsequential (Marceau and Illy 2009: 483–84). These supply-side constraints importantly included, among other things, the inability to cope with the social and economic adjustment costs of commitments already incurred, as well as the inability to enhance production and exports in a competitive manner due to lack of necessary technologies, infrastructure, finances and skilled workforce (Ismail 2007: 90; Page 2007b). At the same time, incurring additional costs through implementing WTO Agreements and entering new ones, only contributed to perpetuating their status quo in terms of poverty.

It, therefore, gradually but clearly emerged that despite the promises of economic growth and development made by the proponents of liberalisation, neither had materialised for D-LDCs according to their expectations. There were severe constraints inherent in the WTO regime, resulting from their unequal capabilities to compete, which hindered their equal participation in MTS and the possibility of them benefitting therefrom. Thus, the overall impact was that the WTO rules and policies intrinsically created a seriously limiting environment for D-LDCs to use their governance space for ensuring growth and development. Unless, those inhibiting factors responsible for the creation of the limiting environment were addressed, it would be impossible for them to benefit from the WTO regime. The consequences of a continuation of the limiting environment were far too portentous than the benefits of participating in the regime.

Introduction to the case study and rationale for choosing it: the Aid for Trade initiative

The continued logjam at the WTO only served to create more doubts about the legitimacy of the organisation and of the free trade agenda. It became clear that the only way to get D-LDCs on board for further market access negotiations was through offering some sort of an aid scheme whereby their supply-side constraints, which inhibited any realistic participation in MTS, were addressed. Thus, the AfT initiative was born as a result of a wedlock between two circumstances feeding on each other – the interest of D-LDCs in making MTS cater to their needs and the interest of DCs to achieve further liberalisation. The former needed to receive aid to address their supply-side constraints, and the latter needed to give aid to get the negotiations running again (Wilkinson 2006). Thus, the dicta of 'trade not aid' and then later 'trade and aid' metamorphosed into 'aid for trade' (UNCTAD 2009: 5).

It is not surprising that several scholars point out that the AfT Initiative was, therefore, a carrot (Page 2006), or a buy-out (Hoekstra and Koopman 2012: 329), by DCs to induce D-LDCs to the negotiating table. Help was received on this front from the Bretton Woods Institutions in early 2005, when the Development Committee of the IMF and WB resolved to incorporate AfT on its agenda and to work with others to develop proposals to help D-LDCs adjust to and take advantage of the Doha Round (IMF and WB 2005). It was apparent that AfT Initiative was linked by the DCs since the outset to the intention of getting D-LDCs to agree to further market openings and concluding the Doha Round. This was made clear at the May 2005 meeting of the G8 Heads of States at Gleneagles, where they agreed to increase their help to D-LDCs to build the physical, human and institutional capacity to trade, including trade facilitation measures, and further committed as follows:

> We are committed to granting additional support for trade capacity building to assist LDCs, particularly in Africa, to take advantage of the new opportunities to trade which will result from a positive conclusion of the DDA. We call on the IFIs to submit proposals to the annual meetings for additional assistance to countries to develop their capacity to trade and ease adjustment in their economies.
>
> (G8 2005: Para. 22)

Later in December 2005, at the Hong Kong Ministerial Conference, the AfT Initiative was formally adopted at the WTO. The Ministerial Declaration included a separate section on AfT – the first time a reference to the initiative was made within the WTO. It welcomed the discussions within the Development Committee of the IMF and WB and stated that 'Aid for Trade should aim to help developing countries, particularly LDCs, to build the supply-side capacity and trade-related infrastructure that they need to assist them to implement and benefit from WTO Agreements and more broadly to expand their trade' (WTO 2005a: Para. 57). It further stated that AfT 'cannot be a substitute for the development benefits that will result from a successful conclusion to the DDA, particularly on market access'; however, 'it can be a valuable complement to the DDA' (WTO 2005a: Para. 57). Finally, the Declaration invited the Director-General to create a task force to provide recommendations by July 2006 on how to operationalise AfT.

The Task Force, thus created, submitted its recommendations in July 2006, and the same was adopted by the WTO. The report of the Task Force is instructive of the rationale, scope, objectives and guiding principles of the AfT Initiative. In terms of the rationale, the Task Force stated:

> Aid for Trade is about assisting developing countries to increase exports of goods and services, to integrate into the multilateral trading system, and to benefit from liberalised trade and increased market access. Effective Aid for Trade will enhance growth prospects and reduce poverty in developing countries, as well as complement multilateral trade reforms

> and distribute the global benefits more equitably across and within developing countries.
>
> (WTO 2006b: Para. B)

With respect to the scope of AfT, the report stated that it should be defined in a way that is both broad enough to reflect the diverse trade needs identified by countries and clear enough to establish a border between AfT and other development assistance of which it is a part. It further stated that projects and programmes should be considered as AfT 'if these activities have been identified as trade-related development priorities in the recipient country's national development strategies' (WTO 2006b: Para. D).

Six categories of AfT were identified as falling within the aforesaid scope, namely trade policy and regulations, trade development, trade-related infrastructure, building productive capacity, trade-related adjustment and a residual category which was termed as 'other trade-related needs' (WTO 2006b: Para. D).

Regarding financing AfT, the report made it clear that this needs to be additional to the general development aid being given to D-LDCs, predictable, sustainable and effective, since these characteristics of financing are 'fundamental for fulfilling the Aid-for-Trade mandate' (WTO 2006b: Para. C). Most importantly, the report also outlined the guiding principles on which AfT must be based. It stated that:

> Aid for Trade should be guided by the Paris Declaration on Aid Effectiveness, applicable to all parties involved (donors, agencies and beneficiaries), including key principles such as country ownership, mutual accountability, aligning aid to national development strategies, effective donor coordination, harmonisation of donor procedures, use of programme-based aid modalities, managing for result, transparency, and predictable and multi-year commitments, which should be built into all programming.
>
> (WTO 2006b: Para. F.2.)

Interestingly, the report directly linked AfT to sustainable development by observing that it 'should be rendered in a coherent manner taking full account, inter alia, . . . of the overall goal of sustainable development' (WTO 2006b: Para. F.2.).

The Task Force also stressed on the importance of monitoring and evaluation of AfT in 'building confidence that increased AfT will be delivered and effectively used' (WTO 2006b: Para. F.6.). It emphasised the need for concrete and visible results on the ground in order to 'provide strong incentives to both donors and recipients to advance the Aid-for-Trade agenda' (WTO 2006b: Para. F.6.). In terms of the mechanisms for monitoring and evaluation, the major elements of its recommendations included a global periodic review, self-reporting by recipient countries as well as donors and the inclusion of an assessment of AfT in the Trade Policy Reviews of WTO members.

Finally, the report recommended delinking the AfT Initiative from the Doha Round negotiations on market access. Specifically, it affirmed that AfT 'is a complement, not a substitute, for a successful Doha Round' and that 'a successful conclusion of the Round will increase the need for assistance to implement new agreements (e.g. Trade Facilitation), to ease adjustment costs, and to make use of new market access' (WTO 2006b: Para. G). It concluded by observing that AfT 'is important in its own right' and that it is 'a complement to the Doha Round, but it is not conditional upon its success' (WTO 2006b: Para. G). The formal separation of the AfT Initiative from the Doha Round negotiations was endorsed by the WTO members in the October 2006 General Council meeting, along with the recommendations of the Task Force.

In terms of the role of WTO in the AfT initiative, the Secretariat made it abundantly clear that 'there is no intention in the Secretariat – and no appetite among Members – to expand the WTO's mandate or to turn the organisation into a development agency' and, therefore, the WTO 'has a catalytic role to play – ensuring that relevant agencies and organisations understand the trade needs of WTO Members and encouraging them to work together more coherently and effectively to address these needs' (WTO 2007). The WTO's webpage on AfT describes its role as encouraging additional flows of AfT from bilateral, regional and multilateral donors to support requests for trade-related capacity building from beneficiary countries, supporting improved ways of monitoring and evaluating the initiative and encouraging mainstreaming of trade into national development strategies by partner countries (WTO 2016b).

Thus, the WTO looks at itself as a 'facilitator' of the AfT initiative and does that by working together with international and regional development banks and agencies and other multilateral and bilateral donors, including governments. Marceau and Illy (2009: 487) have described this role of the WTO as one of advocacy. This role has also been traced to the 'Coherence Mandate' given to the WTO by negotiators of the Uruguay Rounds whereby WTO was asked to promote 'coherence in global economic policy making' (WTO 2016a). Within the WTO, the Enhanced Integrated Framework is the main mechanism through which LDCs access AfT. Additionally, the Standards and Trade Development Facility maintains close contacts with the AfT initiative, by complementing 'this global scheme through projects and monitoring of aid flows at an operational, issue-specific level' (WTO 2016b). The OECD has taken the lead role in monitoring the global flows of AfT through its Creditor Reporting System (OECD 2016). Five Global Reviews have thus far been published by the WTO, references to some of which will be made in the analysis later.

From the governance space point of view, the AfT Initiative brings up two distinct questions for analysis. The first is founded on the position that AfT is indeed an important vehicle for undoing the 'limiting environment' inherent to the WTO system with respect to D-LDCs. In this case, the analysis of the effects of AfT on Governance Space depends entirely on how AfT is designed and implemented on the ground. As the experience with aid in general educates us, wrong design and implementation of aid can lead to adverse consequences for the recipient country; on many occasions worsening the situation more than before receiving aid. Therefore, the first question for analysis is whether the AfT initiative has worked since its formal inception in 2005 in achieving the results aimed for, and, resultantly, whether it has been successful in undoing the 'limiting environment' for D-LDCs. This question is important because adverse results would only mean that the limiting environment is still perpetuating or possibly getting worse.

The second question which the AfT Initiative brings up is founded on the position that AfT, by virtue of it being intended for fulfilling free trade commitments, can only perpetuate the neoclassical model of liberalisation and thus maintain the existing *status quo* in the imbalance between DCs and D-LDCs. By doing so, AfT merely reinforces the inherent 'limiting environment' created by the WTO system vis-à-vis D-LDCs. As such, these States will continue to be incapable of using their governance space, impacting their abilities to fulfil their human rights obligations. The ensuing discussion deals with each of these analytical questions.

Aid for Trade and its effectiveness

While the idea of a targeted AfT within the WTO discourse is formally and institutionally only 11 years old, grant of aid by development agencies for purposes which could be linked to trade is not necessarily a new phenomenon (Cai 2008: 286). Such development aid has for long been a subject of great debate among economists with respect to their effectiveness in achieving results. Critiques of aid have pointed out several flaws in the manner in which the aid industry functions, and there is no reason to consider them inapplicable to AfT. Dambisa Moyo, one of the fiercest critiques of aid, argues that such aid should better be called 'dead aid' since it has only killed the economies of the recipient African countries by creating aid dependency, and, far from alleviating poverty, it has made the situation worse (Moyo 2010: 65–67). William Easterly has observed that around USD 568 billion spent on aid in Africa over 40 years has not lifted average African incomes (Easterly 2005: 3); instead the number of poor people has increased (Easterly 2005; 2006). Contemporary research in this area has increasingly pointed towards aid ineffectiveness, although scholars also agree that it is possible that certain components of aid may be effective.[2]

Apart from aid dependency, scholars have pointed at other reasons that aid can have an adverse impact on the recipient country's economy. For instance, Cai (2008: 303) has pointed out that the sudden increase in the available pool of foreign currency due to aid inevitably leads to a decrease in price, which can lead to an upward pressure on the value of the domestic currency. Because the domestic currency valuation goes up, the country's exports are rendered more expensive and resultantly less competitive (Cai 2008: 303). For small- and medium-sized exporting firms, the change in exchange rate measured in terms of domestic currency can reduce the profits substantially. Similarly, economists like Page (2006) have pointed out that aid inflows can lead to the infamous 'Dutch Disease', whereby a recipient incurs serious social and economic adjustment costs due to temporary nature of the inflow of funds (Ebrahim-zadeh 2003). Unlike long-term aid inflow, development aid leads to quick changes in production patterns, and, once the aid stops, producers in recipient countries find it difficult to readjust production patterns (Cai 2008: 304). Despite these arguments, most critiques, including the ones mentioned earlier, also agree that under the right circumstances, targeted aid which is properly designed, implemented and monitored, can lead to improved welfare results.

With respect to AfT, the question, therefore, is whether such results can be observed since the initiative was launched in 2005. In general, the aid and growth literature has been plagued by econometric problems of proving causation (Rajan and Subramanian 2005). In case of AfT, the problem is compounded much more, because unlike generalised development aid which focuses on poverty reduction and alleviation directly, AfT seeks to spur economic development through free trade, which in turn is expected to alleviate poverty (Suwa-Eisenmann and Verdier 2007). Thus, proving causation in case of AfT involves complex variables making it extremely difficult to evaluate (Cadot *et al.* 2011: 29; Cadot and Newfarmer 2011). Also, the key problem in evaluating the AfT Initiative is that 'it is difficult to ascertain the counterfactual, i.e. what would have happened in its absence?' (Stiglitz and Charlton 2013: 370). These econometric difficulties directly explain why the empirical research by economists on the effectiveness of AfT is inconclusive and indeed many times based on hypothesis rather than facts and figures.

Several factors feed into the difficulties in evaluating the impacts of AfT on the ground, thereby raising doubts about the veracity of claims of success. Both at the aggregate level and at the project level, without evidence of additionality and a clear distinction between projects which would have occurred anyway under development programmes, it is almost impossible to assess whether it is the specific AfT initiative that has delivered incremental benefits to D-LDCs (Stiglitz and Charlton 2013: 370). As noted earlier, the Task Force as well as the Hong Kong Ministerial Declaration clearly indicated that AfT must be additional to existing Official Development Assistance (ODA). The case for additionality includes compensation for the costs of undertaking both current and future WTO commitments and the accompanying inevitable preference erosions (Wijayasiri and Samad 2007). However, the only thing we know is that AfT today constitutes over 30% of ODA (OECD and WTO 2013: 374, table A.15). Despite that, there are serious doubts whether AfT has been additional or 'merely a reallocation rather than an increase in assistance' and 'a relabelling rather than a fundamental reform of the global trade and development framework' (Stiglitz and Charlton 2013: 359). The underlying reasons for this being highly possible is 'because aid is never an obligation on the donor and because generosity can tend to be fungible' and as such 'it is all too easy for a donor to move assistance from one area into another' (UNEP 2009: 91). The political economy of AfT also means that one of its major thrusts is on having to compete with other development aid (Hoekstra and Koopman 2012: 339). For AfT to work, however, it is clear that it must be additional to development assistance, come from additional sources and not compete with existing assistance expenditures in the environmental, trade or other related arenas. Yet, as has been rightly pointed out by Stiglitz and Charlton (2013: 371), since most countries have not reached their commitment of 0.7% of their respective GDPs in ODA, it is hard to see AfT as additional, and, in any case, it is certainly not additional to what they had previously promised to deliver. As a result, they observe that 'development assistance reclassified as AfT' obviously cannot fulfil the motive of compensating D-LDCs from the unfairness of the Uruguay Round and that it only further adds to the unfairness of MTS that assistance which they would have otherwise been receiving is now labelled AfT (Stiglitz and Charlton 2013: 371).

It may be recalled that the Task Force defined AfT in the widest terms permitting anything which a recipient country labelled as AfT to fall within that rubric. A broad definition served the purpose of appealing to a wide range of donors because it allowed them a wider choice between different sorts of projects and forms of aid. But the almost all-encompassing definition also meant that many non-trade motives could creep into AfT projects. For instance, Marceau and Illy (2009: 497) point out that a road project intended to open up a region inside a country for many purposes including social, political and cultural reasons, could easily be passed off as having trade-related benefits. Hallaert (2013: 659) suggests that these sort of overlapping motives resulting from a lack of clear demarcations and foci, resulted in inflating of the reported AfT flows but, on the ground, an infrastructure project is an infrastructure project and not an AfT project. The resulting confusion was the reason that several countries shown as recipients of AfT by donors were officially reported as having responded to a survey that they never received any AfT (OECD and WTO 2009: 39). Another important aspect highlighted by researchers is that the Task Force remained silent on what form of money should be provided, and this further gave leeway to donors to offer AfT in the traditional forms of development assistance such as grants or loans (Adhikari 2011: 3). The problem is only exacerbated because calls from some scholars (Zedillo *et al.* 2005: 5; Stiglitz and Charlton 2006: 22–24; Hoekman 2010: 18), developing countries (Luke, Monge-Roffarello and Varma 2009: 33), LDCs (Laird 2007: 15) and UN bodies such as UNCTAD (Laird 2007: 15) for a dedicated trust fund for AfT were rejected by the WB, IMF and DCs (Nielson 2006: 323).

Despite the broadness of the definition of AfT set out by the Task Force, it did catalogue six categories of measures which are covered by the term. In practice, however, aid flows are not categorised either by donors or recipients along those lines, making it even more difficult to agree on which measures ought to be assessed (Brown 2006: 246–49).

Further, there are no common yardsticks for evaluating AfT projects making it difficult to assess their impacts. Everyone uses different yardsticks in their self-reporting (Cadot and de Melo 2014: 3). While the Task Force exhibited reasonable clarity on the rationale behind monitoring and evaluation, it did not provide any robust methodological tool to evaluate the effectiveness of AfT (Adhikari 2011: 3). This has led to a free-for-all kind of environment for donors and recipients to use any methodologies they prefer to evaluate impacts. Cai points out that 'one of most striking themes to emerge from the OECD and donor self-assessment reports is that there is no agreement on what constitutes a "successful" technical assistance or trade-capacity building result' (Cai 2008: 310). In practice, most evaluation frameworks are weak and do not have defined baselines against which impacts can be assessed (Stiglitz and Charlton 2013: 371).

The result of all of this is that donors and recipients report differently in their self-evaluations. OECD-WTO reports have observed that D-LDCs do not recognise the AfT flows reported by donors (OECD and WTO 2009), and many expressed dissatisfaction with the results of AfT (OECD and WTO 2011: Chapters 2 and 4).

The growing discontent and suspicion among D-LDCs with respect to AfT meant that the WTO Secretariat as well as the OECD needed to show results to bring some faith back into the initiative. Thus, the initial focus on resource mobilisation quickly moved to a focus on demonstrating results even without scientific evaluation methodologies. This was attempted in the 2011 joint report of the OECD and WTO, where 270 case stories of success were published. None of these were based on a common monitoring framework, but only on what donors and recipients having an interest in demonstrating success stated in their self-evaluation reports. As is well known in the aid industry, all stakeholders – whether donors, recipients or the WTO – have an incentive to show success for the industry to keep running (Hallaert 2013: 660). Some scholars have, therefore, labelled this exercise as a 'beauty contest', where only success stories based on whimsical evaluation frameworks are demonstrated, while the myriads of failures are not put forth (Hallaert 2013: 660; Cadot and de Melo 2014: 3). Indeed, a meta-evaluation of AfT projects conducted for the OECD in 2010 illustrated that trade impact of operations was not the main focus of evaluators' work, were not even addressed in a number of cases and were generally extremely superficial (Delpeuch *et al.* 2010).

Recent evaluations of projects branded as AfT and conducted by the European Commission and the Department for International Development (DFID) have starkly demonstrated wholesome flaws in the design, implementation and evaluation of those projects. For instance, one review conducted by Turner and Rovamaa (2012) found that, among other things, there is very little publicly available information on whether AfT projects and programmes are impacting on poverty.

It also found that there is typically a gap between strategic ambitions and statements on poverty reduction and the actual project and programme design, implementation and M&E and that, by and large, causal linkages between what a project delivers and the impact on poverty is based on a series of assumptions and, in some cases, a leap of logic (Turner and Rovamaa 2012: 24). It also flagged a worrying trend that 'both DFID and the EC are moving away from using the term AfT, with DFID more inclined to refer to trade policy, facilitation, regional integration, infrastructure, etc. whilst the EC is reverting to terms such as trade-related assistance and private sector development' (Turner and Rovamaa 2012: 24). Among the key recommendations were calls for more rigorous impact assessments, greater accountability by donors in conducting and publishing robust evaluations, greater transparency by donors in monitoring information and data and better intervention logics behind their projects and programmes (Turner and Rovamaa 2012: 25).

A more recent report by the Independent Commission for Aid Impact (2013) on DFID's trade development work in Southern Africa is even more damning. One of the DFID projects reviewed in this report is a 5-year £100 million TradeMark Southern Africa (TMSA) which supported the establishment of a free trade area in Eastern and Southern Africa and also supported the removal of obstacles to the movement of goods across borders and the development of the North-South Corridor (the road link between Durban and Dar es Salaam). This project was terminated in March 2014, possibly because of the findings of this report. The report is replete with findings of flaws in the design, implementation, monitoring and evaluation of the projects and the funds, including that the targets only monitored activities, but not the impacts. But, worse, it found that TMSA misreported its performance and inflated figures, and DFID did not provide effective oversight of the detail. For instance, the report states that the 'TMSA's summary management report . . . claims that 83% of targets have been met whereas, in fact, we found this figure to be only 21% in its detailed project reports' (Independent Commission for Aid Impact 2013: 2). It further found that weak financial monitoring had led to wasteful spending that contributed little to overall goals and had resulted in an unauthorised grant agreement with and money disbursed to the Government of Zimbabwe. Finally, the report also exposed the lack of consultation by DFID or TMSA with representatives of intended beneficiaries or other stakeholders, 'even though there are well-organised, articulate and representative regional organisations in place' (Independent Commission for Aid Impact 2013: 35).

An important aspect of the AfT debate with respect to its effectiveness has been an assessment of which countries tend to be the bigger recipients of AfT and what motivations lead donors to choose some over the others. Adhikari (2011: 6) points out that although the donors' biases are difficult to fully uncover, an indication of this tendency can be seen from the way AfT resources are allocated to the major recipients of AfT. For instance, in independent validation of his insight done for this study, one can notice that four of the top five recipients of AfT disbursements, according to the 2013 AfT Report, were India, Vietnam, Indonesia and Morocco, which are all emerging markets as well as FDI destinations for DCs (OECD and WTO 2013: 363, Table A.5B). A perusal of the list of top 20 recipients of AfT by actual 'disbursements' in 2011 reveals some interesting statistics. The top 20 recipients, of which only seven are LDCs, constitute 46.2% of all AfT. The top 5 recipients alone constitute 22% of all AfT disbursements. The obvious implication is that, while even China finds a place in the list as the 12th-largest recipient of AfT, several D-LDCs which need AfT the most are not the beneficiaries. A comparison with the list of top 20 beneficiaries by 'commitments' (OECD and WTO 2013: 363, Table A.5A) also shows that there is a huge schism between what is committed under AfT and what is actually disbursed. For instance, the official 2013 report on AfT pompously claims in the Executive Summary that 'Aid-for-trade commitments reached USD 41.5 billion in 2011 up 57% over the 2002–05 baseline'. While the Executive Summary does acknowledge that this was a reduction from commitments in 2009, there is not even a whisper of the fact that actual disbursements only turned out to be USD 33.5 billion – almost a 20% drop (the figure of actual disbursements is only in the annexes). Individual country data also reveals a big gap between commitments and disbursements. For instance, commitments to Bangladesh, a LDC, came to about USD 1.9 billion in AfT, while only USD 479 million was actually disbursed. Similarly, while Haiti ranked eighth on the list of top 20 recipients by commitments which expected AfT of USD 779.3 million, it ended up with actual disbursements of only USD 332.6 million – less than 50% (OECD and WTO 2013: 366).

There have always been suspicions that donor interests – political, strategic and economic – are the major determinants of development aid allocations in general (Alesina and Dollar 2000), and scholars are increasingly pointing towards the same considerations in AfT allocations (International Lawyers and Economists Against Poverty 2007: 12). Any kind of aid, because it is non-binding and beyond the perimeters of an existing institutionally governed design, implementation and evaluation framework, creates an inherent power imbalance between donors and recipients. Donors exercise virtually complete discretion over all aspects of the AfT process, and, if aid is diminished or cut off, recipient has no enforcement mechanism to restore or guarantee the aid (Cai 2008: 306). It is, therefore, not surprising that in contemporary practice, donor interests primarily dictate the AfT process and not the recipient needs (Berthelemy 2006; Brazys 2009; Nunnenkamp and Ohler 2011; Fuchs, Nunnenkamp and Ohler 2015), making the political economy of the whole initiative arguably dubious (Sally 2009).

One of the most significant interests which donors have in choosing whom to grant aid, in which form, under which conditions and for which purpose is whether such aid will enhance donor exports. Almost all empirical studies conducted by economists on whether AfT enhances donor exports to recipients agree that it significantly does (Huhne, Meyer and Nunnenkamp 2013; Pettersson and Johansson 2013).[3] The tying of AfT to donor exports can be manifested in different ways. Sometimes, it can happen directly by requesting or indirectly by creating mechanisms, whereby recipients must spend aid for supplies or services only from the specific donors (Huhne, Meyer and Nunnenkamp 2013). Langan and Scott (2014: 155), for instance, reveal how the EU aid for building roads in Uganda, under the label of AfT, turned out merely a form of 'boomerang-aid' whereby a large chunk of the aid was spent on providing project related contracts to European firms.[4] As such, this direct and indirect tying of AfT to donor exports translates into not only enhancing exports of donors' firms by creating market in goods and services for them, but importantly also subsidising them. Indeed, doubts have been expressed whether such form of export subsidy through indirect tying of aid is legal under the SCM Agreement (Hagemeyer 2014).

Apart from tied aid, there is a good amount of research which shows that untied aid also can increase exports from the donor country to the recipient country due to the 'goodwill' phenomenon (Silva and Nelson 2012). This theory posits that due to 'habit-formation' or 'goodwill' effects of AfT in a recipient country, there may be a shift in its preferences in the following period, as a result of which, 'aid can then be seen as an instrument with the power to influence future consumption of the recipient in a direction that is beneficial to the donor' (Djajic, Lahiri and Raimondos-Moller 2004: 152).

While there is no doubt among scholars that donors' exports to recipients of AfT increase, there is no such consensus on what effect it has on recipients' exports (partly because of the attribution problem). While some are convinced that exports of recipients increase (Cali and te Velde 2011; Helble, Mann and Wilson 2012; Huhne, Meyer and Nunnenkamp 2013), others argue that such increase is not significant (Nowak-Lehmann *et al.* 2009; Pettersson and Johansson 2013), while still some others argue that AfT actually has a negative impact on recipient exports while increasing imports (including due to 'Dutch Disease' phenomenon) (Munemo 2011; Rajan and Subramanian 2011). But even if we accept that recipient exports also increase, how much is it relative to the increase in donor exports? A recent study on this issue by Huhne, Meyer and Nunnenkamp (2013) concludes that AfT increases recipient exports to donors as well as recipient imports from donors. They further suggest that, in quantitative terms, 'a doubling of total AfT would imply that recipient exports increase by about 5% and recipient imports increase by about 3%' (Huhne, Meyer and Nunnenkamp 2013: 1285). Based on this estimation, they conclude that it 'contradicts the sceptical view that donors grant AfT primarily to promote their own export interests'. However, assuming that their quantitative findings are correct, the conclusion appears to be specious, because it compares increase in respective donor and recipient exports in percentiles. Given that the sheer size and value of existing exports from donors is disproportionately higher as compared to imports from recipients, the actual value of the 3% increase for the donors is far higher than the 5% increase for recipients. Thus, the only conclusion which can be made is that the benefits of AfT to donors are significantly high enough for them to continue controlling the political economy of the initiative. As Hoekstra and Koopmann (2012: 340) put it, 'where AfT is needed, it might be unhelpful because necessary institutions to constrain self-interest (formal and informal rules) are lacking'.

Contemporary practice also creates a permissive environment for donor countries to pass off their own interests as those of the recipients. Thus, a road constructed from the port in an LDC to the interiors will definitely permit agricultural produce to reach the port and be exported. However, it also creates deep inroads into the domestic markets of the recipient for the donors' exporters. Thus, what is passed off as an AfT project in the interest of the recipient (cotton producers gaining access to ports) might actually be motivated by donors' export interests (Coca Cola gaining access to the interiors). Also, the form in which AfT is given demonstrates that donors' can benefit significantly at the expense of the recipients. Current practices of ODA allow concessional loans to form part of aid, as long as the package contains at least 25% grant component. Because AfT is currently being given by donors within the framework of ODA, loans can constitute a significant part of AfT. Indeed, the 2013 AfT Report confirms that about half of all ODA is given in the form of loans (OECD and WTO 2013: 76). It stands to logic that if one of the most important functions of AfT is to compensate for the costs of undertaking WTO commitments, loans will only add to the likelihood of many recipient countries augmenting their debts (Adhikari 2011: 7). This is despite the fact that D-LDCs, as well as the UNDP, have for long demanded that AfT should not be debt-creating or on a loan basis, but must be on a grant basis (Luke, Monge-Roffarello and Varma 2009: 32).

Aid for Trade and the reinforcement of capability imbalances between states

As the previous discussion demonstrates, if AfT has not been effective in addressing the main objectives of the initiative, the inherent 'limiting environment' to use governance space is not being undone under contemporary practices. But the impact of this is much more. Not only is the 'limiting environment' not addressed, it is possibly even reinforced more firmly. This is because the schism between the capabilities of DCs and D-LDCs continues to widen constantly instead of narrowing. The AfT initiative then acts as the perfectly camouflaged mechanism by which the current imbalances are reinforced and amplified. One of the ways in which the AfT initiative does so is by purposely focusing only on the domestic supply-side constraints and not the WTO rules themselves, as the main reason for D-LDCs not benefitting adequately from MTS. In other words, AfT Initiative places all its emphasis only on how the inherent limiting environment created by unfair WTO rules can be adapted to by D-LDCs, but it does not deal with the unfairness itself. The focus is on more liberalisation as part of the Doha Round. Once AfT legitimises the continuation of the free trade agenda and the post-Washington template for growth, it essentially impacts on the ability of States to use their governance space in the manner in which they deem necessary. AfT then can be seen merely as an instrument whereby the existing imbalanced *status quo* between the DCs and D-LDCs is perpetuated and constantly reinforced. This is precisely what many post-colonial legal scholars have called neo-colonialism (Gathii 2000a; Balakrishnan 2003; Anghie 2007; Alvarez 2009; Pahuja 2011).

Scholarship from the TWAIL can offer important perspectives on why AfT may be viewed as a tool which perpetuates and amplifies the already wide gulf between DCs and D-LDCs.[5] An essential aspect of TWAIL scholarship is a critique of the emergence and use of international laws for the purpose of recolonisation (Chimni 2006: 3). In this perspective, colonisation is not merely incidental to international law and used to achieve self-interested objectives, but more fundamentally, colonisation has been instrumental in the formation of an unequal international law (Anghie and Chimni 2003: 84). The international law, thus created, then plays a crucial role in legitimising and sustaining the unequal structures and processes that help maintain and exacerbate the divide between DCs and D-LDCs. As a result, International Law, with its binding structure, becomes the principal language in which domination is exercised over D-LDCs (Chimni 2006: 3).

TWAIL scholarship can be described as both reactive and proactive – the former referring to a reaction against international law as an imperial project and the latter referring to its emphasis on internal transformation of conditions in the Third World (Mutua 2000: 38). As a result of both aspects, TWAIL scholarship has evolved through different phases over time (Khosla 2007). Importantly, not all those who identify themselves as TWAILians agree with each other on every issue. Despite that malleability, TWAIL, which can at once be described as both a theory and a method (Okafor 2008), benefits from a common core. The lived history and continuing experience of colonialism and neo-colonialism for people in the Third World is central to how they understand and deconstruct international law. It is that lived experience which makes them 'acutely sensitive to power relations among states and to the ways in which any proposed international rule or institution will actually affect the distribution of power between states and peoples' (Anghie and Chimni 2003: 78). It is also the same lived experience which makes them critically view the Third World post-colonial State, with its rampant human rights abuses against its own people, as a creation of international law. As Gathii puts it, 'The rules of international law are not only Eurocentric, but they create a social and political entity: the post-colonial state . . . the rules are constitutive of this entity; and not only, or merely, a reflection of Eurocentricity' (Gathii 2000b: 266). But the critique of existing international law does not, under TWAIL, automatically lead to a dismissal of the potential opportunity presented by a reformed international legal order to contribute to a more just and equitable world. As Anghie and Chimni (2003: 79) explain, 'By evaluating positivist rules through the lens of the lived experience of Third World peoples, TWAIL scholars seek to transform international law from being a language of oppression to a language of emancipation – a body of rules and practices that reflect and embody the struggles and aspirations of Third World peoples and which, thereby, promotes truly global justice'.

TWAIL scholarship inherently frowns upon 'attempts to confer universality on norms and practices that are European in origin, thought, and experience' because otherwise, 'powerful economic and military interests are able to force their views on the rest of the world and freeze them as eternal, inflexible truths' (Mutua 2000: 38). It is in this backdrop that the AfT project can be critically analysed from a TWAIL perspective. WTO laws, with their standard normative template of open markets for all countries irrespective of their technological and infrastructural capabilities, create a binding international legal order whereby the template itself gets legal sanctity and justification, breach of which can be punished before the DSB. The 'normal order of things' thus created becomes representative of what is perceived as rational, objective and just. AfT helps solidify this new 'normal' by creating a structure where the unfair norms are no more questioned. They are rather internalised as the indisputable norms – the only correct manner – in which MTS ought to be developed. In this way, the already dominant DCs, through the mechanism of AfT, help maintain their domination over D-LDCs by offering aid as a buy-out for more liberalisation. Both the WTO and the OECD play a crucial role in institutionalising these dominant ideas and in helping align aid policies with those dominant ideas.[6] Chimni (2006: 16), in the context of the role which international institutions play in perpetuating the 'culture of international law', notes that the knowledge production and dissemination functions of these institutions are steered by 'the dominant coalition of social forces and States to legitimise their vision of world order'. The primary role assigned to the OECD under the AfT initiative, and the often questionable reports pronouncing success produced by it jointly with the WTO, can be viewed as a thriving example of the critique presented by Chimni previously.

Langan and Scott (2014) make similar arguments using a 'moral political economy' perspective. They explain that the 'moral political economy' theory examines 'how moral norms relating to the "rules" of economic life often contrast, in regressive fashion, with actual economic outcomes in relation to human well-being/ill-being' (Langan and Scott 2014: 145). They draw useful insight from the work of Andrew Sayer (2004; 2007), who argues that:

> economic activity presupposes the establishment of moral economic norms . . .; even where, as in the case of capitalist

> property rights and the capitalist labour-relation, they [economic relations] are products of unequal power, there are generally attempts to legitimise them as just and fair.
>
> (Sayer 2004: 5)

Applying this theoretical framework to an analysis of AfT, Langan and Scott observe that widespread acceptance of the AfT initiative has principally internalised and, thus, legitimised the post-Washington consensus that MTS in its current form is the best way for D-LDCs to address poverty reduction objectives. As such, AfT measures are 'utilised here as a discursive tool to interlock aid and trade policies and to establish common-sense imaginings of free trade agendas as morally just endeavours aimed at raised living standards and reduced poverty' (Langan and Scott 2014: 150).

The authors also do an excellent job in deconstructing how narratives of the moral justness of the current free trade agenda and its ability to address poverty alleviation are systematically constructed through promotion of the AfT mechanism. They provide many examples, but the one which makes it most apparent, is the following quote by Pascal Lamy:

> We need to listen to the development community and make the case why trade is important for economic growth. We can do a better job of explaining why Aid for Trade can support broader policy objectives like poverty alleviation, social welfare, food security, gender empowerment, climate change adaptation, energy generation and sustainable development . . . . [I]n making the case for Aid for Trade, we are really making the argument for the multilateral trading system. Aid for Trade is all about logging onto this world-wide trading system.
>
> (WTO 2011)

As the authors point out, 'Within such narratives, AfT measures once more reinforce post-Washington Consensus imaginings that free trade structures will work for "the poor"' (Langan and Scott 2014: 150). They further observe that because of this 'a broader moral economy is thereby reinforced, creating common-sense images of "poverty alleviation, social welfare, food security" – to name but a few – for both external (public) and internal (official) consumption' (Langan and Scott 2014: 150). This, they argue, 'internally cements officials' willingness to actively pursue free market reforms while externally insulating market-opening agendas from potential public criticism and protest' (Langan and Scott 2014: 151).

Conclusion on AfT and its effectiveness in addressing the 'limiting environment'

The previous discussion demonstrates that while AfT was initiated with the purpose of addressing the supply-side constraints of D-LDCs and, for compensating them for the costs of undertaking WTO commitments, it is quite clear that there are serious doubts about the effectiveness of contemporary AfT practices. To the contrary, there are enough reasons to believe that the principal beneficiaries of AfT happen to be donor countries. Additionally, far from addressing the inherent unfairness of WTO Agreements vis-à-vis D-LDCs, AfT only reinforces the neo-liberal agenda which prescribes free trade as the one-size-fits-all template for all States to prosper. If the recent empirical data on the status of trade of LDCs are any indication, it becomes clear that AfT which has been on the global agenda has not only not worked, but the continuation of the current agenda has only exacerbated the schism between DCs and LDCs. UNCTAD's 2014 LDC Report states that 'in 2013, the current account and merchandise trade of the LDCs as a group were weaker' and 'their current account deficit continued to rise, reaching a historic peak of $40 billion in 2013, and their merchandise trade deficit also widened, escalating by 29 per cent to $21.1 billion' (UNCTAD 2014: III). This only confirms the conclusion that AfT has not been successful in undoing the 'limiting environment' for D-LDCs to use their governance space. The inherent limitations brought about by the undertaking of WTO commitments still continue unabated and, indeed, continue to grow.

The case study of AfT is obviously not the only linkage-issue which may fall under the third linkage-category. Indeed, given that incapabilities of D-LDCs in comparison with DCs are multifaceted, there are many possible candidates, such as the S&D regime, which may be situated within this category. However, as with the previous two chapters, it will be irresponsible to jump to sweeping judgements on any linkage-issue without an exhaustive analysis such as the one presented for AfT in this chapter. Insofar as the case study of AfT is concerned, our conclusions also form the stepping stone for analysing the appropriate approach to finding solutions to issues within this category. The following chapter of this book brings together the discussion on all three linkage-categories and the respective case studies in Chapters 5, 6 and 7, and in the backdrop of the discussions on normative aspects of the linkages debate presented in Chapters 3 and 4, explores the way forward.

Notes

1 These observations are not made by Wacziarg and Welch but by Stiglitz and Charlton (2013: 363) on the basis of the data provided by the former in their article. These observations have been independently verified by me for their correctness.
2 For a meta-literature review on this aspect, see Doucouliagos and Paldam (2011).
3 For pre-AfT initiative studies, see Nilsson (1997) and Wagner (2003).
4 The authors note that the Kampala Northern Bypass Project, funded by AfT by the EU, was partially designed by French firm BCEOM, undertaken by Italian construction firm Salini Constructori Spat and ultimately reviewed by British company TRL.
5 For an exhaustive bibliography on TWAIL scholarship, see Gathii (2011). Also see generally Eslava and Pahuja (2012).
6 On the role of international institutions as tools of new-colonialism, see Rajagopal (2000).

8

THE WAY FORWARD

The right to development approach

The context for analysing approaches to solutions

The analyses carried out in the previous chapters of this book have brought up some important conclusions with respect to the linkages between MTS and human rights. We concluded that the adverse impacts which MTS has on human rights obligations of States cannot be resolved under the framework of normative hierarchy of human rights norms over trade norms. The proposition that human rights obligations of States trump WTO obligations by virtue of Article 103 of the UN Charter, as well as the principle of *jus cogens*, operate only in a limited set of circumstances, which in any case, are not very likely to occur. We also concluded that the appropriate framework for understanding and analysing the linkages between the two fields is through the governance space framework, which allows us to categorise the diverse range of linkage-issues into three linkage-categories. Within each linkage-category, we analysed one linkage-issue as a case study to demonstrate how MTS specifically interacts differently with the governance space of States thereby impacting their abilities to use that space to fulfil their human rights obligations.

The question that beckons us now is about the way forward in terms of addressing each of these linkage-categories in order to resolve the tensions. In Chapter 1, we argued that one of the gaps in existing studies on this topic is a systematic lens for analysing the linkages between MTS and human rights. We, therefore, developed the governance space framework which provides us the theoretical framework for deconstructing and making sense of the different linkages between the two fields. This framework, however, needs to be supplemented by an appropriate *approach* which will ensure that governance space of States is not used or abused in a manner which adversely impacts on their obligations to respect, protect and fulfil human rights. This is especially true since we have observed that the judicial mechanism of the WTO may not be the appropriate forum for resolving such conflicts in light of the limitations placed by WTO members on it. As such, the onus to adopt appropriate approaches to ensuring that impacts of MTS on governance space of States is not adverse lies upon States themselves, both individually and collectively at the WTO.

We have seen throughout the preceding chapters that, unfortunately, States tend to compartmentalise their legal commitments, on the one hand, as WTO members and, on the other, as States parties to human rights treaties under the UN. As Alston has noted in his capacity as the Special Rapporteur on Extreme Poverty and Human Rights, when human rights issues are raised at the WTO, the refrain by States is that they should be rather dealt with at the UNHRC (2015). The rhetorical and policy disconnect between these areas has led most States to disregard their binding human rights obligations while pursuing trade negotiations. The WTO position itself has for a long time been dominated by the 'watertight compartment's view' that the WTO is a trade organisation, not a human rights or even a development organisation (Howse 2004: Para. 20; Lang 2011: 133–34). WTO diplomats and judges have a long-standing preference for avoiding human rights discourse in WTO bodies (Petersmann 2008a: 180). Additionally, States themselves are reluctant to read their human rights obligations into WTO Agreements. It is clear that the adverse impacts of WTO obligations on the use or abuse of governance space of States are a direct result of States not taking into consideration human rights concerns at any stage of the WTO processes.

If, therefore, governance space issues are to be addressed and appropriate solutions found, it is vital that human rights considerations are made intrinsic to the WTO processes. This essentially means that States must take into consideration human rights concerns at all stages of the WTO processes, including pre-negotiation, negotiation and trade policy review. But, given the consistent stand by States and the WTO Secretariat, that WTO is not a human rights or development organisation and that its mandate is free trade, why would States agree to internalise human rights considerations in their WTO processes? In the teeth of the argument that human rights obligations are exogenous to WTO, it is incumbent that we do not provide only moral arguments justifying internalisation of human rights considerations in WTO processes, but also legal arguments. The attempt here is not to insist on the primacy of human rights obligations of States through any legal technique of interpretation. Rather, the legal arguments justifying internalisation of human rights considerations in WTO processes are presented here with the sole objective of ensuring that States do not end up making trade rules and policies which undermine their own human rights obligations.

This rationale can be found in the Preamble of the Marrakesh Agreement, which incorporates 'sustainable development' as one of the principal objectives of the WTO. Thus, WTO's mandate clearly is to frame trade policies and agreements in a manner which would achieve sustainable development. In other words, trade policies and agreements cannot be counterproductive to the very institutional objective of achieving sustainable development. The important point of departure here from current arguments at the WTO is, therefore, acknowledging the fact that free trade and economic growth are not ends in themselves, but are means to achieve sustainable development. And because sustainable development cannot take place if human rights are undermined, the argument is that it is necessary for all WTO processes to internalise human rights considerations.

Sustainable development as the institutional objective of the WTO

The relevant portion of the Preamble of the Marrakesh Agreement, reproduced in Chapter 1, states that 'the Parties to this Agreement . . ., *Recognising* that their relations in the field of trade and economic endeavour should be conducted . . . in accordance with the objective of sustainable development, . . . agree as follows' (Marrakesh Agreement 1994: Preamble, Para. 1).

Thus, when States decided to establish the WTO, it was with a clear understanding that their WTO commitments, which would capture the rules by which their 'relations in the field of trade and economic endeavour' would be conducted, had to be in accordance with the objective of sustainable development. Sustainable development is not merely an incidental objective of MTS; it is a core foundational objective. This is fortified by the third paragraph of the Preamble, which stipulates that States are agreeing to the establishment of WTO and its free trade rules, 'being desirous of contributing to *these objectives* by entering into reciprocal and mutually advantageous arrangements' (Marrakesh Agreement 1994: Preamble, Para. 3).

As such, the implication is that free trade by itself is not the end, but is a means to achieve an end – that end being sustainable development. The Doha Ministerial Declaration is an unequivocal interpretation of the Preamble by WTO members. Therein, members strongly reaffirmed their 'commitment to the objective of sustainable development, as stated in the Preamble to the Marrakesh Agreement' (WTO 2001: Para. 6). They further stated that they are 'convinced that the aims of upholding and safeguarding an open and non-discriminatory multilateral trading system, and acting for the protection of the environment and the promotion of sustainable development can and must be mutually supportive' (WTO 2001: Para. 6). In *US – Shrimp* (AB Report 1998: Para. 129), the AB also stated that the Preamble of the WTO Agreement explicitly acknowledges the objective of sustainable development and that this objective informs not only GATT 1994, but also the other covered agreements. In *China – Raw Materials*, the AB observed that the 'Preamble concludes with the resolution to develop an integrated, more viable and durable multilateral trading system' and that the WTO Agreement, as a whole, reflects 'the balance struck by WTO Members between trade and non-trade-related concerns' (AB Report 2012: Para. 306). As noted in Chapter 7, the AfT Task Force's report directly linked AfT to sustainable development by observing that AfT 'should be rendered in a coherent manner taking full account, inter alia, . . . of the overall goal of sustainable development' (WTO 2006b: Para. F.2). Thus, there is no doubt that WTO rules fostering free trade were intended to have entered into with the objective of sustainable development.[1] The natural corollary to this is that if WTO rules and policies end up militating against sustainable development, then the very institutional objective of the WTO is being undermined by States.

The concept of 'sustainable development' has gained massive policy significance in the last 30 years or so, ever since its famous articulation by the World Commission on Environment and Development, also known as the Brundtland Commission, in its 1987 report titled 'Our Common Future'. In this report, sustainable development was defined as 'development that meets the needs of the present without compromising the ability of future generations to meet their own needs' (World Commission on Environment and Development 1987: 43). It encompasses three general policy areas: social development, economic development and environmental protection (UNGA 1997a). The social development dimension of the concept obviously includes human rights, inasmuch as, it is impossible to have social development and in turn sustainable development if it is accompanied by undermining of human rights (UN Conference on Sustainable Development 2012: Para. 8). The focus on present and future generations involves both intra-generational and inter-generational equity, thereby essentially encompassing human rights within its fold (McGoldrick 1996; French 2001; Shelton 2007; Weiss 2010; Folkesson 2013). Indeed, the

Rio Declaration declared that 'human beings are at the centre of concerns for sustainable development. They are entitled to a healthy and productive life in harmony with nature' (UN Conference on Environment and Development 1992: Principle 1). In the Outcome Document of the 2012 UN Conference on Sustainable Development (Rio+20 Conference), world leaders reaffirmed the importance of UDHR, as well as other international instruments relating to human rights and international law and emphasised 'the responsibilities of all States, in conformity with the Charter of the United Nations, to respect, protect and promote human rights and fundamental freedoms for all' (UN Conference on Sustainable Development 2012: Para. 9). Finally, the 2030 Agenda for Sustainable Development encapsulating the post-2015 SDGs recognises the indispensability of human rights to the concept of sustainable development (UNGA 2015: Preamble and Para. 3, 8, 10, 19, 20, 29, 35, 67, 74).

Whether 'sustainable development' is a legally binding norm under international law has been a subject of debate among scholars (Cordonier Segger and Khalfan 2004; French 2005; Bugge and Voigt 2008; Schrijver 2008; Stephens 2012). In *Gabcikovo – Nagymaros Project* (1997: Para. 140), the ICJ referred to sustainable development as a 'concept' in its majority opinion. In his separate opinion in support of the majority, Justice Weeramantry, however, opined that sustainable development was more than a mere concept and that it was a 'principle with normative value' and an 'integral part of modern international law' (*Gabcikovo – Nagymaros Project*, Separate Opinion of Vice-President Weeramantry 1997: 88–89). In a later case, the ICJ did not go the same extent; however, it did elevate 'sustainable development' from being merely a concept to being an 'objective' under international law (*Pulp Mills on the River Uruguay* 2010: 75–77). For our purposes, whatever be its legal status under the general international law, it is immaterial to its specific status under WTO law inasmuch as it is explicitly recognised as the institutional objective of the WTO in its constituting document.

It needs to be further acknowledged, however, that debates do exist on the precise definition of 'sustainable development', although as mentioned earlier, the definition by Brundtland Commission is the most accepted one. Some scholars even argue that the concept is of an intrinsically evolutive nature and that 'rather than being a weakness, [this] represents the strength of the concept' because 'to be able to function, the contents of sustainable development must evolve, the specificities of each situation and each set of circumstances must be taken into account, and this inherent malleability is not an obstacle to sustainable development's legal classification' (Barrel 2012: 383). Solow has argued that the definition by the Brundtland Commission adopts a narrow focus on 'needs' and should instead be expanded to include 'standards of living' (Solow 1993). Sen argues that even this is inadequate and 'sustainable development' should rather focus on expansion of freedoms and capabilities (Sen 2009: 248–52). Today, it can safely be said that the 17 SDGs and their accompanying 169 targets as outlined in the 2030 Agenda represent a global consensus on what sustainable development entails and that human rights are definitely encompassed therein.

Evolution of the idea of development as a human right

In his rightly celebrated book *Development as Freedom* published in 1999, Amartya Sen challenged the predominant understanding of development existing in the field of economics at the time, which equated it with income, wealth or GDP per capita. He argued that the basic objective of development should be enhancing the lives we lead (our well-being) and the freedoms we enjoy, rather than just the maximisation of income or wealth (Sen 1999: 27). He pointed out that income or wealth is useful, but its usefulness lies only to the extent of the things that it allows us to do – the substantive freedoms it helps us to achieve (Sen 1999: 27). If income or wealth does not lead to enhancing our lives and freedoms, then it is pretty much useless. In his view, any adequate conception of development must not ignore economic growth, but must look beyond it. As such, he argued that enhancement of our freedoms is both the primary end and the principal means of development (Sen 1999: 45). He, therefore, posited that the appropriate factual base is one that focuses on substantive freedoms that people have reason to enjoy and not on income statistics, and this essentially means focusing on capability deprivation of people rather than income deprivation (Sen 1999: 32). A related but important insight provided by Sen was that when development is viewed as freedom, we must focus not only on the outcome achieved, but also on the process through which that outcome is achieved (Sen 1999: 30). In other words, it would be erroneous to claim that we are moving towards development if the outcome of a project or measure results in enhancement of certain freedoms, but in the process of achieving those outcomes, some other freedoms have been violated.

Sen's work has had a huge impact in the field of economics, with even the Bretton Woods organisations now adopting social indicators in their measurement of development. Coupled with studies on development produced by influential writers such as Arturo Escobar (1995) and Martha Nussbaum (2000) and the emergence of the twin concepts of human security and human development (UNDP 1994), a consensus gradually began to grow among economists and development institutions that the concept of development needed to include the human dimension as a central element.

More than a decade prior to Sen's thesis, however, the human rights field had already endorsed a human-centred approach to development when the UNGA adopted the Declaration on the Right to Development (DRTD) on 4 December 1986 (UNGA 1986). DRTD in its Preamble defined development as:

> a comprehensive economic, social, cultural and political process, which aims at the constant improvement of the well-being of the entire population and of all individuals on the basis of their active, free and meaningful participation in development and in the fair distribution of benefits resulting therefrom.
>
> (DRTD 1986: Preamble, Para. 2)

The focus on process and well-being of people in DRTD resonates loudly with the approach to development adopted by Sen, the economist. What, then, happened to the idea of RtD till Sen's work emerged in 1999? Why is it that the right was not operationalised thus far?

In order to understand the concept of RtD in its fullness, it is important to account for the historical context in which it emerged.[2] Unsurprisingly, this had a lot to do with the decolonisation process which was in full swing in the 1960s. Indeed, the first articulation of RtD as a concept is ascribed to the Senegalese foreign minister Doudou Thiam who made an impassioned speech at the opening of the 21st Session of the UNGA in 1966, lamenting the hangover of colonisation which D-LDCs had been left with (UNGA 1966).[3] The emergence of a number of newly independent countries in the 1960s and the 1970s had a bitter-sweet effect on them. The joy of escaping the claws of decolonisation was met with the equally grim realisation that these countries had been born into a global political and economic system which they had neither created, nor was in their interest (Chakravarthi 1990: 52). The then existing global order, including the financial and trading institutions, were created by the victors of WWII with the primary objective of reconstructing post-war Europe. Soon, the initial suspicion which had been generated by debt-creating prescriptions of the WB and IMF and the experience with untimely opening of markets under GATT 1947, led to disillusionment with the overall agenda of DCs and the economic and development organisations they controlled (Chakravarthi 1990: 51). This led to an initial push by D-LDCs to reform the WB, IMF and the GATT 1947, without much success. The only notable exception was the creation of UNCTAD as an organ of the UNGA, however, that was as far as the reformist phase could go. By the 1970s, the reformist phase characterised by feeble attempts to make minor changes to the international economic system had transformed into a restructuring phase characterised by attempts to modify the fundamentals of the entire economic system which perpetuated underdevelopment for D-LDCs (Chakravarthi 1990: 53).

In 1974, the UNGA which by then comprised D-LDCs in the majority, adopted the Declaration on the Establishment of a New International Economic Order (UNGA 1974a). Paragraph 1 thereof reflected the mood of D-LDCs at the time and is pertinent not only for its historical value but also because of its introspective value with respect to the situation existing even today. It stated:

> The developing countries, which constitute 70 per cent of the world's population, account for only 30 per cent of the worlds income. It has proved impossible to achieve an even and balanced development of the international community under the existing international economic order. The gap between the developed and the developing countries continues to widen in a system which was established at a time when most of the developing countries did not even exist as independent States and which perpetuates inequality.
>
> (UNGA 1974a: Para. 1)

The Declaration stressed that 'international co-operation for development is the shared goal and common duty of all countries' (UNGA 1974a: Para. 3) and emphasised that 'one of the main aims of the reformed international monetary system shall be the promotion of the development of the developing countries and the adequate flow of real resources to them' (UNGA 1974a: Para. 4). What is clear from the previous passage is that D-LDCs were convinced by then that the so-called New World Order established in the aftermath of WWII was counterproductive to their interests and catered only to the interests of DCs. This Declaration was soon followed a few months later by the adoption of the Charter of Rights and Duties of States (UNGA 1974b), which also attempted a shift towards understanding international cooperation for development as a common 'duty' of all countries. Despite the obvious discomfiture of DCs with the language of rights and duties introduced in the discourse on development, in 1977, the UNCHR for the first time recognised RtD as a human right and recommended to the ECOSOC that it should request the UNSG to undertake a study of the subject (UNCHR 1977). This led to the creation in 1981 of a Working Group of Government Experts on the Right to Development. However, before the issue could get swallowed by the political marsh, the African block created a *fait accompli* by incorporating RtD as a binding obligation on States in the African Charter on Human and People's Rights (1981: Article 22). With one major continent of the world having recognised RtD as an enforceable human right and having recognised a legal obligation on States to ensure it, the rest of the world could no more ignore the topic. This led, in 1986, to the adoption of the DRTD with 146 countries voting in favour, 8 countries abstaining and only the US voting in opposition. Countries which abstained were Denmark, Finland, Germany, Iceland, Israel, Japan, Sweden and the UK (OHCHR 2013: 500). Clearly, the DCs were not very enthused with the emergence of RtD.

A perusal of some of the provisions of DRTD makes it evident why the DCs were reluctant to be on board. Article 3(1) states that 'States have the primary responsibility for the creation of national and international conditions favourable to the realisation of the right to development'. Recognising responsibility of States to create international conditions favourable to RtD meant recognising responsibility for changing the lopsided rules of international finance and trade and abandoning the asymmetric advantages DCs enjoyed. Article 3(3) was another provision which was problematic. It recognised that 'States have the duty to co-operate with each other in ensuring development and eliminating obstacles to development'. Similarly, Article 4(1) stated that 'States have the duty to take steps, individually and collectively, to formulate international development policies with a view to facilitating the full realisation of the right to development'. The language of duties within the development context was clearly not comfortable to the economic and political interests of DCs.

The sheer open-endedness of the definition of development enshrined in the Preamble of DRTD, and the controversial 'new' duties recognised therein on States, also led to an inevitable polarisation of opinions among scholars. One of the early critiques of DRTD, Jack Donelly, for instance, concluded that RtD was a 'delusion of well-meaning optimists' because the definition of development was vague, the subjects of RtD were unclear and it relied on notions of solidarity and community instead of concrete notions of innate personal dignity (Donnelly 1985: 478, 492). He also argued that DRTD shifts the focus away from States themselves as the biggest perpetrators of human rights violations, to external forces which also contribute to human rights violations (Donnelly 1985: 499).[4] Charlesworth (1992: 196) critiqued DRTD arguing that despite the stated holistic definition of development in DRTD, it was still mostly economic at its heart. Ghai (1994: 10) argued that RtD takes attention away from specific rights, such as speech, assembly and social welfare, to an 'ambiguous portmanteau right to development'.

On the other side of the debate, there were a host of optimistic voices expressing support for DRTD and expressing ways to operationalise the same. In stark contrast with Donnelly, Philip Alston, one of the earliest western supporters of RtD argued that the open-endedness of the definition of development in DRTD was its biggest strength and that it should be welcomed because it allows the concept to evolve as time progresses and be interpreted and applied with flexibility as needed (Alston 1985; 1991: 218). He also did not find that DRTD was vague in terms of its subjects or duties on States. Scholars from D-LDCs and those inclined towards NIEO understandably came out quite strongly in support of RtD, as was reflected vividly in a number of essays published in a voluminous book in 1992, pursuant to a seminar held in Kolkata by the 'Committee on the Legal Aspects of a New International Economic Order' of the International Law Association (Chowdhury, Denters and de Waart 1992). Importantly, for many scholars like Bedjaoui, there was nothing new or astonishing about the concept of RtD, and that it was 'an "inherent" and "built-in" right forming an inseparable part of the right to self-determination' (Bedjaoui 1991: 1184).

While the academic world was feverishly debating the Declaration and its import well into the 1990s, the international economic institutions had maintained a stoic silence on RtD. At the UN, however, the term continued to pop up seasonally at conferences and resolutions of the erstwhile UNCHR. For instance, the 1993 Vienna Declaration and Programme of Action made explicit reference to DRTD and reaffirmed RtD as a universal and inalienable right and an integral part of fundamental human rights (World Conference on Human Rights 1993: Article 10). In the same year, the UNCHR established a working group on RtD for a period of three years (UNCHR 1993), at the end of which, in 1996, it established an inter-governmental working group on RtD for a period of two years (UNCHR 1996). In 1997, the UNGA passed a resolution with 129 States in favour, 12 against and 32 abstaining, whereby a call was made to include the DRTD as part of the International Bill of Human Rights as an appropriate way of celebrating the 50th anniversary of the UDHR (UNGA 1997b). The resolution also called for the establishment of a follow-up mechanism for the implementation of RtD (UNGA 1997b: Para. 15). Soon thereafter, the UNCHR recommended to the ECOSOC that an open-ended working group be created for a period of three years, along with appointment of an independent expert to support the working group (UNCHR 1998). This led to the appointment of Arjun Sengupta as the UN's independent expert on RtD, and it is to his valuable work thereafter that a lot of credit should be due in our understanding of RtD today. His appointment in 1998 and the near simultaneous publication of Sen's Development as Freedom also led to the final convergence of the evolving concept of development from the economics perspective and the human rights perspective.[5]

Debates on the status and content of RtD

Among the first tasks which Sengupta undertook was to explain to States what RtD really meant, what its scope was, whether it was indeed a human right and what the rights and obligations in DRTD entailed. In his first report, Sengupta devoted substantial space to clarifying that RtD is indeed an inalienable human right and that the issue can be considered to have been settled in view of the universal consensus obtained on this point in the 1993 Vienna Declaration (UNCHR 1999: Para. 17). Another aspect which Sengupta took pains to clarify was with respect to arguments by some legal scholars of the positivist school, that if certain rights are not legally enforceable, they cannot be regarded as human rights and at best can be regarded as social aspirations or statements of objectives (UNCHR 1999: Para. 21). The argument therefore raised against RtD was that because it lacks justiciability in many jurisdictions, it is not a human right. In response, Sengupta rightly pointed out that this argument suffers from an equating of human rights with legal rights. In the same tradition as James Nickel (2007: 22–34), he pointed out that there are many human rights recognised in the ICESCR which may not be justiciable in many jurisdictions, but that does not mean they are not human rights.[6] Enforceability before courts only makes a right a legal right, but that is only one way in which a human right can be respected, protected and fulfilled. Other mechanisms include free press, fair elections, non-judicial human rights inquiries, naming and shaming, peer pressure and protests. Thus, justiciability is not determinative of whether a norm is a human right. As Nickel (2007) puts it, enforceability merely makes a human right more effective by providing yet another avenue for holding States accountable in addition to all the others available.

A specific confusion with respect to the status of RtD flows from Article 1(1) of DRTD, which states that:

> [t]he right to development is an inalienable human right by virtue of which every human person and all peoples are entitled to participate in, contribute to, and enjoy economic, social, cultural and political development, in which all human rights and fundamental freedoms can be fully realised.

As one can notice, this provision proclaims that RtD is an inalienable human rights by itself, but also in the same breath states that it is a right in which all human rights and fundamental freedoms – civil, political, economic, social and cultural – can be fully realised. In clarifying the actual import of this provision, Sengupta pointed out that RtD had a two-fold character. It was simultaneously a self-standing human right, as well as inclusive of all other human rights (UNCHR 1999: Para. 46).[7] By the time he submitted his third report, Sengupta had developed a sophisticated 'Vector' approach to understanding RtD (UNCHR 2001: Para. 9–10). He described RtD as a vector composed of various elements including the right to food, the right to health, the right to education, the right to housing and other economic, social and cultural rights, as well as all the civil and political rights together with the rates of growth of GDP and other financial, technical and institutional resources that enable any improvement in the well-being of the entire population and the realisation of the rights to be sustained (UNCHR 2001: Para. 9). He outlined three important characteristics of the Vector approach.

First, each element of the vector is a human right (inclusive of all human rights) just as the vector itself is a human right (self-standing right). This means that 'they all will have to be implemented in a rights-based manner which is transparent, accountable, participatory and non-discriminatory with equity in decision-making and sharing of the fruits or outcomes of the process' (UNCHR 2001: Para. 10).

Second, all the elements are interdependent, both at any specific point in time and over a period of time, in the sense that realisation of one right (say, right to health) depends on the realisation of other rights (say, right to housing). Additionally, and importantly for our context, he pointed out that 'realisation of all these rights in a sustainable manner would depend upon the growth of GDP and other resources, which in turn would depend upon the realisation of the rights to health and education, as well as to freedom of information' (UNCHR 2001: Para. 10). As such, resources for growth including GDP and technology, need to be an integral part of the vector of rights that constitute RtD.

Third, this necessarily requires a holistic approach to human rights, where improvement in one cannot come at the cost of another. Thus, an improvement in the realisation of RtD or an increase in the value of the vector is defined as an improvement in all the elements of the vector (i.e. human rights) or at least in one element of the vector while no other element deteriorates (UNCHR 2001: Para. 10). The value-added of this framework is that it recognises all human rights to be inviolable and equally important and, at the same time, forces us to ensure that one right is not offset against the deterioration of another.

Another valuable insight provided by Sengupta is the focus of RtD not only on outcomes but more importantly on the process aspect. Indeed, he argued that RtD ought to be understood as a right to a process of development (UNCHR 1999: Para. 36). The language of the provisions of DRTD support this observation. For instance, the Preamble as well as Article 2(3) of DRTD clearly indicate that development is a process of 'the constant improvement of the well-being of the entire population and of all individuals, on the basis of their active, free and meaningful participation in development and in the fair distribution of the benefits resulting therefrom'. As Sengupta has pointed out,

> The phrase 'constant improvement of the well-being' not only refers to the notion of 'progressive realisation' which is implied in any idea of achieving the goals of development; it also calls for precise policy formulation that leads to a properly defined process of 'improvement' as well as a properly identified concept of 'well-being.
>
> (UNCHR 2001: Para. 6)

Similarly, the process aspect is underscored by the importance placed to 'active, free and meaningful participation in development'. This does not, however, relegate the outcome aspect of the process to anything less important. This is underscored by the importance placed to 'the fair distribution of the benefits resulting therefrom' through such participation.

DRTD also identifies who the right-holders and the duty-bearers of RtD are, but the same is not necessarily clear on first blush. Article 2(1) states that 'the human person is the central subject of development and should be the active participant and beneficiary of the right to development'. Thus, this provision clearly stipulates that human beings are the right-holders individually of RtD. Article 2(3) of DRTD, however, also mentions that 'States have the right and the duty to formulate appropriate national development policies'. This provision could be misconstrued by some to mean that States have such a right against their own citizens with respect to setting development policies and priorities. However, analysing the language of this provision in the context of Sengupta's elaboration mentioned earlier makes it evident that the State is a holder of RtD only on behalf of (or as an agent of) 'the entire population and of all individuals'. In other words, this right of the State is not exercisable against its own citizens, but against other States or actors who have 'the power to deny or constrain the capacity of the State to formulate national development policies that benefit the entire population and all individuals' (Orford 2001: 137).[8] States continue to have duties with respect to RtD towards their own citizens.

At the same time, this duty extends beyond the States' borders as well and permeates through international decision making at international organisations. This is most explicit in Article 3(1), which stipulates that 'States have the primary responsibility for the creation of national and international conditions favourable to the realisation of the right to development'. States would, therefore, be failing in their obligations if their actions or the policies they support lead to creation of *international* conditions unfavourable to the realisation of RtD. These include the whole gamut of policies supported by States at the UN, IMF, WB and, indeed, the WTO. Article 4(1) clinches the issue by stipulating that 'States have the duty to take steps, *individually and collectively*, to formulate international development policies with a view to facilitating the full realisation of the right to development'.[9] As Sengupta has stressed, 'Making RtD a human right recognised by all Governments, enjoins them to follow a code of conduct that not only restrains them from disrupting the conditions required to fulfil that right but also actively assists and promotes its fulfilment' (UNCHR 1999: Para. 59).

This duty of States is also evident from the provisions related to international cooperation enshrined in DRTD. Article 3(3) lays down that 'States have the duty to co-operate with each other in ensuring development and eliminating obstacles to development'. Specifically, with reference to D-LDCs, DRTD states in Article 4(2) that 'sustained action is required to promote more rapid development of developing countries' and that 'as a complement to the efforts of developing countries, effective international co-operation is essential in providing these countries with appropriate means and facilities to foster their comprehensive development'.[10] Of course, what is important is to ensure that in all these methods of cooperation, the different rights included in RtD are fully protected (UNCHR 1999: Para. 62).

A collective appraisal of all the aforesaid points leads us to the following conclusions with respect to RtD:

1 RtD is an inalienable self-standing human right, and, for that purpose, it is immaterial whether or not it is justiciable.
2 RtD should be understood as a vector, which in turn comprises all other human rights – civil, political, economic, social and cultural – as its elements along with the resources of growth such as GDP and technology. This is not to suggest that RtD is a meta-right. Rather, the vector approach simply means that given the very nature of development as a human right, it cannot be enhanced when there are violations of other human rights.
3 RtD includes both process and outcome aspects.
4 Human beings are individually and collectively the right-holders of RtD against their States as well as other States. States are also right-holders of RtD against other States, as agents of their citizens. The duty-bearers of RtD are States, individually and collectively, including at international organisations. This duty is towards their own citizens as well as towards other States and their citizens.
5 RtD imposes an obligation on States, individually and collectively, to create conditions favourable to the realisation of RtD and refrain from making policies adverse to its realisation.
6 RtD imposes a duty on States with respect to international cooperation to achieve RtD.

Before closing this section, it will be relevant to highlight two related aspects of the discussion on the status of RtD as a human right. First, lack of justiciability of RtD has nothing to do with any particular inherent characteristic of the right itself which might make it unenforceable. To the contrary, the reason for lack of justiciability is simply that many States do not recognise it as an enforceable right under their laws. The fact that RtD is as amenable to being justiciable as any other human right is amply proved by the decision rendered by the African Commission on Human Rights in the *Endorois* case (*Centre for Minority Rights Development (Kenya) and Minority Rights Group International on behalf of Endorois Welfare Council vs. Kenya* 2009;

hereafter, *Endorois* 2009). In this case, the challenge was that illegal usurpation of traditional lands of the Endorois indigenous peoples by the Government of Kenya to build a game reserve, was a violation of their RtD under Article 22 of the Banjul Charter. The Commission relied on the extensive work produced by Sengupta and held that although other individual human rights were violated in this case, RtD was also violated in its capacity as a self-standing right (*Endorois* 2009: Para. 269–98). It would, indeed, not be a far stretch to argue that the reason why more Courts have not enforced RtD is because no one was sure of its actual scope until Sengupta's work as the Independent Expert emerged.[11] In any case, as stated earlier, the fact that RtD is a human right is not dependent at all on whether or not it is justiciable.

The second important point worth highlighting is whether RtD has attained the status of CIL, despite DRTD being only a Declaration. Again, this question is immaterial to a conclusion that RtD is a human right. However, there are strong arguments today that RtD has become part of CIL. The *opinio juris* of States is evident from the fact that 146 countries voted in favour of DRTD and that subsequently all countries voted in its favour in the 1992 Rio Declaration and the 1993 Vienna Declaration, which trend continues in outcome resolutions and declarations from several State conferences, including Resolution 60/251 of the UNGA which created the UN Human Rights Council (UNGA 2006: Para. 4), the UN Declaration on the Rights of Indigenous Peoples (UNGA 2007: Preamble, Para. 6 and Article 23) and the 2030 Agenda.[12] Many scholars argue that States have also confirmed the same in their practice by acting extensively and uniformly in virtually all fields of international law according to the principles set out in DRTD.[13] The UN Millennium Declaration, the emphatic commitment by all States therein to 'making the right to development a reality for everyone' (UNGA 2000: Para. 11) and the resultant MDGs to operationalise the Millennium Declaration's objectives, have been cited as eloquent evidence of State practice (Possel 2008: 192). One may also point out the resolution of the UNGA (1997b) whereby States urged introduction of the DRTD in the International Bill of Human Rights, alongside UDHR, ICCPR and ICESCR, as proof of its acceptance by States as CIL. Lastly, one may note that participation by States in the UNHRC, which lists promotion and protection of RtD as one of its founding mandates, is adequate proof of State practice. Another interesting line of argument highlighted in a 2004 study by Gutto conducted for the erstwhile UNCHR, is that the DRTD could be treated as binding on States if the UNGA Resolution is considered, not as enshrining any new right, but as an authoritative interpretation by member States of the UN Charter, more specifically Article 55(a) thereof which employs the term 'development' (UNCHR 2004: Para. 39–40).[14] On the other hand, scholars like Peter Uvin have trashed RtD as 'catastrophic' and a 'total failure', pointing especially at the lack of political consensus on its scope (Uvin 2007). Thus, while one can clearly notice an increasing acceptance of RtD as CIL, there do remain sceptics. Be that as it may, as has been pointed out earlier, whether or not RtD is CIL has no implications for the position that it is indeed a human right.

RtD and governance space as coterminous

As can be gathered from the aforesaid discussion, the holistic nature of the RtD framework makes it a natural candidate for being considered as the ideal approach to finding solutions to linkage-issues. Indeed, the governance space framework as we have developed in this book is naturally synergetic with different elements of RtD. As discussed in Chapter 2, a key feature underpinning 'governance space' is that, unlike 'policy space', it encompasses both rights and duties of States as the reason for having it. It is this particular aspect of 'governance space' which enables us to identify not just the first linkage-category where MTS limits the space needed by States to respect, protect and fulfil human rights, but the other two linkage-categories as well. Thus, while making a strong argument that MTS seriously limits governance space of States in some respects, the framework also allows us to critique the abuse of governance space by States. At the same time, it also allows us to identify lack of capabilities, especially among D-LDCs, to benefit from MTS as an additional important category which needs to be addressed. Availability of governance space (first linkage-category) as well as the capability to use governance space (third linkage-category) are certainly rights of States, but not abusing governance space which they have (second linkage-category) is also a binding duty.

It is this holistic nature of governance space as a framework for identifying linkage-categories which makes it entirely coterminous with RtD as a framework for approaching solutions. Thus, RtD also focuses on both the right and the duty aspects of States. It allows States, especially D-LDCs, to stake a claim as agents of their citizens that ensuring development within the State is their right and that other States and international organisations have a duty to not undermine the same (coterminous with the first linkage-category). Moreover, acknowledging the lower threshold of infrastructural and technological capabilities which D-LDCs have, RtD also frames international cooperation as a duty of States, particularly the DCs (coterminous with the third linkage-category). On the other hand, however, it also insists that all States, including the D-LDCs, have an obligation to respect, protect and fulfil human rights internally to ensure development and that they cannot pass off violations of the rights of their citizens under the false label of development (coterminous with the second linkage-category).

It is worth highlighting that it is precisely this holistic nature of RtD which sits uncomfortably with both DCs and D-LDCs, thereby leading to attempts by both to politically distort its essential tenets. With respect to D-LDCs, Ibhawoh (2011) points out how D-LDCs have tried to orient an understanding of RtD only in terms of claims against the DCs, while blocking attempts to use it as a tool to evaluate their own human rights record at home. He argues that 'the paradox of the right to development talk coming from the South is that it is at once deployed to demand radical change in the international economic order and to resist change in the national political order' (Ibhawoh 2011: 78).

From a historical point of view, Rajagopal points out that the original demands of D-LDCs relating to the RTD were more focused on 'changes in the international order than on changes within states to achieve rights-based development outcomes' (Rajagopal 2013: 900). However, as he also rightly suggests, any continued interpretation of RtD which focuses only on the international economic order as the main reason for non-fulfilment of human rights, without looking inward as well, will be antithetical to the core essence of the framework.

DCs on the other hand have insisted that the idea of RtD must be essentially equated with an incorporation of human rights principles within development or what is called as human rights–based approach to development or 'rights-based development'.[15] As Fukuda-Parr points out, with respect to RtD, DCs have categorically opposed the creation of a Convention on the grounds that the State has the principal responsibility for the protection and the fulfilment of human rights and have insisted that RtD as a concept is useful only for rights-based development, not beyond that (Fukuda-Parr 2012: 848). Clearly, the attempt here is to orient an understanding of RtD only as a framework for how D-LDCs should be judged in terms of their human rights performance as part of the development process at home, without admitting any responsibility of DCs for changing the international economic system, including MTS, which may limit the abilities of D-LDCs to ensure such development. Thus, in terms of 'governance space', the attempt by D-LDCs is to focus on an understanding of RtD only on the first and third linkage-categories, while the attempt by DCs is to focus exclusive on the second linkage-category.

An accurate and holistic understanding of RtD as discussed in the preceding section, however, allows us to equate development and human rights in all the required dimensions. It allows us to confront distorted political interpretations of RtD and insist on making both DCs and D-LDCs accountable for adverse impacts on human rights. The coterminous nature of RtD with governance space, therefore, allows us to approach solutions to all linkage-categories without the fear of 'leakages'.

Connecting WTO, sustainable development and RtD

A juxtaposition of the aforesaid discussion on RtD with the earlier discussion on sustainable development should make it evident that both are essentially the same concepts in different incarnations. The former gives proper shape and texture to the latter by purposely stressing on the right and duty aspects of sustainable development. By insisting that development is a human right which has clearly identified duty-bearers, RtD hammers down the point that the only way development can be sustainable is if it encompasses all human rights as equally important and ensures that no human right is undermined. Indeed, Gutto's study referred to the above noted that RtD necessarily includes the notion of sustainable development and should be more appropriately called 'Right to Sustainable Development' (UNCHR 2004c: Para. 50). Unsurprisingly, several recent Declarations have directly linked sustainable development with RtD (Association of Southeast Asian Nations 2012: Articles 35–37; UN Conference on Sustainable Development 2012: Para. 8). Most importantly, the 2030 Agenda categorically reaffirms RtD in the context of implementing the SDGs and states that it is informed as well as grounded in the DRTD (UNGA 2015: Para. 10; Kanade 2016a, b).

It is in this factual matrix that the 'internal' link between human rights and MTS can be found through the objective of 'sustainable development' in the Marrakesh Agreement of the WTO itself. States are obliged to take into consideration human rights while operating at the WTO because the institutional objective of WTO to ensure sustainable development mandates so. Human rights are inextricably linked to development, whilst development is inseparably linked to MTS. It may be worthwhile to point out Article 3(3) of DRDT which mandates States to realise their rights and fulfil their duties in such a manner as to promote 'a new international economic order' based on sovereign equality, interdependence, mutual interest and cooperation among all States, as well as to encourage the observance and realisation of human rights. This clause has utmost significance inasmuch as States knew throughout the Uruguay round of negotiations around the same time and while establishing the WTO almost a decade later, that they had committed to establishing a 'new international economic order' in terms of Article 3(3) of DRDT.

In sum, the concept of RtD suggests that the 'appropriate' development strategy is one that conforms to the international human rights framework. This link of development between the human rights regime and MTS should rest to calm all the opposition of States for bringing in exogenous human rights treaties into the WTO processes. The compartmentalisation of human rights obligations and its 'splendid isolation' from WTO processes is against the very institutional objective of WTO and, it is for this reason, that WTO members are under an obligation to ensure that their human rights obligations are not undermined as a result of impacts of MTS on their governance space.

Now, before we proceed to analysing what exactly applying an RtD approach to the three linkage-categories means, it is important to stress what it does not mean. In the context of WTO, the RtD approach does not necessarily permit a claim to be made before the Panels by any State that trade policies of another State are illegal because they breach RtD. First, as we have noted earlier, despite there being agreement among States that RtD is a human right, there is still a doubt among some whether it can be a legally enforceable right by virtue of being CIL. Second, the obligation of States to formulate WTO policies with the aim of fulfilling the RtD, as borne out in the concept of sustainable development, is enshrined in the Preamble of the Marrakesh Agreement. Rules of interpretation of treaties do not accord the same value to Preambles as they do to substantive provisions (Koskenniemi 1999: 27–39). A violation of a substantive provision can be challenged before the Panels, however, the Preamble has a role limited to interpretation of WTO Agreements, namely only to provide the context for interpreting substantive provisions (ILC 1966: 221). Nevertheless, the fact still remains that the Preamble of the Marrakesh Agreement asserts the purposes and institutional objectives of the WTO in no uncertain terms, and, therefore, even if the same cannot be enforced through WTO Panels, States are obliged to ensure that such objectives, including sustainable development, are not being undermined.

Also, it is important to stress that adopting an RtD approach as the way forward to addressing the impacts on governance space does not mean that there is a one-size-fits-all solution. This is only an approach to finding solutions, and clearly solutions under each of the linkage-categories and within those categories cannot be the same. As will be demonstrated later, applying the RtD approach to linkage-issues under the three linkage-categories not only permits, but requires different solutions to be adopted to different problems. While the focus of this book is not on identifying solutions for all linkage-issues arising due to interactions between MTS and human rights, it is certainly necessary for us to indicate the manner in which the RtD approach can be applied to different linkage-categories, before concluding our study.

RtD approach to addressing the shrinking of governance space

As noted in Chapter 5, the first linkage-category comprises linkage-issues where WTO laws limit the governance space of States which they need to fulfil their human rights obligations. In order to be compatible with WTO's institutional objective of sustainable development, the RtD approach means that States are required to ensure that their trade commitments do not shrink their own or other States' governance space in a manner that adversely affects a WTO member's ability to fulfil their human rights obligations. If the governance space is limited by WTO laws, then clearly, States are creating obstacles to the fulfilment of their own objective of sustainable development and, in turn, the obligations enshrined under DRTD.

Normatively, the reasons that the RtD approach obliges States to ensure that such a situation does not arise in the first place can be found in Articles 2(3), 3(1), 3(2), 3(3), 4(1), 6(3), 8(1) and 10, which all require States to ensure RtD in all their domestic and international policies and at international organisations. But how do States ensure that such a situation does not arise, or, if it does arise, it is corrected? It is here that the RtD approach necessitates having systems in place which inform States whether the trade rules they are negotiating might limit their governance space in a manner that their human rights obligations are adversely affected. It is only upon having such systems in place that States can ensure compatibility of free trade as the means and sustainable development as the end. Similarly, systems need to be in place which inform States whether an existing Agreement creates a situation whereby the governance space of States to adequately deal with their human rights concerns is limited as a result of WTO obligations. If such situations are found to exist, the RtD approach obliges

States to remove such limitations by subsequent efforts, without which the 'means' cannot achieve the 'ends'.

Given this position, such systems need to be incorporated not at any one stage of the WTO processes, but at all stages, including the stages of pre-negotiation, negotiation and trade policy review. Adopting the RtD approach also necessitates that such systems ensure the vector model, whereby all human rights are considered as equally important and no trade-off is permitted between them. It also requires a participatory approach whereby engagement with all stakeholders (the right-holders) is crucial to the 'process' of development.

In the field of human rights, such systems are called as human rights impact assessments (HRIA). HRIA has grown today to be a sophisticated technique whereby impacts of specific policies affecting development can be assessed through targeted human rights indicators.[16] Specifically with respect to trade, HRIA has a lot to offer in terms of our knowledge of what impacts WTO rules have on human rights (Harrison and Goller 2008; Walker 2009; The Berne Declaration *et al.* 2010). Indeed, human rights treaty bodies and special procedures of the UNHRC such as the UN Committee on the Elimination of Discrimination Against Women (2007: Para. 29), the UN Committee on Economic, Social and Cultural Rights (2004: Para. 55–56) and the UN Committee on the Rights of the Child (2004: Para. 48) have called upon States to conduct HRIA of the trade and investment agreements they conclude. In particular, de Schutter, in his capacity as the Special Rapporteur on the Right to Food, has insisted on the use of HRIA by States in evaluating the impact of trade policies on human rights (UNHRC 2009b: Para. 37–38) and has provided extensive general guidance to States on how HRIA should be conducted (UNHRC 2011a). The following principles related to HRIA highlighted by de Schutter are important for our purposes and directly applicable to the RtD approach:

1 HRIA is a 'tool to ensure consistency and coherence between the obligations of States under international law and other international agreements to which they are parties, and thus to overcome, or at least mitigate, the problems resulting from the fragmentation of international law' (UNHRC 2011a: Para. 1.1).
2 HRIA, by serving to inform public debate, seeks to fulfil the right of every citizen to take part in the conduct of public affairs recognised under Article 25(a) of ICCPR. In the context of WTO, this implies that no trade or investment agreement should be concluded in the absence of a public debate (UNHRC 2011a: Para. 1.2).

3 All States are under a legal duty to prepare HRIA *prior* to the conclusion of trade agreements because they have pre-existing human rights obligations, and must ensure that trade commitments do not come into 'conflict' with them, lest Article 103 of the UN Charter or the principle of *jus cogens* may become applicable (UNHRC 2011a: Para. 1, 1.3).

4 HRIA should measure the potential impact of WTO agreements on human rights outcomes and on the capacity of States to meet their human rights obligations, as well as on the capacity of individuals to enjoy their rights (UNHRC 2011a: Para. 2.1). This is also in conformity with the expectation that States shall 'maintain adequate domestic policy space to meet their human rights obligations when pursuing business-related policy objectives with other States' as observed in the UN Guiding Principles on Business and Human Rights (UNHRC 2011b: Principle 9).

5 States owe obligations to not adversely affect human rights through WTO rules, with respect to both individuals on their territory and individuals on the territory of other States with whom they conclude a trade agreement (UNHRC 2011a: Para. 2.6). To support this proposition, de Schutter cites the Committee on Economic, Social and Cultural Rights, which in its concluding observations on Switzerland, recommended that 'the State party undertake an impact assessment to determine the possible consequences of its foreign trade policies and agreements on the enjoyment by the population of the State party's partner countries, of their economic, social and cultural rights' (UN Committee on Economic, Social and Cultural Rights 2010: Para. 24).

6 HRIA should be prepared *prior* to the conclusion of the agreements and in time to influence the outcomes of the negotiations, but should also be conducted *post* the implementation of the agreements to measure actual impacts (UNHRC 2011a: Para. 3).

7 There is no one-size-fits-all solution which will apply to all situations. Based on the results of HRIA, '[A] range of responses exist where an incompatibility is found', including but not limited to 'termination of the agreement', 'amendment of the agreement', 'insertion of safeguards in the agreement', 'provision of compensation by third-State parties' and 'adoption of mitigation measures' (UNHRC 2011a: Para. 3).

8. Any trade-offs while prioritising certain human rights 'must never result in a deprivation of the ability of people to enjoy the essential content of their human rights'. Therefore, 'no provision is acceptable that might deprive people of their current income sources

unless a credible, realistic and sustainable alternative is offered that would allow for the continued enjoyment of human rights in full dignity' (UNHRC 2011a: Para. 6.5).

In terms of the RtD approach, it is clear that the information which can be derived from HRIA based on the aforesaid principles, has an instrumental role in informing States whether their governance space is being limited by undertaking certain WTO commitments. Gathering this information is an obligation on States not only because they must avoid 'conflicts' with pre-existing human rights obligations. It is an obligation even when such 'conflicts' do not arise, because shrinking of governance space to fulfil human rights obligations directly and adversely impacts the institutional objective of WTO.

As we have noted earlier, de Schutter suggests that HRIA must be conducted by States prior to and post-WTO agreements. However, I suggest that HRIA needs to be conducted at least at four stages of the WTO processes, namely pre-negotiation, negotiation, implementation and trade policy review and by different actors. Importantly, in line with the RtD approach, it is essential that civil society organisations are made inherent part of the process by States, as appropriate, in collecting and analysing data.

First, HRIA needs to be conducted at pre-negotiation stage by all WTO members because without knowledge of possible human rights impacts, it is rather difficult to adopt initial negotiating positions which ensure compatibility between potential trade rules and human rights. As discussed in Chapter 3, States need to undertake this exercise anyway in order to ensure that potential trade obligations which may be negotiated will not be in 'conflict' with human rights so as to make Article 103 of the UN Charter and the principle of *jus cogens* invokable.

Second, it needs to be conducted at the negotiation stage of a WTO agreement before the final negotiated draft is adopted by members. At this stage, HRIA must be conducted not only by States but also by the Committee on Trade and Development (CTD) of the WTO. The Doha Ministerial Declaration, in fact, expressly mandated the CTD to 'act as a forum to identify and debate developmental . . . aspects of the negotiations, in order to help achieve the objective of having sustainable development appropriately reflected' (WTO 2001: Para. 51).

Third, HRIA must be conducted at implementation stage by each WTO member, at an appropriate time before (at the design stage) or after the implementation of the commitments. This needs to be conducted by a State because that is when the actual, not just the anticipated, impacts on the ground will be noticed.

Finally, HRIA needs to be conducted at the full membership level of the WTO as part of the review of WTO commitments. The need for such review is to assess whether or not WTO obligations by States are advancing the objectives of MTS, namely sustainable development. Fortunately, WTO's basic structure already provides a mechanism where this can be done, and, as such, there is no need to reinvent the wheel by creating new procedures or bodies for this purpose. Specifically, the Agreement on Trade Policy Review Mechanism (TPRM Agreement) provides for the establishment of a periodic peer review process so as to enable 'the regular collective appreciation and evaluation of the full range of individual Members' trade policies and practices and their impact on the functioning of MTS (TPRM Agreement 1994: Article A(i)).[17] If 'the function of the review mechanism is to examine the impact of a Member's trade policies and practices on the multilateral trading system' (TPRM Agreement 1994: Article A(ii)), it follows that the assessment must be of a *systemic* nature which includes both the implementation of trade rules and their impacts on the institutional objective of sustainable development. Clearly, trade policies and practices of States will have an adverse impact on MTS, if their implementation results in undermining this institutional objective. In terms of who should conduct the HRIAs, the TPRM also provides the appropriate procedures. It states that the Trade Policy Review Body (TPRB) 'shall base its work' (TPRM Agreement 1994: Article C(v)) on two documentations. The first is a full report supplied by the member/s under review (TPRM Agreement 1994: Article C(v)(a)). The second is a 'report, to be drawn up by the Secretariat on its own responsibility, based on the information available to it and that provided by the Member/s concerned' (TPRM Agreement 1994: Article C(v)(b)). For this second documentation, the TPRM also provides that the Secretariat should seek clarification from the member/s concerned of their trade policies and practices. The TPRB Rules of Procedure stipulate that these documentations are to be circulated not less than five weeks in advance of the relevant meetings to all other members, 'who should submit written questions to the Member under review at least two weeks before the review meeting, to allow time to prepare replies' (WTO 2008: Rule 11–12). Once the review is undertaken, the documentation by the member under review and by the Secretariat, together with the minutes of the respective meeting of the TPRB, are required to be 'published promptly' (TPRM

Agreement 1994: Article C(vi)), and all these documents are required to be 'forwarded to the Ministerial Conference, which shall take note of them' (TPRM Agreement 1994: Article C(vii)). These procedures which generally apply to trade policy reviews of members with respect to implementation of their WTO commitments are also appropriate for assessing their impacts on WTO's institutional objective of sustainable development. As such, at the trade policy review stage, it is suggested that both States and the Secretariat must conduct HRIA. This mechanism should also act as a check and balance against the tendency of States to underplay human rights impacts of their trade policies, especially when such impacts are on other countries. It needs to be noted that the mechanism on trade policy review, as conceived in TPRM Agreement, applies to review of an individual member's trade policy and practices. One may, therefore, argue that these reviews may not be helpful at the broader level of evaluating whether Agreements and the obligations therein have adverse impacts on human rights as a general trend. However, this argument may not be correct since the maximum impacts on human rights of trade policies and practices are those of the biggest economies, who are reviewed more often than others. Reports of the impacts of their trade policies and practices on human rights, internally and externally, will generally be indicative of the larger picture and this will form the necessary information required for Ministerial Conferences to reassess WTO rules. Also, group reviews have become a regular feature of TPRM in order to maximise efficiency and identify common issues (WTO 2016c: Para. 16).[18] In fact, the 2005 report on the second appraisal of the TPRM welcomed 'the use of grouped reviews as an instrument to make a more efficient use of resources and generate greater interest in the reviews of smaller Members' and encouraged 'the identification of further opportunities for reviews of geographically or economically close trading partners, while taking due account of their rights and obligations as individual WTO Members' (WTO 2005b: Para. 14). Additionally, the mechanism also requires that an annual overview of developments in the international trading environment which are having an impact on MTS shall be undertaken by the TPRB (TPRM Agreement 1994: Para. G). It further provides that 'the overview is to be assisted by an annual report by the Director-General setting out major activities of the WTO and highlighting significant policy issues affecting the trading system'. This is clearly an avenue for the TPRB to produce HRIA reports at the generic level, assisted by the Director-General's annual report. However, because these generic reports can only be based on HRIA at the individual and group levels, the primary focus ought to be on the trade policy reviews of WTO member/s. A last point fortifying the appropriateness of TPRB in conducting HRIAs is that the Agreement expressly negates a possible fear that the findings of the review might 'serve as a basis for the enforcement of specific obligations under the Agreements or for dispute settlement procedures, or to impose new policy commitments on Members' (TPRM Agreement 1994: Para. A(i)).[19]

As stated earlier, the primary purpose of HRIAs is to inform States on whether they are undermining the institutional objective of the WTO. Ideally, States should ensure that WTO Agreements are adopted only after HRIAs at the pre-negotiation and negotiation stages are conducted and considered. However, if HRIAs at the implementation and trade policy review stages demonstrate the need for course correction, *post facto* measures will need to be undertaken through negotiations. What the nature and form of those course correction measures ought to be will vary according to the impact at hand, and, as such, it is a futile exercise to pre-judge all of them. As de Schutter (UNHRC 2011a) has noted, a range of responses exist including but not limited to termination of the agreement, amendment of the agreement, insertion of safeguards in the agreement, provision of compensation by third-State parties and adoption of mitigation measures. What is indispensable is the adoption of the RtD approach to addressing shrinking of governance space, since it is the only way in which options for course correction can even be brought to the negotiating table.

Thus, the RtD approach to the shrinking of governance space due to the manner in which Article XX(b) of GATT is framed would have required an HRIA to be conducted at the pre-negotiation stage by all WTO members and at the negotiation stage by the members as well as the CTD (although the CTD did not exist at the time Article XX(b) was negotiated first, it is applicable to all new negotiations). If that had been done, it might have come to light that the provision may not necessarily allow and may instead shrink the necessary governance space which States need to protect human health as a result of trade agreements. At the very least, it would have made for an informed negotiation and the shrinking of governance space could have been avoided. If States still would have gone ahead with the language as it exists today, they would have at least done so with full consciousness and understanding of the impacts the provision may have on their governance space. However, since those stages have long elapsed now, it does not mean that course correction ought not to be done. In fact, it is necessary in accordance with the RtD approach. As such, if HRIAs were conducted at appropriate junctures, that is by States at the early stages of design and implementation of the measures necessary to protect human health, as well as by States and the Secretariat at the trade policy review stages, the necessity to amend the provisions might have been on the table. It may be recalled that in Chapter 5, an argument was made that the requirement of 'necessity' in Article XX(b) is extremely strict and there is no reason that the 'related to' test in Article XX(g) ought not to be adopted. It was also demonstrated that the language of the Chapeau of Article XX seriously limits the governance space which States need to adopt measures in order to protect human health. All these aspects, if identified and brought to the negotiating table through HRIAs at the appropriate time, would have led to a realisation that the provision probably needs to be amended in a suitable manner such that governance space of States is not limited by it.

In any case, there is already enough jurisprudence and research by scholars pointing towards the difficulty States face in invoking Article XX(b) successfully. The clear implication is that the provision and the obligations enshrined therein (necessity test and Chapeau requirements) undermine the institutional objective of sustainable development because they limit the governance space of States to take measures to protect human health. An RtD approach necessitates that States re-negotiate the provision with a view to ensuring that it does not limit the governance space of States as it presently does. This is the most appropriate way in which States can ensure that Article XX(b) is compatible with the objective of sustainable development.

RtD approach to addressing the permissive environment to abuse governance space

As we noted in Chapter 6, the linkage-issues arising in this linkage-category relate mostly to the impact on labour standards as a result of participation by States in MTS. In these cases, WTO laws neither limit, nor do they create any sort of limiting environment for States to safeguard labour rights of their workers. To the contrary, they create the permissive environment for States to be able to violate labour rights. As such, States end up abusing the governance space they already have for abiding by their labour rights obligations. Solutions for linkage-issues arising in this category cannot obviously be the same for linkage-issues arising due to WTO laws limiting governance space of States.

RtD approach necessitates that States do not permit regression of labour standards by businesses in order to expand exports. Economic growth at the cost of labour rights is antithetical to RtD and cannot even be justified as 'development' within the meaning of DRTD or, for that matter, in terms of the 2030 Agenda. An RtD approach requires that States – DCs and D-LDCs – do not abuse their governance space by not implementing their labour rights obligations.

However, that fact does not necessarily mean that the 'appropriate' policy response is at the WTO. The point of departure here from the solutions we discussed with respect to the first linkage-category is that linkage-issues of labour rights do not arise because governance space of States is limited by WTO laws, which will require those laws to be amended in some way or the other. In terms of governance space to abide by labour obligations, all States have ample of it, with or without WTO obligations. If WTO obligations have no impact on the governance space of States to abide by their labour obligations, there is no a priori reason to assume that solutions for the first linkage-category would work for the second linkage-category. In other words, amending WTO provisions when they have no adverse impact on governance space of States ought not to be the starting point for finding solutions.

In order to fulfil the institutional objective of sustainable development and the inherent RtD obligations, it is not enough that States merely adopt development policies. Such policies need to be 'appropriate' as well (UNGA 1986: Article 2(3)). The appropriateness of development policies must account for several factors, the first among which is whether the policy is productive or counterproductive to the realisation of the right concerned. As has been extensively argued in Chapter 6, incorporating social clauses in WTO Agreements to regulate and enforce labour obligations of D-LDCs is not only incapable of improving labour standards in those countries; it is, in fact, counterproductive to the livelihoods of those very workers who are sought to be protected by those clauses. Article 3(1) of DTRD places the 'primary responsibility for the creation of national and international conditions *favourable* to the realisation' of RtD on States. If enforcing labour standards through WTO will undermine the protection of workers, it can only be *unfavourable* to the realisation of RtD.

Appropriateness of development policies must also include the choice of institution through which the policies will be implemented, the general direction of available political will and the greatest common good. We have already seen why D-LDCs have consistently opposed incorporation of labour clauses in WTO agreements and for valid reasons. Many of those are indeed indefeasible arguments on why labour standards should be enforced through the organisation created for that purpose, that is the ILO, and not through an entirely different organisation like the WTO. An RtD approach insists on participation of those whose rights are affected by any development policy. WTO processes do not accommodate any possibility for participation by workers in policy and decision making. On the other hand, the structure of ILO is certainly more representative than the WTO, with workers' organisations having a direct say in its agreements and policies.[20] Thus, the chances of striking the right balance to achieve the greatest common good are much more with the ILO. Additionally, as argued in Chapter 6, it would be far more pragmatic to successfully amend the ILO Constitution in accordance with Article 36 thereof in order to put in place strong enforcement and supervisory mechanisms, rather than attempt the impossibility of getting all WTO members on board to amend WTO Agreements. Inherent in the concept of RtD is a requirement that solutions which are realistic and more effective be pursued, rather than running after a mirage.

A brief note may also be made about the UN's Business and Human Rights agenda, which among other human rights impacts of corporations also includes violations of labour rights. An important portion of the UN Guiding Principles on Business and Human Rights (UNGP) focuses on the *responsibility* of corporations to respect human rights, including labour rights (UNHRC 2011b: Part II). States obviously have the legal *duty* to protect workers from their labour rights being violated by companies (UNHRC 2011b: Part I), however, laws alone are insufficient to ensure compliance if companies are not on board. As such, responsibility by companies to respect human rights is an indispensable tool in the efforts to ensure compliance by States of their labour obligations. I have elsewhere strongly critiqued the UNGPs and have argued that businesses not only have a moral responsibility but also a legal duty to respect human rights under international law (Kanade 2014). The DRTD gives support to this proposition as well. It states that:

> nothing in the present Declaration shall be construed as being contrary to the purposes and principles of the United Nations, or as implying that any State, group or person has a right to engage in any activity or to perform any act aimed at the violation of the rights set forth in the Universal Declaration of Human Rights and in the International Covenants on Human Rights.
>
> (UNGA 1986: Para. 9)

Businesses enjoy legal personality and, as such, do not have the right to violate human rights of workers. However, irrespective of the debate whether companies have binding obligations under international law to respect human rights or not, it is clear that the problem of labour standards compliance needs to factor in businesses as well. As stated earlier, the WTO is not in a position to do so. The ILO, on the other hand, with its tripartite structure represented by all three constituencies, is in a much better position to align with the UN Human Rights System and promote the business and human rights agenda insofar as labour rights are concerned, rather than the WTO.

From whichever perspective the matter is looked at, it is clear that for linkage-issues within this category where WTO laws and policies neither limit nor create a limiting environment for use of governance space by States, amending WTO laws is not the appropriate solution. From an RtD perspective, more appropriate solutions include a combination of compliance of obligations by States and businesses, the most appropriate body for which is the ILO.

RtD approach to addressing the limiting environment to use governance space

In Chapter 7, we discussed how MTS also creates an inherent limiting environment for D-LDCs to use their governance space because of their lower technological, infrastructural and other supply-side capabilities. Similar to the earlier discussion, the solutions for this last linkage-category clearly cannot be the same as those for either of the two other linkage-categories. The key point characterising this linkage-category is that the limiting environment to use governance space is created by MTS by requiring everyone to open their markets irrespective of their capabilities. It is also created by perpetuation of the existing capability deficiencies in D-LDCs, ironically through the very mechanisms which aim to enhance the competitive capabilities of D-LDCs. By way of case study, we analysed how the AfT Initiative was the product of a realisation that such inherent limiting environment exists for D-LDCs and that it must be removed by providing aid. We analysed also how the AfT Initiative suffers from serious deficiencies which only perpetuate the existing imbalances between the DCs and the D-LDCs.

As we have seen, increased inequality between and within States is contrary to the goal of sustainable development. Unless the limiting environment inherent to MTS is addressed, it is impossible for States to move in the direction of sustainable development as the institutional objective of WTO. Additionally, if current initiatives such as AfT perpetuate the limiting environment instead of removing it, the only implication can be that WTO is going in exactly the opposite direction of its own institutional objective of sustainable development.

One of the biggest problems we have identified with the effectiveness of the AfT Initiative is that aid by donors to D-LDCs remains predominantly in the control of the former, and recipients hardly have ownership over the use of such aid. Also, a significant amount of AfT is tied and even then, the flow, sectors and choice of recipient countries depends entirely on the interests of the donor countries. AfT then becomes a privilege or generosity conferred by donors upon recipients and not a duty. A juxtaposition of the current issues in AfT with DRTD exposes all the flaws innate to the initiative which inhibit its proper use in addressing the limiting environment to use governance space by D-LDCs.

As we have seen in the discussion on the first linkage-category, DRTD enjoins all States, especially DCs, to ensure that international policies promote RtD and do not diminish it. But more importantly, as our discussion on Article 2(3) of DRTD highlights, D-LDCs have the right against DCs to formulate appropriate national development policies. The stated purpose of recognising this right is to ensure 'the constant improvement of the well-being of the entire population and of all individuals, on the basis of their active, free and meaningful participation in development and in the fair distribution of the benefits resulting therefrom' (UNGA 1986: Article 2(3)). Therefore, an RtD approach to AfT requires that recipients have full ownership over how and where the aid received by them ought to go. This ability to set their own development priorities is not only a privilege but a right inherent to the idea of RtD.

Second, as analysed in this chapter, there is a corresponding duty on DCs to ensure that D-LDCs are able to enjoy their RtD. Specifically, in the context of development aid, however, DRTD goes further and clearly identifies duties on DCs to ensure international cooperation to realise RtD in D-LDCs. Thus, Article 3(3) stipulates that 'States have the duty to co-operate with each other in ensuring development and eliminating obstacles to development'. Article 6(1) further stresses that 'all States should co-operate with a view to promoting, encouraging and strengthening universal respect for and observance of all human rights and fundamental freedoms'. With respect to D-LDCs, Article 4(2) reminds us that 'sustained action is required to promote more rapid development of developing countries' and that 'as a complement to the efforts of developing countries, effective international co-operation is essential in providing these countries with appropriate means and facilities to foster their comprehensive development'. Sengupta argues that this provision should be read in conjunction with the opening sentence of the Preamble to DTRD which refers to the purposes and principles of the UN Charter relating to the achievement of international cooperation in solving international problems of an economic, social, cultural and humanitarian nature, and in promoting and encouraging respect for human rights and fundamental freedoms (UNCHR 1999: Para. 43). He points out that the reference is clearly to the obligation of international cooperation under Article 1 of the UN Charter read with Articles 55 and 56 which require joint and separate action by States.

Thus, if AfT is conceived to be part of international cooperation, it cannot simply operate within the framework of generosity which gives total control of what happens with such aid to donor countries. AfT needs to be understood as a duty of DCs and for this purpose, as Stiglitz and Charlton (2013: 359–60, 376) point out, the RtD approach needs to be mainstreamed into the initiative if it is to be successful. The RtD approach requires the international community, and particularly the DCs, to meet the obligations of such international cooperation (UNCHR 2001: Para. 33). Indeed, Sengupta in his third report clearly noted the unfulfilled commitment of DCs to ensure 0.7% of GNP as foreign aid as a violation of the duty of international cooperation inherent to RtD (UNCHR 2001: Para. 34). The same argument which Sengupta applied to ODA in 2001, applies with equal force to AfT post-2005.

Thus, applying the RtD approach to AfT Initiative points to the broader picture that, in general, removing the limiting environment which D-LDCs suffer from as a result of participating in MTS must be understood as an obligation upon all States, especially the DCs. It is only when development is viewed as a right of D-LDCs and their people, and the need for removing the limiting environment is viewed as a duty of DCs, can the institutional objective of sustainable development be promoted through the WTO.

Final observations on the way forward

This chapter has argued that in view of the explicit commitment by States to promote sustainable development as the institutional objective of WTO, the appropriate approach to finding solutions to issues within the three linkage-categories identified in this book is through an RtD approach. This is especially because the RtD and the governance space frameworks are coterminous on account of their holistic natures. Both inherently imbibe the necessary aspects of rights as well as duties of States. Adopting the RtD approach enables us to identify the distinct, yet appropriate, solutions to linkage-issues within each of the three categories. This book has used case studies to explain the three categories as well as to make suggestions on how RtD approach could be utilised to resolving them. This is not to say that the same solutions will necessarily apply to all linkage-issues which may emerge within the respective linkage-categories, although their broad characteristics may remain the same. Each linkage-issue under discussion will require at least as detailed an analysis as has been conducted in this book with respect to the three case studies. While doing that for all possible linkage-issues is beyond the mortal capabilities of any one researcher, the governance space theory and the accompanying RtD approach to solutions provides the necessary framework to begin embarking on that process in a coherent and systematic manner.

It is important to remember that while the distinction between the three linkage-categories is crucial in understanding how they emerge and what solutions to issues within them could be, the categories themselves are not compartmentalised in a watertight and inflexible manner. As suggested in Chapter 1, it is entirely possible for one linkage-issue to contain strands which may fall under more than one linkage-category. For instance, it was suggested that if the linkage-issue is that WTO laws requiring D-LDCs to open up their markets have an adverse impact on human right to livelihood, it could be argued that it falls under the first category because WTO law limits the governance space of such States by not permitting adoption of protectionist measures when needed. At the same time, it was suggested that the issue could clearly also fall under the third category, if the focus is on the capability deficiencies of D-LDCs and the resultant limiting environment to use governance space to address right to livelihood. If we now analyse this linkage-issue falling under two linkage-categories from the RtD perspective, it will become clear that the overlap is neither superfluous nor inconsequential. It is, in fact, vital to a proper application of the RtD approach if we are to find holistic solutions for addressing the linkage-issue. As we have seen earlier in this chapter, each linkage-category needs a different approach to identifying solutions, and the overlap may simply mean that the linkage-issue needs more than one policy response to be resolved using the RtD approach. Thus, if we apply an RtD approach to this specific linkage-issue of D-LDCs facing an adverse impact on the human right to livelihood due to opening their markets, it may require a solution under the first as well as third linkage-categories. In other words, it may be possible to address the linkage-issue only if we amend WTO laws to bring in more flexibility for D-LDCs to adopt a mix of appropriate protectionist and open trade policies as deemed necessary for ensuring their own RtD, but also simultaneously if we address their capability deficiencies through an RtD approach to aid. This example demonstrates the significant value a theoretical framework such as governance space accompanied by a coterminous approach to solutions such as RtD can bring in. Not only does it allow the most effective and appropriate solutions to linkage-issues to be identified, it also ensures that 'leakages' can be arrested by identifying all the different ways in which governance space of States may be impacted through a specific linkage-issue.

Notes

1 See generally Gehring and Cordonier Segger (2005) and Voig (2009).
2 For an excellent overview of the historical context in which RtD emerged, see Orford (2001); OHCHR (2013: Chapters 1–4); and Whelan (2015).
3 For a discussion on the speech, see Whelan (2015: 93–94). Some scholars also identify Senegalese jurist, Kéba M'Baye, as the one who coined and developed the concept of RtD. See M'baye (1972).
4 This line of argument found empirical support from Ghai and Pao (1989), when they argued that many repressive regimes in Asia used the language of rights in the Declaration to emphasise priority of economic development over human rights.
5 In his first report, Sengupta, in fact, took note of Sen's theorisation of development and observed that Sen had 'approached this problem almost entirely from the point of view of the right to development'. See UNCHR (1999: Para. 55).
6 See also Sengupta (2002: 859), for a more elaborate discussion on the proposition that, in order to be a human right, it is not necessary that it be also recognised as a legal right.
7 See also UNCHR (2000b: Para. 22).
8 See also Qerimi (2012: 117–18).
9 See also Article 10. 'Steps should be taken to ensure the full exercise and progressive enhancement of the right to development, including the formulation, adoption and implementation of policy, legislative and other measures at the national and international levels.'
10 See also Article 6(1) of DRTD (UNGA 1986).
11 For instance, in the landmark Ogoniland case, there was no claim raised regarding the violation of Article 22 of the African Charter by the petitioners. See *The Social and Economic Rights Action Center and the Center for Economic, and Social Rights vs. Nigeria* (2001).
12 For instance, the 2002 World Summit on Sustainable Development; the 1995 World Summit for Social Development; the 1994 Programme of Action of the International Conference on Population and Development, the 1995 Beijing Platform for Action; and the 2012 United Nations Conference on Sustainable Development ('Rio+ 20'), as well as the follow-up to these conferences, including the outcomes of the 2011 Fourth United Nations Conference on the Least-Developed Countries, the 2014 Third International Conference on Small Island Developing States; the 2014 Second United Nations Conference on Landlocked Developing Countries;

and the 2015 Third UN World Conference on Disaster Risk Reduction, all make references to the right to development.

13 For a detailed analysis of RtD as Customary International Law, see Chimni (2003: 260). For the extreme proposition that the right to development is a *jus cogens* norm, see Bedjaoui (2008: 1447).

14 See also Macklem (2014: 16). For the general proposition that when a resolution of the UNGA touches on subjects dealt with in the UN Charter, it may be regarded as an authoritative interpretation of the Charter, see Crawford (2012: 193).

15 I have argued elsewhere that the RtD approach, accurately framed, goes beyond a 'Human Rights-Based Approach to Development' (HRBA). HRBA focuses merely on linking and aligning the objectives of development projects to specific human rights norms, standards and principles. RtD approach goes further and makes development itself a human right. Therefore, while an RtD approach encompasses HRBA within its fold, it also requires understanding that States have duties to ensure development as a matter of human right. This includes both national and international action (Kanade 2016a; b).

16 For good analyses, see Harrison (2011) and Nordic Trust Fund and World Bank (2013).

17 Article C(ii) of TPRM Agreement provides that the first four biggest entities in terms of world trade share (counting the European Communities as one) shall be subject to review every two years; the next 16 shall be reviewed every four years; and other members shall be reviewed every six years.

18 The TPRB has conducted group reviews of the WTO members of the South African Customs Union, the Organisation of Eastern Caribbean States and the East African Community, along with group reviews of pairs such as Switzerland and Liechtenstein, Cameroon and Gabon, Benin, Burkina Faso and Mali, Niger and Senegal and Guinea and Mauritania.

19 WTO Panels have also decidedly ignored and rejected reliance by States on TPRB documents and reports in dispute settlement proceedings. See *Canada – Aircraft* (Panel Report 1999: Para. 9.274–9.275); *Chile – Price Band System* (Panel Report 2002: Footnote 664).

20 For an overview of the tripartite structure of the ILO, including States, workers' organisations and employers' organisations, see ILO (2016).

9

CONCLUSION

This book began with the ambition to unravel the complex muddle created by the myriads of interactions between MTS and human rights and bring about a systematic order to the otherwise scattered study on linkages. The detailed analysis conducted through the preceding eight chapters has sought to achieve precisely that. As was contended in the first chapter, regulation under the WTO of several 'trade-related' areas of economic activity has meant that the impacts of MTS have permeated into the lives of human beings in multifaceted ways. While WTO members have the duty to comply with their legal obligations under MTS, the principal obligation under international law to deal with the adverse impacts of MTS on human rights also lies on those very States. This necessarily calls for synergies to be established between MTS and human rights. As has been demonstrated throughout this book, however, States tend to compartmentalise their trade-related obligations under the WTO and their human rights obligations under the UN, thus leading to 'splendid isolation' of the two regimes.

One of the challenges identified in this book was that, in general, solutions proposed by scholars to the linkage-issues have suffered from either a complete issue-by-issue segregation so that there is no coherent and holistic theoretical framework for analysing the linkages or from a collective dealing of all human rights issues affected by MTS as if they were a single issue which deserved a common solution. The reason for this was identified as the lack of a comprehensive theory on linkages. This book, therefore, not only developed a theoretical framework for analysing linkages conceived of as the 'governance space' framework, but also identified three linkage-categories within which linkage-issues arise. Case studies were used to further elaborate on each of the linkage-categories. Our focus in this book was consciously on the adverse impacts on human rights. This does not mean that MTS has no positive impacts whatsoever on human rights. It could well be argued that MTS, with its focus on transparency in tariff and trade-related non-tariff policies of States, promotes the right to information. If properly oriented, MTS can also advance the right to property and the right to livelihood for a significant number of participants in the system. However, we have also seen that benefits of MTS in the existing form are deeply asymmetric and much needs to be done to orient it towards promotion of human rights.

The ambition of this book was not merely to provide an explanation for why things are the way they are. It also aimed at providing the appropriate approach to resolving linkage-issues arising within the three linkage-categories identified by us. The fundamental premise was that the governance space framework needs to be supplemented by an appropriate 'approach' that will ensure that governance space of States is not used or abused in a way which adversely impacts on their obligations to respect, protect and fulfil human rights. This is especially important since, as concluded in Chapter 4, the judicial mechanism of the WTO may not be the appropriate forum for resolving tensions between MTS and human rights due to the limitations placed by WTO members on it. The onus to adopt appropriate approaches to ensuring that the impacts of MTS on governance space of States are not adverse, therefore, lies upon States themselves, both individually and collectively.

In light of this, it was argued that if governance space issues are to be addressed and appropriate solutions found, it is vital that human rights considerations are made intrinsic to the WTO processes. This essentially means that States must take into consideration human rights concerns at all stages of the WTO processes, including pre-negotiation, negotiation and trade policy review. To do so, however, it was important for us to provide moral as well as legal arguments justifying internalisation of human rights considerations in WTO processes. That justification was found in the Marrakesh Agreement itself which incorporates 'sustainable development' as one of its principal objectives. The important point of departure here from current arguments at the WTO is, therefore, acknowledging the fact that free trade and economic growth are not ends in themselves but are intended to be means to achieve sustainable development. And because sustainable development cannot be promoted if human rights are undermined, it is necessary for all WTO processes to internalise human rights considerations. To systematically establish the link between sustainable development and human rights, an exhaustive analysis of RtD was undertaken whereby development itself was presented as a human right. It was contended that RtD gives proper shape and texture to the institutional objective of WTO by purposely stressing on the rights and duties aspects of sustainable development. By insisting that development is a human right which has clearly identified duty-bearers including both DCs and D-LDCs, the RtD approach drives home the point that the only way development through MTS can be sustainable is if it encompasses all human rights as equally important and ensures that no human right is undermined.

As we have seen in this book, the concepts of governance space and RtD are coterminous because both focus equally on the rights as well as duties of States. As demonstrated in Chapter 2, availability of governance space (first linkage-category) as well as the capability to use governance space (third linkage-category) are certainly rights of States, but not abusing governance space which they have (second linkage-category) is also a binding duty. It is precisely this holistic nature of governance space as a framework for identifying linkage-categories which makes it entirely coterminous with RtD as an approach to finding solutions. This is because, as demonstrated in Chapter 8, the focus of RtD as well on both the rights and the duties of States allows them, and D-LDCs, in particular, to stake a claim as agents of their citizens that ensuring development within the State is their right and that other States and international organisations have a duty to not undermine the same (coterminous with the first linkage-category). Moreover, acknowledging the lower threshold of infrastructural and technological capabilities which D-LDCs have, RtD also frames international cooperation as a duty of States, particularly the DCs (coterminous with the third linkage-category). On the other hand, it also insists that all States, including the D-LDCs, have an obligation to respect, protect and fulfil human rights internally to ensure development and that they cannot pass off violations of the rights of their citizens under a distorted label of development (coterminous with the second linkage-category).

Because of this specific coterminosity, RtD provides the perfect approach to identify the distinct, yet appropriate, solutions to linkage-issues within each of the three linkage-categories under the governance space framework. This is not to say that the same solutions will necessarily apply to all linkage-issues which may emerge within the respective linkage-categories, although, their broad characteristics may remain the same. This is also not to say that a given linkage-issue may fall in clinical precision only within one of the three linkage-categories and that there can be no overlaps. As was pointed out, that is indeed possible and is, in fact, the biggest value-added of the coterminous nature of RtD approach and the governance space framework. Overlap of a linkage-issue between two or more linkage-categories helps us identify and acknowledge that solutions thereto may need more than one policy response.

Before concluding this book and in order to prevent myself doing grave disservice to all the arguments raised herein, I find it particularly important to caution WTO members against embarking on what I believe is a disturbing recent development – the concerted attempt by DCs, particularly the US, to sound the death-knell for the DDA during and in the aftermath of the tenth WTO Ministerial Conference held at Nairobi in December 2015 (Kanade 2016c). Indeed, the intention to do so was made abundantly clear by Michael Froman, the US Trade Representative, in an op-ed published in the *Financial Times* just two days prior to the Conference (Froman 2015). In this piece suggestively entitled 'We are at the End of the Line on the Doha Round of Trade Talks', Froman argued that 'Doha was designed in a different era, for a different era, and much has changed since' and that 'it is time for the world to free itself of the strictures of Doha', before concluding in a presagious manner that 'Nairobi will mark the end of an era' (Froman 2015). Froman, directly connected the deadlock in the Doha Round with the proliferation of RTAs, ironically led by his own country. He reminded everyone that the US had 'recently concluded the Trans-Pacific Partnership, which raises standards and tackles emerging issues across nearly 40 per cent of the global economy' and that 'the US and the EU are moving forward with the world's largest bilateral agreement' (Froman 2015). With these RTAs led by the US put forth as proof for the fact that 'trade initiatives outside the WTO have become the norm', Froman then went on to argue that the Doha Round must be buried if multilateralism has to have a chance of succeeding (Froman 2015). An excellent description of this stand is provided by Chakravarthi Raghavan, who is quoted as stating that 'the US/EU arguments to abandon Doha because of the deadlock reminded him of the story of a son convicted for murdering his parents to get at their property who asks the court for leniency on the grounds that he was an orphan!' (Patnaik 2015).

Regretfully, while the Nairobi Ministerial Declaration adopted in the end by WTO members insisted on the 'pre-eminence of WTO as the global forum for trade rules setting and governance' (WTO 2015b: Para. 3) and on the 'need to ensure that RTA's remain complementary, not a substitute for, the multilateral trading system' (WTO 2015b: Para. 28), it refrained from reaffirming the DDA and its mandate. The Declaration, in fact, acknowledged that members 'have different views' on how to address the future of the Doha Round negotiations and that while many members reaffirm the DDA, 'other Members do not reaffirm the Doha mandates, as they believe new approaches are necessary to achieve meaningful outcomes in multilateral negotiations' (WTO 2015b: Para. 30). At the same time, the Declaration loosened the lid on the question of whether the WTO should consider new issues beyond those contained in the DDA, even without resolving those first. Unsurprisingly, a compromise arrangement was arrived at, which included an acceptance that WTO members may raise new issues at the WTO, however, a consensus would be required for launching these new negotiations (WTO 2015b: Para. 34).

There are two implications of the Nairobi Declaration. First, it has opened up the opportunity for DCs to place new issues relating to further liberalisation on the agenda, even if the Doha issues are not negotiated upfront. Of course, D-LDCs will need to agree to negotiate these new issues, but the Declaration has now officially provided DCs with the legal justification for elevating non-Doha issues to the same level as Doha issues. Second, and more importantly, it has provided the opportunity to DCs, their policy think-tanks and media outlets to claim that DDA is dead and buried, and it is time now to move on to further liberalisation. Indeed, an editorial in the *Financial Times* took precious little time in ecstatically declaring the death-knell for the DDA and the Doha Round itself. In its obituary, laden with celebratory overtones, the editorial stated:

> After a death scene so drawn-out it would have done credit to a Victorian melodrama, the curtain has finally come down on one of the longest-running farces in global policymaking. The so-called Doha round, the programme of multilateral trade talks that started in 2001, was last week declared dead by World Trade Organisation members after nearly a decade spent comatose.
>
> (*Financial Times* 2015)

In light of this deeply offensive and invidious onslaught upon the hopes and aspirations of the Global South, D-LDCs will need to put up a collective front in order to ensure that the DDA and its issues are not relegated to the backburner. The Nairobi Declaration contains some language which may yet salvage the situation. Despite the concessions on new issues, it states that 'nevertheless, there remains a strong commitment of all Members to advance negotiations on the remaining Doha issues' and that 'this includes advancing work in all three pillars of agriculture, namely domestic support, market access and export competition, as well as non-agriculture market access, services, development, TRIPS and rules' (WTO 2015b: Para. 31).

It is worthwhile highlighting that the DDA did not give birth to the development mandate of the WTO; the Marrakesh Agreement itself did. It did so by recognising sustainable development as the WTO's institutional objective. The DDA was nothing but an attempt to reorient MTS towards fulfilment of that institutional objective. The adoption of the ambitious 2030 Agenda and the accompanying 17 SDGs by world leaders in September 2015 has for the first time provided shape and texture to this institutional objective of the WTO. SDG 17.1, in particular, requires promoting 'a universal, rules-based, open, non-discriminatory and equitable multilateral trading system under the World Trade Organisation, including through the conclusion of negotiations under its Doha Development Agenda' (UNGA 2015). If the conclusion of negotiations under the DDA is what the world leaders agreed is required for sustainable development, it is clear that the Nairobi Declaration adopted just three months later cannot be interpreted to mean that the DDA is dead and buried, as Froman and the *Financial Times* would have us believe. Any such interpretation would directly militate against not only the 2030 Agenda but also the very institutional objective of the WTO. D-LDCs must remain vigilant against such attempts; for it would be impossible to later exhume and reconstruct the skeleton of the DDA limb by limb.

As noted earlier, this book has attempted to fill a theoretical void in the study of linkages between MTS and human rights, but simultaneously, has also attempted to be policy-oriented in terms of approaches to solutions. The analysis conducted herein has sought to present a balanced perspective on different contentious issues in the debates on linkages. However, search for balance often necessarily implies resistance from those who seek to maintain the imbalance. At the very least, it is hoped that the governance spaces theory and its accompanying RtD approach to solutions presented in this book will influence the debates on this topic at the WTO, at the UN and in the civil society and academia, with respect to the way forward in this increasingly complex globalised world.

APPENDIX: LIST OF CASES

WTO and GATT 1947 cases

Argentina – Poultry Anti-Dumping Duties

Argentina – Definitive Anti-Dumping Duties on Poultry from Brazil, Report of the Panel, World Trade Organization, WT/DS241/R, 22 April 2003.

Brazil – Retreaded Tyres

Brazil – Measures Affecting Imports of Retreaded Tyres, Report of the Panel, World Trade Organization, WT/DS332/R, 12 June 2007.

Brazil – Measures Affecting Imports of Retreaded Tyres, Report of the Appellate Body, World Trade Organization, WT/DS332/AB/R, 3 December 2007.

Canada – Aircraft

Canada – Measures Affecting the Export of Civilian Aircraft, Report of the Panel, World Trade Organization, WT/DS70/R, 14 April 1999.

Canada – Dairy

Canada – Measures Affecting the Importation of Milk and the Exportation of Dairy Products, Report of the Appellate Body, World Trade Organization, WT/DS103/AB/R, 13 October 1999.

Canada – Herring and Salmon

Canada – Measures Affecting Exports of Unprocessed Herring and Salmon, Report of the Panel, BISD 35S/98, L/6268, 22 March 1998.

China – Intellectual Property Rights

China – Measures Affecting the Protection and Enforcement of Intellectual Property Rights, Report of the Panel, WT/DS362/R, 26 January 2009.

China – Publications and Audiovisual Products

China – Measures Affecting Trading Rights and Distribution Services for Certain Publications and Audiovisual Entertainment Products, Report of the Appellate Body, World Trade Organization, WT/DS363/AB/R, 21 December 2009.

China – Rare Earths

China – Measures Related to the Exportation of Rare Earths, Tungsten, and Molybdenum, Report of the Panel, World Trade Organization, WT/DS431/R, 26 March 2014.

China – Measures Related to the Exportation of Rare Earths, Tungsten, and Molybdenum, Report of the Appellate Body, World Trade Organization, WT/DS431/AB/R, 7 August 2014.

China – Raw Materials

China – Measures Related to the Exportation of Various Raw Materials, Report of the Panel, World Trade Organization, WT/DS394/R, 5 July 2011.

China – Measures Related to the Exportation of Various Raw Materials, Report of the Appellate Body, World Trade Organization, WT/DS394/AB/R, 30 January 2012.

Chile – Price Band System

Chile – Price Band System and Safeguard Measures Relating to Certain Agricultural Products, Report of the Panel, World Trade Organization, WT/DS207/R, 3 May 2002.

EC – Approval and Marketing of Biotech Products

European Communities – Measures Affecting the Approval and Marketing of Biotech Products, Report of the Panel, World Trade Organization, WT/DS291/R, 29 September 2006.

EC – Asbestos

European Communities – Measures Containing Asbestos and Asbestos Containing Products, Report of the Panel, World Trade Organization, WT/DS135/ R, 18 September 2000.

European Communities – Measures Containing Asbestos and Asbestos Containing Products, Report of the Appellate Body, World Trade Organization, WT/DS135/AB/R, 12 March 2001.

EC – Bananas III

European Communities – Regime for the Importation, Sale, and Distribution of Bananas, Report of the Panel, World Trade Organization, WT/DS27/R/ECU, 22 May 1997.

European Communities – Regime for the Importation, Sale, and Distribution of Bananas, Report of the Appellate Body, World Trade Organization, WT/DS27/AB/R, 9 September 1997.

EC – Chicken Cuts

European Communities – Customs Classification of Frozen Boneless Chicken Cuts, Report of the Appellate Body, World Trade Organization, WT/DS286/AB/R, 12 September 2005.

EC – Commercial Vessels

European Communities – Measures Affecting Trade in Commercial Vessels, Report of the Panel, World Trade Organization, WT/DS301/R, 22 April 2005.

EC – Computer Equipment

Ireland – Customs Classification of Certain Computer Equipment, Report of the Appellate Body, World Trade Organization, WT/DS68/AB/R, 5 June 1998.

EC – Hormones (22.6)

European Communities – Measures Concerning Meat and Meat Products (Hormones) (Article 22,6 – EC), Report of the Appellate Body, World Trade Organization, WT/DS26/ARB, 12 July 1999.

EC – Poultry

European Communities – Measures Affecting the Importation of Certain Poultry Products, Report of the Appellate Body, World Trade Organization, WT/DS69/AB/R, 13 July 1998.

EC – Seal Products

European Communities – Measures Prohibiting the Importation and Marketing of Seal Products, Report of the Panel, World Trade Organization, WT/DS400/R, 25 November 2013.

European Communities – Measures Prohibiting the Importation and Marketing of Seal Products, Report of the Appellate Body, World Trade Organization, WT/DS400/AB/R, 22 May 2014.

EC and Certain Member States – Large Civil Aircraft

European Communities – Measures Affecting Trade in Large Civil Aircraft, Report of the Panel, World Trade Organization, WT/DS316/R, 30 June 2010.

European Communities – Measures Affecting Trade in Large Civil Aircraft, Report of the Appellate Body, World Trade Organization, WT/DS316/AB/R, 18 May 2011.

EC – Tariff Preferences

European Communities – Conditions for the Granting of Tariff Preferences to Developing Countries, Report of the Panel, World Trade Organization, WT/DS246/R, 1 December 2003.

Japan – Alcoholic Beverages II

Japan – Taxes on Alcoholic Beverages, Report of the Appellate Body, World Trade Organization, WT/DS8/AB/R, 4 October 1996.

Korea – Alcoholic Beverages

Korea – Taxes on Alcoholic Beverages, Report of the Panel, World Trade Organization, WT/DS84/R, 17 September 1998, as modified by Report of the Appellate Body, WT/DS84/AB/R, 18 January 1999.

Korea – Procurement

Korea – Measures Affecting Government Procurement, Report of the Panel, World Trade Organization, WT/DS163/R, 19 June 2000.

Korea – Various Measures on Beef

Korea – Measures Affecting Imports of Fresh, Chilled and Frozen Beef, Report of the Appellate Body, World Trade Organization, WT/DS161/AB/R, 11 December 2000.

Mexico – Soft Drinks

Mexico – Tax Measures on Soft Drinks and Other Beverages, Report of the Appellate Body, World Trade Organization, WT/DS308/AB/R, 6 March 2006.

Philippines – Distilled Spirits

Philippines – Taxes on Distilled Spirits, Report of the Panel, World Trade Organization, WT/DS396/R, 15 August 2011, as modified by Report of the Appellate Body, World Trade Organization, WT/DS396/AB/R, 21 December 2011.

Thailand – Cigarettes

Thailand – Restrictions on Importation of and Internal Taxes on Cigarettes, Report of the Panel, BISD 37S/200, DS10/R, 7 November 1990.

Thailand – Cigarettes (Philippines)

Thailand – Customs and Fiscal Measures on Cigarettes from the Philippines, Report of the Panel, World Trade Organization, WT/DS371/R, 15 November 2010, as modified by Report of the Appellate Body, WT/DS371/AB/R, 17 June 2011.

Turkey – Textiles

Turkey – Restrictions on Imports of Textile and Clothing Products, Report of the Panel, World Trade Organization, WT/DS34/R, 31 May 1999.

US – Anti-Dumping and Countervailing Duties (China)

United States – Definitive Anti-Dumping and Countervailing Duties on Certain Products from China, Report of the Appellate Body, World Trade Organization, WT/DS379/AB/R, 11 March 2011.

US – Clove Cigarettes

United States – Measures Affecting the Production and Sale of Clove Cigarettes, Report of the Panel, World Trade Organization, WT/DS406/R, 2 September 2011, as modified by Report of the Appellate Body, WT/DS406/AB/R, 4 April 2012.

US – FSC (21.5)

United States – Tax Treatment for 'Foreign Sales Corporations', Recourse to Article 21,5 of the DSU by the European Communities, Report of the Appellate Body, World Trade Organization, WT/DS108/AB/RW, 14 January 2002.

US – Gambling

United States – Measures Affecting the Cross-Border Supply of Gambling and Betting Services, Report of the Appellate Body, World Trade Organization, WT/DS285/AB/R, 7 April 2005.

US – Gasoline

United States – Standards for Reformulated and Conventional Gasoline, Report of the Panel, World Trade Organization, WT/DS2/R, 29 January 1996.

United States – Standards for Reformulated and Conventional Gasoline, Report of the Appellate Body, World Trade Organization, WT/DS2/AB/R, 29 April 1996.

US – Section 337

United States – Section 337 of the Tariff Act of 1930, Report of the Panel, BISD 36S/345, L/6439, 7 November 1989.

US – Shrimp

United States – Import Prohibition of Certain Shrimp and Shrimp Products, Report of the Appellate Body, World Trade Organization, WT/DS58/AB/R, 12 October 1998.

US – Shrimp (21.5)

United States – Import Prohibition of Certain Shrimp and Shrimp Products, Recourse to Article 21,5 of the DSU by Malaysia, Report of the Panel, World Trade Organization, WT/DS58/RW, 15 June 2001.

United States – Import Prohibition of Certain Shrimp and Shrimp Products, Recourse to Article 21,5 of the DSU by Malaysia, Report of the Appellate Body, World Trade Organization, WT/DS58/AB/RW, 22 October 2001.

US – Tuna Dolphin I

United States – Restrictions on Imports of Tuna, Report of the GATT Panel, DS21/R – 39S/155, 3 September 1991.

US – Tuna Dolphin II

United States – Restrictions on Imports of Tuna, Report of the GATT Panel, DS29/R, 16 June 1994.

Other cases

Centre for Minority Rights Development (Kenya) and Minority Rights Group International on behalf of Endorois Welfare Council vs. Kenya, African Commission on Human and Peoples' Rights, 276/2003, 4 February 2010.

Constitution of the Maritime Safety Committee of the Inter-Governmental Maritime Consultative Organization, Advisory Opinion, International Court of Justice, *I.C.J. Reports 1960*, 150–72.

The Gabčíkovo-Nagymaros Project (Hungary/Slovakia), Judgement, International Court of Justice, *I.C.J. Reports 1997*, 7–84.

The Gabčíkovo-Nagymaros Project (Hungary/Slovakia), Separate Opinion of Vice-President Weeramantry, International Court of Justice, *I.C.J. Reports 1997*, 88–119.

Interpretation of the Convention of 1919 Concerning Employment of Women during the Night, Advisory Opinion, Permanent Court of International Justice, *P.C.I.J. Series A/B50, 1932*, 365–82.

Legality of the Threat or Use of Nuclear Weapons, Advisory Opinion, International Court of Justice, *I.C.J. Reports 1996*, 226–67.

Maritime Delimitation and Territorial Questions between Qatar and Bahrain (Qatar vs. Bahrain), Jurisdiction and Admissibility, Judgment, International Court of Justice, *I.C.J. Reports 1995*, 6–26.

Pulp Mills on the River Uruguay (Argentina vs. Uruguay), Judgement, International Court of Justice, *I.C.J. Reports 2010*, 14–107.

Questions of Interpretation and Application of the 1971 Montreal Convention Arising from the Aerial Incident at Lockerbie (Libyan Arab Jamahiriya vs. United States of America), Preliminary Objections, Judgement, International Court of Justice, *I.C.J. Reports 1992*, 115–37.

The Social and Economic Rights Action Center and the Center for Economic, and Social Rights vs. Nigeria, African Commission on Human and Peoples' Rights, 155/96, 27 October 2001.

Territorial Dispute Case (Libyan Arab Jamahiriya/Chad), Judgement, International Court of Justice, *I.C.J. Reports 1994*, 6–43.

BIBLIOGRAPHY

International and regional treaties/agreements

'African Charter on Human and Peoples' Rights', 27 June 1981, CAB/LEG/67/3 rev. 5, *International Legal Materials*, 21.1 (1982): 58–68.

'Agreement on Subsidies and Countervailing Measures', 15 April 1994, *United Nations Treaty Series*, 1869: 14–56.

'Agreement on Technical Barriers to Trade', 15 April 1994, *United Nations Treaty Series*, 1868: 120–40.

'Agreement on the Application of Sanitary and Phyto-Sanitary Measures', 15 April 1994, *United Nations Treaty Series*, 1867: 493–507.

'Agreement on Trade Policy Review Mechanism', Annex 3 to the Agreement Establishing the WTO, 15 April 1994, *United Nations Treaty Series*, 1869: 480–2.

'Agreement on Trade-Related Aspects of Intellectual Property Rights', Annex 1C to the Agreement Establishing the World Trade Organization, 15 April 1994, *United Nations Treaty Series*, 1869: 299–331.

'Charter of the United Nations', 24 October 1945, *United Nations Treaty Series*, 1: XVI.

'Constitution of the International Labour Organisation (ILO)', Adopted by the *Peace Conference*, Paris, 1 April 1919.

'Convention (No. 105) Concerning the Abolition of Forced Labour', 25 June 1957, *United Nations Treaty Series*, 320: 291–300.

'Convention (No. 182) Concerning the Prohibition and Immediate Action for the Elimination of the Worst Forms of Child Labour', 17 June 1999, *United Nations Treaty Series*, 2133: 161–7.

'Convention Against Torture and Other Cruel, Inhuman or Degrading Treatment or Punishment', 10 December 1984, *United Nations Treaty Series*, 1465: 113–22.

'Convention on the Elimination of All Forms of Discrimination Against Women', 18 December 1979, *United Nations Treaty Series*, 1249: 14–23.

'Convention on the Rights of Persons With Disabilities', 13 December 2006, *United Nations Treaty Series*, 2515: 70–96.

'Convention on the Rights of the Child', 20 November 1989, *United Nations Treaty Series*, 1577: 44–61.

'Fourth ACP-EC Convention of Lomé Signed at Lomé on 15 December 1989'. As Revised by the Agreement Signed in Mauritius on 4 November 1995, *Official Journal of the European Union*, 156: 3–106.

'General Agreement on Tariffs and Trade', 30 October 1947, *United Nations Treaty Series*, 55: 187–316.

'General Agreement on Tariffs and Trade', Annex 1A to the Agreement Establishing the World Trade Organization, 15 April 1994, *United Nations Treaty Series*, 1867: 190–1.

'General Agreement on Trade in Services', Annex 1B to the Agreement Establishing the World Trade Organization, 15 April 1994, *United Nations Treaty Series*, 1869: 183–218.

'Havana Charter for an International Trade Organization', Adopted at the United Nations Conference on Trade and Employment, Havana, Cuba, 21 November 1947–24 March 1948, U.N. Doc. E/CONF.2/78.

'International Convention for the Protection of All Persons From Enforced Disappearance', 20 December 2006, *United Nations Treaty Series*, 2716: 56–74.

'International Convention on the Elimination of All Forms of Racial Discrimination', 7 March 1966, *United Nations Treaty Series*, 660: 212–38.

'International Convention on the Protection of the Rights of All Migrant Workers and Members of Their Families', 18 December 1990, *United Nations Treaty Series*, 2220: 92–127.

'International Covenant on Civil and Political Rights', 16 December 1966, *United Nations Treaty Series*, 999: 172–86.

'International Covenant on Economic, Social and Cultural Rights', 16 December 1966, *United Nations Treaty Series*, 993: 3–12.

'Marrakesh Agreement Establishing the World Trade Organization', 15 April 1994, *International Legal Materials*, 33.5 (1994): 1144–53, *United Nations Treaty Series*, 1867: 154–64.

'North American Free Trade Agreement', 17 December 1992, *International Legal Materials*, 32.1 (1993): 296–456.

'Partnership Agreement Between the Members of the African, Caribbean and Pacific Group of States of the One Part, and the European Community and Its Member States, of the Other Part, Signed in Cotonou on 23 June 2000', *Official Journal of the European Union*, 317: 3–353.

'Statute of the International Court of Justice', Annexed to the Charter of the United Nations, 24 October 1945, *United Nations Treaty Series*, 1: XVI.

'Understanding on Rules and Procedures Governing the Settlement of Disputes', Annex 2 to the Agreement Establishing the WTO, 15 April 1994, *United Nations Treaty Series*, 1869: 401–25.

'United Nations Convention on the Law of the Sea', 10 December 1982, *United Nations Treaty Series*, 1833: 397–581.

'Vienna Convention on the Law of Treaties', 23 May 1969, *United Nations Treaty Series*, 1155: 331–52.

Books and articles

Aaronson, Susan and Zimmerman, Jamie. 2008. *Trade Imbalance: The Struggle to Weigh Human Rights Concerns in Trade Policymaking*. Cambridge: Cambridge University Press.

Abbott, Frederick, Kaufmann, Christine and Cottier, Thomas (eds). 2006. *International Trade and Human Rights: Foundations and Conceptual Issues*. Michigan: University of Michigan Press.

Adhikari, Ratnakar. 2011. 'Evaluating Aid for Trade Effectiveness on the Ground: A Methodological Framework', *International Centre for Trade and Sustainable Development Issue Paper Series*, 20: 1–35.

AFL-CIO. 2004. 'Section 301 Petition Against China: Executive Summary', *New Labor Forum*, 13(3): 86–89.

AFL-CIO. 2013. 'Resolution 12: America and the World Need a New Approach to Trade and Globalization', www.aflcio.org/About/Exec-Council/Conventions/2013/Resolutions-and-Amendments/Resolution-12-America-and-the-World-Need-a-New-Approach-to-Trade-and-Globalization (accessed on 1 October 2016).

AFL-CIO. 2014. 'Declaration of Joint Principles by AFL-CIO and the European Trade Union Confederation (ETUC) on the Trans-Atlantic Trade and Investment Partnership', www.aflcio.org/content/download/132421/3553131/AFL-CIO+TTIP+Report_6+(2).pdf (accessed on 1 October 2016).

Akyuz, Yilmaz. 2009. 'Multilateral Disciplines and the Question of Policy Space', *Third World Network Trade & Development Series*, 38: 1–88.

Alben, Elissa. 2001. 'GATT and the Fair Wage: A Historical Perspective', *Columbia Law Review*, 101(6): 1410–47.

Alesina, Alberto and Dollar, David. 2000. 'Who Gives Foreign Aid to Whom and Why?', *Journal of Economic Growth*, 5(1): 33–63.

Alexander, Lisa. 2010. 'Reflections on Success and Failure in New Governance and the Role of the Lawyer', *Wisconsin Law Review*, 2: 737–74.

Alston, Philip. 1985. 'The Shortcomings of a "Garfield the Cat" Approach to the Right to Development', *California Western International Law Journal*, 15(3): 510–18.

Alston, Philip. 1991. 'Revitalising United Nations Work on Human Rights and Development', *Melbourne University Law Review*, 18(2): 216–57.

Alston, Philip. 2004. 'Core Labour Standards and the Transformation of the International Labour Rights Regime', *European Journal of International Law*, 15(3): 457–522.

Alvarez, Jose. 2001. 'How Not to Link: Institutional Conundrums of an Expanded Trade Regime', *Widener Law Symposium Journal*, 7: 1–20.

Alvarez, Jose. 2009. 'Contemporary International Law: An "Empire of Law" or the "Law of Empire"?', *American University International Law Review*, 24(5): 811–42.

Anghie, Antony. 1999. 'Universality and the Concept of Governance in International Law', in Edward Quashigah and Obiora Okafor (eds), *Legitimate*

Governance in Africa: International and Domestic Legal Perspectives, pp. 21–40. The Hague: Kluwer Law International.

Anghie, Antony. 2000. 'Civilization and Commerce: The Concept of Governance in Historical Perspective', *Villanova Law Review*, 45(5): 887–912.

Anghie, Antony. 2007. *Imperialism, Sovereignty and the Making of International Law*. Cambridge: Cambridge University Press.

Anghie, Antony and Chimni, Bhupinder. 2003. 'Third World Approaches to International Law and Individual Responsibility in Internal Conflicts', *Chinese Journal of International Law*, 2(1): 79–103.

Annan, Kofi. 2003. 'Message of the UN Secretary-General, Mr. Kofi Annan, to the WTO Ministerial Meeting, Cancun'. WT/MIN(03)/12. 10 September 2003.

Anuradha, R.V. and Dutta, Nimisha. 2012. 'Trade and Labour Under the WTO and FTAs', *Centre for WTO Studies Discussion Paper Series*, 9: 1–42.

Arend, Jan-Michael and Riedel, Eibe. 2012. 'Article 55(c)', in Bruno Simma *et al.* (eds), *The Charter of the United Nations: A Commentary*, Volume II, pp. 1565–602. Oxford: Oxford University Press.

Association of Southeast Asian Nations. 2012. 'ASEAN Human Rights Declaration'. Adopted on 18 November 2012 at Phnom Penh, Cambodia.

Aust, Anthony. 2013. *Modern Treaty Law and Practice*. Cambridge: Cambridge University Press.

Bagwell, Kyle and Staiger, Robert. 2000. 'The Simple Economics of Labor Standards and the GATT', in Alan Deardorff and Robert Stem (eds), *Social Dimensions of US Trade Policies*, pp. 195–231. Michigan: University of Michigan Press.

Bal, Salman. 2001. 'International Free Trade Agreements and Human Rights: Reinterpreting Art XX of the GATT', *Minnesota Journal of Global Trade*, 10(1): 62–108.

Balakrishnan, Rajagopal. 2003. *International Law From Below: Development, Social Movements and Third World Resistance*. Cambridge: Cambridge University Press.

Banks, Kevin. 2006. 'The Impact of Globalization on Labour Standards: A Second Look at the Evidence', in John Craig and Michael Lynk (eds), *Globalization and the Future of Labour Law*, pp. 77–107. Cambridge: Cambridge University Press.

Barrel, Virginie. 2012. 'Sustainable Development in International Law: Nature and Operation of an Evolutive Legal Norm', *The European Journal of International Law*, 23(2): 377–400.

Barry, Christian and Reddy, Sanjay. 2008. *International Trade and Labor Standards: A Proposal for Linkage*. New York: Columbia University Press.

Bartels, Lorand. 2002. 'Article XX of GATT and the Problem of Extraterritorial Jurisdiction: The Case of Trade Measures for the Protection of Human Rights', *Journal of World Trade*, 36(2): 353–403.

Bartels, Lorand. 2011. 'Jurisdiction and Applicable Law Clauses in International Law: Where Does a Tribunal Find the Principal Norms Applicable to the Case

Before It?', in Tomer Broude and Yuval Shany (eds), *Multi-Sourced Equivalent Norms in International Law*, pp. 115–41. Oxford: Hart Publishing.

Bartels, Lorand. 2014. 'Jurisdiction and Applicable Law in WTO', *University of Cambridge Legal Studies Research Paper Series*, 59: 1–23.

Basu, Kaushik. 2001. 'The View From the Tropics', *Boston Review*, February/March, http://new.bostonreview.net/BR26.1/basu.html (accessed on 01 October 2016).

Bedjaoui, Mohammed. 1991. *International Law: Achievement and Prospects*. Paris: UNESCO.

Bedjaoui, Mohammed. 2008. 'The Right to Development', in Henry Steiner, Philip Alston and Ryan Goodman (eds), *International Human Rights in Context*, pp. 1447–8. Oxford: Oxford University Press.

Bell, Stephen. 2002. *Economic Governance and Institutional Dynamics*. Oxford and Melbourne: Oxford University Press.

Bello, Walden and Legrain, Phillipe. 2000. 'Should the WTO Be Abolished?', *The Ecologist*, 30(9): 20–23.

The Berne Declaration *et al.* 2010. 'Human Rights Impact Assessment for Trade and Investment Agreements'. *Report of the Expert Seminar*, 23–24 June, Geneva, Switzerland, http://www2.ohchr.org/english/issues/food/docs/report_hria-seminar_2010.pdf (accessed on 2 October 2016).

Berthelemy, Jean-Claude. 2006. 'Bilateral Donors' Interest vs. Recipients' Development Motives in Aid Allocation: Do all Donors Behave the Same?', *Review of Development Economics*, 10(2): 179–94.

Bevir, Mark. 2013. *Governance: A Very Short Introduction*. Oxford: Oxford University Press.

Bhagwati, Jagdish. 2000. *The Wind of the Hundred Days: How Washington Mismanaged Globalization*. Cambridge: MIT Press.

Bhagwati, Jagdish. 2002. 'Afterword: The Question of Linkage', *American Journal of International Law*, 96(1): 126–34.

Bhagwati, Jagdish. 2007. 'America's Bipartisan Battle Against Free Trade', www.ft.com/content/0dae9606-e5e9-11db-9fcf-000b5df10621 (accessed on 01 October 2016).

Bhagwati, Jagdish. 2008. *Termites in the Trading System: How Preferential Agreements Undermine Free Trade*. Oxford: Oxford University Press.

Bhagwati, Jagdish and Hudec, Robert. 1996. *Fair Trade and Harmonization: Prerequisites for Free Trade?* Cambridge: MIT Press.

Bhagwati, Jagdish *et al.* 1999. 'Third World Intellectuals and NGOs Statement Against Linkage', *The Earth Times*, 8(17): 16–30.

Bhala, Raj. 1998. 'Clarifying the Trade-Labor Link', *Columbia Journal of Transnational Law*, 37(1): 11–56.

Blackett, Adelle. 2007. 'Trade Liberalization, Labour Law and Development: A Contextualization', *International Institute for Labour Studies Discussion Paper Series*, 179: 1–30.

Block, Richard, Roberts, Karen and Ormiston, Russell. 2002. 'Economic Perspectives on International Labour Standards', *Michigan State University – Detroit College of Law's Journal of International Law*, 11(3): 417–26.

Boie, Bertram. 2012. 'Labour Related Provisions in International Investment Agreements', *ILO Employment Working Paper Series*, 126: 1–48.

Borgen, Christopher. 2005. 'Resolving Treaty Conflicts', *George Washington International Law Review*, 37(1): 573–648.

Brazys, Samuel. 2009. 'Evaluating the Impact of Trade Capacity Building: Evidence for the Donor-Interest or Recipient-Need Theory of Foreign Aid?'. Paper Presented at the Conference *Exploring the Past, Anticipating the Future*, New York, 15 February.

Broude, Tomer. 2008. 'Fragmentation of International Law: On Normative Integration as Authority Allocation', in Tomer Broude and Yuval Shany (eds), *The Shifting Allocation of Authority in International Law: Considering Sovereignty, Supremacy and Subsidiarity*, pp. 99–121. Portland: Hart Publishing.

Brown, Drusilla. 2000. 'International Trade and Core Labour Standards: A Survey of the Recent Literature', *OECD Labour Market and Social Policy Occasional Papers Series*, 43: 1–62.

Brown, Kathy-Ann. 2006. 'Can Donors Help Countries to Negotiate and Maintain Their Rights Under Trade Agreements?', in Sheila Page (ed), *Trade and Aid: Partners or Rivals in Development Policy?*, pp. 245–73. London: Cameron May.

Bugge, Hans Christian and Voigt, Christina. 2008. *Sustainable Development in International and National Law: What Did the Brundtland Report Do to Legal Thinking and Legal Development, and Where Can We Go From Here?* Groningen: Europa Law Publishing.

Cadot, Olivier and de Melo, Jaime. 2014. *Aid for Trade: What We Have Learnt? Which Way Ahead?* London: CEPR Press and FERDI.

Cadot, Olivier and Newfarmer, Richard. 2011. 'Does It Work? Aid for Trade Through the Evaluation Prism', *Trade Negotiations Insights*, 10(7): 10–11.

Cadot, Olivier *et al.* 2011. *Where to Spend the Next Million? Applying Impact Evaluation to Trade Assistance*. Washington, DC: The World Bank.

Cai, Phoenix. 2008. 'Aid for Trade: A Roadmap for Success', *Denver Journal of International Law and Policy*, 36(3–4): 283–324.

Cali, Massimiliano and te Velde, Dirk. 2011. 'Does Aid for Trade Really Improve Trade Performance?', *World Development*, 39(5): 725–40.

Cappuyns, Elizabeth. 1998. 'Linking Labor Standards and Trade Sanctions: An Analysis of Their Current Relationship', *Columbia Journal of Transnational Law*, 36(3): 659–86.

Carnegie Endowment for International Peace and Trade Policy Group of the Inter-American Dialogue. 2001. 'Breaking the Labor-Trade Deadlock', *Carnegie Foundation Working Paper Series*, 17: 1–20.

Cassimatis, Anthony. 2007. *Human Rights Related Trade Measures Under International Law: The Legality of Trade Measures Imposed in Responses to Violations of Human Rights Obligations Under General International Law*. Leiden: Martinus Nijhoff Publishers.

Chakravarthi, Raghavan. 1990. *Recolonization: GATT, the Uruguay Round and the Third World*. London: Zed Books.

Chang, Ha-Joon. 2002. *Kicking Away the Ladder: Development Strategy in Historical Perspective*. London: Anthem Press.

Chang, Ha-Joon. 2005. 'Policy Space in Historical Perspective – With Reference to Trade and Industrial Policies', www.ase.tufts.edu/gdae/about_us/leontief/Chang_remarks.pdf (accessed on 29 September 2016).

Chang, Ha-Joon. 2007. *Bad Samaritans: Rich Nations, Poor Policies, and the Threat to the Developed World*. London: Random House.

Charlesworth, Hillary. 1992. 'The Public/Private Distinction and the Right to Development in International Law', *Australian Yearbook of International Law*, 12: 190–204.

Charnovitz, Steve. 1987. 'The Influence of International Labour Standards on the World Trading Regime: A Historical Overview', *International Labour Review*, 126(5): 565–84.

Charnovitz, Steve. 1997. 'The Moral Exception in Trade Policy', *Virginia Journal of International Law*, 38(4): 689–746.

Charnovitz, Steve. 2002. 'Triangulating the World Trade Organization', *American Journal of International Law*, 96(1): 28–55.

Charny, David. 2001. 'Regulatory Competition and the Global Coordination of Labour Standards', in Daniel Esty and Damien Geradin (eds), *Regulatory Competition and Economic Integration: Comparative Perspectives*, pp. 311–29. Oxford: Oxford University Press.

Chartres, Renee and Mercurio, Bryan. 2012. 'A Call for an Agreement on Trade-Related Aspects of Labor: Why and How the WTO Should Play a Role in Upholding Core Labor Standards', *North Carolina Journal of International Law and Commercial Regulation*, 37(3): 665–724.

Chatterjee, Mihir. 2007. 'Re-Negotiating Trade and Labor Standards in a Post Hong Kong Scenario', *Asian Journal of WTO and International Health Law and Policy*, 2(2): 473–500.

Chimni, Bhupinder. 2003. 'Development and Migration', in Alexander Aleinikoff and Vincent Chetail (eds), *Migration and International Legal Norms*, pp. 255–70. The Hague: T.M.C. Asser Press.

Chimni, Bhupinder. 2006. 'Third World Approaches to International Law: A Manifesto', *International Community Law Review*, 8: 3–27.

Choudhury, Barnali *et al.* 2011. 'A Call for a WTO Ministerial Decision on Trade and Human Rights', in Thomas Cottier and Panagiotis Delimatsis (eds), *The Prospects of International Trade Regulation: From Fragmentation to Coherence*, pp. 323–58. Cambridge: Cambridge University Press.

Chowdhury, Subrata Roy, Denters, Erik and de Waart, Paul. 1992. *The Right to Development in International Law*. Leiden: Martinus Nijhoff.

Cleveland, Sarah. 2001. 'Human Rights Sanctions and the World Trade Organization', in Francesco Francioni (ed), *Environment, Human Rights and International Trade*, pp. 199–262. Oxford: Hart Publishing.

Collier, Debbie and Bamu, Pamhidzai. 2012. 'Linking Trade to Labour Standards: A Promising Synergy or a Double-Edged Sword?', *Acta Juridica*, 2012(1): 326–47.

Commission on Global Governance. 1995. *Our Global Neighbourhood.* Oxford: Oxford University Press.

Compa, Lance and Diamond, Stephen (eds). 2003. *Human Rights, Labour Rights, and International Trade.* Pennsylvania: University of Pennsylvania Press.

Cooper, Richard. 1968. *The Economics of Interdependence: Economic Policy in the Atlantic Community.* New York: McGraw Hill for the Council on Foreign Relations.

Cordonier Segger, Marie-Claire and Khalfan, Ashfaq. 2004. *Sustainable Development Law: Principles, Practices, and Prospects.* Oxford: Oxford University Press.

Cottier, Thomas, Pauwelyn, Joost and Burgi, Elisabeth (eds). 2005. *Human Rights and International Trade.* Oxford: Oxford University Press.

Council and Member States of the European Communities. 1991. 'Resolution of the Council and of the Member States Meeting in the Council on Human Rights, Democracy and Development', *Bulletin of the European Communities*, 11(1): 122. 28 November 1991.

Crawford, James. 2012. *Brownlie's Principles of Public International Law.* Oxford: Oxford University Press.

Credit Suisse. 2015. *Global Wealth Report, 2014.* Zurich: Credit Suisse.

Crowell, E.H. 1950. 'The Declaration of Human Rights, the United Nations Charter and Their Effect on the Domestic Law of Human Rights', *Virginia Law Review*, 36(8): 1059–84.

Cullen, Holly. 1999. 'The Limits of International Trade Mechanisms in Enforcing Human Rights: The Case of Child Labour', *International Journal of Child Rights*, 7(1): 1–30.

Delimatsis, Panagiotis. 2011. 'The Fragmentation of International Trade Law', *Journal of World Trade*, 45(1): 87–116.

Delpeuch, Claire *et al.* 2010. *Aid for Trade: A Metaevaluation.* Paris: OECD.

de Schutter, Olivier. 2010. 'Human Rights and the Rise of International Organizations: The Logic of Sliding Scales in the Law of International Responsibility', *La Cellule de Recherche Interdisciplinaire en Droits de L'homme (CRIDHO) Working Paper, 2010/4*: 1–68.

de Schutter, Olivier. 2011. 'International Trade in Agriculture and the Right to Food', in Olivier de Schutter and Kaitlin Cordes (eds), *Accounting for Hunger: The Right to Food in the Era of Globalisation*, pp. 137–92. Oxford: Hart Publishing.

de Schutter, Olivier. 2014. *International Human Rights Law: Cases, Materials, Commentary.* Cambridge: Cambridge University Press.

Dine, Janet and Fagan, Andrew. 2006. *Human Rights and Capitalism: A Multidisciplinary Perspective on Globalisation.* Cheltenham: Edward Elgar Publishing.

Djajic, Slobodan, Lahiri, Sajal and Raimondos-Moller, Pascalis. 2004. 'Logic of Aid in an Intertemporal Setting', *Review of International Economics*, 12(1): 151–61.

Dollar, David. 1992. 'Outward-Oriented Developing Economies Really Do Grow More Rapidly: Evidence From 95 LDCs, 1976–85', *Economic Development and Cultural Change*, 40(3): 523–44.

Dommen, Caroline. 2004. 'The WTO, International Trade and Human Rights', www.choike.org/documentos/WTOmainstreamingHR.pdf (accessed on 29 September 2016).

Donnelly, Jack. 1985. 'In Search of the Unicorn: The Jurisprudence and Politics of the Right to Development', *California Western International Law Journal*, 15(3): 473–509.

Doucouliagos, Hristos and Paldam, Martin. 2011. 'The Ineffectiveness of Development Aid on Growth: An Update', *European Journal of Political Economy*, 27(2): 399–404.

Drache, Daniel and Jacobs, Lesley (eds). 2014. *Linking Global Trade and Human Rights: New Policy Space in Hard Economic Times*. Cambridge: Cambridge University Press.

Drahos, Peter and Braithwaite, John. 2003. *Information Feudalism*. New York: New Press.

Easterly, William. 2005. 'Can Foreign Aid Save Africa?', *Saint John's University Clemens Lecture Series 2005*, 17: 1–29.

Easterly, William. 2006. *White Man's Burden: Why the West's Efforts to Aid the Rest Have Done So Much Ill and So Little Good*. New York: Penguin Press.

Ebert, Franz Christian and Posthuma, Anne. 2011. 'Labour Provisions in Trade Arrangements: Current Trends and Perspectives', *International Institute for Labour Studies Discussion Paper Series*, 205: 1–37.

Ebrahim-zadeh, Christine. 2003. 'Dutch Disease: Too Much Wealth Managed Unwisely', *Finance and Development*, 40(1), www.imf.org/external/pubs/ft/fandd/2003/03/ebra.htm (accessed on 1 October 2016).

ECOSOC. 2000. 'The Realization of Economic, Social and Cultural Rights: Globalization and Its Impact on Full Achievement of Human Rights'. E/CN.4/Sub.2/2000/13. 15 June 2000.

ECOSOC. 2004. 'Economic, Social and Cultural Rights: The Right of Everyone to the Enjoyment of the Highest Attainable Standard of Physical and Mental Health – Report of the Special Rapporteur Paul Hunt, Addendum: Mission to the World Trade Organization'. E/EC.4/2004/49/Add.1. 1 March 2004.

ECOSOC. 2006. 'Definition of Basic Concepts and Terminologies in Governance and Public Administration: Note by the Secretariat'. E/C.16/2006/4. 5 January 2006.

Edwards, Sebastian. 1998. 'Openness, Productivity and Growth: What Do We Really Know?', *The Economic Journal*, 108(447): 383–98.

Ehrenberg, Daniel. 1995. 'The Labour Link: Applying the International Trading System to Enforce Violations of Forced and Child Labour', *Yale Journal of International Law*, 20(2): 361–418.

Elliott, Kimberly and Freeman, Richard. 2003. *Can Labor Standards Improve Under Globalization?* Washington, DC: Peterson Institute for International Economics.

Eres, Tatjana. 2004. 'The Limits of GATT Article XX: A Back Door for Human Rights?', *Georgetown Journal of International Law*, 35(3): 597–636.

Escobar, Arturo. 1995. *Encountering Development: The Making and Unmaking of the Third World*. New Jersey: Princeton University Press.

Eslava, Luis and Pahuja, Sundhya. 2012. 'Beyond the (Post)Colonial: TWAIL and the Everyday Life of International Law', *Journal of Law and Politics in Africa, Asia and Latin America*, 45(2): 195–221.

Ewing-Chow, Michael. 2007. 'First Do No Harm: Trade Sanctions and Human Rights', *Northwestern Journal of International Human Rights*, 5(2): 153–80.

Fastenrath, Ulrich. 1993. 'Relative Normativity in International Law', *European Journal of International Law*, 4: 305–40.

Feenstra, Robert and Hanson, Gordon. 1999. 'The Impact of Outsourcing and High-Technology Capital on Wages: Estimates for the United States, 1979–1990', *Quarterly Journal of Economics*, 114(3): 907–40.

Financial Times. 2015. 'The Doha Round Finally Dies a Merciful Death', 21 December, www.ft.com/content/9cb1ab9e-a7e2-11e5-955c-1e1d6de94879 (accessed on 11 October 2016).

Finger, Michael and Schuler, Philip. 2000. 'Implementation of the Uruguay Round: The Development Challenge', *The World Economy*, 23(4): 511–25.

Finnis, John. 1980. *Natural Law and Natural Rights*. Oxford: Oxford University Press.

Finnis, John. 1998. *Aquinas: Moral, Political, and Legal Theory*. Oxford: Oxford University Press.

Flanagan, Robert. 2003. 'Labour Standards and International Competitive Advantage', in Robert Flanagan and William Gould IV (eds), *International Labor Standards: Globalization, Trade and Public Policy*, pp. 15–60. Stanford: Stanford University Press.

Flanagan, Robert. 2006. *Globalization and Labor Conditions: Working Conditions and Worker Rights in a Global Economy*. Oxford: Oxford University Press.

Folkesson, Emelie. 2013. 'Human Rights Courts Interpreting Sustainable Development: Balancing Individual Rights and the Collective Interest', *Erasmus Law Review*, 6(2): 142–54.

Fominaya, Cristina. 2014. *Social Movements and Globalization: How Protests, Occupations and Uprisings Are Changing the World*. New York: Palgrave MacMillan.

Ford, Christie and Condon, Mary. 2011. 'Introduction to New Governance and the Business Organization', *Law & Policy*, 33(4): 449–58.

Francioni, Francesco (ed). 2001. *Environment, Human Rights, and International Trade*. Portland: Hart Publishing.

French, Duncan. 2001. 'International Environmental Law and the Achievement of Intragenerational Equity', *Environmental Law Reporter*, 31(5): 10469–485.

French, Duncan. 2005. *International Law and Policy of Sustainable Development.* Manchester: Manchester University Press.

Friedrich, Georg. 1841. *The National System of Political Economy.* Translated From German Into English by Sampson Lloyd. 1885. London: Longmans, Green, and Company.

Froman, Michael. 2015. 'We Are at the End of the Line on the Doha Round of Trade Talks', *Financial Times*, 13 December, www.ft.com/cms/s/0/4ccf5356-9eaa-11e5-8ce1-f6219b685d74.html (accessed on 11 October 2016).

Fuchs, Andreas, Nunnenkamp, Peter and Ohler, Hannes. 2015. 'Why Donors of Foreign Aid Do Not Coordinate: The Role of Competition for Export Markets and Political Support', *World Economy*, 38(2): 255–85.

Fukuda-Parr, Sakiko. 2012. 'Right to Development: Reframing a New Discourse for the Twenty-First Century', *Social Research: An International Quarterly*, 79(4): 839–64.

G8. 2005. 'Communique on Africa', *Gleneagles*, July 8.

Gallagher, Kevin. 2005. *Putting Development First: The Importance of Policy Space in the WTO and IFIs.* London: Zed Books.

Gallagher, Kevin. 2013. *The Clash of Civilizations: Essays on the Political Economy of Trade and Development Policy.* London: Anthem Press.

Garcia, Frank. 1999. 'The Global Market and Human Rights: Trading Away the Human Rights Principle', *Brooklyn Journal of International Law*, 25: 51–97.

Gathii, James. 1999. 'Good Governance as a Counter-Insurgency Agenda to Oppositional and Transformative Social Projects in International Law', *Buffalo Human Rights Law Review*, 5: 107–77.

Gathii, James. 2000a. 'Neoliberalism, Colonialism and International Governance: Decentering the International Law of Governmental Legitimacy', *Michigan Law Review*, 98(6): 1996–2055.

Gathii, James. 2000b. 'Alternative and Critical: The Contribution of Research and Scholarship on Developing Countries to International Legal Theory', *Harvard International Law Journal*, 41(2): 263–76.

Gathii, James. 2001. 'Re-Characterizing the Social in the Constitutionalization of the WTO: A Preliminary Analysis', *Widener Law Symposium Journal*, 7: 137–73.

Gathii, James. 2011. 'TWAIL: A Brief History of Its Origins, Its Decentralized Network, and a Tentative Bibliography', *Trade Law and Development*, 3(1): 26–64.

Gehring, Markus and Cordonier Segger, Marie-Claire. 2005. *Sustainable Development in World Trade Law.* The Hague: Kluwer Law International.

Ghai, Yash. 1994. 'Human Rights and Governance: The Asia Debate', *Australian Yearbook of International Law*, 15: 1–34.

Ghai, Yash and Pao, Y.K. 1989. *Whose Human Right to Development?* London: Commonwealth Secretariat.

Gonzalez-Pelaez, Ana. 2005. *Human Rights and World Trade: Hunger in International Society*. London: Routledge.

Gould IV, William. 2001. 'Labour Law for a Global Economy: The Uneasy Case for International Labour Standards', *Nebraska Law Review*, 80(4): 715–53.

Graber, Christoph, Kuprecht, Karolina and Lai, Jessica. 2012. *International Trade in Indigenous Cultural Heritage: Legal and Policy Issues*. Cheltenham: Edward Elgar Publishing.

Granger, Clotilde and Siroen, Jean-Marc. 2006. 'Core Labour Standards in Trade Agreements From Multilateralism to Bilateralism', *Journal of World Trade*, 40(5): 813–36.

Gray, John. 2002. *False Dawn: The Delusions of Global Capitalism*. London: Granta Books.

Green, Leslie. 2007. 'The Duty to Govern', *Legal Theory*, 13(3–4): 165–85.

Grimwade, Nigel. 2004. 'The GATT, the Doha Round and Developing Countries', in Homi Katrak and Roger Strange (eds), *The WTO and Developing Countries*, pp. 11–37. New York: Palgrave MacMillan Publishing.

Gunningham, Neil. 2009. 'Environmental Law, Regulation and Governance: Shifting Architectures', *Journal of Environmental Law*, 21(2): 179–212.

Guzman, Andrew. 2003. 'Trade, Labor, Legitimacy', *California Law Review*, 91(3): 885–902.

Haberli, Christian, Jansen, Marion and Monteiro, José-Antonio. 2012. 'Regional Trade Agreements and Domestic Labour Market Regulation', *ILO Employment Working Paper Series*, 120: 1–62.

Hagemeyer, Teoman. 2014. 'Tied Aid: Immunization for Export Subsidies Against the Law of the WTO?', *Journal of World Trade*, 48(2): 259–94.

Hallaert, Jean-Jacques. 2013. 'The Future of Aid for Trade: Challenges and Options', *World Trade Review*, 12(4): 653–68.

Harrison, James. 2007. *The Human Rights Impacts of the World Trade Organisation*. Portland: Hart Publishing.

Harrison, James. 2011. 'Human Rights Measurement: Reflections on the Current Practice and Future Potential of Human Rights Impact Assessment', *Journal of Human Rights Practice*, 3(2): 162–87.

Harrison, James and Goller, Alessa. 2008. 'Trade and Human Rights: What Does "Impact Assessment" Have to Offer', *Human Rights Law Review*, 8(4): 587–615.

Hart, Herbert. 1955. 'Are There Natural Rights?', *Philosophical Review*, 64(2): 175–91.

Helble, Matthias, Mann, Catherine and Wilson, John. 2012. 'Aid-for-Trade Facilitation', *Review of World Economics*, 148(2): 357–76.

Henkin, Louis. 1990. *The Age of Rights*. New York: Columbia University Press.

Hepple, Bob. 2007. 'The WTO as a Mechanism for Labour Regulation', in Brian Bercusson and Cynthia Estlund (eds), *Regulating Labour in the Wake of Globalization: New Challenges, New Institutions*, pp. 161–78. Portland: Hart Publishing.

Hernandez-Truyol, Berta and Powell, Stephen. 2009. *Just Trade: A New Covenant Linking Trade and Human Rights*. New York: New York University Press.

Hestermeyer, Holger. 2007. *Human Rights and the WTO: The Case of Patents and Access to Medicines*. Oxford: Oxford University Press.

Hiatt, Jonathan and Greenfield, Deborah. 2004. 'The Importance of Core Labour Rights in World Development', *Michigan Journal of International Law*, 26(1): 39–62.

Hirst, Paul. 2000. 'Democracy and Governance', in Jon Pierre (ed), *Debating Governance: Authority, Steering, and Democracy*, pp. 13–35. Oxford: Oxford University Press.

Hoekman, Bernard. 2010. 'Aid for Trade: Why, What, and Where Are We?', http://siteresources.worldbank.org/INTRANETTRADE/Resources/239054-1273092281133/Bernard_Hoekman_Aid_For_Trade.pdf (accessed on 01 October 2016).

Hoekman, Bernard and Kostecki, Michel. 1995. *The Political Economy of the World Trading System: From GATT to the WTO*. Oxford: Oxford University Press.

Hoekman, Bernard and Kostecki, Michel. 2001. *The Political Economy of the World Trading System: WTO and Beyond*. Oxford: Oxford University Press.

Hoekstra, Ruth and Koopmann, Georg. 2012. 'Aid for Trade and the Liberalization of Trade', *Journal of World Trade*, 46(2): 327–66.

Howse, Robert. 1999. 'The World Trade Organization and the Protection of Workers' Rights', *Journal of Small and Emerging Business Law*, 3: 131–72.

Howse, Robert. 2002a. 'From Politics to Technocracy – and Back Again: The Fate of the Multilateral Trading Regime', *American Journal of International Law*, 96: 94–117.

Howse, Robert. 2002b. 'The Appellate Body Rulings in the Shrimp/Turtle Case: A New Legal Baseline for the Trade and Environmental Debate', *Columbia Journal of Environmental Law*, 27(2): 491–519.

Howse, Robert. 2003. 'Back to the Court After Shrimp/Turtle? Almost but Not Quite Yet: India's Short Lived Challenge to Labour and Environmental Exceptions in the European Union's Generalized System of Preferences', *American University International Law Review*, 18(6): 1333–81.

Howse, Robert. 2004. 'Mainstreaming the Right to Development Into International Trade Law and Policy at the World Trade Organization'. UN Doc. E/CN.4/Sub.2/2004/17. 9 June 2004.

Howse, Robert. 2007. *The WTO System: Law, Politics and Legitimacy*. London: Cameron May.

Howse, Robert. 2008. 'Human Rights, International Economic Law and Constitutional Justice: A Reply', *European Journal of International Law*, 19(5): 945–53.

Howse, Robert, Langille, Brian and Burda, Julien. 2006. 'The World Trade Organization and Labor Rights: Man Bites Dog', in Virginia Leary and Daniel Warner (eds), *Social Issues, Globalisation and International Institutions: Labour Rights and the EU, ILO, OECD and WTO*, pp. 157–232. Leiden: Martinus Nijhoff Publishers.

Howse, Robert and Mutua, Makau. 2000. 'Protecting Rights in a Global Economy: Challenges for the World Trade Organization', *Human Rights in Development Yearbook – The Millennium Edition*, 63: 51–82.

Howse, Robert and Regan, Donald. 2000. 'The Product/Process Distinction - An Illusory Basis for Disciplining "Unilateralism" in Trade Policy', *European Journal of International Law*, 11(2): 249–89.

Hufbauer, Gary, Schott, Jeffrey and Elliott, Kimberly Ann. 1990. *Economic Sanctions Reconsidered – History and Current Policy*. Washington, DC: Peterson Institute for International Economics.

Hughes, Steve and Wilkinson, Rorden. 1998. 'International Labour Standards and World Trade: No Role for the World Trade Organisation?', *New Political Economy*, 3(3): 375–89.

Huhne, Philipp, Meyer, Birgit and Nunnenkamp, Peter. 2013. 'Who Benefits From Aid for Trade? Comparing the Effects on Recipient Versus Donor Exports', *The Journal of Development Studies*, 50(9): 1275–88.

Human Rights Caucus. 2005. 'Statement of the Human Rights Caucus of 10 December 2005', www.aidslaw.ca/site/wp-content/uploads/2013/04/WTOHRCaucusStatement2005+-+ENG.pdf (accessed on 28 September 2016).

Iacovides, Marios. 2014. 'Marginal Consumers, Marginalized Economics: Whose Tastes and Habits Should the WTO Panels and Appellate Body Consider When Assessing "Likeness"?', *Journal of World Trade*, 48(2): 323–50.

Ibhawoh, Bonny. 2011. 'The Right to Development: The Politics and Polemics of Power and Resistance', *Human Rights Quarterly*, 33(1): 76–104.

ILC. 1966. 'Draft Articles on the Law of Treaties With Commentary', *Yearbook of the International Law Commission, 1966*, II: 187–274.

ILC. 1977. 'Sixth Report on State Responsibility by Mr. Roberto Ago, Special Rapporteur – The Internationally Wrongful Act of the State, Source of International Responsibility'. Doc. No. A/CN.4/302 and Add.1, 2 & 3.

ILC. 1999. 'Report of the International Law Commission on the Work of Its Fifty-First Session, 3 May–23 July 1999'. Doc. No. A/54/10.

ILC. 2001. 'Articles on Responsibility of States for Internationally Wrongful Acts', *Yearbook of the International Law Commission, 2001*, II(2): 20–143.

ILC. 2006a. 'Fragmentation of International Law: Difficulties Arising From Diversification and Expansion of International Law: Report of the Study Group of the International Law Commission'. A/CN.4/L.702. 18 July 2006.

ILC. 2006b. 'Fragmentation of International Law: Difficulties Arising From Diversification and Expansion of International Law: Report of the Study Group of the International Law Commission'. A/CN.4/L.682. 13 April 2006.

ILO. 1998. 'Declaration on the Fundamental Principles and Rights at Work'. Adopted by the International Labour Conference at its Eighty-Sixth Session, Geneva, 18 June 1998.

ILO. 2016. 'How the ILO Works', http://www.ilo.org/global/about-the-ilo/how-the-ilo-works/lang--en/index.htm (accessed on 2 October 2016).

IMF and World Bank. 2005. 'Development Committee Communiqué, 2005 Annual Meetings', 25 September, www.imf.org/en/news/articles/2015/09/28/04/51/cm092505 (accessed on 1 October 2016).

Independent Commission for Aid Impact. 2013. 'DFID's Trade Development Work in Southern Africa', Report No. 30, http://icai.independent.gov.uk/wp-content/uploads/DFIDs-Trade-Development-Work-in-Southern-Africa-Report.pdf (accessed on 1 October 2016).

Institute for Agriculture and Trade Policy. 2000. 'WTO Director-General Hits Back at UN for Critical Human Rights Report', http://iatp.org/news/wto-director-general-hits-back-at-un-for-critical-human-rights-report (accessed on 28 September 2016).

International Federation for Human Rights. 1999. 'Position Paper – The WTO and Human Rights', https://business-humanrights.org/en/the-world-trade-organisation-and-human-rights-position-paper (accessed on 14 September 2016).

International Federation for Human Rights. 2005. 'Understanding Global Trade and Human Rights', www.un-ngls.org/orf/FIDH.pdf (accessed on 30 September 2016).

International Lawyers and Economists Against Poverty. 2007. 'Aid for Trade: A New Issue in the WTO', *Negotiation Advisory Brief*, 16: 1–22.

Irish, Maureen. 2011. 'Special and Differential Treatment, Trade and Sustainable Development', *The Law and Development Review*, 4(2): 71–98.

Irwin, Douglas. 1996. *Against the Tide: An Intellectual History of Free Trade*. New Jersey: Princeton University Press.

Ismail, Faizel. 2007. *Mainstreaming Development in the WTO: Developing Countries in the Doha Round*. Jaipur: CUTS International and Frederick Ebert Stiftung.

Joseph, Sarah. 2011. *Blame It on the WTO? A Human Rights Critique*. Oxford: Oxford University Press.

Joseph, Sarah, Kinley, David and Waincymer, Jeff (eds). 2009. *The World Trade Organization and Human Rights: Interdisciplinary Perspectives*. Cheltenham: Edward Elgar Publishing.

Kanade, Mihir. 2014. 'UN Guiding Principles on Business and Human Rights: Presenting the Problem as the Solution', in Mirian Vilela and Laura Westra (eds), *The Earth Charter, Ecological Integrity, and Social Movements*, pp. 39–49. New York: Routledge.

Kanade, Mihir. 2016a. 'Advancing Peace, Rights and Well-being: A Right to Development Approach to SDGs as the Way Forward'. Speech Delivered at the Event *In Search of Dignity and Sustainable Development for All*, Geneva, United Nations, 29 February.

Kanade, Mihir. 2016b. 'Operationalizing the Right to Development for Implementing the SDGs'. Presentation Made at the 32nd Session of the UN Human Rights Council at the Event *Commemoration of the 30th Anniversary of the Right to Development*, Geneva, United Nations, 15 June.

Kanade, Mihir. 2016c. 'Chronicles of the Doha Wars: The Battle of Nairobi – Appraisal of the Tenth WTO Ministerial', *Strathmore Law Journal*, 2(1): 155–64.

Karkkainen, Bradley. 2004. 'New Governance in Legal Thought and the World: Some Splitting as Antidote to Overzealous Lumping', *Minnesota Law Review*, 89: 471–97.

Kaufmann, Christine. 2007. *Globalisation and Labour Rights: The Conflicting Relationship Between Core Labour Rights and International Economic Law*. Portland: Hart Publishing.

Kaufmann, Daniel and Kraay, Aart. 2008. 'Governance Indicators: Where Are We, Where Should We Be Going?', *The World Bank Research Observer*, 23(1): 1–30.

Kaufmann, Daniel, Kraay, Aart and Zoido-Lobaton, Pablo. 1999. *Aggregating Governance Indicators*. Washington, DC: World Bank.

Kelsen, Hans. 1950. *The Law of the United Nations: A Critical Analysis of Its Fundamental Problems*. New York: Frederick A. Praeger, Inc.

Khosla, Madhav. 2007. 'The TWAIL Discourse: The Emergence of a New Phase', *International Community Law Review*, 9(3): 291–304.

Kinley, David. 2009. *Civilising Globalisation*. Cambridge: Cambridge University Press.

Klein, Naomi. 2000. *No Logo: Taking Aim at the Brand Bullies*. Toronto: Vintage Canada.

Kolben, Kevin. 2006. 'The New Politics of Linkage: India's Opposition to the Worker's Rights Clause', *Indiana Journal of Global Legal Studies*, 13(1): 225–60.

Kolben, Kevin. 2010. 'The WTO Distraction', *Stanford Law and Policy Review*, 21(3): 461–92.

Kong, Qingjiang. 2005. 'A Human Rights Approach to Trade? Some Reflections', in Thomas Cottier, Joost Pauwelyn and Elisabeth Burgi (eds), *Human Rights and International Trade*, pp. 232–5. Oxford: Oxford University Press.

Konstantinov, Boyan. 2009. 'Human Rights and the WTO: Are They Really Oil and Water?', *Journal of World Trade*, 43(2): 317–38.

Koskenniemi, Martii. 1999. 'The Preamble to the Universal Declaration on Human Rights', in Gudmundur Alfredsson and Asbjorn Eide (eds), *The Universal Declaration on Human Rights: A Common Standard of Achievement*, pp. 27–39. The Hague: Kluwer.

Koskenniemi, Martti. 2004. 'Letter to the Editors of the Symposium', *Studies on Transnational Legal Policy*, 1: 110–25.

Kozul-Wright, Richard and Rayment, Paul. 2008. *The Resistible Rise of Market Fundamentalism: Rethinking Development Policy in an Unbalanced World*. London: Zed Books and Third World Network.

Krugman, Paul and Obstfeld, Maurice. 2008. *International Economics: Theory & Policy*. 8th Edition. Boston: Pearson-Addison-Wesley.

Kryvoi, Yaraslau. 2008. 'Why European Trade Sanctions Do Not Work', *Minnesota Journal of International Law*, 17(2): 209–46.

Kuijper, Pieter. 1994. 'The Law of the GATT as a Special Field of International Law: Ignorance, Further Refinement or Self-Contained System of International Law?', *Netherlands Yearbook of International Law*, 25(1): 227–57.

Laird, Sam. 2007. 'Aid for Trade: Cool Aid or Kool-Aid?', *G-24 Discussion Paper Series*, 48: 1–24.

Lang, Andrew. 2011. *World Trade Law After Neo-Liberalism: Reimagining the Global Economic Order*. Oxford: Oxford University Press.

Langan, Mark and Scott, James. 2014. 'The Aid for Trade Charade', *Cooperation and Conflict*, 49(2): 143–61.

Langille, Brian. 1997. 'Eight Ways to Think About International Labour Standards', *Journal of World Trade*, 31(4): 27–53.

Langille, Brian. 2005. 'Core Labour Rights – The True Story (Reply to Alston)', *European Journal of International Law*, 16(3): 409–38.

Lauren, Paul. 1983. 'First Principles of Racial Equality: History and the Politics and Diplomacy of Human Rights Provisions in the United Nations Charter', *Human Rights Quarterly*, 5(1): 1–26.

Lauterpacht, Hersch. 1950. *International Law and Human Rights*. New York: Frederick A. Praeger, Inc.

Leader, Sheldon. 2005. 'Human Rights and International Trade', in Patrick Macrory, Arthur Appleton and Michael Plummer (eds), *The World Trade Organization: Legal, Economic and Political Analysis*, Volume II, pp. 664–95. New York: Springer.

Leary, Virginia. 1996. 'Workers' Rights and International Trade: The Social Clause', in Jagdish Bhagwati and Robert Hudec (eds), *Fair Trade and Harmonization: Prerequisites for Free Trade?*, Volume 2, pp. 177–230. Cambridge: MIT Press.

Leary, Virginia. 1997. 'The WTO and the Social Clause: Post-Singapore', *European Journal of International Law*, 8(1): 118–22.

Lennard, Michael. 2002. 'Navigating by the Stars: Interpreting the WTO Agreements', *Journal of International Economic Law*, 5(1): 17–89.

Lim, Hoe. 2001. 'The Social Clause: Issues and Challenges', http://training.itcilo.it/actrav_cdrom1/english/global/guide/hoelim.htm (accessed on 1 October 2016).

Lobel, Orly. 2004. 'The Renew Deal: The Fall of Regulation and the Rise of Governance in Contemporary Legal Thought', *Minnesota Law Journal*, 89: 262–390.

Loukaides, Loukes. 1995. *Essays on the Developing Law of Human Rights*. Leiden: Martinus Nijhoff Publishers.

Luke, David, Monge-Roffarello, Luca and Varma, Sabrina. 2009. 'Perspectives on Aid for Trade', in Philippe de Lombaerde and Lakshmi Puri (eds), *Aid for Trade: Global and Regional Perspectives*, pp. 29–38. Berlin: Springer.

MacDonald, Theodore. 2006. *Health, Trade and Human Rights*. Oxon: Radcliffe Publishing.

Macklem, Patrick. 2014. 'Global Poverty and the Right to Development in International Law', *International Law Journal of London*, 1(1): 1–76.

Marceau, Gabrielle. 1999. 'A Call for Coherence in International Law', *Journal of World Trade*, 33(5): 87–152.

Marceau, Gabrielle. 2001. 'Conflicts of Norms and Conflicts of Jurisdictions: The Relationship Between the WTO Agreement and MEAs and Other Treaties', *Journal of World Trade*, 35(6): 1081–131.

Marceau, Gabrielle. 2002. 'WTO Dispute Settlement and Human Rights', *European Journal of International Law*, 13(4): 753–814.

Marceau, Gabrielle. 2006. 'Fragmentation of International Law: The Relationship Between WTO and General International Law – A Few Comments From a WTO Perspective', *Finnish Yearbook of International Law*, 17: 5–20.

Marceau, Gabrielle and Illy, Ousseni. 2009. 'Global Administrative Law Perspective of the WTO Aid for Trade Initiative', *International Organizations Law Review*, 6(2): 479–98.

Marks, Stephen. 2009. 'Access to Essential Medicines as a Component of the Right to Health', in Andrew Clapham and Mary Robinson (eds), *Realizing the Right to Health: Swiss Human Rights Book*, pp. 80–99. Zurich: Ruffer and Rub.

Maskus, Keith. 1997. 'Should Core Labor Standards Be Imposed Through International Trade Policy?', *World Bank Policy Research Working Paper Series*, 1817: 1–92.

Mavroidis, Petros. 2004. 'Human Rights, Developing Countries and the WTO Constraint: The Very Thing That Makes You Rich Makes Me Poor?', in Eyal Benvenisti and Moshe Hirsch (eds), *The Impact of International Law on International Cooperation: Theoretical Perspectives*, pp. 244–60. Cambridge: Cambridge University Press.

Mavroidis, Petros. 2008. 'No Outsourcing of Law? WTO Law as Practiced by WTO Courts', *American Journal of International Law*, 102(3): 421–74.

Mayer, Jorg. 2008. 'Policy Space: What, for What, and Where?', *UNCTAD Discussion Paper No. 191*. UNCTAD/OSG/DP/2008/6.

M'baye, Keba. 1972. 'Le Droit au Développement comme un Droit de l'Homme', *Revue des Droits de l'Homme*, 5(1): 503–34.

McCrudden, Christopher and Davies, Anne. 2000. 'A Perspective on Trade and Labour Rights', *Journal of International Economic Law*, 3(1): 43–62.

McGee, Robert and Yoon, Yeomin. 2009. 'Incorporating Labor Standards Into Trade Agreements: An Ethical Analysis', in Robert McGee (ed), *Essays in International Trade*, pp. 222–34. Hyderabad: The ICFAI University Press.

McGoldrick, Dominic. 1996. 'Sustainable Development and Human Rights: An Integrated Conception', *International and Comparative Law Quarterly*, 45(4): 796–818.

Meron, Theodor. 1989. *Human Rights and Humanitarian Norms as Customary Law*. Oxford: Clarendon Press.

Milberg, William. 2008. 'Trade Theory Dissidents', *Challenge*, 51(4): 119–26.

Moyo, Dambisa. 2010. *Dead Aid: Why Aid Is Not Working and How There Is a Better Way for Africa*. New York: Farrar, Straus and Giroux.

Munemo, Jonathan. 2011. 'Foreign Aid and Export Diversification in Developing Countries', *Journal of International Trade and Economic Development*, 20(3): 339–55.

Mutua, Makau. 2000. 'What Is TWAIL?', *Proceedings of the Annual Meeting (American Society of International Law)*, 94: 31–38.

Narlikar, Amrita. 2005. *The World Trade Organization: A Very Short Introduction*. New York: Oxford University Press.

NeJaime, Douglas. 2009. 'When New Governance Fails', *Ohio State Law Journal*, 70(2): 323–99.

Nickel, James. 2007. *Making Sense of Human Rights*. Oxford: Blackwell Publishing.

Nielson, Julia. 2006. 'Aid for Trade', in Richard Newfarmer (ed), *Trade, Doha and Development: A Window Into the Issues*, pp. 319–28. Washington, DC: World Bank.

Nilsson, Lars. 1997. *Essays on North-South Trade*. Lund: Lund University Publications.

Nordic Trust Fund and World Bank. 2013. 'Human Rights Impact Assessments: A Review of the Literature, Differences With Other Forms of Assessments and Relevance for Development', http://siteresources.worldbank.org/PROJECTS/Resources/40940-1331068268558/HRIA_Web.pdf (accessed on 2 October 2016).

Nowak-Lehmann, Felicitas *et al.* 2009. 'Aid and Trade: A Donor's Perspective', *Journal of Development Studies*, 45(7): 1184–202.

Nunnenkamp, Peter and Ohler, Hannes. 2011. 'Aid Allocation Through Various Official and Private Channels: Need, Merit and Self-Interest as Motives of German Donors', *World Development*, 39(3): 308–23.

Nussbaum, Martha. 2000. *Women and Human Development: The Capabilities Approach*. Cambridge: Cambridge University Press.

OECD. 1996. *Trade, Employment and Labour Standards: A Study of Core Workers' Rights and International Trade*. Paris: OECD Publishing.

OECD. 2000. *International Trade and Core Labour Standards*. Paris: OECD Publishing.

OECD. 2016. 'Creditor Reporting System', http://stats.oecd.org/Index.aspx?DataSetCode=crs1 (accessed on 1 October 2016).

OECD and WTO. 2009. *Aid for Trade at a Glance 2009: Maintaining Momentum*. Paris and Geneva: OECD and WTO.

OECD and WTO. 2011. *Aid for Trade at a Glance 2011: Showing Results*. Paris and Geneva: OECD and WTO.

OECD and WTO. 2013. *Aid for Trade at a Glance: Connecting to Value Chains*. Paris: OECD Publishing.

OHCHR. 1996. 'The International Bill of Human Rights', *Fact Sheet No. 2 (Rev.1)*, www.ohchr.org/Documents/Publications/FactSheet2Rev.1en.pdf (accessed on 28 September 2016).

OHCHR. 2002. 'Liberalisation of Trade and Services and Human Rights – Report of the High Commissioner'. E/CN.4/Sub.2/2002/9. 25 June 2002.

OHCHR. 2007. *Good Governance Practices for the Protection of Human Rights*. Geneva: United Nations.

OHCHR. 2013. *Realizing the Right to Development: Essays in Commemoration of 25 Years of the United Nations Declaration on the Right to Development*. Geneva: United Nations.

OHCHR. 2016a. *Human Rights Bodies*, www.ohchr.org/EN/HRBodies/Pages/HumanRightsBodies.aspx (accessed on 29 September 2016).

OHCHR. 2016b. *Good Governance and Human Rights*, www.ohchr.org/EN/Issues/Development/GoodGovernance/Pages/GoodGovernanceIndex.aspx (accessed on 29 September 2016).

Okafor, Obiora. 2008. 'Critical Third World Approaches to International Law: Theory, Methodology or Both?', *International Community Law Review*, 10(1): 371–8.

Orford, Anne. 2001. 'Globalization and the Right to Development', in Philip Alston (ed), *People's Rights*, pp. 127–84. Oxford: Oxford University Press.

Oxfam. 2002. 'Rigged Rules and Double Standards', http://policy-practice.oxfam.org.uk/publications/rigged-rules-and-double-standards-trade-globalisation-and-the-fight-against-pov-112391 (accessed on 28 September 2016).

Oxfam. 2006. 'Patents Versus Patients: Five Years After the Doha Declaration', *Oxfam Briefing Papers 95*, http://policy-practice.oxfam.org.uk/publications/patents-versus-patients-five-years-after-the-doha-declaration-114562 (accessed on 30 September 2016).

Oxfam. 2015. 'Oxfam Response to Credit Suisse Global Wealth Report', www.oxfam.org/en/pressroom/reactions/oxfam-response-credit-suisse-global-wealth-report (accessed on 1 October 2016).

Page, Sheila. 2006. *Trade and Aid: Partners or Rivals in Development Policy?* London: Cameron May.

Page, Sheila. 2007a. 'Policy Space: Are WTO Rules Preventing Development', *Overseas Development Institute Briefing Paper*, 14: 1–4.

Page, Sheila. 2007b. 'The Potential Impact of the Aid for Trade Initiative', *G-24 Discussion Paper Series*, 45: 1–37.

Pahuja, Sundhya. 2011. *Decolonising International Law: Development, Economic Growth and the Politics of Universality*. Cambridge: Cambridge University Press.

Panagariya, Arvind. 2001. 'Labor Standards and Trade Sanctions: Right End Wrong Means'. Paper Presented at the Conference *Towards an Agenda for Research on International Economic Integration and Labor Markets*. Hawaii, 15–16 January.

Patnaik, Biraj. 2015. 'How Sitharaman Served up India Instead of Using WTO High Table to Block US Agenda', *The Wire*, 25 December, http://thewire.in/17894/the-ugly-american-and-compliant-indian/ (accessed on 11 October 2016).

Pauwelyn, Joost. 2001. 'The Role of Public International Law in WTO: How Far Can We Go?', *American Journal of International Law*, 95(3): 535–78.

Pauwelyn, Joost. 2003a. 'Bridging Fragmentation and Unity: International Law as a Universe of Inter-Connected Islands', *Michigan Journal of International Law*, 25(1): 903–16.

Pauwelyn, Joost. 2003b. 'How to Win a World Trade Organization Dispute Based on Non-World Trade Organization Law?', *Journal of World Trade*, 37(6): 997–1030.

Pauwelyn, Joost. 2003c. *Conflict of Norms in Public International Law: How WTO Law Relates to Other Rules of International Law*. Cambridge: Cambridge University Press.

Pauwelyn, Joost. 2005. 'Human Rights in WTO Dispute Settlement', in Thomas Cottier, Joost Pauwelyn and Elisabeth Burgi (eds), *Human Rights and International Trade*, pp. 205–31. Oxford: Oxford University Press.

Petersmann, Ernst-Ulrich. 2001. 'Time for Integrating Human Rights Into the Law of Worldwide Organizations: Lessons From European Integration Law for Global Integration Law', *Jean Monnet Working Paper 7/01*: 1–45.

Petersmann, Ernst-Ulrich. 2008a. 'The Development Objectives of the WTO: State-Centred Versus Human Rights Approaches', in Gary Sampson and Bradnee Chambers (eds), *Developing Countries and the WTO*, pp. 169–91. Tokyo: UNU Press.

Petersmann, Ernst-Ulrich. 2008b. 'Human Rights, International Economic Law and Constitutional Justice', *European Journal of International Law*, 19(4): 769–98.

Pettersson, Jan and Johansson, Lars. 2013. 'Aid, Aid for Trade, and Bilateral Trade: An Empirical Study', *Journal of International Trade and Economic Development*, 22(6): 866–94.

Pierre, Jon. 2000. *Debating Governance: Authority, Steering, and Democracy*. Oxford: Oxford University Press.

Pogge, Thomas. 2008. *World Poverty and Human Rights*. 2nd Edition. Cambridge: Polity Press.

Possel, Jens. 2008. 'A Human Rights Approach to "Sustainable Development" Within WTO', in Gary Sampson and Bradnee Chambers (eds), *Developing Countries and the WTO*, pp. 192–228. Tokyo: UNU Press.

Qerimi, Qerim. 2012. *Development in International Law: A Policy-Oriented Inquiry*. Leiden: Martinus Nijhoff.

Rajagopal, Balakrishnan. 2000. 'From Resistance to Renewal: The Third World, Social Movements, and the Expansion of International Institutions', *Harvard International Law Journal*, 41(2): 531–78.

Rajagopal, Balakrishnan. 2013. 'Right to Development and Global Governance: Old and New Challenges Twenty-Five Years on', *Human Rights Quarterly*, 35(4): 893–909.

Rajan, Raghuram and Subramanian, Arvind. 2005. 'Aid and Growth: What Does the Cross-Country Evidence Really Show?', *The Review of Economics and Statistics*, 90(4): 643–65.

Rajan, Raghuram and Subramanian, Arvind. 2011. 'Aid, Dutch Disease, and Manufacturing Growth', *Journal of Development Economics*, 94(1): 106–18.

Ramcharan, B.G. 1989. *The Concept and Present Status of International Protection of Human Rights: Forty Years After the Universal Declaration*. London: Martinus Nijhoff Publishers.

Ratner, Steven and Slaughter, Anne-Marie. 2004. 'Appraising the Methods of International Law: A Prospectus for Readers', *Studies on Transnational Legal Policy*, 1: 1–22.

Reinert, Erik. 2007. *How the Rich Countries Got Rich . . . and Why Poor Countries Remain Poor*. New York: Carroll and Graf.

Ricardo, David. 1817. *On the Principles of Political Economy and Taxation*. London: John Murray Publications.

Robinson, Mary. 2001. 'Making the Global Economy Work for Human Rights', in Gary Sampson (ed), *The Role of the World Trade Organization in Global Governance*, pp. 209–22. Tokyo: UNU Press.

Rodriguez, Francisco and Rodrik, Dani. 2000. 'Trade Policy and Economic Growth: A Sceptic's Guide to the Cross-National Evidence', in Ben Bernanke and Kenneth Rogoff (eds), *NBER Macroeconomics Annual 2000*, pp. 261–368. Cambridge: MIT Press.

Rodrik, Dani. 1997. *Has Globalization Gone Too Far?* Washington, DC: Peterson Institute for International Economics.

Rosenau, James and Czempiel, Ernst Otto. 1992. *Governance Without Government: Order and Change in World Politics*. Cambridge: Cambridge University Press.

Ruggie, John. 1982. 'International Regimes, Transactions, and Change: Embedded Liberalism in the Postwar Economic Order', *International Organization*, 36(2): 379–415.

Ruggie, John. 2014. 'Global Governance and "New Governance Theory": Lessons From Business and Human Rights', *Global Governance*, 20: 5–17.

Sachs, Jeffrey and Warner, Andrew. 1995. 'Economic Reform and the Process of Global Integration', *Brookings Papers on Economic Activity*, 1: 1–118.

Sadat-Akhavi, Seyed Ali. 2003. *Methods of Resolving Conflicts between Treaties*. Leiden: Martinus Nijhoff Publishers.

Salazar-Xirinachs, Jose. 2000. 'The Trade-Labor Nexus: Developing Countries' Perspectives', *Journal of International Economic Law*, 3(2): 377–86.

Sally, Razeen. 2009. 'Introduction: Trade Liberalization in the Twenty-First Century', in Peter Draper, Philip Alves and Razeen Sally (eds), *The Political Economy of Trade Reform in Emerging Markets*, pp. 1–30. Cheltenham: Edward Elgar.

Sampson, Gary. 2005. *The WTO and Sustainable Development*. Tokyo: UNU Press.

Samuelson, Paul. 1938. 'Welfare Economics and International Trade', *The American Economic Review*, 28(2): 261–66.

Sayer, Andrew. 2004. 'Moral Economy', Published by the Department of Sociology, Lancaster University, www.lancaster.ac.uk/fass/resources/sociology-online-papers/papers/sayer-moral-economy.pdf (accessed on 2 October 2016).

Sayer, Andrew. 2007. 'Moral Economy as Critique', *New Political Economy*, 12(2): 261–70.

Schachter, Oscar. 1951. 'The Charter and the Constitution: The Human Rights Provisions in American Law', *Vanderbilt Law Review*, 4(3): 643–59.

Schrijver, Nico. 2008. *The Evolution of Sustainable Development in International Law: Inception, Meaning and Status*. Leiden: Martinus Nijhoff.

Schwelb, Egon. 1965. 'The United Nations and Human Rights', *Howard Law Journal*, 11(2): 356–72.

Sen, Amartya. 1999. *Development as Freedom*. Oxford: Oxford University Press.

Sen, Amartya. 2009. *The Idea of Justice*. London: Penguin.

Sengenberger, Werner. 2006. 'International Labor Standards in the Globalized Economy: Obstacles and Opportunities for Achieving Progress', in John Craig and Michael Lynk (eds), *Globalization and the Future of Labor Law*, pp. 331–55. Cambridge: Cambridge University Press.

Sengupta, Arjun. 2002. 'On the Theory and Practice of the Right to Development', *Human Rights Quarterly*, 24(4): 837–89.

Shelton, Dinah. 2007. 'Equity', in Daniel Bodansky, Jutta Brunnee and Ellen Hey (eds), *The Oxford Handbook of International Environmental Law*, pp. 639–62. Oxford: Oxford University Press.

Silva, Simone and Nelson, Douglas. 2012. 'Does Aid Cause Trade? Evidence From an Asymmetric Gravity Model', *World Economy*, 35(5): 545–77.

Simma, Bruno and Alston, Philip. 1989. 'The Sources of Human Rights Law: Custom, "Jus Cogens", and General Principles', *Australian Yearbook of International Law*, 12: 82–108.

Sinclair, Timothy. 2004. *Global Governance: Critical Concepts in Political Science*. New York: Routledge.

Skyes, Alan. 2003. 'International Trade and Human Rights: An Economic Perspective', *University of Chicago Law School's John M. Olin Law and Economics Working Paper Series*, 188: 1–32.

Smarzynska, Beata and Wei, Shang-Jin. 2001. 'Pollution Havens and Foreign Direct Investment: Dirty Secret or Popular Myth?', *World Bank Policy Research Working Paper Series*, 2673: 1–32.

Smith, Adam. 1776. *The Wealth of Nations*. Reprinted Edition, 1937. New York: Modern Library Edition.

Smith, Jackie. 2002. 'Globalizing Resistance: The Battle of Seattle and the Future of the Social Movements', in Jackie Smith and Hank Johnston (eds),

Globalization and Resistance: Transnational Dimensions of Social Movements, pp. 207–27. Lanham: Rowman & Littlefield Publishers.
Sohn, Louis. 1975. 'The Human Rights Law of the Charter', *Texas International Law Journal*, 12(2–3): 129–40.
Sohn, Louis. 1982. 'The New International Law: Protection of the Rights of Individuals Rather Than States', *American University Law Review*, 32: 1–64.
Solow, Robert. 1993. *An Almost Practical Step Toward Sustainability*. Washington, DC: Resources for the Future Press.
South Centre. 2005. 'Policy Space for the Development of the South', *T.R.A.D.E. Policy Brief*, 1: 1–8.
South Centre. 2011. 'The Doha Declaration on TRIPS and Public Health – Ten Years Later: The State of Implementation', *South Centre Policy Brief*, 7: 1–18.
Staiger, Robert. 2003. 'A Role for the WTO', in Kaushik Basu, Henrik Horn, Lisa Roman and Judith Shapiro (eds), *International Labor Standards: History, Theory and Policy Options*, pp. 273–303. Malden, MA: Blackwell Publishing.
Standing, Guy. 1999. *Global Labour Flexibility: Seeking Distributive Justice*. New York: Palgrave MacMillan.
Stephens, Tim. 2012. 'International Courts and Sustainable Development: Using Old Tools to Shape a New Discourse', in Brad Jessup and Kim Rubenstein (eds), *Environmental Discourses in Public and International Law*, pp. 195–217. Cambridge: Cambridge University Press.
Stern, Robert and Terrell, Katherine. 2003. 'Labour Standards and the World Trade Organization', *University of Michigan RSIE Discussion Paper Series*, 499: 1–13.
Stiglitz, Joseph. 2002. *Globalization and Its Discontents*. London: Penguin Press.
Stiglitz, Joseph and Charlton, Andrew. 2004. 'The Doha Round of Trade Negotiations: An Agenda to Promote Development and Facilitate Adjustment', in *Commonwealth Finance Ministers Reference Report 2004*, pp. 174–83. London: Henley Media Group.
Stiglitz, Joseph and Charlton, Andrew. 2006. *Aid for Trade: A Report for the Commonwealth Secretariat*. London: Commonwealth Secretariat.
Stiglitz, Joseph and Charlton, Andrew. 2013. 'The Right to Trade: Rethinking the Aid for Trade Agenda', in Mohammad Razzaque and Dirk te Velde (eds), *Assessing Aid for Trade: Effectiveness, Current Issues and Future Directions*, pp. 359–86. London: Commonwealth Secretariat.
Stirling, Patricia. 1996. 'The Use of Trade Sanctions as an Enforcement Mechanism for Basic Human Rights: A Proposal for Addition to the WTO', *American University Journal of Law and Policy*, 11(1): 1–46.
Stoll, Tobias. 2012. 'Article 56', in Bruno Simma *et al.* (eds), *The Charter of the United Nations: A Commentary*, Volume II, pp. 1603–10. Oxford: Oxford University Press.

Stone, Katherine. 2008. 'Flexibilization, Globalization, and Privatization: Three Challenges to Labour Rights in Our Time', in Brian Bercusson and Cynthia Estlund (eds), *Regulating Labour in the Wake of Globalization: New Challenges, New Institutions*, pp. 115–36. Portland: Hart Publishing.

Summers, Clyde. 2001. 'Battle in Seattle: Free Trade, Labor Rights, and Societal Values', *University of Pennsylvania Journal of International Economic Law*, 22(1): 61–90.

Sutherland, Johanna. 1998. 'International Trade and the GATT/WTO Social Clause: Broadening the Debate', *Queensland University of Technology Law Journal*, 14: 83–107.

Suwa-Eisenmann, Akiko and Verdier, Thierry. 2007. 'Aid and Trade', *Oxford Review of Economic Policy*, 23(3): 481–507.

Tandon, Yash. 1999. 'The World Trade Organization and Africa's Marginalization', *Australian Journal of International Affairs*, 53(1): 83–94.

Tarullo, Daniel. 1985. 'Logic, Myth and the International Economic Order', *Harvard International Law Journal*, 26(2): 533–52.

Thirlway, Hugh. 2014. *The Sources of International Law*. Oxford: Oxford University Press.

Thomas, Chantal. 2004. 'Should the WTO Incorporate Labor and Environmental Standards?', *Washington and Lee Law Review*, 61(1): 347–404.

Thomas, Janet. 2000. *The Battle in Seattle: The Story Behind and Beyond the WTO Demonstrations*. Golden: Fulcrum Publishing.

Topalova, Petia. 2010. 'Factor Immobility and Regional Impacts of Trade Liberalization: Evidence on Poverty From India', *American Economic Journal: Applied Economics*, 2(4): 1–41.

Trachtman, Joel. 1999. 'The Domain of WTO Dispute Resolution', *Harvard International Law Journal*, 40(2): 333–78.

Trachtman, Joel. 2004. '"Book Review", Review of Conflict of Norms in Public International Law: How WTO Law Relates to Other Rules of International Law, by Joost Pauwelyn', *American Journal of International Law*, 98(3): 855–61.

Trebilcock, Michael. 2011. *Understanding Trade Law*. Cheltenham: Edward Elgar Publishing.

Trebilcock, Michael and Howse, Robert. 2005. 'Trade Policy and Labor Standards', *Minnesota Journal of Global Trade*, 14(2): 261–300.

Turner, Liz and Rovamaa, Laura. 2012. 'Aid for Trade: Reviewing EC and DFID Monitoring and Evaluation Practices'. *Study Commissioned by Traidcraft and Conducted by Saana Consulting*, www.enterprise-development.org/wp-content/uploads/Aid_for_Trade_Report.pdf (accessed on 1 October 2016).

UNCHR. 1977. 'Question of the Realization of the Economic, Social and Cultural Rights Contained in the Universal Declaration of Human Rights and in the International Covenant on Economic, Social and Cultural Rights, and Study of Special Problems Relating to Human Rights in Developing Countries'. Resolution 4 (XXXIII). 21 February 1977.

UNCHR. 1993. 'The Right to Development'. E/CN.4/RES/1993/22. 4 March 1993.

UNCHR. 1996. 'The Right to Development'. E/CN.4/RES/1996/15. 11 April 1996.

UNCHR. 1998. 'The Right to Development'. E/CN.4/RES/1998/72. 22 April 2998.

UNCHR. 1999. 'Study on the Current State of Implementation of the Right to Development Submitted by Mr. Arjun Sengupta, Independent Expert'. E/CN.4/1999/WG.18/2. 27 July 1999.

UNCHR. 2000a. 'The Role of Good Governance in the Promotion of Human Rights'. Resolution 2000/64. 26 April 2000.

UNCHR. 2000b. 'Report of the Independent Expert on the Right to Development, Mr. Arjun Sengupta'. A/55/306. 17 August 2000.

UNCHR. 2001. 'Third Report of the Independent Expert on the Right to Development, Mr. Arjun Sengupta'. E/CN.4/2001/WG.18/2. 2 January 2001.

UNCHR. 2004a. 'The Role of Good Governance in the Promotion of Human Rights'. Resolution 2004/70. 21 April 2004.

UNCHR. 2004b. 'The Role of Good Governance in the Promotion of Human Rights: Note by the United Nations High Commissioner for Human Rights'. E/CN.4/2005/97. 14 December 2004.

UNCHR. 2004c. 'The Legal Nature of the Right to Development and Enhancement of Its Binding Nature'. E/CN.4/Sub.2/2004/16. 1 June 2004.

UN Committee on Economic, Social and Cultural Rights. 1990. 'The Nature of State Parties' Obligations'. General Comment No. 3. E/1991/23. 14 December 1990.

UN Committee on Economic, Social and Cultural Rights. 1999. 'Right to Adequate Food'. General Comment 12. E/C.12/1999/5. 12 May 1999.

UN Committee on Economic, Social and Cultural Rights. 2000. 'Right to the Highest Attainable Standard of Health'. General Comment 14. E/C.12/2000/4. 11 August 2000.

UN Committee on Economic, Social and Cultural Rights. 2002. 'The Right to Water'. General Comment 15. E/C.12/2002/11. 20 January 2003.

UN Committee on Economic, Social and Cultural Rights. 2004. 'Concluding Observations of the Committee: Ecuador'. E/C.12/1/Add.100. 7 June 2004.

UN Committee on Economic, Social and Cultural Rights. 2010. 'Concluding Observations of the Committee: Switzerland'. E/C.12/CHE/CO/2–3. 26 November 2010.

UN Committee on the Elimination of Discrimination Against Women. 2007. 'Concluding Comments of the Committee: Colombia'. CEDAW/C/COL/CO/6. 2 February 2007.

UN Committee on the Rights of the Child. 2004. 'Concluding Observations: El Salvador'. CRC/C/15/Add.232. 30 June 2004.

UN Committee on the Rights of the Child. 2013. 'The Right of the Child to Have His or Her Best Interests Taken as a Primary Consideration'. General Comment No. 14. CRC/C/GC/14. 29 May 2013.

UN Conference on Environment and Development. 1992. 'Rio Declaration on Environment and Development'. A/CONF.151/26 (Vol. I). 12 August 1992.

UN Conference on Sustainable Development. 2012. 'The Future We Want'. A/RES/66/288. 1 September 2012.

UNCTAD. 2004a. 'Notes on the Concept of Economic Policy Space'. 4 March 2004.

UNCTAD. 2004b. 'São Paulo Consensus'. TD/410. 18 June 2004.

UNCTAD. 2006. 'Trade and Development Report 2006'. UNCTAD/TDR/2006.

UNCTAD. 2009. 'Aid for Trade and Development', in Philippe de Lombaerde and Lakshmi Puri (eds), *Aid for Trade: Global and Regional Perspectives*, pp. 5–28. Berlin: Springer.

UNCTAD. 2014. 'The Least Developed Country Report 2014 – Growth With Structural Transformation: A Post-2015 Development Agenda'. UNCTAD/LDC/2014.

UNDP. 1994. *Human Development Report 1994*. New York: Oxford University Press.

UNDP. 1997a. *Governance for Sustainable Human Development: A UNDP Policy Document*. New York: UNDP.

UNDP. 1997b. *Human Development Report 1997*. New York: Oxford University Press.

UNDP. 2003. *Poverty Reduction and Human Rights: A Practical Note*. New York: UNDP.

UNEP. 2009. 'Aid for Trade for Sustainable Development', in Philippe de Lombaerde and Lakshmi Puri (eds), *Aid for Trade: Global and Regional Perspectives*, pp. 87–98. Berlin: Springer.

UNGA. 1948. 'Universal Declaration of Human Rights'. 217 A (III). 10 December 1948.

UNGA. 1966. 'Official Records, 1414th Plenary Meeting, Twenty-First Session'. A/PV.1414. 23 September 1966.

UNGA. 1974a. 'Declaration on the Establishment of a New International Economic Order'. A/RES/S-6/3201. 1 May 1974.

UNGA. 1974b. 'Charter of Rights and Duties of States'. A/RES/29/3281. 12 December 1974.

UNGA. 1986. 'Declaration on the Right to Development'. A/RES/41/128. 4 December 1986.

UNGA. 1997a. 'Resolution of the General Assembly: Programme for the Further Implementation of Agenda 21'. A/RES/S-19/2. 28 June 1997.

UNGA. 1997b. 'Human Rights Questions, Including Alternative Approaches for Improving the Effective Enjoyment of Human Rights and Fundamental Freedoms'. A/52/644/Add.2. 5 December 1997.

UNGA. 2000. 'United Nations Millennium Declaration'. A/RES/55/2. 8 September 2000.

UNGA. 2006. 'Human Rights Council'. A/RES/60/251. 3 April 2006.

UNGA. 2007. 'Declaration on the Rights of Indigenous Peoples'. A/RES/61/295. 13 September 2007.

UNGA. 2015. 'Transforming Our Word: The 2030 Agenda for Sustainable Development'. Resolution A/RES/70/1. Adopted on 25 September 2015.

UNHRC. 2008a. 'The Role of Good Governance in the Promotion of Human Rights'. Resolution 7/11. 27 March 2008.

UNHRC. 2008b. 'Protect, Respect and Remedy: A Framework for Business and Human Rights: Report of the Special Representative of the Secretary-General on the Issue of Human Rights and Transnational Corporations and Other Business Enterprises'. A/HRC/8/5. 7 April 2008.

UNHRC. 2009a. 'Report of the Special Rapporteur on the Right of Everyone to the Enjoyment of the Highest Attainable Standard of Physical and Mental Health, Anand Grover'. A/HRC/11/12. 31 March 2009.

UNHRC. 2009b. 'Report of the Special Rapporteur on the Right to Food on His Mission to the World Trade Organization'. A/HRC/10/5/Add.2. 4 February 2009.

UNHRC. 2011a. 'Guiding Principles on Human Rights Impact Assessments of Trade and Investment Agreements: Report of the Special Rapporteur on the Right to Food, Olivier De Schutter'. A/HRC/19/59/Add.5. 19 December 2011.

UNHRC. 2011b. 'Guiding Principles on Business and Human Rights: Implementing the United Nations "Protect, Respect and Remedy" Framework: Report of the Special Representative of the Secretary-General on the Issue of Human Rights and Transnational Corporations and Other Business Enterprises'. A/HRC/17/31. 21 March 2011.

UNHRC. 2012a. 'The Role of Good Governance in the Promotion of Human Rights'. Resolution 19/20. 25 April 2012.

UNHRC. 2012b. 'Final Draft of the Guiding Principles on Extreme Poverty and Human Rights'. A/HRC/21/39. 18 July 2012.

UNHRC. 2015. 'Report of the Special Rapporteur on Extreme Poverty and Human Rights, Philip Alston'. A/HRC/29/31. 27 May 2015.

UNHRC. 2016. 'Report of the Special Rapporteur on Extreme Poverty and Human Rights, Philip Alston'. A/HRC/32/31. 28 April 2016.

UN Human Rights Committee. 2004. 'The Nature of the General Legal Obligation Imposed on States Parties to the Covenant'. General Comment No. 31(80). CCPR/C/21/Rev.1/Add. 13.

Uvin, Peter. 2007. 'From the Right to Development to the Rights-Based Approach: How "Human Rights" Entered Development', *Development in Practice*, 17(4–5): 597–606.

van der Heijden, Jeroen. 2013. 'Looking Forward and Sideways: Trajectories of New Governance Theory', *Amsterdam Law School Legal Studies Research Paper*, 2013(4): 1–26.

Vasquez, Carlos Manuel. 2003. 'Trade Sanctions and Human Rights – Past, Present, and Future', *Journal of International Economic Law*, 6(4): 797–840.

Vierdag, E.W. 1988. 'The Time of Conclusion of a Multilateral Treaty', *British Yearbook of International Law*, 59(1): 75–111.

Voig, Christina. 2009. *Sustainable Development as a Principle of International Law: Resolving Conflicts Between Climate Change and WTO Laws*. Leiden: Martinus Nijhoff Publishers.

Wacziarg, Romain and Welch, Karen. 2008. 'Trade Liberalization and Growth: New Evidence', *World Bank Economic Review*, 22(2): 187–231.

Wagner, Don. 2003. 'Trade and Aid – An Empirical Study', *Journal of Japanese and International Economies*, 17(2): 153–73.

Walker, Simon. 2009. *The Future of Human Rights Impact Assessments of Trade Agreements*. Brussels: Intersentia.

Watson, Peter. 1994. 'The Framework for the New Trade Agenda', *Law and Policy in International Business*, 25(4): 1237–58.

WB. 1994. *Governance: The World Bank's Experience*. Washington, DC: World Bank.

WB. 2016a. 'What Is Governance?', http://go.worldbank.org/G2CHLXX0Q0 (accessed on 29 September 2016).

WB. 2016b. 'World Wide Governance Indicators Project', http://info.worldbank.org/governance/wgi/index.aspx#home (accessed on 29 September 2016).

Weil, Prosper. 1983. 'Towards Relative Normativity in International Law', *American Journal of International Law*, 77(3): 413–42.

Weiss, Edith Brown. 2010. 'Implementing Intergenerational Equity', in Malgosia Fitzmaurice, David Ong and Panos Merkouris (eds), *Research Handbook on International Environmental Law*, pp. 100–16. Cheltenham: Edward Elgar.

Weiss, Edith Brown and Sornarajah, Ahila. 2012. 'Good Governance', in *Max Planck Encyclopedia of Public International Law*. Oxford: Oxford University Press.

Weiss, Thomas. 2000. 'Governance, Good Governance and Global Governance: Conceptual and Actual Challenges', *Third World Quarterly*, 21(5): 795–814.

Weiss, Thomas. 2013. *Global Governance: Why? What? Whither?* Cambridge: Polity Press.

Whelan, Daniel. 2015. '"Under the Aegis of Man": The Right to Development and the Origins of the New International Economic Order', *Humanity: An International Journal of Human Rights, Humanitarianism, and Development*, 6(1): 93–108.

Wijayasiri, Janaka and Samad, Shihana. 2007. 'Preference Erosion and Aid for Trade: A South Asian Perspective', www.ips.lk/intecon/research/wto_doha/briefing_paper.pdf (accessed on 1 October 2016).

Wilkinson, Rorden. 2006. 'The WTO in Hong Kong: What It Really Means for the Doha Development Agenda', *New Political Economy*, 11(2): 291–303.

Wilkinson, Rorden and Hughes, Steve. 2002. *Global Governance: Critical Perspectives*. New York: Routledge.

Wilson Center. 2007. 'The Policy Space Debate: Does a Globalized and Multilateral Economy Constrain Development Policies?', www.wilsoncenter.

org/publication/the-policy-space-debate-does-globalized-and-multilateral-economy-constrain-development (accessed on 29 September 2016).

Winters, L. Allen, McCulloch, Neil and McKay, Andrew. 2004. 'Trade Liberalisation and Poverty: The Evidence So Far', *Journal of Economic Literature*, 42(1): 72–115.

Wolfrum, Rudiger. 2011. 'Obligation of Result Versus Obligation of Conduct: Some Thoughts About the Implementation of International Organizations', in Mahnoush Arsanjani *et al.* (eds), *Looking to the Future: Essays on International Law in Honor of W. Michael Reisman*, pp. 363–83. Leiden: Martinus Nijhoff Publishers.

World Commission on Environment and Development. 1987. *Our Common Future*. Oxford: Oxford University Press.

World Conference on Human Rights. 1993. 'Vienna Declaration and Programme of Action'. Adopted on 25 June 1993.

WTO. 1996. 'Singapore Ministerial Declaration'. WT/MIN(96)/DEC. 18 December 1996.

WTO. 1999. 'Preparations for the 1999 Ministerial Conference: Summary of Proposals'. JOB(99)/4797/Rev.3. 18 November 1999.

WTO. 2001. 'Doha Ministerial Declaration'. WT/MIN(01)/DEC/l. 20 November 2001.

WTO. 2005a. 'Hong Kong Ministerial Declaration'. WT/MIN(05)/DEC. 22 December 2005.

WTO. 2005b. 'Second Appraisal of the Operation of the Trade Policy Review Mechanism: Report to Ministers by Chairman Don Stephenson'. WT/MIN(05)/1. 21 September 2005.

WTO. 2006a. 'Fact Sheet on TRIPS and Pharmaceutical Patents', www.wto.org/english/tratop_e/trips_e/factsheet_pharm00_e.htm (accessed on 30 September 2016).

WTO. 2006b. 'Recommendations of the Task Force on Aid for Trade'. WT/AFT/1. 27 July 2006.

WTO. 2007. 'WTO Work Programme on Aid-for-Trade: Background Note Prepared by the WTO Secretariat'. WT/AFT/W/26. 29 May 2007.

WTO. 2008. 'Rules and Procedures for Meetings of the Trade Policy Review Body'. WT/TPR/6/Rev.2. 14 November 2008.

WTO. 2011. 'Lamy Hails "Encouraging" Third Global Review of Aid for Trade', www.wto.org/english/news_e/sppl_e/sppl201_e.htm (accessed on 30 September 2016).

WTO. 2015a. *Understanding the WTO: The Basics*. Geneva: WTO Publications.

WTO. 2015b. 'Nairobi Ministerial Declaration'. WT/MIN(15)/DEC. 19 December 2015.

WTO. 2016a. 'Aid for Trade Fact Sheet', www.wto.org/english/tratop_e/devel_e/a4t_e/a4t_factsheet_e.htm (accessed on 29 September 2016).

WTO. 2016b. 'Aid for Trade', www.wto.org/english/tratop_e/devel_e/a4t_e/aid4trade_e.htm (accessed on 01 October 2016).

WTO. 2016c. 'WTO Analytical Index: Trade Policy Review', www.wto.org/ENGLISH/res_e/booksp_e/analytic_index_e/tprm_01_e.htm (accessed on 30 September 2016).
WTO and WB. 2015. *The Role of Trade in Ending Poverty*. Geneva: WTO.
Yuen, E., Burton-Rose, D. and Katsiaficas, G.N. 2001. *The Battle of Seattle: The New Challenge to Capitalist Globalization*. New York: Soft Skull Press.
Zagel, Gudrun. 2005. 'WTO and Human Rights: Examining Linkages and Suggesting Convergence', *Voices of Development Jurists*, 2(2): 1–37.
Zaheer, Daniel. 2004. 'Breaking the Deadlock: Why and How Developing Countries Should Accept Labor Standards in the WTO', *Stanford Journal of Law, Business and Finance*, 9(1): 69–104.
Zedillo, Ernesto *et al.* 2005. *Strengthening the Global Trade Architecture for Economic Development: An Agenda for Action*. New Haven: Development and the Global Trade Architecture Project/Yale Center for the Study of Globalization.

INDEX

abusing governance space, permissive environment to 136–67; *see also* Aid for Trade Initiative (AfT)
Adhikari, Ratnakar 186
AFL-CIO *see* American Federation of Labor and Congress of Industrial Organizations (AFL-CIO)
African-Caribbean-Pacific (ACP) countries 35, 50n8, 86
Agency for Trade and Labor Standards (ATLAS) 163, 164
Ago, Roberto 66–8
Agreement on Subsidies and Countervailing Measures 85, 94, 96, 153; Article 1.1(a)(1) of 86–7; Article 5 of 95
Agreement on Trade Policy Review Mechanism (TPRM Agreement) 219–21
Agreement on Trade-Related Aspects of Labour (TRILS) 162
agreements, WTO 12, 55; Article 103 of the UN Charter and 59–60; covered agreements 79–80; DSB and 80; HRIA and 217, 218–21; human rights arguments 79–82; international law and 89–91; *lex posterior* 78–9; *lex specialis* 76–8; social clause 12, 159–62; *see also* World Trade Organisation (WTO)
Aid for Trade Initiative (AfT) 170, 176–94; addressing limiting environment 193–4; capability imbalances 189–93; effectiveness 180–9; introduction 176–80; RtD approach to 225–7
Alston, Philip 150, 196, 204
American Federation of Labor and Congress of Industrial Organizations (AFL-CIO) 160–1
Annan, Kofi 175
applicable law: interpretation and 84–7; jurisdiction and 88–97
approaches, analysing 195–7
Argentina – Poultry Anti-Dumping Duties 93–4, 237
Article 1(1) of DRTD 206
Article 1 of the UN Charter 227
Article 2(1) of DRTD 207–8
Article 2(3) of DRTD 207, 208, 226
Article 3(1) of DRTD 203, 208, 223
Article 3(3) of DRTD 203, 208, 213–14, 226
Article 4(1) of DRTD 203, 208
Article 4(2) of DRTD 208–9, 226
Article 6(1) of DRTD 226
Article 22 of the Banjul Charter 210
Article 25(a) of ICCPR 216
Article 28 of the UDHR 11
Article 36 of ILO 166, 224
Article 38(1) of the Statue of ICJ 47
Article 55(a) of the UN Charter 10, 62
Article 55(c) of the UN Charter 60, 62
Article 55 of the UN Charter 10–11, 60–5; Article 56 *vs.* 61–2; obligations on states under Article 56

and 65–8; obligations on UN 60, 61; purposes set forth 62–5
Article 56 of the UN Charter 60–2; Article 55 *vs.* 61–2; important parts 61; obligations on states under 65–8; taking action 61–2
Article 103 of UN Charter 68–9, 75, 195, 218; human rights argument 60–1; *lex superior* 59–60
Article II of GATT 1994 8
Article VI of the Treaty on the Non-Proliferation of Nuclear Weapons 68
Article VI of Treaty on the Non-Proliferation of Nuclear Weapons 68
Article X of the Marrakesh Agreement 165–6
Article XI of GATT 1994 9
Article XII of the Marrakesh Agreement 17n2
Article XX of GATT 79, 162, 165, 167–8n4; Chapeau 125–34; clause (a) 108, 158–9; clause (b) 107–8, 109–19; clause (g) 119–25; general exceptions clause 106–10
Article XX(a) of GATT 108; labour standards as 'public morals' 158–9
Article XX(b) of GATT 43, 55, 107–8, 221, 222; extra-territorial measures under 157–8; textual and jurisprudential analysis 110–19
Article XX(d) of GATT 111, 112
Article XX(g) of GATT 119–25, 222
ATLAS *see* Agency for Trade and Labor Standards (ATLAS)
autonomy 144

Banjul Charter, Article 22 of 210
Banks, Kevin 143
Barry, Christian 163
Battle of Seattle 3
beggar-thy-neighbour policies 3
Bell, Stephen 30
Bevir, Mark 30
Bhagwati, Jagdish 142, 147, 149, 151, 161
Brandt Commission 30
Brazil – Retreaded Tyres 112–15, 116, 119, 130–2, 237
Brundtland Commission 198, 199–200
business corporations: governance and 31

Canada – Aircraft 237
Canada – Dairy 237
Canada – Herring and Salmon 120, 237
Chang, Ha-Joon 22–3
Chapeau of Article XX of GATT 1994 125–34
Charlesworth, Hillary 204
Charlton, Andrew 171, 172, 182
Charter of the United Nations 4, 5, 9, 51–2; Article 1 of 227; Preamble to DTRD 226–7; *see also* Article 55 of the UN Charter
Chartres, Renee 162
Chile – Price Band System 238
Chimni, Bhupinder 39, 191
China – Intellectual Property Rights 238
China – Publications and Audiovisual Products 93, 238
China – Rare Earths 118, 121–3, 124, 238
China – Raw Materials 117–18, 120, 123, 124–5, 198, 238
CIL *see* Customary International Law (CIL)
civil society 2; governance and 31
CLS *see* core labour standards (CLS)
Commission on Global Governance *see* Brandt Commission
Committee on Trade and Development of the WTO (CTD) 218
comparative advantage, theory of 7, 18n9, 171
competition: lower labour standards and 142–3; unfair 145, 148
conflict resolution: *lex posterior* 78–9; *lex specialis* 76–8
consumer autonomy 144
Convention on the Rights of the Child 141

core labour standards (CLS) 140, 141, 144, 145, 148, 149, 150, 152, 155, 159
Costa Rica 7–9
Crawford, James 67
Creditor Reporting System (OECD) 180
Customary International Law (CIL) 2, 25, 78, 210, 211

Declaration on Fundamental Principles and Rights at Work 140, 150
Declaration on the Right to Development (DRTD) 25, 201–5; Article 1(1) 206; Article 2(1) 207–8; Article 2(3) 207, 208, 226; Article 3(1) 203, 208, 223; Article 3(3) 203, 208, 213–14, 226; Article 4(1) 203, 208; Article 4(2) 208–9, 226; Article 6(1) 226; Preamble 203; *see also* right to development (RtD) approach
de Schutter, Olivier 60, 70–1, 72, 74n8, 216–18, 221
developing and least-developed countries (D-LDC) 22–3; AfT Initiative 170, 176–94; good governance 38–9; labour standards (*see* labour standards); limiting environment 169–94; RtD approach (*see* right to development (RtD) approach); trade liberalisation and 172–6
development: as freedom 144–5, 200; human-centred approach to 201; as human right 200–5
Development as Freedom (Sen) 144, 200
dispute settlement body (DSB) 14, 75–101
Doha Development Round 173, 174–9, 189, 234
Doha Ministerial Declaration 141, 197–8, 218
Donnelly, Jack 203–4
DSU (understanding disputes settlement) 6, 12, 79–101; dispute over 82–3; interpretation and applicable law 84–7; jurisdiction and applicable law 88–97; potential scenarios 79–82

EC and Certain Member States – Large Civil Aircraft 94–6, 100–1, 240
EC – Approval and Marketing of Biotech Products 98–9, 238
EC – Asbestos 85–6, 115–16, 125, 133, 153–4, 156, 238–9
EC – Bananas III 86, 239
EC – Chicken Cuts 239
EC – Commercial Vessels 93, 239
EC – Computer Equipment 100, 239
EC – Hormones 239
Economic and Social Council (ECOSOC) 2, 4
economic growth, free trade and 171–2
ECOSOC *see* Economic and Social Council (ECOSOC)
EC – Poultry 80, 239
EC – Seal Products 113–15, 127–8, 132–3, 155–6, 158, 239–40
EC – Tariff Preferences 117, 240
EC Temporary Defensive Mechanism for Shipbuilding 93
embedded liberalism 144
Endorois case 209–10
Escobar, Arturo 201
European Commission 184–5
export protectionism 147–8
extra-territorial measures, under Article XX(b) of GATT 157–8

Fair Labour Standards 138
Feenstra, Robert 149
financial institutions 20
Finger, Michael 173
Flanagan, Robert 148–9
fragmentation of international law 53–6
freedom, development as 144–5, 200
free trade: agenda 3, 170; D-LDCs 172–6; economic growth and

171–2; poverty alleviation 170; Ricardian theory of 170
Froman, Michael 234

Gabcikovo – Nagymaros Project 199
GATT *see* General Agreement on Tariffs and Trade (GATT)
General Agreement on Tariffs and Trade (GATT) 3, 6, 10–11
general exceptions clause, in Article XX of GATT 1994 106–10
Generalised System of Preferences (GSP) 174
globalisation 2–3, 20
good governance 34–41; European Union (EU) 34–5; governance, governance space and 38–41; human rights 34–8; OHCHR 36–8; UN 34, 35–8; UNCHR on 35–6; World Bank 34
Good Governance Practices for the Protection of Human Rights (OHCHR) 36–7
governance: Brandt Commission on 30; business corporations 31; defined 29–30; good 34–41; governance space, good governance and 38–41; non-State actors 31; scholarly definition 30; State and 31–3; UNDP on 30; World Bank (WB) on 29
governance space 27–9; abusing, permissive environment to 136–67; framework 41–5; governance, good governance and 38–41; instrumental function 45; linkage-category 42–5; shrinking 105–35
Great Depression of 1930 3
GSP *see* Generalised System of Preferences (GSP)
Guzman, Andrew 162–3

Hanson, Gordon 149
Harrison, James 13, 54, 159
Havana Charter for an International Trade Organisation 3, 10, 138
Heckscher, Eli 18n9
Heckscher-Ohlin theorem 18n9
Hirst, Paul 30
Hoekstra, Ruth 188
Holocaust 3
Hong Kong Ministerial Conference 177
Howse, Robert 11, 145–6, 148, 150, 155, 158–9, 162
HRIA *see* human rights impact assessments (HRIA)
Hudec, Robert 142
human development 201
human rights: policy space and 24–7
human rights, MTS and 1; Harrison's analysis/methodology 14; linkages between 1–4; treaties and 2
human rights impact assessments (HRIA) 216–22
human security 201
Hungary 172–3

Ibhawoh, Bonny 212
ICCPR *see* International Covenant on Civil and Political Rights (ICCPR)
ICESCR *see* International Covenant on Economic, Social and Cultural Rights (ICESCR)
intellectual property rights 2, 6, 23, 172–3
International Bill of Human Rights 5
International Court of Justice (ICJ) 47; *Legality of the Threat or Use of Nuclear Weapons* 68; *Lockerbie* case 83, 84
International Covenant on Civil and Political Rights (ICCPR) 4–5
International Covenant on Economic, Social and Cultural Rights (ICESCR) 2, 4–5
International Labour Organization (ILO) 138, 139–42, 150; Declaration on Fundamental Principles and Rights at Work 140, 150; enforcement mechanisms 139, 146; UN Human Rights System and 225; WTO *vs.* 164–6, 223–5; *see also* labour standards
international law, fragmentation of 53–6

International Law Commission (ILC) 53–6
International Monetary Fund (IMF) 3
International Trade Organisation (ITO) 3, 5–6, 10
interpretation, and applicable law 84–7
ITO *see* International Trade Organisation (ITO)

Japan – Alcoholic Beverages II 82–3, 240
jurisdiction and applicable law 88–97
jurisprudential analysis of Article XX(b) 110–19
jus cogens norms 71–2

Kaufmann, Daniel 30
Kicking Away the Ladder (Chang) 22
Kolben, Kevin 144–5, 147
Koopmann, Georg 188
Korea – Alcoholic Beverages 156, 240
Korea – Procurement 90–1, 240
Korea – Various Measures on Beef 111–12, 114, 240
Koskenniemi, Martii 48, 53
Kraay, Aart 30

labour costs 143, 145, 147
Labour Ministers of Non-Aligned and Other Developing Countries (1995) 139
labour standards 137–67; arguments by opponents 147–52; arguments by proponents 142–6; case study 137; history 137–42; overview 137; rules and exclusion 152–62; WTO *vs.* ILO 164–6
Langan, Mark 187, 191–3
laws/legal binding: case study 106–10; clause (b) of Article XX 110–19; clause (g) of Article XX 119–25; general exceptions clause in Article XX 106–10; overview 105–6
Legality of the Threat or Use of Nuclear Weapons (ICJ) 68
lex generalis 77, 78
lex posterior 76, 78–9
lex specialis 76–8
liberalisation 7–8, 23, 171–6; D-LDC and 172–6; neoclassical theory and 172–4
liberal trading regime 145–6
like products 152–7
limiting environment 169–94; *see also* Aid for Trade Initiative (AfT)
linkage-category 42–5, 169–70
Lockerbie case 83, 84, 88
lower labour standards: competition 142–3; race to the bottom 143
low labour costs 143, 147

Marceau, Gabrielle 72, 81–2, 99, 100, 179, 183
Marrakesh Agreement 3, 10, 232; on free trade and D-LDCs 174; Preamble of 197, 214
MERCOSUR 93, 131
Mercurio, Bryan 162
methods of international law 47–8
Mexico – Soft Drinks 80, 240
MFN *see* most favoured nation (MFN)
Millennium Declaration 36, 210
most favoured nation (MFN) 8–9, 152–7
MTS *see* multilateral trading system (MTS)
multilateral trading system (MTS) 1; human rights and 20; nation-state system and 20; permeating nature 20
multinational corporations 20

NAFTA *see* North American Free Trade Agreement (NAFTA)
Nairobi Ministerial Declaration 234–6
national treatment (NT) 8, 9, 152–7
necessary measures: determining, in Article XX(b) 110–19; weighing and balancing process 112–15
neoclassical theory 172–4
neo-colonialism 39

New World Order 3
Nickel, James 205–6
normative hierarchy debate 51–73; distractions 73; fragmentation of international law 53–6; *jus cogens* 71–2; overview 51–3; rules for resolving conflicts 56–9
North American Free Trade Agreement (NAFTA) 80
NT *see* National Treatment Principle (NT)
Nussbaum, Martha 201

obligations of conduct/means 66–8
obligations of results/ends 66–8
ODA *see* Official Development Assistance (ODA)
OECD *see* Organisation for Economic Co-Operation and Development (OECD)
Office of the High Commissioner for Human Rights (OHCHR) 5, 36–8
Official Development Assistance (ODA) 182, 188–9, 227
OHCHR *see* Office of the High Commissioner for Human Rights (OHCHR)
Ohlin, Bertil 18n9
Organisation for Economic Co-Operation and Development (OECD) 148, 174, 180, 184, 191
Our Common Future (Brundtland Commission) 198
Outcome Document of the UN Conference on Sustainable Development (2012) 199

Panagariya, Arvind 148, 150–1, 161
panels, WTO 79–82
parties: in Article 31(3)(c) of VCLT 97–102
patenting obligations 105–6
Pauwelyn, Joost 81, 83, 87–90, 91–2, 99–100, 103n3
Peer and Partner Review Committees (PPRC) 163
permissive environment, to abuse governance space 136–67; *see also* labour standards
Peru – Agricultural Products 97, 101
Philippines – Distilled Spirits 156, 241
Pierre, Jon 30
pledge by States 61–2, 63, 65
policy space 20–1; concept 21–4; limitations 24–7; limiting effect 23–4; official status 21
Policy Space for the Development of the South 21
poor governance 34
poverty: alleviation 170; free trade and 172; human rights and 170–1
PPRC *see* Peer and Partner Review Committees (PPRC)
Preamble of DRTD 203
Preamble of Marrakesh Agreement 197, 214
Preamble of UDHR 4, 64
preferential market access schemes 174
preferential trade agreements (PTA) 142, 164
PTA *see* preferential trade agreements (PTA)

Questions of Interpretation and Application of the 1971 Montreal Convention Arising from the Aerial Incident at Lockerbie (Libya v. US) see *Lockerbie* case
quotas 9

race to the bottom 143
Raghavan, Chakravarthi 234
Rajagopal, Balakrishnan 32–3, 212
Reddy, Sanjay 163
Ricardian theory of free trade 170
Ricardo, David 7, 18n9
right to development (RtD) approach 17, 47, 201–29, 232–3; to AfT Initiative 225–7; governance space and 211–13; HRIA 216–22; to labour standards/rights 222–5; status and content 205–11; sustainable development and 213–15
Rio Declaration 85, 199, 210
Robinson, Mary 2
Rodriguez, Francisco 171
Rodrik, Dani 171

'The Role of Good Governance in the Promotion of Human Rights' (UNCHR) 36
'The Role of Trade in Ending Poverty' 170
Rovamaa, Laura 184–5
Ruggie, John 32, 49n1, 144

Samuelson, Paul 170
Sao Paulo Consensus of 2004 21, 22
Sayer, Andrew 191–2
Schuler, Philip 173
SCM Agreement *see* Agreement on Subsidies and Countervailing Measures
Scott, James 187, 191–3
Sen, Amartya 144, 200–1
Sengupta, Arjun 205, 206, 207, 208, 210, 226–7
shrinking of governance space 105–35; *see also* laws/legal binding
Singapore Ministerial Declaration (1996) 139–42, 151, 158, 160
Skyes, Alan 149–50
Smith, Adam 17n8
social clause 12, 159–62
social development 198
social dumping 142
Sornarajah, Ahila 34
South Centre of G77 21–2
States: multilateral trade obligations 55
Stiglitz, Joseph 171, 172, 182
Sub-Saharan Africa 174
sustainable development 197–200, 232–3; defined 198, 199; ICJ on 199; policy significance 198; RtD and 213–15
sustainable development goals (SDG) 21, 236

taking action 65–6; obligation to 66
TDM Regulation *see* EC Temporary Defensive Mechanism for Shipbuilding
Thailand – Cigarettes 111, 241
Thailand – Cigarettes (Philippines) 156, 241
Theory of Absolute Advantage 17n8
theory of comparative advantage *see* comparative advantage, theory of
Thiam, Doudou 201
Third World Approaches to International Law (TWAIL) 48, 189–91
Third World Intellectuals and NGOs Statement Against Linkage (Bhagwati) 147
TMSA *see* TradeMark Southern Africa (TMSA)
Tokyo Round Subsidies Code 95, 96
TPRB *see* Trade Policy Review Body (TPRB)
TPRM Agreement *see* Agreement on Trade Policy Review Mechanism (TPRM Agreement)
trade law and human rights law 14
trade liberalisation 11
TradeMark Southern Africa (TMSA) 185
Trade Policy Review Body (TPRB) 219–21, 230n18
trade protectionism 23
'Transforming Our World: the 2030 Agenda for Sustainable Development' 21, 199
Trans-Pacific Partnership 234
treaties 2
Treaty on the Non-Proliferation of Nuclear Weapons 68
Trebilcock, Michael 145–6, 148, 150, 155, 158–9, 162
TRILS *see* Agreement on Trade-Related Aspects of Labour (TRILS)
TRIPS Agreement 42, 57, 105, 162, 173
Turkey – Textiles 80–1, 241
Turner, Liz 184–5
TWAIL *see* Third World Approaches to International Law (TWAIL)

UDHR *see* Universal Declaration of Human Rights (UDHR)
UK Department of International Development 184–5
UN Committee on Economic, Social and Cultural Rights 26, 216
UN Committee on the Elimination of Discrimination Against Women 216

UN Committee on the Rights of the Child 216
UN Declaration on the Rights of Indigenous Peoples 210
Understanding on Rules and Procedures Governing the Settlement of Disputes *see* DSU
unfair competition 146, 148
UN Human Rights Council 210
United Nations (UN) 2, 3–4; approach of 4–5; DRTD (*see* Declaration on the Right to Development (DRTD)); Millennium Declaration 36, 210; *see also* Charter of the United Nations
United Nations Commission on Human Rights (UNCHR) 35–7, 203, 204–11
United Nations Conference on Trade and Development (UNCTAD) 21
United Nations General Assembly (UNGA) 4
Universal Declaration of Human Rights (UDHR) 4–5, 199
Uruguay Round of negotiations (1980s) 6
US – Anti-Dumping and Countervailing Duties (China) 86–7, 241
US – Clove Cigarettes 156–7, 241
US – FSC (21.5) 85, 241
US – Gambling 115, 242
US – Gasoline 82, 107, 108–9, 111, 116–17, 120–4, 126, 128, 130, 242
US – Section 337 110–11, 242
US – Shrimp 85, 100, 120–1, 124, 126, 129–30, 158, 159, 242
US – Shrimp (21.5) 133–4, 242
US – Tuna Dolphin I 157, 242
US – Tuna Dolphin II 157, 242
Uvin, Peter 211

Vienna Convention on the Law of Treaties (VCLT): Article 26 91; Article 30 78; Article 31(3) 89; Article 31(3)(c) 83, 96, 97–102; Article 41 81; Article 53 71; Articles 31 82–3, 85, 90; Articles 32 90

Wacziarg, Romain 171
wages of unskilled workers 149
The Wealth of Nations (Smith) 17n8
weighing and balancing process 112–15
Weiss, Edith Brown 34
Weiss, Thomas 29, 30
Welch, Karen 171
Wolfrum, Rudiger 68
World Bank (WB) 3
World Commission on Environment and Development *see* Brundtland Commission
world economic growth 6–7
World Trade Organisation (WTO) 2–4; Aid for Trade (*see* Aid for Trade Initiative (AfT)); approach of 5–9; Battle of Seattle 3; comparative advantage, theory of 7; criticism and protest against 2–3; free trade agenda 3; globalisation 2–3, 20; human rights and 11–13, 46–7; ILO *vs.* 164–6, 223–5; labour standards 137–66; legal architecture 8, 107; limiting environment 169–94; panels 79–82; shrinking of governance space 105–35; sustainable development 197–200; unique feature 17n2
Worldwide Governance Indicators Project 30
WTO *see* World Trade Organisation (WTO)
WWII 3

Zoido-Lobaton, Pablo 30